The Multiculturalism Question

Debating Identity in 21st-Century Canada

Edited by

Jack Jedwab

Queen's Policy Studies Series
School of Policy Studies, Queen's University
McGill-Queen's University Press
Montreal & Kingston • London • Ithaca

SCHOOL OF
Policy Studies

Publications Unit
Robert Sutherland Hall
138 Union Street
Kingston, ON, Canada
K7L 3N6
www.queensu.ca/sps/

Library and Archives Canada Cataloguing in Publication

The multiculturalism question : debating identity in 21st-century Canada / edited by Jack Jedwab.

(Queen's policy studies series / School of Policy Studies, Queen's University)
Includes bibliographical references and index.
Issued in print and electronic formats.

ISBN 978-1-55339-422-8 (pbk.). – ISBN 978-1-55339-423-5 (epub). –
ISBN 978-1-55339-424-2 (pdf)

1. Multiculturalism – Canada. 2. Minorities – Government policy – Canada.
3. Immigrants – Government policy – Canada. 4. Ethnicity – Canada. 5. Nationalism – Canada. 6. Canada – Ethnic relations. I. Jedwab, Jack, 1958-, editor of compilation II. Queen's University (Kingston, Ont.). School of Policy Studies III. Series: Queen's policy studies series

FC105.M8M89 2014   305.800971   C2013-906975-5
                                                C2013-906976-3

In partnership with

CONTENTS

ACKNOWLEDGEMENTS

I want to begin by thanking all of the authors who contributed to this book. I set out to try to offer the readers a publication that would provide a path through the contours of the debate – the pros and the cons – surrounding multiculturalism in Canada. Upon completion, I discovered that there may be more upon which we agree than disagree. In effect, there is considerable room for dialogue, and the conversation will inevitably continue.

I want to thank Keith Banting of the School of Policy Studies at Queen's University, Kingston, Ontario, and acknowledge Valerie Jarus and Mark Howes in the Publications Unit for their tireless efforts to ensure that this volume attain the highest possible standards. My particular appreciation goes to copy editor Stephanie Stone for the excellent work she has done in this regard. The anthology owes much of its intellectual inspiration to the deliberations at the 2013 National Metropolis Conference, and, in part, it is fair to describe it as a Metropolis project. I would also like to thank my multi-ethnic staff at the Association for Canadian Studies for their ongoing support, especially Sarah Kooi, James Ondrick, Julie Perrone, and Victoria Chwalek. Finally, I would like to thank my wife, Louise, and my four children – Tamara, Romy, David, and Ashley – who have shown me the way to truly celebrate diversity.

Jack Jedwab

CONTRIBUTORS

YASMEEN ABU-LABAN is professor in the Department of Political Science at the University of Alberta.

JOHN W. BERRY is professor emeritus of psychology at Queen's University. He was recently appointed research professor at the National Research University Higher School of Economics, Moscow, Russia.

JOHN BILES is special advisor to the Director General Integration/Foreign Credentials Referral Office at Citizenship and Immigration Canada.

RICHARD J.F. DAY is associate professor in Cultural Studies/Global Development Studies/Sociology at Queen's University.

RANDALL HANSEN is Canada Research Chair in Immigration and Governance in the Department of Political Science and Director of the Centre for European, Russian and Eurasian Studies, Munk School of Global Affairs, University of Toronto.

EVE HAQUE is associate professor in the Department of Languages, Literatures and Linguistics at York University.

SUSAN W. HARDWICK is professor emerita in the Department of Geography at the University of Oregon.

JACK JEDWAB is executive director of the Association for Canadian Studies.

GENEVIÈVE NOOTENS is Canada Research Chair in Democracy and Sovereignty in the Department of Social Sciences at the Université du Québec à Chicoutimi.

JEFFREY G. REITZ is professor of sociology; R.F. Harney Professor of Ethnic, Immigration and Pluralism Studies; and on the faculty of the Munk School of Global Affairs at the University of Toronto.

PHIL RYAN is associate professor at the School of Public Policy and Administration, Carleton University.

Daniel Weinstock is professor in the Faculty of Law at McGill University.

Elke Winter is associate professor in the Department of Sociology and Anthropology at the University of Ottawa and research director of the thematic focus Migration, Ethnic Pluralism and Citizenship at the University of Ottawa's Centre for Interdisciplinary Research on Citizenship and Minorities.

INTRODUCTION

Jack Jedwab

Canada is widely regarded as the first country to enact a policy of multi-culturalism. But since this policy was first introduced in 1971, debating the theory and practice of multiculturalism has become part of the country's national pastime. At first, several Quebec francophone opinion leaders insisted that multiculturalism unjustly placed French culture on an equal footing with the country's minority ethnic cultures. Such concerns were not allayed when, in 1969, the Liberal government of Pierre Elliott Trudeau recognized French and English as the country's two official languages, and the acknowledgement of the French language without official recognition of the French culture has been a source of persistent opposition to multiculturalism amongst many francophone Quebecers. Paradoxically, leaders of some minority ethnic groups articulated their opposition to multiculturalism in somewhat inverse terms. They contended that the government's recognition of multiple cultures was incomplete without some official acknowledgement of languages other than English or French.

But despite the criticism, during the 1970s and 1980s, multiculturalism was embraced by many Canadians as a fundamental marker of Canadian identity. There remained less enthusiasm toward multiculturalism amongst francophone Quebecers, but the province's non-francophones strongly supported it. Sykes and Kunz suggest that each decade has been marked by important changes in the direction of multicultural policy. During the 1970s, the policy promoted the value of minority ethnic identities and the celebration of cultural differences, which Kunz and Sykes describe as "ethnicity multiculturalism."[1] In the 1980s, the priority was removing institutional barriers to the economic participation of ethnic

The Multiculturalism Question: Debating Identity in 21st-Century Canada, ed. Jack Jedwab. Kingston: School of Policy Studies, Queen's University. © 2014 The School of Policy Studies, Queen's University at Kingston. All rights reserved.

and racial minorities, which the authors refer to as "equity multicultural-ism."[2] This objective was reinforced by the introduction of the *Canadian Charter of Rights and Freedoms* in 1982, the *Employment Equity Act* in 1986, and the *Canadian Multiculturalism Act* in 1988.

The *Canadian Charter of Rights and Freedoms* included a provision stating that it should be interpreted in a manner consistent with the preservation and enhancement of the multicultural heritage of Canadians. Although that relevant section of the Charter did not come with a promise of meaningful financial support for minority ethnic groups, it nonetheless offered a symbolic victory for supporters of the idea of multicultural-ism. Political support for multiculturalism initially transcended federal party lines as, similar to the previous Liberal government, the federal Conservatives under Prime Minister Brian Mulroney continued to en-dorse multiculturalism as a pillar of Canadian identity by introducing the *Canadian Multiculturalism Act*.

In the 1990s, the promotion of a sense of shared citizenship and a sense of belonging to Canada were prioritized, ushering in the era of "civic multiculturalism."[3] By 1991, as the country faced serious challenges to national unity, the Citizens' Forum on Canada's Future concluded that while Canadians valued cultural diversity, citizens wanted a definition of being Canadian that encompassed many different origins. They called for a refocusing of official multiculturalism that welcomed all Canadians into an evolving mainstream. The Citizens' Forum recommended that future government funding of multiculturalism be confined to immigrant integration, fighting racism, and promoting equality.[4] In short, funds were no longer to be directed toward minority ethnic organizations engaged in the preservation and enhancement of specific cultures.

As noted, Canada was the first country in the world to introduce an official multicultural policy, and shortly thereafter, a number of countries followed suit. While Canada consistently used the term *multiculturalism* to describe its approach to managing the relationship between diversity and identities, over time the meaning of *multiculturalism* evolved, and, by the end of the 20th century, much of immigrant-receiving Europe began abandoning the term. Gradually, debate in Canada became a microcosm of a broader global discussion on how immigrant-receiving countries could best deal with issues of newcomer integration and its impact on national identity. National conversation about multiculturalism increas-ingly touched upon integration and whether encouraging immigrants and their children to preserve customs and traditions was detrimental to building a common or shared national culture. What emerged in the first decade of the 20th century has been described as "integrative multiculturalism."[5]

Policy-makers and intellectuals increasingly warned of societies facing problems of social cohesion and the appearance of fault lines between ma-jority and minority groups. As regards immigrants, these loosely defined issues seemingly implied that newcomers undercut the majority, or host, community's sense of solidarity, shared citizenship, and purported adherence to a set of common values. Talk of problems of cohesion morphed into warnings about the erosion of shared values that were presumably under siege by the persistence of immigrant cultures. Heath contends that values frequently get defined in abstract ways, such as "sharing," "democracy," or "dialogue."[6] When values are defined as such, sharing them is relatively uncomplicated. Yet the perceived need to reconcile those values purportedly held by immigrants with those presumably held by members of the host society sometimes encompasses a harmful "us versus them" stereotype in which the problem of social cohesion – however defined – becomes a self-fulfilling prophesy.

Ethnic and religious-based conflicts in Europe and North America have seen increased government attention directed at immigrant integration. Popular American political scientist Robert Putnam argued in his essay "E Pluribus Unum [Out of the Many One]: Diversity and Community in the Twenty-First Century" that in highly diverse cities, "people living in ethnically diverse settings appear to 'hunker down' – that is, to pull in like a turtle."[7] He proposed that the United States redefine its "we" more broadly and renew shared identity and social solidarity. Detractors of multiculturalism in Canada and elsewhere were quick to seize upon Putnam's conclusions, although, paradoxically, the United States describes itself as a melting pot.

Since the beginning of the 21st century, globalization and security have undoubtedly influenced public opinion and policy-making on multiculturalism, notably after the terrorist attacks of 11 September 2001. Surveys conducted by the firm Leger Marketing in 2012 and 2013 reveal that some 54 percent of Canadians agree that there is an irreconcilable conflict between Western societies and Muslim societies (33 percent disagree, and 12 percent do not know).[8] Similar views are quite certainly held in other immigrant-receiving countries. Security concerns are increasingly evoked in public debates about immigration. The first decade of the 21st century has witnessed a growing perception that multiculturalism will offer certain individuals justification for practices that are contrary to the laws of the country. Raising this spectre has been effective in fostering attacks on multiculturalism, even though the same criticism might be directed at the freedom-of-religion provisions of the Charter.

As regards public opinion in Canada, since the 1990s, perhaps the most commonly asked question touching on multiculturalism included in public opinion surveys asks some variation of whether Canadians agree or disagree that immigrants or minority groups should preserve their cultures and/or customs and traditions or become more like us, the majority, or most Canadians. It is worth noting that the question does not include the word *multiculturalism*. However, the question reflects the way several opinion leaders have constructed the debate, and it attempts to capture the thought process that tends to underlie the national integration/identity paradigm.

Canadians are generally divided in their response to such a question, with Quebec francophones and the country's baby boomers somewhat more likely to agree that immigrants and minorities should become more like the majority. The formulation of the question suggests that the societal choice confronting immigrants is between preserving culture and customs and becoming like the majority. Yet some observers see both paths as viable, and, indeed, when the two propositions are submitted separately to the population, a majority of Canadians agree that it is legitimate to preserve one's culture and also agree that it is important to encourage immigrants to become more like the majority.[9]

Is the perceived need for greater cohesion a euphemism for a desire for cultural assimilation of newcomers and their children? It is difficult to say as a number of the more painful periods in our country's history involve efforts at assimilating Aboriginal and French Canadians. Hence, the term *assimilation* resonates negatively with many Canadians. Paradoxically, many Quebec francophone opinion leaders who vehemently oppose multiculturalism also abhor the idea of cultural assimilation and go so far as to describe themselves as global advocates of cultural diversity.[10]

In the absence of a shift in orientation, the dominant paradigm in this second decade of the 21st century might be described as socially cohesive multiculturalism. In 2009, then immigration minister Jason Kenney made the following statement: "We have shifted our program of multiculturalism ... to focus precisely on integration toward liberal democratic values to remove any confusion that may have existed that our approach to multiculturalism justifies abhorrent cultural practices and the expression of hatred."[11]

Criticism of multiculturalism has increasingly moved on from the policy and instead targets its presumed message. This is probably a good thing since relatively few Canadians are familiar with the substance of the policy. A survey conducted by Leger Marketing for the Association for Canadian Studies in 2010 revealed that 64 percent of Canadians said they "didn't know" (the figure was 90 percent in Quebec, the home of its biggest detractors) when asked, "What are actions taken by the Government of Canada to promote multiculturalism?"[12] Indeed, those who claimed that they did know what actions were taken by the federal government often incorrectly identified such things as direct funding of ethnic groups, a measure that had been dropped two decades earlier. The term *multiculturalism* was considered sufficiently evocative that in October 2010, a lead *Globe and Mail* editorial went so far as to suggest a form of self-censorship by calling for its banning from our national vocabulary.[13] That Canada's leading national newspaper thought it necessary to suggest such a radical stand is not to be taken lightly even if surveys reveal that some three in four Canadians react positively to the word *multiculturalism* (amongst others, a survey done by Leger Marketing in June 2010).[14] Respected Canadian scholars Keith Banting and Will Kymlicka point out that while the "m word" is now virtually taboo in some countries and may be irretrievable, the underlying principles and policies of a liberal-democratic multicultural citizenship are still in place in Western democracies, irrespective of the vocabulary used to describe them.[15]

A considerable number of Canadian researchers export knowledge to many countries, share experiences, and vaunt our practices in immigrant integration and diversity management. In a February 2008 survey carried out by Leger Marketing, some 68 percent of Canadians stated that the rest of the world should learn from Canada's multiculturalism policy, while some 52 percent agreed that Canada could also learn a lot from the way other countries deal with cultural diversity.[16]

Despite all the domestic wrangling over the limits of multiculturalism and problems of cohesion, Canada consistently ranks near the top in global assessments of integration policies. It finished third in 2010 in the Migrant Integration Policy Index when compared with countries in the European Union and with the United States.[17]

Today, public debates about multiculturalism in Canada tend to invite participants to say whether they are for or against it. Yet despite this apparent polarization, there is a broader spectrum of opinion in debates amongst academics and policy-makers. Yes, there are unconditional supporters of multiculturalism and unconditional critics. Between these two ends of the spectrum is what might be described as soft supporters of multiculturalism, who raise questions about its meaning and impact, and soft critics, who have serious concerns about multiculturalism but do not reject it outright.

Multiple meanings are attributed to multiculturalism in Canada and abroad. Very often, the attributed meaning determines whether multiculturalism elicits favourable or unfavourable views. Its critics continue to insist that governments are simply not doing enough to discourage immigrants from preserving their cultures of origin; others believe that immigrants should determine the pace and process of cultural retention; and a relatively smaller group of thinkers wants governments to actively support the preservation of minority cultures, which they claim was the original intent. In some ways, the multicultural policy might be described as a "project in the works" as its direction was never firmly established. Underlying all this is a debate about what it means to be Canadian.

This collection of essays from some of the country's leading thinkers about issues of identity attempts to capture the contours of the current debate as the authors reflect on multiculturalism as policy, ideology, and message. The essays in this volume aim to help Canadians better understand the essence of a debate that is likely to remain with us for the foreseeable future. Short summaries are provided below of these essays, which are designed to stimulate ongoing reflection about multicultural-ism and its impact on Canada.

John Biles traces the evolution of Canada's multicultural policy along thematic lines. These themes take place within the parameters of three interrelated elements of what he calls the Canadian inclusion reflex: a desire to create a framework for an inclusive national identity; a desire to ensure the full participation of all Canadians in the social, economic, cultural, and civic facets of Canadian society; and a commitment to the reduction of systemic barriers and discrimination.

Elke Winter argues that during the 1990s, multiculturalism owed its success to a tacit alliance among the republican, liberal-pluralist, and liberal-multiculturalist perspectives on national identity and multiculturalism sharing opposition to Quebec's allegedly "ethnically nationalist" model. The important differences among the three identi-fied perspectives resurfaced in the first decade of the 21st century as the salience of Québécois nationalism has given way to fears about Muslim fundamentalism, and, as a consequence, recent negotiations concerning multiculturalism are marked by debates about religious accommodation, gender equality, and national security.

Randall Hansen contends that Canada has an assimilation policy masquerading as an integration policy, and it is the failure to clarify this situation that partly explains the ongoing debate between opponents and supporters of multiculturalism. In practice, multiculturalism means that a migrant's culture is not merely passively tolerated; it is actively encour-aged and fostered. Critics describe multiculturalism as it is supposed to be and not what the policy corresponds to in the Canadian context. Paradoxically, its supporters have, in the end, defended the broader and far more important set of assimilationist policies into which current Canadian multiculturalism policies are actually nested.

Phil Ryan examines John Rawls's thoughts on pluralism and offers a Rawlsian speculation on the prospects for liberal multiculturalism. Ryan contends that serious flaws mar much of the criticism of Canadian multiculturalism. He cites immigrants' attachment to homeland as a phenomenon that existed long before the introduction of multiculturalism and the false nostalgia about an imagined time when Canadians were united by a shared identity and sense of history. This certainly does not mean that all criticism of multiculturalism is mistaken.

Jeffrey G. Reitz contends that multicultural policies have had little im-pact, either positive or negative, on support for minority cultures. Yet he contends that multicultural discourse plays a part in the scale of national commitment to immigration, the extent of public support, and the success of immigrants in integrating into society. Celebrating multiculturalism as a national ideal reflects Canadians' enthusiasm for immigration and its cultural and economic benefits. While popular multiculturalism re-inforces support for immigration as a national project, evidence indicates that it does not materially influence barriers to the social and economic integration of immigrant minorities into the community.

Richard J.F. Day suggests that liberal multiculturalism must prove to be considerably better at accommodating differences arising from various expressions of identity other than those of race and ethnicity. He worries that multiculturalism promotes hierarchies and relativism, wherein importance is not thoughtfully directed toward the broad spectrum of identities that are reflected in the country's plural landscape.

Yasmeen Abu-Laban notes that since its inception, multiculturalism has been mainly a symbolic policy, and while symbolism should not be discounted in meeting real and legitimate interests, the policy has clearly not always been effective in ameliorating material inequities stemming from race, class, or gender, amongst other forms of social inequality. As such, the content and meaning of multiculturalism is also shaped by state actors and social actors with unequal power as well as by shifting political circumstances. Abu-Laban contends that Canada's Conservative government has engaged in a systematic remaking of select symbols and discourses relating to Canadian identity. When it comes to multiculturalism, she describes the government's agenda as "reform by stealth." Rather than directly attacking multiculturalism policy, the government has reformulated it through, for example, changes to immigration and citizenship policies.

Geneviève Nootens suggests that the divergent approaches to immigrant integration and diversity are a microcosm of the conflict between the respective nationalist visions of Quebec and Canada. Canadian multiculturalism is seen as emphasizing pluralism and diversity, while Quebec interculturalism stresses integration in support of the French-speaking majority. The fact that Canadian multiculturalism does not explicitly call for the assertion of the majority does not detract from the presence of majority norms and institutions to which new Canadians are asked to adapt, amongst them the adoption of English as the common public language. In Quebec, the francophone population's status as a political minority in Canada requires that it assert its majority status and more explicitly define the parameters of immigrant integration for those newcomers who settle in Quebec.

Daniel Weinstock argues that interculturalist critics of multiculturalism have mistakenly characterized the relationship as pitting opposing models of diversity management against each other. Far from constituting a distinct political philosophy or ideology, multiculturalism is best thought of as resulting from the application of core liberal principles to circumstances of cultural diversity. Interculturalism is best thought of not as a policy-relevant set of principles but rather as an attractive vision of the kind of society that might emerge from one ordered by just principles, including multicultural principles, given the presence of the right mix of sociological characteristics.

Eve Haque contends that from the outset, the ratification of official languages before the enactment of multiculturalism ensured a hierarchy of language in support of dual-white-settler dominance and hence an extension of the British and French colonization of Canada. Non-official languages were deemed to be a problematic outcome of multiculturalism and their use a threat to official languages. Ultimately, minority ethnic groups did not succeed in advancing an inclusive multilingual vision that would offer a truly meaningful expression of multiculturalism.

John W. Berry reviews the dominant hypotheses reflected in Canadian and international research about the potential effects of multiculturalism: the *multiculturalism hypothesis*, the *integration hypothesis*, and the *contact hypothesis*. The multiculturalism hypothesis posits that when individuals and societies are confident in, and feel secure about, their own cultural identities and their place in the larger society, more positive mutual attitudes will result; in contrast, when these identities are threatened, mutual hostility will result. The integration hypothesis proposes that there will be more successful psychological and social outcomes for individuals and societies when strategies and policies that support double cultural engagement (i.e., with both the heritage and the national cultures) are pursued. The contact hypothesis suggests that greater contact among members of cultural groups will lead to more positive mutual regard under most contact circumstances. There appears to be sufficient empirical support, both within Canada and around the world, to consider these hypotheses to be general principles that can serve as a basis for developing multiculturalism policies and programs, something that may, in turn, lead to an improvement in intercultural relations in plural societies.

Finally, Susan W. Hardwick and I argue that the comparisons between Canadian multiculturalism and the American melting pot is no longer a useful metaphor for comparing the two countries with respect to issues of immigration, integration, and diversity. We look specifically at studies done in the two countries on residential concentration of ethnic and racial minorities and insist that the differences in this regard are not associated with the respective populations' preferred models of diversity. We conclude that it is time to invent a new paradigm to promote comparative research between Canadians and Americans on the vital questions of immigration and national identity.

NOTES

[1] Jean Lock Kunz and Stuart Sykes, *From Mosaic to Harmony: Multicultural Canada in the 21st Century – Results of Regional Roundtables* (Ottawa: Government of Canada, Policy Research Initiative, 2007).

[2] Ibid.

[3] Ibid.

[4] Yasmeen Abu-Laban and Daiva Stasiulis, "Ethnic Pluralism under Siege: Popular and Partisan Opposition to Multiculturalism," *Canadian Public Policy* 18, no. 4 (December 1992):365–386.

[5] Kunz and Sykes, *From Mosaic to Harmony*.

[6] Joseph Heath, *The Myth of Shared Values in Canada* (Ottawa: Canadian Centre for Management Development, 2003).

[7] Robert Putnam, "*E Pluribus Unum*: Diversity and Community in the Twenty-First Century – The 2006 Johan Skytte Prize Lecture," *Scandinavian Political Studies* 30, no. 2 (June 2007):149.

[8] Leger Marketing, survey conducted for the Association for Canadian Studies, 25–29 April 2013.

[9] Leger Marketing, survey conducted for the Association for Canadian Studies, 4–10 October 2007.

[10] Louise Beaudoin (Ministre d'état Aux Relations Internationales, Gouvernement du Québec), speech delivered to the Colloque Panaméricain, Montreal, 22–24 April 2002, at http://www.er.uqam.ca/nobel/gricis/actes/panam/Beaudoin.pdf, accessed 16 December 2013.

[11] Jason Kenney (Minister of Citizenship, Immigration and Multiculturalism), opening remarks at the Global Forum for Combating Anti-Semitism, Jerusalem, 16–17 December 2009.

[12] Leger Marketing, survey conducted for the Association for Canadian Studies, 21 May 2010.

[13] *Globe and Mail*, editorial, 8 October 2010.

[14] Leger Marketing, survey conducted for the Association for Canadian Studies, June 2010.

[15] Keith Banting and Will Kymlicka, "Is There Really a Retreat from Multiculturalism Policies? New Evidence from the Multiculturalism Policy Index," *Comparative European Politics* 11, no. 5 (2013):1–22.

[16] Leger Marketing, survey conducted for the Association for Canadian Studies, 6–11 February 2008.

[17] Migrant Integration Policy Index, "MIPEX III Key Findings" (Brussels: Migration Policy Group, 2010), at http://www.mipex.eu/research, accessed 16 December 2013.

THE GOVERNMENT OF CANADA'S MULTICULTURALISM PROGRAM: KEY TO CANADA'S INCLUSION REFLEX?

JOHN BILES[1]

INTRODUCTION

Multiculturalism as official government of Canada policy dates to its promulgation by then prime minister Pierre Trudeau on 8 October 1971 in the House of Commons. However, recognition of the cultural diversity of the Canadian population and a need for policy responses predate this announcement by decades, a point made by several authors in this volume and elsewhere.[2] Canada, Canadians, their governments, and institutions obviously look dramatically different 40 years later. Curiously, both proponents and opponents of multiculturalism have framed their engagement with multiculturalism through a lens that appears to have varied little over the intervening four decades, even though the exact contours of what is meant by *multiculturalism* appear to have broadened significantly.[3]

While multiculturalism has broadened to include policies at all levels of government, many major institutions, and a powerful public idea that the majority of Canadians believe is central to Canadian identity, the policy itself has remained remarkably consistent with the central aspects of the 1971 policy, which became embedded in the *Canadian Multiculturalism Act* of 1988. This consistency is all the more surprising given that the Multiculturalism Program has been managed by four different departments (Secretary of State, Multiculturalism and Citizenship, Canadian

The Multiculturalism Question: Debating Identity in 21st-Century Canada, ed. Jack Jedwab. Kingston: School of Policy Studies, Queen's University. © 2014 The School of Policy Studies, Queen's University at Kingston. All rights reserved.

Heritage, and Citizenship and Immigration Canada), each with its own corporate culture and focus. Five constant themes can be found in the policy: a need to assist minority communities to contribute to Canada; overcoming barriers to participation; promoting interaction amongst Canadians of diverse backgrounds; promoting the use of both official languages; and working with partners, whether other orders of government or federal institutions, to advance the objectives of the policy.[4] These themes are outlined in Table 1 below.

It is interesting that the act includes more of an emphasis on cultural contributions and heritage languages, typically subsumed within the concept of ethnic maintenance, which most typologies identify as the focus of multiculturalism programming in the 1970s.[5] Similarly, the emphasis on the role that multiculturalism plays in national identity and in constructing Canada's future is evident in both the act and the inclusion of multiculturalism in the *Canadian Charter of Rights and Freedoms*, although it was not included in the 1971 multiculturalism policy.[6]

In this chapter, I will argue that this flexible policy framework, promulgated in 1971 and legislated in 1988, has enabled the development of chameleon-like programming, which has allowed for extraordinary heterogeneity in the foci of the federal government's Multiculturalism Program as it sought to assist the government and its institutions to adjust to the uneven needs of a rapidly evolving population across Canada. I will adopt a different strategy than that pursued in several recent evaluations, which focused primarily on short periods of time and on whether the Grants and Contributions Program could demonstrate concrete outcomes.[7] Rather, by taking a broader view over the four decades of multiculturalism as policy and programming, I will point to a series of vital successes. I do not claim to have solved the causality challenges that bedevil evaluations of the program, merely that examining initiatives as a whole over an extended period of time can more effectively demonstrate change over time.[8]

I will focus in this chapter solely on federal multiculturalism policy and programming. It is critical to note that this is not to diminish the tremendous importance of multiculturalism that has taken root as a powerful public idea across Canada and found voice in some form in nearly every government and institution.[9] Nor is there much to be gained from rehearsing the evolution of the policy and program in a strict chronological fashion.[10] Instead, I have approached this expanse of time and history along the thematic lines that have cut across multiculturalism programming over the last four decades: knowledge, research, and data development; historical redress; cultural expression; reducing barriers and tackling discrimination; civic participation; and marketing the Canadian model on the world stage. It is my contention that the major themes that are present across this complex canvas bring greater clarity to the kinds of foci that the Multiculturalism Program has pursued and the

TABLE 1
Multiculturalism Policy Reflected in the 1971 Multiculturalism Policy and the 1988
Canadian Multiculturalism Act

Multiculturalism Policy (1971)	*Canadian Multiculturalism Act* (1988)
"First, resources permitting, the government will seek to assist all Canadian cultural groups that have demonstrated … a capacity to grow and contribute to Canada, and a clear need for assistance, the small and weak groups no less than the strong and highly organized.	"(*a*) recognize and promote the understanding that multiculturalism reflects the cultural and racial diversity of Canadian society and acknowledges the freedom of all members of Canadian society to preserve, enhance and share their cultural heritage;
Second, the government will assist members of all cultural groups to overcome cultural barriers to full participation in Canadian society.	(*b*) recognize and promote the understanding that multiculturalism is a fundamental characteristic of the Canadian heritage and identity and that it provides an invaluable resource in the shaping of Canada's future;
Third, the government will promote creative encounters and interchange among all Canadian cultural groups in the interest of national unity.	(*c*) promote the full and equitable participation of individuals and communities … in the continuing evolution and shaping of all aspects of Canadian society and assist them in the elimination of any barrier to that participation;
Fourth, the government will continue to assist immigrants to acquire at least one of Canada's official languages in order to become full participants in Canadian society.…	(*d*) recognize the existence of communities whose members share a common origin and their historic contribution to Canadian society, and enhance their development;
We are also ready and willing to work cooperatively with the provincial governments toward implementing those recommendations that concern matters under provincial or shared responsibility.…	(*e*) ensure that all individuals receive equal treatment and equal protection under the law, while respecting and valuing their diversity;
An Inter-Agency Committee of all those agencies involved will be established to coordinate the federal effort."	(*f*) encourage and assist the social, cultural, economic and political institutions of Canada to be both respectful and inclusive of Canada's multicultural character;
	(*g*) promote the understanding and creativity that arise from the interaction between individuals and communities of different origins;
	(*h*) foster the recognition and appreciation of the diverse cultures of Canadian society and promote the reflection and the evolving expressions of those cultures;
	(*i*) preserve and enhance the use of languages other than English and French, while strengthening the status and use of the official languages of Canada; and
	(*j*) advance multiculturalism throughout Canada in harmony with the national commitment to the official languages of Canada."

Source: Canada, Parliament, House of Commons, *Debates,* 28th Parliament, 3rd Session, 1970–1972, vol. 8 (Ottawa: Queen's Printer, 8 October 1971), 8545; and Canada, *Canadian Multiculturalism Act,* c. 31 (1988), s. 3(1).

outcomes it has obtained. These themes take place within the parameters of three interrelated, overarching elements of what I term the Canadian inclusion reflex: a desire to create a framework for an inclusive national identity; a desire to ensure the full participation of all Canadians in the social, economic, cultural, and civic facets of Canadian society; and a commitment to the reduction of systemic barriers and discrimination. This chapter seeks to help us understand how we developed this reflex.

AN INCLUSIVE NATIONAL IDENTITY

There is no doubt that the desire to craft a more inclusive Canadian national identity is woven throughout the four decades of multiculturalism as official policy in Canada. We can easily discern a well-worn pathway from the outset of demands for multiculturalism policy, whereby Canadians and their governments sought both to actively expand the historical gaze to better reflect the diversity of the Canadian populace and to address the most egregious acts of the past that have singled out a few Canadian communities in a manner inconsistent with our desire to construct an inclusive present and future. This pathway can be charted through a long-standing commitment to investing in knowledge through research and data development, through a more contemporary concern with redressing past wrongs, and how the government of Canada positions Canada's approach to diversity on the world stage.

Knowledge: Research and Data Development

Any trip through Canadian historiography finds a predominance of white, upper-class, English- and sometimes French-origin and -speaking Christian males until the late 1960s and early 1970s, when this comfortable, if monotonous, history was abruptly disrupted.[11] The "other" ethnic groups demanded to be heard by the Royal Commission on Bilingualism and Biculturalism. In its response to the commission's findings, the government of Canada committed to funding "histories specifically directed to the background, contributions and problems of various cultural groups in Canada."[12] This commitment has been met through a variety of means over the last 40 years, including publications, research chairs, research grants, and support for research networks. Across all activities, there is a discernible evolution from ethnic-specific activities to those that are either thematic or multicultural.

In terms of publications, the promised support materialized in at least two series. The first was a book series sponsored by the Department of the Secretary of State, edited by Jean Burnet and Howard Palmer, entitled Generations: A History of Canada's Peoples,[13] and the second was a series of 20 booklets entitled Canada's Ethnic Groups, produced in partnership with the Canadian Historical Association.[14] The latter booklets addressed thematic issues rather than ethno-specific histories. Little is formally known about the impact of these publications. However, as they continue to be referenced by work in this field and have been followed by hundreds of similar studies, it can be surmised that they have had some impact.

The government of Canada has also invested significant resources in its Canadian Ethnic Studies Program. Initially, this consisted of visiting professorships and lectureships and ethnic research, with the subsequent addition of endowment assistance.[15] The Visiting Professorships and Lectureships Program was designed to "assist in the initiation and development of studies and research related to Canada's ethnocultural diversity and multiculturalism."[16] It met with mixed success. For example, when conducting an evaluation of the program in 1978, Evelyn Kallen found that two major factors inhibited the participation of Canadian academics and universities: first, the requirement that 20 percent of costs were to be borne by a university and, second, the surprising number of participants in the evaluation who had never heard of the program. In addition, researchers consulted thought that the definition of ethnic studies itself, the "ethnic particularist focus," and the requirement that participants be Canadian also comprised obstacles to uptake of the program. It is interesting to note that the scholars surveyed were also divided about the desirability of more actively engaging communities and whether an Ottawa-based think tank or regionally dispersed ethnic research centres would be more effective; these themes continue to echo 30 years later.

This trend of an evolution from ethno-specific to thematic or multicultural approaches can also be seen in the 28 chairs of ethnic studies funded by the Department of the Secretary of State and successor departments.[17] The chairs were created over 20 years (1977–1995) "in order to assist ethno-cultural communities in their efforts to maintain their ancestral heritage and to make Canadian society more aware of the history, language, culture and contribution to Canadian life of the many groups that consider Canada their home."[18] Canadian universities or voluntary organizations were invited to submit proposals for endowed chairs, with federal government contributions of between $300,000 and $400,000.

The overall Canadian Ethnic Studies Program cost $10 million. In return, each university was required to provide a financial audit and a full evaluation of the chair's stated objectives at the end of five years, but no further commitments for accountability were required. However, the Department of Canadian Heritage undertook an evaluation of the program in 1996–1997 as part of a strategic review of multiculturalism programming. The evaluation found that the chairs had supervised almost 200 graduate students between 1990 and 1996, had produced a significant volume of research, had fostered extensive relationships with the voluntary sector, and had legitimized the study of ethnic groups. It also found that the department needed to expend more energy bringing the chairs together and ensuring that they were informed of policy changes. Despite efforts in the late 1990s to engage the chairs more systematically, these efforts bore little fruit; government interest in the chairs dwindled, and the program was phased out.[19]

A third component of the Canadian Ethnic Studies Program was the allocation of resources to academics to pursue specific studies. In 1973, Howard Palmer and Harold Troper were commissioned by the Department of the Secretary of State to undertake a study on the current state of ethnic studies in Canada. They surveyed university administrators and academics across the country and found that while there was a division of opinion on whether resources should be concentrated in one national or several regional research centres,[20] there was agreement that there was a need for interdisciplinary coordination to both give visibility to Canadian ethnic studies and establish the area as a legitimate research and teaching field. One of the report's recommendations was to establish a Canadian Ethnic Studies Advisory Committee, which could advise the department on what kind of research it should fund. Of all research initiatives undertaken under the rubric of multiculturalism, this committee would have the greatest longevity.

The evolution of this program is captured well by James Cameron.[21] Cameron reports the impact of this modest program as "substantial," and he observes that its "legacy is strongest at those universities where it assisted the establishment of ethnic studies chairs."[22] The impact of this program on the evolution of the field of ethnic studies is detailed by a range of scholars, including Howard Palmer, John Berry and Jean Laponce, and most recently by Leo Driedger.[23] To establish that ethnic studies had indeed become a bona fide area of academic inquiry, Cameron observes that at the outset of this program, the Social Sciences and Humanities Research Council of Canada (SSHRC) and its predecessor, the Canada Council, "rarely supported ethnic/immigration research," but by the time the state-of-the-art research on ethnicity compendium was published in 1994, its editors, John Berry and Jean Laponce, were able to observe, "We [the contributors] are in general agreement in our overall assessment: ethnic and multicultural studies are remarkably well-developed in Canada."[24]

The success of the Canadian Ethnic Studies Program is attributed to the longevity of funding (nearly 35 years), the calibre of the research produced and of the researchers involved, and the longevity of many of the key bureaucrats and researchers involved with the program. For example, only three people chaired the Canadian Ethnic Studies Advisory Committee: Jean Burnet, 1973–1987; Raymond Breton, 1987–1989; and John Edwards, 1990–1999. This committee of six to eight prominent scholars met three or four times a year to assess research applications and to advise the minister responsible for multiculturalism which proposals merited funding. Over the period 1973–1997, the committee recommended

350 projects for funding, which yielded 480 articles or book chapters in its first 15 years alone.[25] In addition, committee members were occasionally consulted for policy advice, including for a working paper on the development of the *Canadian Multiculturalism Act*; programming components, or the 1996–1997 strategic review of the program.[26] Related to this was ongoing support for both the Canadian Ethnic Studies Association, which has held biennial conferences since 1971, and the journal *Canadian Ethnic Studies*, which has been published continuously since that era.[27]

Despite its many successes, the Canadian Ethnic Studies Program faced diminishing resources following the strategic review. This was, in part, a result of the government's overall cuts to research during the cross-government program review; in part a result of investments in a new initiative, the Metropolis Project; and, most important, a result of increasing competition for shrinking resources within the broader Canadian Heritage portfolio, which saw a sizable portion of multiculturalism funds "reprofiled" to meet other departmental priorities.[28]

Subsequent research endeavours of the Multiculturalism Program were more modest. These included a brief three-year partnership with SSHRC (2002–2004) to fund multiculturalism-focused research and a quartet of policy-research seminars designed to help focus research efforts on the strategic goals of the renewed program: civic participation, social justice, and identity.[29]

Ultimately, however, apart from some modest research contracts, the majority of the research efforts of the Multiculturalism Program over the last decade are to be found in the Metropolis Project. The 15 years of funding for this initiative clearly accomplished its objectives of increasing the volume of research on immigration and diversity, the policy-relevance of this research, and the number of researchers working in this field.[30]

What direction future efforts will take remains unclear, although a piece commissioned from Will Kymlicka suggests future directions for research.[31] The Multiculturalism Program was transferred from Canadian Heritage to Citizenship and Immigration Canada (CIC) in 2008, and multiculturalism-specific research efforts have subsequently been integrated into the broader departmental research agenda. CIC's Research and Evaluation Branch maintains a multiculturalism research framework to guide its work in this field.

Interspersed among these various research efforts was a significant effort to develop large-scale data sets that could guide multiculturalism programming and policy development. This included a survey of individuals on multiculturalism and ethnic attitudes in the mid-1970s[32] and one on non-official-language use.[33] In the 1990s, a major survey was funded on Canadians' attitudes toward multiculturalism.[34]

Perhaps most significant was the continuous objective of maintaining an ethnic-origin question on the Canadian census. Every five years sees an intense debate among proponents and opponents of the question, with proponents arguing that its inclusion is essential for guiding policy-making and program design to meet the needs of an increasingly diverse populace and opponents arguing that the concepts are fuzzy and lack statistical reliability.[35] Following the debate surrounding the 2001 census, a post-censual survey, the Ethnic Diversity Survey, was implemented in order to shed light on this ubiquitous debate. The resulting data set is the single most important data set undertaken on the subject. The 42,000 responses on a wide range of issues has been used extensively in program and policy development since its release in 2003.[36]

In addition, the Multiculturalism Program has regularly supported demographic projections.[37] These are typically used in program and policy development, but also in awareness-raising activities. For example, in 2005, the program organized a government-wide policy forum focused on what the 2017 demographic projections augured for the government of Canada.[38] It is important to note that the projections for 2017 and later for 2030 have included projections for both visible minorities and religious diversity; multiculturalism had long been critiqued for overlooking the significance of religious diversity.

In summary, the Multiculturalism Program has effectively established ethnic studies as a bona fide field of academic inquiry in Canada. Thousands of studies, academic publications, and graduate theses[39] have been produced, and, today, this mature field of study has resulted in the regular granting of funds from the major research-granting councils. In the wake of the phasing-out of the Metropolis network, there is some encouraging signs that smaller research networks such as the Association for Canadian Studies and the Canadian Ethnic Studies Association have begun to collaborate to ensure forward momentum on research on diversity in Canada.

The evidence produced with the assistance of the Multiculturalism Program has provided a robust knowledge platform for developing policies and programs designed to meet the evolving needs of an increasingly diverse Canadian populace. This more complex and inclusive history has also laid the groundwork upon which a more inclusive Canadian national identity has been forged.

Redress

The development of a more complex historiography and understanding of Canadian society was an endeavour fraught with difficulties and controversy. However, these challenges were minor compared to those confronted over the demands for redress of past wrongs by certain ethnic groups. The ideological clash on this front was far less esoteric and far more political, although it, too, featured interpretations of the past (through the lens of both professional historians as well as novelists and other cultural producers). The two poles are best represented by, at one end of the spectrum, former prime minister Pierre Trudeau, who on his last day in the House of Commons observed, "I do not see how I can apologize for some historical event to which we or these people in this House were not a party,"[40] and at the other end by former prime minister Brian Mulroney and current Prime Minister Stephen Harper, who have actively pursued redress for past injustices (in the case of the former, the Japanese Canadian Redress Agreement[41] and an apology to Italian Canadians[42] and, under the leadership of the latter,[43] redress for the "head tax" for Chinese Canadians[44] and a much more comprehensive historical recognition program[45]).

One additional approach to multicultural redress implicated both major parties in Canada, suggesting that opinions do not cleanly follow party lines. The *Internment of Persons of Ukrainian Origin Recognition Act* was introduced by Conservative Member of Parliament Inky Mark as a private member's bill, which was passed into law in 2005, during Paul Martin's time as prime minister.[46]

It is interesting to note that while academics played an active role in many redress campaigns,[47] most notably those of the Japanese Canadians, Ukrainian Canadians, Italian Canadians, and Chinese Canadians, it is novelists and other cultural creators who may have had the greatest impact. For example, Joy Kogawa's novel *Obasan* is often credited with raising public awareness of the need for Japanese Canadian redress.[48] Similarly, a National Film Board and Canadian Broadcasting Corporation (CBC) documentary, *Barbed Wire and Mandolins,* assisted the Italian Canadians in their efforts to raise public awareness.[49] The CBC also played a role in the Ukrainian Canadian campaign with a 1994 airing of a documentary entitled *Freedom Had a Price: Canada's First Internment Operation.* This effort was augmented by "The Barbed Wire Solution," a historical exhibit of the Ukrainian Canadian Research and Documentation Centre, and artist Sophia Isajiw's exhibit entitled "History's Exiles."[50]

While debate has tended to focus on a range of issues, including historical revisionism, individual versus collective rights, and a fear that opening Pandora's box of apologies would lead to an endless and destructive series of requests for apologies,[51] at its core the debate has been about Canadian identity and the place of Canada's diverse citizenry in the development of the country.[52] For example, the government of Canada's new citizenship guide, *Discover Canada: The Rights and Responsibilities of Citizenship,*[53] references the regrettable internment of Canadians of Austro-Hungarian origin (mostly Ukrainians) in the First World War, Japanese Canadians during the Second World War, as well as the discrimination faced by Chinese immigrants through the so-called head tax imposed upon them following the completion of the Canadian Pacific Railway. Inclusion of these references in the "official" history of Canada represents the acceptance and inclusion sought by activists from these communities for decades. Of course, other communities remain outside the official history and continue to lobby for formal redress from the government. For example, in 2005, the Canadian Race Relations Foundation identified 13 ethnic and religious groups that had launched redress claims.[54]

Redress is a highly contested idea and one that even supporters approach warily. As political scientist Matt James details, at its core is a concern among some critics that the politics of recognition have trumped those of redistribution. In other words, systemic inequalities like poverty have been sacrificed to identity-based recognition claims like redress.[55] James remains unconvinced, however, by these critiques and suggests, "Canadian redress movements are clearly part of a historical movement toward more demanding understandings of what equal citizenship entails."[56] In the end he concludes,[57] "For the federal government, therefore, demands that Canada must revisit unflattering episodes and practices of its past afford an opportunity. This opportunity is to seek to realize in a more thorough and inclusive manner the potential of the most basic instrument of connectedness that we have. Struggles over respect and recognition are often discomforting, but they are premised on the desire to pursue the project of a common citizenship."[58]

James chronicles how Japanese Canadian redress gave rise to a more confident and civically active Japanese Canadian population,[59] and he suggests that this was also true of Chinese Canadians even before their redress claim was settled by the federal government.[60] In other words, redress of past injustices, far from "sanitizing the present," can actually lay the groundwork for active participation of ethnic minorities in Canadian civic structures, as envisioned in both the multiculturalism policy of 1971 and the *Canadian Multiculturalism Act* of 1988.

Marketing Canadian Pluralism on the World Stage

A third arrow in the government of Canada's inclusive national identity quiver was its efforts to project multiculturalism as a component of the Canadian brand.[61] This has been done most extensively, perhaps, through initiatives like the Metropolis Project, the International Council for Canadian Studies, and the Forum of Federations, but it has also been advanced through investments in culture and promotional efforts to globalize that cultural output. International governments, in turn, regularly flock to Canada to ascertain how our multicultural model is designed and implemented and how it impacts outcomes of inclusion and integration for newcomers and minorities.

Scholars like Harald Bauder have argued that efforts at inclusion, particularly of newcomers, are critical to the development of national identities; or, as he describes it, "immigration policies and debates serve to imagine the nation."[62] In this view, Canadians can construct a national identity through the development of both immigration and citizenship policies, but also in the international reflections upon Canada as a generous, pluralistic society. This can be extended to multiculturalism policy as well. For example, Will Kymlicka hypothesizes that the government of Canada promoted its multicultural model for three interrelated reasons: projecting Canadian values onto the world stage and ensuring Canada's ability to play an international role; attracting business, immigrants, and entrepreneurs; and quieting domestic critiques by invoking international plaudits.[63]

In analyzing the success of these different motivations, Kymlicka concludes that the "broad goal of enhancing Canada's international reputation as a diversity friendly country has certainly had some success."[64] He lists the establishment of the Agha Khan Foundation's Global Centre for Pluralism in Ottawa, and the extent to which international organizations hold up Canadian multiculturalism as an ideal, as proof of this bolstering of Canada's image on the international stage. However, he is far more skeptical that this critical acclaim has been linked to government-funded initiatives (which, in the case of both Metropolis and the International Council for Canadian Studies, have subsequently been phased out as government-funded initiatives), that this enhanced image has actually increased Canada's capacity to tackle underlying global humanitarian issues, or, for that matter, that the Canadian multiculturalism model has been of use to other countries in tackling integration and inclusion.

On the other two motivations, he is more certain. In terms of attracting business, immigrants, and entrepreneurs, Kymlicka notes that "there is anecdotal evidence that some immigrants and foreign students have chosen Canada over other countries because of our reputation for multicultural tolerance," particularly since the terrorist attacks of 11 September 2001.[65] In terms of quieting domestic critiques, he concludes, "If nothing else, the awareness of international support for Canada's policies helps shift the burden of proof in public debate, putting domestic critics of these policies on the defensive."[66]

In addition to the ideas proposed by Kymlicka, an examination of how multiculturalism programming has assisted Canadians and Canadian governments in handling moments of crisis reveals a substantive success that has not gone unnoticed on the world stage. These recent moments of crisis have included the terrorist attacks in New York and Washington on 9/11 and the subsequent attacks in London, Madrid, and Bali; the civil unrest in Parisian suburbs, in northern British towns, and on Australian beaches; the two high-profile assassinations in the Netherlands; and European leaders' subsequent speeches on the demise of multiculturalism and the perils of "sleepwalking to segregation." In all cases, a backlash was felt in Canada, as it was in other immigrant-receiving societies, but its manifestations were weaker, and the uniquely Canadian inclusion reflex that has developed over 40 years of official multiculturalism policy in Canada resulted in less precipitous declines in public support for immigration, a muted level of xenophobia evident in political discourse, and no appreciable long-term increase in racism or discrimination.[67]

Attribution to multiculturalism policy or programming is impossible to prove. However, as Jeff Reitz concludes, Canadian pride in multiculturalism (along with belief in the economic contribution of newcomers) is one of the core reasons why Canadian public opinion differs so profoundly from European opinion on the question of immigration.[68] Canada appears to have taken British philosopher Bhikhu Parekh's observation to heart: "A political crisis is like a magnifying mirror reflecting some of the deeper trends and tendencies developing in a society. A wise nation meditates on it and uses it as a means for self-knowledge."[69]

FULL PARTICIPATION

A second component of Canada's developing inclusion reflex is a consistent focus on the full participation of all Canadians in all walks of Canadian life. It is possible to discern a commitment to civic engagement across the last 40 years. Indeed, there are researchers who trace this connection back to the Second World War.[70]

The means of fostering full participation of all Canadians in all facets of our society run the gamut of programming from support for cultural expression, through assisting newcomers to obtain linguistic aptitude in one or both of Canada's official languages, to the encouragement of minorities to participate actively in the formal electoral process, and everything in between. I will consider just three examples of this programming spectrum: cultural programming, programming designed to foster civic participation, and an initiative to reduce barriers and tackle discrimination.

Cultural Expression: How Multiculturalism Became a Public Idea

One of the most over-cited critiques of multiculturalism pertains to the "song and dance," "red-boots," or "saris, samosas, and steel drums" approach to multiculturalism.[71] In general, this critique focuses on the failings of a multicultural approach that begins and ends with cultural expression. However, it is a weak "straw horse" in the Canadian context as the multiculturalism policy and program have always aimed for a broader approach. In addition, this dismissive critique appears particularly at odds with an increasing belief in the importance of cultural citizenship in both the symbolic and the economic spheres.[72]

To be sure, the Multiculturalism Program did have a programming stream focused on cultural expression from the mid-1970s until a strategic review of the entire program was concluded in 1997 and separate funding streams were subsequently rolled into one generic Grants and

Contributions Program. The emphasis of this cultural expression funding shifted over this 30-year span from a greater emphasis on community-oriented programming to more of a focus on institutional adaptation.[73] It should be underscored that these twin objectives (cultural expression and institutional adaptation) were embedded in the Writing and Publications Program (WPP), which was launched in 1977–1978 along with the Performing and Visual Arts Program. Thus, as in most programming areas, it is more a question of emphasis than wholesale shifts in priorities.

According to the program brochure for the WPP, these objectives were listed as "to encourage the writing and publishing efforts of writers who use the non-official languages for their creative work as well as those writers who use the official languages but who have a specific cultural experience to convey" and "to encourage the Canadian literary establishment and the reading public in general to view this literature as an aspect of Canadian literature."[74] The program was never large, with ceilings of $5,000 for writing, $7,500 for conferences and publishing, and $1,500 for promotional activities.[75] In 1990, these two programs were amalgamated into the Creative and Cultural Expression Program, which was mandated to "promote greater opportunity within and equal access to Canada's arts, cultural institutions and industries for artists from a diversity of cultural backgrounds" and "to support and promote writing and publishing [performing arts, visual arts, audio-visual, and film] projects that reflect or foster appreciation for the cultural diversity of Canadian society."[76]

How successful was the Multiculturalism Program at accomplishing the tasks set out by its cultural expression programming? First, let us consider whether the supply of cultural products by minority artists, writers, and other creators increased. Judy Young, who worked in the program from its outset, lists many of its achievements, including anthologies of poetry and fictional works in German, Hungarian, Polish, Spanish, Ukrainian, and Yiddish; many translations from so-called heritage languages into English or French, or both; many works published in English and French by diverse authors; curriculum materials, including anthologies, special issues of magazines, and various series of children's books; and a series on the writers and writing activities of various communities.[77] She observes that the *Resource Guide of Publications Supported by Multiculturalism Programs 1973–1992* lists over 1,300 publications, and this excludes the last five years of the program's investments as well as grants for writing, translations, conferences, and promotional grants awarded over the life of this program.[78] She also chronicles a litany of former recipients of multiculturalism grants who are today recognizable as stars in the Canadian literary firmament, including, ironically, some who have become well-known critics of multiculturalism.

An observer more removed from the program, literary critic Enoch Padolsky, concludes in his analysis of "Canadian Ethnic Minority

Literature in English" in the mid-1990s, "Today, Canadian literature reflects a much broader proportion of a changing Canadian society and both the number of writers and the group experiences represented have expanded dramatically."[79] Similarly, Sherry Simon and David Leahy observe that "it was only in the 1980s that there came into critical existence a category designating authors of immigrant or culturally diverse origins" in Quebec.[80]

That said, critics argue that the parallel structure established by multicultural funding further marginalized minority cultural creators[81] and thus no structural change can be noted among "mainstream" institutions and systems. However, others contend that mainstream arts, cultural, and heritage institutions have adapted, at least partially, to the new reality of a diverse Canadian pool of cultural creators. Young tackles the very premise of the marginalization argument when she observes that causality is a challenge for critics since "marginalization was a fact of life before the Multiculturalism policy."[82] Others, like Carol Tator, Frances Henry, and Winston Mattis, conclude, "Despite all the efforts by cultural agencies and authorities to contain the challenges to their institutions and systems, there have been some gains."[83] Putting it in concrete terms, Young observes that "many of the writers funded by the Program in earlier years were now [1990] receiving grants from the 'regular' agencies such as the Canada Council or provincial arts councils. Many ... had 'arrived'; several won major literary prizes, had gone on to do cultural funding decision jury duty, were teaching in the universities or creative writing courses, and were representing Canada abroad."[84] Further, she observes that "the Canada Council (and the provincial arts councils) have moved a great distance toward more inclusive policies in the last ten years. They have increased the diversity of staff and juries."[85]

Young also details how the Multiculturalism Program actively targeted mainstream organizations by developing partnerships like a multi-year project with the Canadian Museums Association to help museums and galleries address cultural diversity effectively; working with the Alliance of Canadian Cinema, Television and Radio Artists to develop its first mainstream talent director featuring artists of diverse backgrounds; and launching the Gemini Awards/Prix Gémeaux with the Academy of Canadian Cinema and Television.[86] An additional feather in the program's cap in this area was the inclusion of multiculturalism in the 1991 *Broadcasting Act*, leading Eric Thomas to claim, "After 20 years, multiculturalism is now an integral part of Canadian cultural policy," although he also cautions, "The task is now to translate such policies into actual reality."[87]

Young concludes, "I believe that taken together, the activities described amounted to a process of institutional change in writing and publishing in Canada or at least speeded up a process that was going to take place anyway." She articulates the complexity of institutional change and the need for long-term investment: "Once there was enough of a body of work by a writer, then a book could be published; once there were enough writers (of a particular origin, region of Canada, region of the world, language, gender, or dealing with particular issues deriving from the immigrant or ethnic or racial experience) then anthologies or special issues of journals could be published; once there were enough works reflecting the diversity of Canada, then they would be noticed and reviewed, there would be critical appraisals; once there were enough critical reviews, then these works and authors would come to the attention of the general reading public, they would be in the daily media, the authors would do public readings and win prizes, be asked to sit on grant juries, represent Canada abroad, and generally become active participants in the cultural life of the country."[88] This theory of institutional change, in which the entire chain is identified and targeted in order to arrive at an end result, is something that has been less evident in other areas of multiculturalism programming over the years.

Finally, it is worth observing that the investments in cultural production had interesting connections with other aspects of multiculturalism programming discussed in this chapter. For example, by supporting minority artists, writers, and other cultural producers, the Multiculturalism Program fundamentally altered the mirror in which Canadians see themselves and created a cadre of opinion-leading voices, just as the Ethnic Studies Program did with academics. Until its recent elimination following Budget 2012, the International Council for Canadian Studies was composed of many academic organizations around the world with an interest in Canada. The vast majority of these were in literature departments as Canadian literature was seen as a window on how Canada had successfully fashioned a multicultural identity for itself. Similarly, as Tator, Henry, and Mattis show in their case studies of cultural clashes in Toronto in the decade between the mid-1980s and -1990s, culture has spurred on the civic engagement and activism of many marginalized communities.

However, active investment in this area by the Multiculturalism Program has significantly receded in recent years. In a comprehensive analysis of multiculturalism grants and contributions and comparing investments from the early 1980s to the debut of the 21st century, McAndrew and colleagues found that "the idea that the Policy might still be in a 'songs-and-dances' phase and might still emphasize the *elsewhere* and the *bygone days* is contradicted first, by the quasi-total disappearance of any support for minority languages and cultures, and, second by the fact that within the mainstream organizations category, organizations with a cultural mandate have been replaced by organizations with a social mandate."[89]

Festivals constitute an interesting exception to this change in funding priorities. They have sometimes been included in the same area of activity, often with significant derision. For example, Will Kymlicka observed that "Canadians have come to realize that institutional adaptation and civic participation are more important to successful integration than ethnic festivals."[90] Other scholars, however, are less certain that festivals are solely aimed at cultural retention. For example, Bramadat argues that festivals can serve multiple purposes that facilitate integration.[91] The government of Canada would appear to agree with Bramadat as it introduced an events stream for smaller communities to the Multiculturalism Program's Grants and Contributions Program, which was rebranded Inter-Action in 2010. Amongst other objectives, this program change was designed to engage Canadians in raising awareness in their communities.[92] In the first year of the Inter-Action events stream (2010–2011), the program had provided $901,753 to support 94 events across Canada.[93]

It will be interesting to observe whether Canadian cultural producers and institutions continue to diversify as the Canadian population shifts through continued mass migration or whether those communities that were ascendant during government funding for the kinds of initiatives described here have joined a more complex mainstream that is still unwilling to create space for more recently arrived Canadians.

Inclusive cultural participation and representation is key to our Canadian inclusion reflex, yet recent examples, including the relative lack of diversity at the opening and closing ceremonies of the Vancouver Winter Olympics,[94] and the brouhaha surrounding the Asian appearance of the scientist to appear on the $100 bill[95] during the Bank of Canada's focus-group testing on its proposed new banknotes, suggest that we have more work to do.

Civic Participation

Equally central to the Canadian inclusion reflex is a desire to ensure that our diversity is reflected at decision-making tables. However, the participation of minorities in elite decision-making is often perceived as threatening and gives rise to the accusation of crass political self-interest (on behalf of both elected officials and ethnic community leaders).[96] Critics try to damn newcomers and minorities whether they do or do not participate: they maintain that "ethnic politics" leads governments to pander to special interest groups, while at the same time suggesting that newcomers and minorities do not share democratic values with Canadians. Despite these critiques, the government of Canada has actively sought to engage newcomers and minorities through civic engagement and empowerment initiatives, citizenship education, and institutional-change strategies.

In the case of civic engagement and empowerment, investments by the Multiculturalism Program can be tracked back to the 1970s, most notably with core funding for ethnocultural organizations, which continued until the strategic review of the program in 1996–1997. This support was critical to fostering the active participation of minority communities in all facets of Canadian life, as envisioned by both the 1971 policy and the *Canadian Multiculturalism Act* of 1988. Even Audrey Kobayashi, in an otherwise scathing chapter on the efficacy of multiculturalism, observes, "The most valuable aspect of the policy, nonetheless, has been to empower (primarily through funding) the minority ethnocultural groups to advance their own causes."[97] Kobayashi in her chapter and Leslie Pal in his *Interests of State* provide comprehensive case studies of the first 20 years on the national stage of the Canadian Ethnocultural Council (CEC).[98] Pal reports that "the CEC was designed to be a vehicle for the co-ordinated representation of ethnic groups' interests in the policy process, particularly around constitutional issues, immigration, race relations, heritage languages, and multiculturalism."[99] Like the National Association of Japanese Canadians, discussed above by James, Kobayashi and Pal describe how the CEC has contributed on a wide range of issues, not just those specifically focused on entrenching multiculturalism in legislation and the Constitution.

Pal goes on to observe that the CEC was a community response to concern that "the Canadian Consultative Council on Multiculturalism (which was later replaced by the Canadian Multicultural Council) was considered unsatisfactory by many ethnic group leaders because its members were government appointees without any clear mandate to speak for their respective communities."[100] This tension highlights a challenge faced by all governments when seeking to include a diverse range of voices in consultations. Typically, the constellation of organizations is too vast to include all organizations, yet governments are often suspicious of which populations ethnocultural organizations actually represent,[101] and, equally, those same organizations are often concerned about the perceived partisanship of government-selected representatives. The federal government has gone back and forth on this and is currently considering striking a third multiculturalism advisory committee to fill a perceived void.

By the mid-1980s, government support for advocacy activities was strongly contested, and concerns about core support were evident, especially for ethno-specific organizations. One evaluation found that "some managers view core funding as a straight-forward tool which allows them to respond to the needs of Canadians. Others view it from the opposite perspective, as an entangled umbilical cord which ties the Department to a plethora of organizations and which will be dangerous to sever or straighten for the fear of hue and cry of organizations who feel that their very existence would be threatened by any attempt to rationalize their relationship with the Secretary of State Department."[102] This tension would remain evident until the relaunch of the Multiculturalism Program following the strategic review of 1996–1997, when core funding was phased out.

This discomfort with ethno-specific organizations may also be seen to be part of a larger trend in multiculturalism programming, as described earlier in the discussion of the ethnic chairs program. Over time, core funding shifted away from ethno-specific organizations and initiatives toward more cross-cultural or multicultural organizations and initiatives. To the extent that ethno-specific funding continued, it shifted from the "old ethnics" from Europe[103] toward the "new ethnics," which were most often rapidly growing visible-minority communities.[104]

Another aspect of civic participation programming focused on citizenship education and encouraging the active participation of individuals rather than ethnic groups. Reva Joshee and others suggest that this interest extends at least as far back as the Second World War. Leslie Pal chronicles the work of first the Social Action Branch and then the Citizenship Branch of the Department of the Secretary of State in the 1950s through to the 1980s. He suggests that the civic participation programs introduced following the report of the Royal Commission on Bilingualism and Biculturalism were motivated by genuine interest in active engagement to tackle unrest and not to create "vote-buying machines," although the initial ardour quickly cooled when it became clear that, most often, participation involved critiquing government directions.[105]

The brief tenure of the Department of Multiculturalism and Citizenship increased the government's focus on civic education and participation, including launching a broad citizenship participation initiative replete with extensive resource materials for non-governmental organizations to use across the country. Unfortunately, little came of this initiative as the department was disbanded and its components distributed to Canadian Heritage and CIC, neither of which was resourced to support broad participation initiatives in the wake of the government-wide program review.

As a result, more recent government of Canada investment in civic participation has been more modest. An analysis of multiculturalism grants reveals "a drastic decrease of projects aimed at integration into society and participation by members of minority groups"; curiously, however, it also notes that a sub-component – projects focused on political participation and social involvement – has increased from 1.8 percent to 6.7 percent of the total budget over the course of the 1990s, albeit to a very modest $657,140 in total expenditures.[106] To some extent, this modest growth was augmented by the short-lived Action Plan to Promote Diversity, Respect and Connections between Canadians and Build Social Cohesion and Shared Citizenship (2002–2005), which was created after the events of 11 September 2001 and provided some resources for an interdepartmental committee dedicated to these issues. More recently, the introduction of a new version of the citizenship guide, *Discover Canada*, in 2009 and its attendant promotions have also breathed new life into this strand of encouraging participation.

Throughout the 40 years of multiculturalism, a myriad of projects have been funded through the regionally administered Grants and Contributions Program; however, as recent government evaluations have concluded, each project may contribute to increased participation for a small number of participants, but it is exceptionally difficult to ascertain the impact on societal outcomes. That said, societal outcomes are, for the most part, quite positive, with most indicators of civic participation for newcomers trending toward the Canadian-born average over ten to 15 years.[107] Even if electoral politics reveals a gap in mirror representation of the diversity of the Canadian populace,[108] as Will Kymlicka observes, "ethnocultural groups participate in Canadian politics. They do not form separate ethnic-based parties, either as individual groups or coalitions, but participate overwhelmingly in pan-Canadian parties."[109] This is in stark contrast to many other immigrant-receiving societies, such as Israel, where ethno-specific parties have become established.

A third approach to civic participation programming has focused on institutional change, so that institutions are now more welcoming to newcomers and minorities, and they design their programs to address the needs of the increasingly diverse population. As the 1989 Strategy to Eliminate Racial Discrimination proposed, "Institutions act to serve as a society's corporate memory, maintaining historical values and attitudes, set standards and determine acceptable norms of behaviour" and "Within an evolving society, there is a requirement that institutional policies and practices also 'evolve' if they are to serve appropriate social, cultural, economic and political functions and contribute to national cohesion, harmony and development."[110] This strategy recognized both the need for change across the federal government that is embedded in the *Canadian Multiculturalism Act* and also the necessity of tackling external institutions such as police and justice, business, media, education,[111] health and social services, culture, and labour institutions.[112] Investments in grants and contributions for institutional change increased from 14.3 percent of program funding in 1991–1993 to 25.6 percent in 1999–2000/2001–2002.[113] Space constraints preclude an examination across all of these institutions;[114] however, along with the cultural institutions that have been discussed above, a brief consideration of the evolution of federal institutions will serve to illustrate the tremendous distance that they have travelled and the ongoing challenges they face.

Government of Canada institutions are required to report each year to the Multiculturalism Program, which, in turn, must table in the House of Commons every February an annual report on the operation of the *Canadian Multiculturalism Act*. Will Kymlicka describes this practice as "innovative," and he concludes that "while Multiculturalism is itself a very small program, it has had a significant impact throughout the federal government, because other departments are required to report each year on how well their policies and programs conform to the principles of the Multiculturalism Act."[115] This might be overly generous, but the contents of these reports do demonstrate an extraordinary breadth of initiatives across the federal family.

These initiatives have varied considerably over time, with the annual reports chronicling best practices from across the government and occasionally signalling ongoing challenges that need to be addressed. In addition, many of the initiatives described above have been undertaken by the Multiculturalism Program in partnership with other federal institutions. Individual initiatives like the cross-cutting Family Violence Initiative[116] and the Metropolis Project contributed to institutional change.

Despite these successes, it would appear that ongoing system-wide engagement has been far more difficult to foster. For example, the most recent evaluation of the Multiculturalism Program found that "the majority of work undertaken within the institutional component is limited to organizing meetings and developing the annual report. Given the limited scope of activities undertaken, there has been little impact on increasing federal organizations' responsiveness to a diverse society."[117] If Kymlicka was overly generous, this conclusion may be overly harsh as it overlooks the plethora of initiatives that have moved the federal government in the direction of greater inclusion.

The Multiculturalism Program has sought various strategies over its four decades to fulfill its mandate as the multiculturalism champion for the whole government of Canada.[118] These efforts have included establishing project-specific interdepartmental committees; setting up a cross-governmental secretariat; developing funding pots for related initiatives; establishing external advisory committees; developing a Multiculturalism Champions Network; and undertaking surveys of federal government employees' attitudes toward diversity, research to ascertain how minorities are faring in hiring and promotion within the public service, and the demographic projection studies described above; as well as cross-government strategies approved by Cabinet. Individually, none of these initiatives has been able to demonstrate significant outcomes.[119] A review of the annual reports on the functioning of the *Canadian Multiculturalism Act* describes a tremendous amount of activity across the federal family, but it constitutes an inventory of best practices without any means of demonstrating the outcomes of any given initiative.

That said, in tandem with the increasingly diverse nature of both the Canadian population and the Canadian public service, and this panoply of activities and initiatives, we can at least conclude that multiculturalism and its underlying tenets of fostering inclusion has attained a broad level of awareness.[120] In a 2004 survey of federal public servants, 95 percent of respondents reported that they considered the country to be multicultural to a moderate or great extent; 70 percent reported that the needs of ethnocultural and ethno-racial communities were different than the population as a whole; only 10 percent reported that they were not well informed about Canada's diversity; 71 percent reported that they were moderately (43 percent) or very (28 percent) well equipped to address the needs of a multicultural population; 73 percent reported that they had seen a positive change in attitudes toward diversity over the last decade; and 85 percent believed that their departments had responded to Canada's diversity moderately (38 percent) or to a great extent (47 percent). More senior respondents were the most likely to be positive about their department's response, while visible-minority public servants were the least likely to hold this view.[121]

REDUCING BARRIERS AND TACKLING DISCRIMINATION

A third major component of the Canadian inclusion reflex is the desire to reduce barriers and tackle discrimination. This has been highly controversial, with critics often decrying "reverse discrimination" or an overreliance on what separates Canadians rather than bringing them together. Accordingly, federal government attention to anti-racism initiatives has ebbed and flowed over time. A comprehensive treatment of this subject is beyond the scope of this chapter, and I will concentrate on just the most long-standing initiative – the March 21 Campaign.

Public Education: Combatting Racism and Discrimination

While the Multiculturalism Program has funded many youth-oriented initiatives over the last four decades, none had the longevity of initiatives designed to engage youth in commemorating March 21 as the International Day for the Elimination of Racial Discrimination. The campaign was born out of a 1988 commitment of federal, provincial, and territorial ministers responsible for human rights to do something to combat racism in Canadian society.[122] Initiatives were created each year from March 1989 until they were discontinued in April 2011, as part of a broader shift of federal government interests in the area of multiculturalism away from understanding and accommodation and toward integration and social cohesion.[123]

The campaign had three explicit goals at the outset: to raise public awareness of the need to eradicate racism and racial discrimination, educate the public on race relations issues, and assist community advocacy and other efforts to improve racial harmony and equality. Under the slogan of "Together We're Better!," the campaign was launched with media articles, a booklet entitled "Eliminating Racial Discrimination in Canada," and a statement in the House of Commons. In addition, the Federation of Canadian Municipalities encouraged members to proclaim the day, and *TG Magazine* launched a campaign for "winning ideas" that would be circulated to schools the following year. In 1990, the Award of Excellence in Race Relations was added.[124]

The first five years of the March 21 Campaign focused on general messaging, and, by 1994, it had come to focus explicitly on youth. It began modestly, with an investment of $1.3 million and one full-time-equivalent position. In 1992, it had a relatively modest impact, with just 6.5 percent of awareness, which after nearly a decade of initiatives climbed to 31 percent of general youth public awareness in 1998.[125] The campaign was guided by advisory committees and gathered partners over the years. The ideas of the initial 1989 campaign were embellished over time to include broader advertising and, in 1993, the addition of a T-shirt-designing contest sponsored by Benetton and MuchMusic/MusiquePlus.

By 1995, it was concluded that the public had been sensitized to the existence of racism and discrimination, and the campaign shifted to other objectives: to promote the understanding that everyone can play a positive role in building an inclusive society that benefits Canadians, to increase institutional commitment to developing and implementing programs and practices adapted to the needs of a diverse and evolving society, and to help promote a strong sense of Canadian identity within a diverse society. It is interesting that two initiatives were introduced in 1994–1995 and continued until the end of the program in 2011: a desire to more fully engage corporate partners that had hitherto been mostly involved only in the provision of prizes as well as a more articulated strategy to engage the broader federal family of departments and agencies.[126]

The March 21 initiative hit its peak with an Action 2000 campaign designed to raise its profile; its budget was estimated to start at $2 million before building in regional events and activities to prepare for the 2001 World Conference against Racism. Accordingly, in 1999, a social marketing campaign was incorporated into the initiative, targeting youth aged 12 to 18. A highlight was a "Mandela and the Children" event at Toronto's Skydome, broadcast on CBC and with a live audience of 40,000. This was accompanied by a promotional mailing to 30,000 schools and organizations across Canada; ads in parliamentarian householders and other publications; information booklets; brochures; teacher's guides; flyers, stickers, and posters; and features on MuchMusic/MusiquePlus.[127] In 2000, the March 21 Millennium Youth Initiative ran throughout the year in partnership with the YWCA of Canada and the Boys and Girls Clubs of Canada; it included a Youth Challenge to End Racism, the Stop Racism National Video competition, a Tour Canada Youth Challenge, a Concert and Awards Program,[128] a specialized website, a cyber petition, and an international Stop Racism Youth Forum.[129]

Following this major investment, a review of the March 21 Campaign was undertaken that led to the development of a new strategy calling for additional partnerships, a link to the broader multiculturalism Grants and Contributions Program, engaging the broader federal family, and shifting from an operational role to one of facilitator and convenor. In a critical move, the review also proposed that the campaign should be embedded in an inclusive approach to "shared citizenship" and that its focus should shift from only raising awareness to one designed to change behaviours.[130] In addition, the campaign was expanded to include the Mathieu Da Costa Challenge in order to capture a younger demographic. Eventually, the public engagement and outreach activities grew to include Black History Month, Asian Heritage Month, and the Paul Yuzyk Award for Multiculturalism; however, none of these initiatives had the same resources devoted to them, the specific youth focus of March 21, or the focus on children of Mathieu Da Costa.[131]

The last decade of the March 21 Campaign saw an increasing focus on connections with the broader initiatives of the Multiculturalism Program, including the Grants and Contributions Program, managed primarily from the regional offices,[132] and the addition of a YouTube channel. McAndrew and colleagues observe "a notable increase in initiatives focused on the fight against racism, whose share of the total budget grows, between 1991–1993 and 1999–2000/2001–2002, from 9.6% to 29.1%."[133] While interest in the video competition remained high (in 2008–2009, more than 1,200 young people contributed 340 submissions, the second-highest number in the competition's history),[134] the overall support afforded to the campaign appeared to wane in favour of other public engagement and outreach activities after the Multiculturalism Program moved from Canadian Heritage to CIC in 2008,[135] and both the March 21 video campaign and the Mathieu Da Costa Challenge were discontinued in 2011.

So what did the March 21 Campaign 1989–2011 accomplish? We can examine whether general awareness and attitudes toward racism shifted, whether awareness of the campaign increased, and whether Canadian children and youth felt empowered to effect change within their communities. Evaluations of the March 21 Campaign were carried out in 1992, 1999, and 2001 and academic explorations of the initiative in 2001 and 2007.[136]

The 1992 evaluation found that demand for the kits had grown substantially from year to year and that it could be anticipated to grow at an annual rate of approximately 50 percent; that 67 percent of users reported that the kits were highly useful; and that nearly half of kit users were repeat users. This same evaluation found tensions between those who believed that raising awareness would lead to behavioural change and those who did not. It also found that general public awareness of the campaign was low (6.5 percent), although it was encouraging that an increasing number of initiatives had not required government support – a trend that would continue across the decades. Within just one year, public awareness of the campaign doubled to 11 percent.[137]

The 1999 evaluation reported that 91 percent of the adult population believed that racism was a problem in Canada, and 66 percent reported that the federal government should take more action to eliminate racial discrimination. General public awareness of the campaign itself had climbed to 16 percent and, within the key target demographic, 12-to-18-year-olds, this reached 31 percent. A full 80 percent of respondents reported that they believed the campaign impacted attitudes and behaviours, and 62 percent agreed that the campaign contributed to resolving racial conflict. However, just as with the 1992 evaluation, the 1999 evaluation found that the majority of resources still served the goal of raising awareness rather than effecting behavioural change, and it recommended more emphasis on the latter.[138] The evaluation also proposed the development of more partnerships and a year-round focus, with a crescendo of activity on March 21st – elements also recommended in a March 21 marketing strategy that was commissioned in 2000.[139]

A pair of evaluation studies that took place after the Action 2000 Campaign concluded that the campaign was not reaching the school saturation that it should and called for some substantive changes to campaign processes as well as materials. In addition, the disconnect between the March 21 Campaign and the myriad regional anti-racism projects funded by the regional offices was highlighted.[140] For example, the 2006 evaluation of the Multiculturalism Program tabulated over 300 funded projects in the period between 2000 and 2004, with an estimated reach of approximately 1 million people and a cost per person of roughly $14. As the evaluation concluded, "Although it is difficult to draw a firm conclusion about program impacts in the area of communities and the public combating racism, there is reason to believe that program supported activities have contributed to the planned result in this area."[141] Not connecting the national campaign to these projects constituted a serious missed opportunity.

The efforts to engage children and youth in combatting racism and discrimination were also complemented by a cross-program emphasis on countering racism and discrimination through a wide array of initiatives, including institutional change. The major milestones in this regard were a Strategy to Eliminate Racial Discrimination, proposed jointly in 1989 by the deputy ministers of both the Department of the Secretary of State and the Department of Multiculturalism and Citizenship;[142] the launch of the Canadian Race Relations Foundation in 1996;[143] the preparatory work undertaken before the World Conference against Racism in 2001; and Canada's Action Plan Against Racism (CAPAR), which ran from 2005 to 2010.[144] Subsequently, according to the recent evaluation of CAPAR, the government of Canada's priorities have shifted away from anti-racism to "an increased focus on social cohesion and equal access to economic opportunity."[145]

In sum, considerable time and energy has been expended on countering racism and discrimination, primarily focused on engaging children and youth. It is encouraging that public support for multiculturalism in Canada remains far higher among the young than among those longer in the tooth. For example, in one poll conducted in March 2012, 74 percent of respondents aged 18–24 have a favourable opinion of official multiculturalism versus only 47 percent of those over the age of 65. This support seems to persist over time as young people age.[146] The dividends from this investment may be felt far into the future as this generation advances through the life cycle and takes up prominent leadership positions in Canadian society.

REFLECTING BACKWARD AND LOOKING FORWARD

Reflecting Backward

Despite a plethora of critiques and admonishments that have been launched at multiculturalism over the last 40 years by those who argue that it has not gone far enough and those who argue that it has gone too far, I believe that the federal government's Multiculturalism Program has facilitated significant progress, despite the meager resources that have been allocated to it.

Through investments in knowledge, data, and research, Canadians, their institutions, and governments have come to recognize the demographic reality that Canada is a multicultural society. By investing in a more complete and inclusive understanding of our national history, by redressing activities that are no longer in accordance with our aspirations to be an inclusive and equitable society, and in the way we project our approach to diversity on the world stage, we have forged an inclusive national identity. By sharing our experiences with an international audience, we contribute to the global policy and program-solution sets available to tackle challenges around the world, and we hold our own feet to the fire to ensure that we also strive for improvement.

Through investments in the artistic and cultural articulations of who we are and who we would like to be, Canadians' conception of who could or should be active members of our society and on what terms have expanded. Similarly, as a result of decades of investments in identifying barriers and obstacles to the full participation of all Canadians, raising awareness of these challenges, and equipping Canadians and Canadian institutions to combat them, we continue to make progress toward an integrated society of active, connected, and productive citizens.

Multiculturalism is a means of managing ubiquitous change, not an attainable end state. As Will Kymlicka argues, multiculturalism "is a deeply (and intentionally) transformative project, both for minorities and majorities,"[147] or, as elegantly stated by a participant in a focus group during a review of the Multiculturalism Program in the mid-1990s, "We're talking about the nature of Canada's soul."[148]

Looking Forward

The Multiculturalism Program has successfully adapted to its environment over the last four decades by constantly striving to create a framework for an inclusive national identity; to ensure the full participation of all Canadians in the social, economic, cultural, and civic facets of Canadian society; and to pursue the reduction of systemic barriers and discrimination to the full participation of all Canadians, regardless of their background. This chapter has described some of the successes that the program has had over the last 40 years.

Key challenges that I can see include the following:

First and foremost, while the integration of newcomers has always been present in multiculturalism programming,[149] the commitment of the government of Canada to unprecedented levels of immigration to Canada over a sustained period has led to a far greater need for a co-ordinated approach across multiculturalism, immigrant settlement, and citizenship policies and programs. The movement of the Multiculturalism Program from Canadian Heritage to CIC, and the addition of the tagline "Promoting Integration" to all of the annual reports on the operation of the *Canadian Multiculturalism Act* since Jason Kenney was first designated as the minister responsible for multiculturalism in 2007, suggest that this connection has already been forged at a political level. At the bureaucratic level, the inclusion of the program in one departmental strategic outcome ("fostering an integrated society") is an encouraging start. However, further work clearly remains to be done to ensure that both sides of the two-way street of integration are equally well nourished, particularly as newcomers increasingly settle into a wider range of communities and the "host" population itself becomes increasingly diverse.

Second, while the seeds of government programming to promote interactions among Canadians of diverse backgrounds have been evident since the first stirrings of what would become multiculturalism, the need for opportunities for communities to come together across their differences has never been greater.

Third, this rapid demographic change and the aging of data collected from major surveys such as the Ethnic Diversity Survey and the Longitudinal Survey of Immigrants to Canada, combined with the challenges of measuring performance for the multiculturalism and settlement programs, means that a robust data and information infrastructure needs to be implemented and monitored over time. Similarly, with the demise of the Metropolis Project, a forward-looking research strategy needs to be developed to both undertake the necessary research and ensure connectivity with the many smaller research networks that have emerged in its wake. The replacement of the long form of the 2011 census with the Voluntary Household Survey raises potential concerns about data quality and will also pose policy-development challenges.

Fourth, religious pluralism is an increasing reality in Canada and one for which we are generally poorly prepared. Many of the flashpoints that have emerged in public discourse in recent years have been framed in terms of religion, and the development of effective responses has often been impaired by what Bramadat refers to as religious illiteracy.[150]

Fifth, racism and discrimination have not disappeared. A sizable portion of the population reports experiencing racism and/or discrimination, particularly in the workplace. Leaving this issue unaddressed is unlikely to serve us well in the long term.

Sixth, while the majority of Canadian identity-building work appears to have been accomplished, with the renewed marriage of multiculturalism and citizenship as a single branch within CIC and discussion of an updated *Citizenship Act*, this may be the occasion for multiculturalism to become fully embedded in citizenship legislation that is more wide-reaching than simply regulating naturalization. This was an idea first championed by David Crombie in the mid-1980s, but still awaiting implementation.

Seventh, spaces for informed public dialogue are in short supply. Their absence allows unsubstantiated critiques to propagate unexamined in the silence. A series of national multiculturalism conferences[151] was held at the outset of multiculturalism as official state policy, and, for 15 years, this role was filled by the national Metropolis conferences; it is unclear where this important dialogue will take place in the future.[152]

Eighth, engaging a wider range of actors (provinces, municipalities, employers, francophone-minority communities, and local communities) in a systematic manner remains an outstanding challenge for the Multiculturalism Program. Over the last 40 years, many initiatives have been attempted, both in Ottawa and through the small grants and contributions managed in the regions, but any sense of a systematized approach has always seemed to elude it. Now, with the program's closer proximity to its long-estranged sister, the settlement program, and its service-delivery network of organizations in almost all major Canadian centres, it may be an occasion for greater synergies between these programs. Through initiatives like Settlement Workers in Schools and Local Immigration Partnership programs, CIC has built up a sustained network that could be used to disseminate best practices resulting from small multiculturalism grants and contributions or to launch institutional-change programs.

Finally, perhaps the time has come to examine a more proactive effort to develop a whole-of-government approach to multiculturalism. CAPAR sowed the seeds of such an approach, but it was stillborn for a range of complex reasons, not the least of which was the institutional and political instability that marred the Multiculturalism Program's efforts in the early years of the 21st century.[153]

For 40 years, the federal government's Multiculturalism Program has sought to inculcate a Canadian inclusion reflex in generations of Canadians. The next 40 years is theirs to write.

NOTES

[1] The views expressed in this chapter are those of the author and do not necessarily reflect those of Integration Branch, Citizenship and Immigration Canada, or the government of Canada.

[2] John Biles and Effie Panousos, "The Snakes and Ladders of Canadian Diversity" (Ottawa: Department of Canadian Heritage, 1999); N.F. Dreisziger, "The Rise of a Bureaucracy for Multiculturalism: The Origins of the Nationalities Branch, 1939–1941," in *On Guard for Thee: War, Ethnicity, and the Canadian State, 1939–1945* (Ottawa: Ministry of Supply and Services, 1988); Reva Joshee, "Federal Policies on Cultural Diversity and Education, 1940–1971" (PhD diss., University of British Columbia, 1995); Richard J.F. Day, *Multiculturalism and the History of Canadian Diversity* (Toronto: University of Toronto Press, 2000); and Christopher P. Champion, *The Strange Demise of British Canada: The Liberals and Canadian Nationalism, 1964–1968* (Montreal: McGill-Queen's University Press, 2010).

[3] For example, Fries and Gingrich argue that "it can refer to any of policy, program, practice, educational approach, sociological concept, symbol, ideal, ideology, theory or description of Canadian society"; see Christopher J. Fries and Paul Gingrich, "A 'Great' Large Family: Understandings of Multiculturalism among Newcomers to Canada," *Refuge* 27, no. 1 (2010):37.

[4] While the acquisition of official languages by newcomers to Canada and interactions among Canadians of diverse backgrounds have also been promoted over the last 40 years, the Multiculturalism Program has not been a major actor in these fields – far larger budgets at Canadian Heritage and CIC have been deployed to obtain these ends, so I will not discuss them in detail here.

[5] Perhaps the most commonly cited typology is found in Jean Lock Kunz and Stuart Sykes, *From Mosaic to Harmony: Multicultural Canada in the 21st Century* (Ottawa: Policy Research Initiative, 2007), 21.

[6] For the most comprehensive exploration of how multiculturalism policy came to be fused with the government of Canada's interests in Canadian identity, see Varun Uberoi, "Multicultural Nation-Building: A Canadian Way to Foster Unity amongst British Citizens" (PhD diss., Oxford University, 2006).

[7] Canadian Heritage, "Summative Evaluation of the Multiculturalism Program" (Gatineau: Canadian Heritage, 28 June 2006); and Citizenship and Immigration Canada, "Evaluation of the Multiculturalism Program" (Ottawa: CIC, March 2012). The evaluation conducted by Brighton Research and submitted to Canadian Heritage in 1996 was more broad-based than either of these two more recent evaluations, but its emphasis was on the evolution of broader societal context than the evolution of multiculturalism programming per se; see Brighton Research, "Strategic Evaluation of Multiculturalism Programs" (Hull: Corporate Review Branch, Department of Canadian Heritage, March 1996).

[8] Several researchers have identified the lack of studies of program and policy to be a void in the literature – for example, Fries and Gingrich, "A 'Great' Large Family"; and Irene Bloemraad, Anna Korteweg, and Gökçe Yurdakul, "Citizenship and Immigration: Multiculturalism, Assimilation, and Challenges to the Nation-State," *Annual Review of Sociology* 34 (2008):153–179.

[9] For an excellent account of the evolution of provincial policies, consult Joseph Garcea and Neil Hibbert, "Policy Frameworks for Managing Diversity in Canada: Taking Stock for Action," in *Integration and Inclusion of Newcomers and Minorities across Canada*, ed. John Biles, Meyer Burstein, James Frideres, Erin Tolley, and Rob Vineberg (Montreal: McGill-Queen's University Press, 2012), 45–76.

[10] Much of this critical work can be found in graduate theses – for example, John Jaworsky, "A Case Study of the Canadian Federal Government's Multiculturalism Policy" (master's thesis, Carleton University, 1979); Beate Schiffer-Graham, "The Federal Policy of Multiculturalism in Canada (1971–1988)" (master's thesis, University of Manitoba, 1989); and John Biles, "It's All a Matter of Priority: Multiculturalism under Mulroney (1984–1988)" (master's research paper, Carleton University, 1997).

[11] This disruption was not welcomed by all historians; indeed, it remains a major concern for some. It is most infamously captured in J.L. Granatstein, *Who Killed Canadian History?* (Toronto: HarperCollins, 1998).

[12] Baha Abu-Laban, "Editors' Introduction," in *An Olive Branch on the Family Tree: The Arabs in Canada* (Toronto: McClelland and Stewart, 1980), vi.

[13] According to Leo Driedger, "Multiculturalism: Bridging Ethnicity, Culture, Religion and Race," *Forum on Public Policy* (22 March 2008), at http://forum onpublicpolicy.com/archivespring08/driedger.pdf, accessed 17 September 2012, this series included the Scottish (1976), Polish (1976), Portuguese (1976), Arabs (1980), Norwegians (1980), Chinese (1982), Ukrainians (1982), Hungarians (1982), Croatians (1982), South Asians (1985), Estonians (1985), Dutch (1988), and a summary volume entitled "Coming Canadians" (1988).

[14] These booklets, published from 1982 to 1991, included brief histories of the Scots, Portuguese, Japanese, Poles, East Indians, West Indians, Jews, Finns, Chinese, Ukrainians, Germans, Irish, Italians, and Belgians in Canada as well as booklets addressing some thematic topics, such as ethnocultural transition in the Eastern Townships of Quebec, Canadian immigration policy since Confederation, immigrant domestic servants in Canada, ethnicity and politics in Canada since Confederation, Quebec and the question of immigration, and ethnic minorities during the two world wars.

[15] Evelyn Kallen, "Academics, Politics and Ethnics: University Opinion on Canadian Ethnic Studies," *Canadian Ethnic Studies* XIII (1981):112–123.

[16] Ibid., 114.

[17] These chairs are in Hungarian and Ukrainian Studies (1978); Mennonite Studies (1979); Acadian Studies (1980); Gaelic, Native and Aboriginal Cultures of Atlantic Canada; and Italian-Canadian Studies (1983); Celtic and Irish Studies (1985); Estonian Studies (1986); Punjabi Language, Literature and Sikh Studies; and Urdu Language and Cultural Studies (1987); German-Canadian Studies; Hindu Studies; and Ethnicity, Immigration and Pluralism (1989); Slovak History and Culture; Icelandic-Canadian; Canadian Ethnicity and Ethnic Relations; and Multicultural Education (1990); Black Canadian Studies; Intercultural, Ethnic and Race Relations; Multi-Ethnic Studies; Education and Multi-ethnic Research

(1991); Modern Greek and Greek-Canadian Studies (1992); Canadian-Jewish Studies; and Cultural Pluralism and Health Studies (1993); and Arts in a Pluralist Society; and Canadian Ethnic Studies (1995); see Corporate Review Branch, "Lessons Learned: Chairs of Ethnic Studies (Volume 1)" (Ottawa: Department of Canadian Heritage, 1997), 9.

[18] Ibid., 4.

[19] During the strategic review of the Multiculturalism Program in the late 1990s, Secretary of State Hedy Fry invited the ethnic studies chairs to participate in a number of meetings to discuss program directions; a sizable number of them did not even reply to the invitation.

[20] The discussion of the desirability of a research-centre structure that might have included ethnic studies, as advanced by J.J. Loubser, and potentially immigration as well (a proposal had also been advanced by Freda Hawkins at this time) foreshadowed the creation of the Metropolis Project in the mid-1990s, which would bring these two fields together; see Kallen, "Academics, Politics and Ethnics," 118.

[21] James D. Cameron, "Ethnicizing Atlantic Canadian Universities: The Regional Impact of the Canadian Ethnic Studies Program, 1973–1997," *Canadian Ethnic Studies* 34, no. 2 (2002):1–24.

[22] Ibid., 1.

[23] Howard Palmer, "Canadian Immigration and Ethnic History in the 1970s and 1980s," *Journal of Canadian Studies* 17 (1982):35; J.W. Berry and J.A. Laponce, eds., *Ethnicity and Culture in Canada: The Research Landscape* (Toronto: University of Toronto Press, 1994); and Driedger, "Multiculturalism."

[24] Berry and Laponce, *Ethnicity and Culture in Canada*, 11.

[25] Cameron, "Ethnicizing Atlantic Canadian Universities," 10.

[26] Ibid., 6.

[27] Driedger, "Multiculturalism," 16.

[28] This reprofiling of resources would reoccur for a couple of years once the program moved to the Department of Citizenship and Immigration, where only 37.5 percent of funds allocated to the Multiculturalism Program was spent on it in 2008–2009 and 36 percent in 2009–2010; see Andrew Griffith, *Policy Arrogance or Innocent Bias* (Ottawa: Anar Press, 2013), 107.

[29] Each of these seminars brought together researchers, community partners, and policy-makers to ascertain the state of contemporary knowledge and to identify knowledge gaps and strategies to fill them in the near term. Background papers, proceedings, and subsequent publications have been distributed in the hundreds of thousands since they became available. A seminar on civic participation was held in conjunction with the Second National Metropolis Conference and the Canadian Ethnic Studies Association Conference in Montreal in 1997 (at http:// canada.metropolis.net/events/civic/intro_e.html, accessed 16 January 2014); a seminar on Social Justice was held in Ottawa in 1999; an identity seminar was held in conjunction with the Canadian Ethnic Studies Association Biennial Conference in Halifax in 2001 (at http://canada.metropolis.net/events/ethnocultural/proceedings/Identity%20Seminar%20-Evolume%201.pdf, accessed 16 January 2014); and a two-day seminar on Intersections of Diversity was held in Niagara Falls in 2003 (at http://canada.metropolis.net/events/diversity/diversity_index_e.htm, accessed 16 January 2014).

[30] Metropolis was funded for three five-year terms and phased out on 31 March 2012. In the first period, the Multiculturalism Program provided $100,000 a year,

$150,000 a year for the second phase, and $200,000 a year for the third and final phase. The returns on this investment (for multiculturalism resources and the other dozen federal agencies that provided resources to Metropolis) can be found in John Biles, "The International Metropolis Project: A Model Worth Emulating," in *Managing Immigration and Diversity in Canada: A Transatlantic Dialogue in the New Age of Migration*, ed. Dan Rodriguez-Garcia (Montreal: McGill-Queen's University Press, 2012), 325–356.

[31] These themes included adapting multiculturalism to religious diversity, racism and discrimination, labour market integration, immigration beyond the metropolis, implications of security issues for multiculturalism, the future of multiculturalism, relating multiculturalism to Aboriginal people, vulnerable groups (women and youth, second generation), patterns of ethnic community formation, and multicultural readiness in service delivery; see Will Kymlicka, *The Current State of Multiculturalism in Canada and Research Themes on Canadian Multiculturalism 2008–2010* (Ottawa: Citizenship and Immigration Canada, 2010), at http://www.cic.gc.ca/english/pdf/pub/multi-state.pdf, accessed 18 September 2012.

[32] John W. Berry, Rudolf Kalin, and Donald M. Taylor, *Multiculturalism and Ethnic Attitudes in Canada* (Ottawa: Ministry of Supply and Services, 1976).

[33] K.G. O'Bryan, Jeffrey G. Reitz, and O. Kuplowska, *Non-Official Languages: A Study in Canadian Multiculturalism* (Ottawa: Department of Secretary of State, 1976).

[34] Angus Reid, "Multiculturalism and Canadians: Attitude Survey 1991," survey conducted for the Department of Multiculturalism and Citizenship, 1991.

[35] These long-standing debates are well captured in a special issue of *Canadian Diversity/Diversité canadienne* 2, no. 2 (Summer 2003).

[36] Statistics Canada, "Ethnic Diversity Survey: Portrait of a Multicultural Society" (Ottawa: Statistics Canada, 2003). The data on discrimination is perhaps the most widely used. Some examples of widely cited research using this data include Richard Y. Bourhis, Annie Montreuil, Denise Helly, and Lorna Jantzen, "Discrimination et linguicisme au Québec: Enquête sur la diversité ethnique au Canada," *Canadian Ethnic Studies* 39, no. 1–2 (2007):31–49; and Jeffrey G. Reitz, Raymond Breton, Karen Kisiel Dion, and Kenneth L. Dion, eds., *Multiculturalism and Social Cohesion: Potentials and Challenges of Diversity* (The Netherlands: Springer, 2009).

[37] See, for example, Nordicity Group Ltd., "Population Projections of Ethnic Groups, Canada, Provinces and Territories, 1991–2006" (Ottawa: Nordicity Group, 1995); Alain Belanger and Éric Caron Malenfant, "Population Projections of Visible Minority Groups, Canada, Provinces and Regions 2001–2017," Catalogue no. 91-541-XIE 2005 (Ottawa: Statistics Canada, 2005); Éric Caron Malenfant, Andre Lebel, and Laurent Martel, "Projections of the Diversity of the Canadian Population 2006 to 2031," Catalogue no. 91-551-X 2010 (Ottawa: Statistics Canada, 2010).

[38] Multiculturalism Program, Discussion Papers for 2017 Policy Forum: Serving Canada's Multicultural Population for the Future, 22–23 March (Ottawa: Department of Canadian Heritage, 2005).

[39] For the most comprehensive coverage of relevant graduate theses and dissertations, see Mary-Lee Mulholland, "Annotated Bibliography of Canadian Theses and Dissertations on Diversity (1980–2001)" (Ottawa: Canadian Heritage, 2001). For inventories of research projects funded by the Multiculturalism Program, consult Daniel Woolford, "Research Projects Supported by the Canadian Ethnic Studies Program 1973–1992" (Ottawa: Minister of Supply and Services, 1993)

and Nabila Abou Najm, "Research Retrospective: A Survey of Research Projects (1996–1999) Funded by the Multiculturalism Program" (Hull: Strategic Research and Analysis, Department of Canadian Heritage, 2002). Information regarding materials produced by Metropolis can be found in the annual activity reports from the five Metropolis centres, at http://www.metropolis.net/centres/index_e. html, accessed 16 January 2014; or a high-level overview can be found in Biles, "International Metropolis Project."

[40] Canada, Parliament, House of Commons, *Debates*, 32nd Parliament, 2nd Session, vol. 4 (1984), 5306–5307.

[41] The history of the campaign for redress culminating in the Japanese Canadian Redress Agreement is well told in a number of sources – for example, Roy Miki, *Redress: Inside the Japanese Canadian Call for Justice* (Vancouver: Raincoast Books, 2004); Rosa Sevy and John Torpey, "Commemoration, Redress, and Reconciliation in the Integration of Immigrant Communities: The Cases of Japanese-Canadians and Japanese-Americans," Research on Immigration and Integration in the Metropolis, Working Paper Series, No. 04-01 (Vancouver: Vancouver Centre of Excellence, 2004); and Ian Radforth, "Ethnic Minorities and Wartime Injustices: Redress Campaigns and Historical Narratives in Late Twentieth-Century Canada," in *Settling and Unsettling Memories: Essays in Canadian Public History*, ed. Nicole Neatby and Peter Hodgins (Toronto: University of Toronto Press, 2012), 369–418.

[42] Prime Minister Mulroney apologized to Italian Canadians on 4 November 1990 at a Toronto luncheon. Since it did not take place in the House of Commons and did not include individual restitution, it did not successfully extinguish the redress claim of the community; see Radforth, "Ethnic Minorities and Wartime Injustices," 386–387.

[43] Prime Minister Paul Martin also announced an agreement in principle with the Ukrainian community and the launch of a $2.5 million Acknowledgement, Commemoration and Education Program, although his government was defeated before the program was fully implemented; see ibid., 392.

[44] Matt James, "Recognition, Redistribution and Redress: The Case of the 'Chinese Head Tax,'" *Canadian Journal of Political Science* 37, no. 4 (2004):883–902; and Peter Li, "Reconciling with History: The Chinese-Canadian Head Tax Redress," *Journal of Chinese Overseas* 4, no. 1 (May 2008):127–140.

[45] On 22 June 2006, the government announced the Community Historical Recognition Program (CHRP) and the National Historical Recognition Program (NHRP) to commemorate and educate Canadians about the historical experiences and contributions of ethnocultural communities affected by wartime measures and immigration restrictions that had been applied in Canada. The CHRP funds community-based commemorative and educational projects that recognize the experiences of ethnocultural communities affected by historical wartime measures, and/or immigration restrictions applied in Canada, and that promote these communities' contributions to building Canada (at http://www.cic.gc.ca/english/multiculturalism/programs/community-projects.asp, accessed 16 January 2014). The NHRP funds federal departments and agencies to undertake national projects that educate Canadians, particularly youth, about the history related to wartime measures and/or immigration restrictions and the contribution of affected communities to the building of Canada.

[46] Radforth, "Ethnic Minorities and Wartime Injustices," 402–403.

[47] Like all identity claims and efforts to establish public memories, redress campaigns and their research underpinnings were often contested. For example, while the Japanese Canadian community itself was initially somewhat divided on the appropriate approach to pursue for redress for internment, the historical record was relatively uncontested compared to other communities seeking redress, although even in the Japanese Canadian case, a group of historians challenged the dominant narrative constructed in Ann Gomer Sunahara, *The Politics of Racism: The Uprooting of Japanese Canadians during the Second World War*, 1st ed. (Toronto: James Lorimer, 1981), which the National Association of Japanese Canadians relied upon heavily to articulate the need for redress. In other communities, this contestation was far more pronounced. For example, in their edited volume, *Enemies Within: Italian and Other Internees in Canada and Abroad* (Toronto: University of Toronto Press, 2000), historians Franca Iacovetta, Roberto Perin, and Angelo Principe took great exception to the narrative advanced by the National Congress of Italian Canadians in its "A National Shame: The Internment of Italian Canadians" (unpublished submission to the government of Canada, January 1990), which claimed that none of the Italian Canadian internees were dangerous. In fact, these historians argue that many internees were in fact fascists who had been persecuting their fellow Italian Canadians, so no blanket claim for redress could be accepted. A similar discomfort among some academics can also be seen in the case of the Ukrainian Canadian community campaign for redress. On the one hand, Lubomyr Luciuk's *A Time for Atonement: Canada's First National Internment Operations and the Ukrainian Canadians, 1914–1920* (Kingston, ON: Limestone Press, 1988) and Bohdan S. Kordan and Craig Steven Mahovsky's *A Bare and Impolitic Right* (Montreal: McGill-Queen's Press, 2004), among others, sought to advance the position of all internees as victims. By contrast, historian Frances Swyripa was less than comfortable with the glossing over of a complex history; see Frances Swyripa, "The Politics of Redress: The Contemporary Ukrainian-Canadian Campaign," in *Enemies Within: Italian and Other Internees in Canada and Abroad*, ed. Franca Iacovetta, Roberto Perin, and Angelo Principe (Toronto: University of Toronto Press, 2000), 355–378.

[48] Joy Kogawa, *Obasan* (Markham, ON: Penguin, 1983).

[49] Radforth, "Ethnic Minorities and Wartime Injustices," 410, note 63.

[50] Ibid., 400.

[51] Roy Brooks, *The Controversy over Apologies and Reparations for Human Injustice: When Sorry Isn't Enough* (New York: New York University Press, 1999); Elazar Barkan, *The Guilt of Nations: Restitution and Negotiating Historical Injustices* (New York: W.W. Norton, 2000); John Torpey, ed. *Politics and the Past: On Repairing Historical Injustices* (Oxford: Rowman & Littlefield, 2003); J. Angelo Corlett, *Race, Racism and Reparations* (Ithaca, NY: Cornell University Press, 2003); John Torpey, *Making Whole What Has Been Smashed: On Reparations Politics* (Cambridge, MA: Harvard University Press, 2006); and Jennifer Henderson and Pauline Wakeham, eds. *Reconciling Canada: Critical Perspectives on the Culture of Redress* (Toronto: University of Toronto Press, 2012).

[52] Matt James, "Redress Politics and Canadian Citizenship," in *Canada: The State of the Federation 1998/99 – How Canadians Connect*, ed. Harvey Lazar and Tom McIntosh (Montreal: McGill-Queen's University Press, 1999), 247–282; and Nicole Neatby and Peter Hodgins, eds., *Settling and Unsettling Memories: Essays in Canadian Public History* (Toronto: University of Toronto Press, 2012).

[53] Citizenship and Immigration Canada, *Discover Canada: The Rights and Responsibilities of Canadian Citizenship* (Ottawa: CIC, 2012).

[54] See the Canadian Race Relations Foundation website at http://www.crr.ca/en/policy-a-research/position-papers/211-a-background-paper-on-the-crrfs-policy-on-redress-a-reparations-, accessed 16 January 2014.

[55] James, "Recognition, Redistribution and Redress"; and Matt James, "Do Campaigns for Historical Redress Erode the Canadian Welfare State?" in *Multiculturalism and the Welfare State: Recognition and Redistribution in Contemporary Democracies*, ed. Keith Banting and Will Kymlicka (Montreal: McGill-Queen's University Press, 2006), 222–246.

[56] James, "Redress Politics and Canadian Citizenship," 267.

[57] Ibid., 269.

[58] Ibid., 271.

[59] Ibid., 261.

[60] James, "Recognition, Redistribution and Redress," 896–898.

[61] In 2009, Cabinet approved new policy directions for the Multiculturalism Program, including sharing Canada's approach to diversity in international forums.

[62] Harald Bauder, *Immigration Dialectic: Imaging Community, Economy and Nation* (Toronto: University of Toronto Press, 2011), 33.

[63] Will Kymlicka, "Marketing Canadian Pluralism in the International Arena," *International Journal* 59, no. 4 (2004):829–852.

[64] Ibid., 833.

[65] Ibid., 834.

[66] Ibid., 835.

[67] For the best collection on this backlash against multiculturalism, see Steven Vertovec and Susanne Wessendorf, eds., *The Multiculturalism Backlash: European Discourses, Policies and Practices* (New York: Routledge, 2010).

[68] Jeffrey G. Reitz, "Pro-immigration Canada: Social and Economic Roots of Popular Views," *IRPP Study* 20 (October 2011), at http://www.irpp.org/pubs/IRPPstudy/IRPP_Study_no20.pdf, accessed 19 October 2012.

[69] Bhikhu Parekh, "The Mutual Suspicions Which Fuelled the Rushdie Affair," *The Independent* (London), 23 February 1989.

[70] Nora Sobel, "Constructing Canadian Citizens: A Textual Analysis of Canadian Citizenship Guides in English 1947–2012" (master's thesis, University of Manitoba, 2013); Joshee, "Federal Policies on Cultural Diversity and Education"; and Dreisziger, "Rise of a Bureaucracy for Multiculturalism."

[71] "Song and dance" multiculturalism is most famously critiqued by Neil Bissoondath, *Selling Illusions: The Cult of Multiculturalism in Canada* (Toronto: Penguin Books, 1994); "red-boots multiculturalism" in reference to Ukrainian dancers was popularized by Audrey Kobayashi, "Multiculturalism: Representing a Canadian Institution," in *Place/Culture/Representation*, ed. James S. Duncan and David Ley (New York: Routledge, 1993: 205–231); and "saris, samosas and steel drums" is a ubiquitous phrase in British multiculturalism literature that has begun to seep into Canadian discourse – see, e.g., Will Kymlicka, "Multiculturalism: Success, Failure, and the Future" (Washington, DC: Migration Policy Institute, 2012), at http://www.migrationpolicy.org/pubs/Multiculturalism.pdf, accessed 24 October 2012.

[72] Marjorie Stone, Helene Destrempes, John Foote, and M. Sharon Jeannotte, "Immigration and Cultural Citizenship: Responsibilities, Rights and Indicators,"

in *Immigration and Integration in Canada in the Twenty-First Century*, ed. John Biles, Meyer Burstein, and James Frideres (Montreal: McGill-Queen's University Press, 2008), 103–135.

[73] Judy Young, "No Longer 'Apart'? Multiculturalism Policy and Canadian Literature," *Canadian Ethnic Studies* 33, no. 2 (2001):88–116.

[74] Ibid., 97.

[75] Ibid., 100.

[76] Ibid., 101.

[77] Ibid.

[78] Ibid., 100.

[79] Enoch Padolsky, "Canadian Ethnic Minority Literature in English," in *Ethnicity and Culture in Canada: The Research Landscape*, ed. J.W. Berry and J.A. Laponce (Toronto: University of Toronto Press, 1994), 361.

[80] Sherry Simon and David Leahy, "La recherche au Québec portant sur l'écriture ethnique," in *Ethnicity and Culture in Canada: The Research Landscape*, ed. J.W. Berry and J.A. Laponce (Toronto: University of Toronto Press, 1994), 387.

[81] Peter Li, "A World Apart: The Multicultural World of Visible Minorities and the Art World in Canada," *Canadian Review of Sociology and Anthropology* 31, no. 4 (1994):365–391.

[82] Young, "No Longer 'Apart'?," 107.

[83] Carol Tator, Frances Henry, and Winston Mattis, *Challenging Racism in the Arts: Case Studies of Controversy and Conflict* (Toronto: University of Toronto Press, 1998), 262.

[84] Young, "No Longer 'Apart'?," 102.

[85] For example, consider the Canada Council's "Report and Recommendations of the Second Advisory Committee for Racial Equality in the Arts at the Canada Council" (Ottawa: Canada Council, 8 July 1996), which includes an annex detailing changes at the council since 1989; see Young, "No Longer 'Apart'?," 107.

[86] Ibid., 102–103.

[87] Eric Thomas, "Canadian Broadcasting and Multiculturalism: Attempts to Accommodate Ethnic Minorities," *Canadian Journal of Communications* 17 (1992):291. The 1991 *Canadian Broadcast Act* stipulates that the Canadian broadcasting system should "through its programming and the employment opportunities arising out of its operations, serve the needs and interests, and reflect the circumstances and aspirations, of Canadian men and women and children, including equal rights, the linguistic duality and multicultural nature of Canadian society and the special place of Aboriginal peoples within that society."

[88] Young, "No Longer 'Apart'?," 106.

[89] Marie McAndrew, Denise Helly, Caroline Tessier, and Judy Young, "From Heritage Languages to Institutional Change: An Analysis of the Nature of Organizations and Projects Funded by the Canadian Multiculturalism Program (1983–2002)," *Canadian Ethnic Studies* 40, no. 3 (2008):165.

[90] Will Kymlicka, *Finding Our Way: Rethinking Ethnocultural Relations in Canada* (Toronto: Oxford University Press, 1998), 45.

[91] Paul Bramadat, "Shows, Selves and Solidarity: Ethnic Identity and Cultural Spectacles in Canada" (Ottawa: Department of Canadian Heritage, 2001), at http://canada.metropolis.net/events/ethnocultural/publications/shows_shelves.pdf, accessed 19 October 2012.

[92] Details of this program can be found at http://www.cic.gc.ca/english/multiculturalism/funding/events.asp, accessed 16 January 2014.

[93] Citizenship and Immigration Canada, *Annual Report on the Operation of the Canadian Multiculturalism Act 2010–2011* (Ottawa: CIC, 2012).

[94] Craig Takeuchi, "Vancouver 2010 Olympics: The Great White, er, Multicultural North?," straight.com (blog), 20 February 2010, at http://www.straight.com/print/blogra/vancouver-2010-olympics-great-white-er-multicultural-north, accessed 21 June 2013.

[95] CBC News, "Asian-Looking Woman Scientist Image Rejected for $100 Bills," 17 August 2012, at http://www.cbc.ca/news/canada/story/2012/08/17/pol-cp-100-dollar-bills-asian-scientist-image.html, accessed 21 June 2013.

[96] For examples of authors who make reference to explicit political rationales for supporting multiculturalism, see Leslie Pal, *Interests of State: The Politics of Language, Multiculturalism, and Feminism in Canada* (Montreal: McGill-Queen's Press, 1993); Brooke Jeffrey, *Divided Loyalties: The Liberal Party of Canada, 1984–2008* (Toronto: University of Toronto Press, 2010); Champion, *Strange Demise of British Canada*; and Uberoi, "Multicultural Nation-Building."

[97] Audrey Kobayashi, "Advocacy from the Margins: The Role of Minority Ethnocultural Associations in Affecting Public Policy in Canada," in *The Nonprofit Sector in Canada: Roles and Relationships*, ed. Keith Banting (Montreal: McGill-Queen's University Press, 2000), 236.

[98] The CEC continues to function today with project-by-project funding, most recently from Health Canada. For more information, visit http://www.ethnocultural.ca/, accessed 16 January 2014.

[99] Pal, *Interests of State*, 204.

[100] Ibid. These consultative bodies were unwieldy and often accused of political partisanship. For example, Pal notes, "The Canadian Consultative Council on Multiculturalism, originally comprising between 12 and 15 members when first proposed, was established after the 1972 elections with 101 members, many of whom had clear connections to the Liberal party," 119. In 1983, this body was renamed the Canadian Multiculturalism Council, and membership was reduced to 30 members and then more than doubled to 65 members in 1985. However, this committee was critiqued by Liberal MP Sergio Marchi, who accused all of the members of being "committed supporters of the Progressive Conservative Party of Canada" as a result of a report drafted by the council chair, Peter McCreath, in which he claimed this partisanship as an advantage; see Joe O'Donnell, "Ottawa-Funded Group All Tory Backers: Report," *Toronto Star*, 16 October 1986, A2. This body was, in turn, replaced in 1990 with the Canadian Multiculturalism Advisory Committee but was discontinued shortly after the Liberals formed the government again in 1993.

[101] For example, Varun Uberoi quotes David Crombie's chief of staff, Ron Doering's, reflections of Crombie's beliefs about so-called professional multiculties: "David had his own biases against these groups. He had seen them at work in Toronto and at Indian and Northern Affairs … and he knew that these people didn't speak for anyone"; see Uberoi, "Multicultural Nation-Building," 150.

[102] Secretary of State, "A Framework for Cross-Sectoral Evaluation of Core Funding in the Secretary of State" (Hull: Department of Secretary of State, 1986: 15–16).

[103] Pal reports that a 1976 internal report for the Multiculturalism Program found, "Almost half (43 per cent) of all monies under the grants program went to five

ethnic groups (Ukrainians, Poles, Germans, Italians and Blacks), with Ukrainians receiving 'almost twice as many grants as the next largest group (Poles)'"; see Pal, *Interests of State*, 190.

[104] McAndrew, Helly, Tessier, and Young, "From Heritage Languages to Institutional Change."

[105] Pal, *Interests of State*, 121.

[106] McAndrew, Helly, Tessier, and Young, "From Heritage Languages to Institutional Change," 161.

[107] John Biles, Annie Carroll, Radostina Pavlova, and Margaret Sokol, "Canada: Fostering an Integrated Society?" in *International Perspectives: Integration and Inclusion*, ed. James Frideres and John Biles (Montreal: McGill-Queen's University Press, 2012), 79–110.

[108] For the most comprehensive treatment of this subject to date, see Caroline Andrew, John Biles, Myer Siemiatycki, and Erin Tolley, eds., *Electing a Diverse Canada: The Representation of Immigrants, Minorities and Women* (Vancouver: UBC Press, 2008).

[109] Kymlicka, *Finding Our Way*, 18.

[110] "A Strategy to Eliminate Racial Discrimination," memo to the Secretary of State and Minister of State (Multiculturalism and Citizenship), 21 July 1989, 3.

[111] For an overview of the breadth of multiculturalism program work in education, consult Secretary of State, "Multiculturalism in Education Projects 1977–1984" (Hull, Secretary of State, 1984); Secretary of State, "Multiculturalism in Education Projects 1984–1987" (Hull, Secretary of State, 1987); and Multiculturalism and Citizenship Canada, "Répertoire des projets sur le multiculturalisme et l'antiracisme dans l'enseignement 1987–1990" (Hull: Multiculturalism and Citizenship Canada, 1990). In addition, the massive expansion of the Settlement Workers in Schools programming of Citizenship and Immigration Canada's Integration Branch is largely attributable to injection of funds through CAPAR.

[112] An excellent example of working with labour organizations includes the Canadian Labour Congress's National Anti-Racism Task Force, which ran from 1994 to 1998 and, among other initiatives, produced a series of five booklets on racism in unions and communities; see Canadian Labour Congress, "National Anti-Racism Strategy: Framework for Action" (Ottawa: CLC, 1997).

[113] McAndrew, Helly, Tessier, and Young, "From Heritage Languages to Institutional Change," 160.

[114] Institutional engagement on multiculturalism across the federal government has been undertaken a number of times. For example, the Standing Committee on Multiculturalism and Citizenship issued a report in 1993 entitled "Study of the Implementation of the *Canadian Multiculturalism Act* in Federal Institutions," and Canadian Heritage undertook an evaluation in 1995, "Evaluation of Activities to Promote and Report on Multiculturalism in Federal Institutions."

[115] Kymlicka, *Finding Our Way*, 48.

[116] The Multiculturalism Family Violence Program (1997–2002) was part of the overall federal Family Violence Initiative launched in 1988. It was designed to "coordinate family violence prevention policy and programming across departments at the federal level and to influence players to contribute to the reduction of family violence in Canada." Roughly $7 million a year was shared across departments, including Canadian Heritage, which received $460,000 a year for the Aboriginal Women's Program, the Multiculturalism Program, and some

evaluation work. The Multiculturalism Program sought to raise awareness of family violence within minority communities through access to information and services to reduce incidents and to "encourage other federal departments, with responsibilities related to family violence, to ensure that their programs benefit Canadians of all ethnic origins"; see Positive Outcomes Consulting Services, "Evaluation of the Family Violence Initiative: Multiculturalism Program," final report submitted to Canadian Heritage (North Vancouver: Positive Outcomes Consulting Services, 18 September 2002). The Metropolis Project (1996–2012) was a cross-government initiative focused on policy research investigating immigration, integration, and diversity in cities in Canada and around the world. It engaged more than a dozen federal departments and agencies over 15 years in discussions on how best to facilitate the integration of newcomers; see Biles, "International Metropolis Project."

[117] CIC, *Annual Report 2010–2011*, 36.

[118] Indeed, Uberoi quotes Richard Clippingdale, the assistant under secretary of state tasked with leading the team that drafted the *Canadian Multiculturalism Act*, when he reflected on the cross-government aspects of the act, "The cross governmental commitment is very weak, it didn't give the bill teeth, it gave it false teeth.... The approach was we bring the institutions of the Federal Government along with us gently"; see Uberoi, "Multicultural Nation-Building," 160. Uberoi also suggests that decisions about the development of the first annual report on the operation of the *Canadian Multiculturalism Act* deliberately focused on a gradual approach to engaging the broader federal family; see ibid., 173–174.

[119] One of the most commonly cited indicators of success of the Multiculturalism Program is the level of hiring of visible minorities into the federal public service. However, this reflects the confusion over the interactions between multiculturalism and employment equity, which are governed by separate legislation (the *Canadian Multiculturalism Act* and the *Employment Equity Act*) and have always been managed by different departments.

[120] It should, however, be noted that persistent critiques levelled at the government's approach to multiculturalism include the absence of a commissioner, such as the commissioners of official languages and human rights; the absence of mandatory five-year reviews, as required by the *Employment Equity Act*; and the absence of a mandatory element of memoranda to Cabinet such as those focused on gender, Aboriginal persons, federal-provincial-territorial relations, and environmental impacts, amongst others. For example, in 1995, the Canadian Ethnocultural Council concluded, "Multiculturalism has not been integrated successfully into the full operations of government"; see Canadian Ethnocultural Council, "The 42% Solution: Making Equality a Reality" (Ottawa: Canadian Ethnocultural Council, 6 December 1995), 26.

[121] Environics, "2005 Survey of Federal Government Employees on Multiculturalism" (Ottawa: Canadian Heritage, August 2005); also Jack Jedwab, "Official's Multiculturalism: Canadian Civil Servants Views on Diversity" (Montreal: Association for Canadian Studies, n.d.).

[122] In 1960, 70 peaceful demonstrators against apartheid were killed and 180 wounded in Sharpeville, South Africa. In 1966, the United Nations proclaimed March 21 as the International Day for the Elimination of Racial Discrimination.

[123] Griffith, *Policy Arrogance or Innocent Bias*, 27.

[124] Frances Abele, Judith Madill, and Joan Murphy, "The March 21 Campaign and Action 2000: An Interpretive Case History" (Ottawa: Canadian Heritage, 21 November 2000).

[125] Fernando Mata, "Segmentation Analysis of the Young Audience of the March 21 Campaign" (Gatineau: Government of Canada, 26 January 1999).

[126] In 1992–1993, 19 percent of demand for products and information on March 21 came from federal organizations. An interdepartmental symposium on "Sharing Effective Practices for Strengthening Race Relations" attracted 120 representatives in 1993–1994 – a 50 percent increase over the previous year; see Marilyn Collins, "Review of Draft Plan for March 21 Campaign 1995" (Gatineau: Government of Canada, 1 August 1994).

[127] "Multiculturalism: Fact Sheet 1999 March 21 Campaign for the Elimination of Racial Discrimination" (Gatineau: Multiculturalism Program, Department of Canadian Heritage, 1999).

[128] Not all aspects of the Action 2000 campaign were a resounding success; for example, the concert had trouble attracting an audience; see Lynn Saxberg, "Music with a Message Takes Aim at Racism," *Ottawa Citizen,* 4 March 2000, E3; and Zev Singer, "Free Tickets Fuel Concert," *Ottawa Citizen,* 4 March 2000, A3.

[129] "March 21 Millennium Youth Initiative" (Gatineau: Multiculturalism Program, Department of Canadian Heritage, 2000).

[130] "A Strategy for Re-orienting March 21" (Gatineau: Multiculturalism Program, Department of Canadian Heritage, 20 June 2001); and "A Framework for Renewing March 21" (Gatineau: Multiculturalism Program, Department of Canadian Heritage, 15 February 2001).

[131] Citizenship and Immigration Canada, "Evaluation of the Multiculturalism Program" (Ottawa: CIC, March 2012). The Mathieu Da Costa campaign ran from 1996 to 2011 and encouraged children and youth between 9 and 18 to submit an original piece of writing celebrating the contributions to Canada of African, Aboriginal, or other ethnocultural-background Canadians. In 2007, it attracted more than 1,000 entries from across the country; see Citizenship and Immigration Canada, *Annual Report on the Operation of the Canadian Multiculturalism Act 2006–2007* (Ottawa: CIC, 2008). Black History Month and Asian Heritage Month (AHM) are loosely coordinated sets of activities undertaken by Canadians and their communities across Canada. In 2010–2011, CIC participated in 27 AHM-related activities across the country between late April and early May 2010; see CIC, *Annual Report 2010–2011.* The Paul Yuzyk Award was launched in 2009 and recognizes the lifetime achievement of a Canadian who has made exceptional contributions to multiculturalism and integration of newcomers. The recipient can nominate a Canadian not-for-profit organization to receive a $20,000 grant.

[132] The Multiculturalism Program's year-round youth engagement on anti-racism activities was undertaken by the regional offices. The extent of these activities was well captured in 1998 in a report on the 1998 campaign, which included annexes of activities developed by all five regions. For example, the Quebec region reported engaging 300 partners, 30 school boards, and eight regions within Quebec and reached more than 4,000,000 people; see Canadian Heritage, "Report on the 1998 March 21 Campaign" (Gatineau: Canadian Heritage, 2008).

[133] McAndrew, Helly, Tessier, and Young, "From Heritage Languages to Institutional Change," 159.

[134] Citizenship and Immigration Canada, *Annual Report on the Operation of the Canadian Multiculturalism Act 2007–2008* (Ottawa: CIC, 2009).

[135] The March 21 Campaign does not even appear in CIC's annual reports on the operation of the *Canadian Multiculturalism Act* for 2007–2008 or 2010–2011.

[136] Judith Madill and Frances Abele, "From Public Education to Social Marketing: The Evolution of the Canadian Heritage Anti-Racism Social Marketing Program," *Journal of Nonprofit & Public Sector Marketing* 17, no. 1–2 (2007):27–53.

[137] Tao Research Associates Inc., "An Evaluation of the March 21, 1992 Anti-Racism Campaign" (Ottawa: Department of Multiculturalism and Citizenship, 1992); and March 21 Anti-Racism Campaign: Some Highlights of Evaluation Results 1992 & 1993 (Ottawa: Department of Multiculturalism and Citizenship, n.d.).

[138] Canadian Heritage, "Evaluation of March 21 Campaign for the International Day for the Elimination of Racial Discrimination" (Gatineau: Corporate Review Branch, Canadian Heritage, July 1999).

[139] CMG Canada, "March 21 Sponsorship Strategy Final Report" (Gatineau: Canadian Heritage, 22 November 2000).

[140] WME Consulting Associates, "Evaluation of the Multiculturalism Program's March 21 Campaign for the Elimination of Racial Discrimination: School and Youth Targeted Campaign Efforts" (Gatineau: Canadian Heritage, 28 November 2001); and Environics Research Group, "Focus Group Evaluation of the Multiculturalism Program's March 21 Campaign for the Elimination of Racial Discrimination" (Gatineau: Canadian Heritage, 28 November 2001).

[141] Canadian Heritage, "Summative Evaluation of the Multiculturalism Program" (Gatineau: Canadian Heritage, 28 June 2006), 48–50.

[142] This strategy proposed five interrelated action areas: i) promotion of institutional change, ii) use of human rights instruments, iii) support for visible-minority communities, iv) effective communications strategies, and v) intervention in racial crisis situations; see "Strategy to Eliminate Racial Discrimination."

[143] The CRRF was a component of the Japanese Canadian Redress Agreement signed in 1988, but was not implemented until the government proclaimed the *Canadian Race Relations Foundation Act* in 1996 and actual work commenced in 1997.

[144] CAPAR proposed a six-part action strategy: i) assist victims and groups vulnerable to racism and related forms of discrimination, ii) develop forward-looking approaches to promote diversity and combat racism, iii) strengthen the role of civil society, iv) strengthen regional and international co-operation, v) educate children and youth on diversity and anti-racism, and vi) counter hate and bias; see Government of Canada, "Canada's Action Plan Against Racism: A Canada for All (Gatineau: Department of Canadian Heritage, 2005). Recent evaluations of the strategy concluded that while some initiatives were successful, the cross-government approach was never fully implemented and little coordination among funded projects was discernible; see Citizenship and Immigration Canada, "Evaluation of Canada's Action Plan Against Racism" (Ottawa: CIC, 2010) and Government Consulting Services, "Horizontal Evaluation of Canada's Action Plan Against Racism: Methodology Report" (Ottawa: CIC, February 2010).

[145] Citizenship and Immigration Canada, "Evaluation of Canada's Action Plan Against Racism," v.

[146] Association for Canadian Studies, "Younger Canadians Believe Multiculturalism Works; Older Canadians, Not So Sure," at http://www.acs-aec.ca/en/social-research/multiculturalism-diversity/, accessed 15 October 2012.

[147] Will Kymlicka, "The Rise and Fall of Multiculturalism? New Debates on Inclusion and Accommodation in Diverse Societies," in *The Multiculturalism Backlash: European Discourses, Policies and Practices*, ed. Steven Vertovec and Susanne Wessendorf (New York: Routledge, 2010), 39.

[148] Brighton Research, "Strategic Evaluation of Multiculturalism Programs," 67.

[149] For example, acquiring an official language was one of four objectives of the policy promulgated in the House of Commons on 8 October 1971 by Pierre Trudeau. Greg Gauld notes, "During the war years [Second World War], the government became concerned about hastening the integration of immigrants, and with relations between groups"; see Greg Gauld, "Multiculturalism: The Real Thing?" in *20 Years of Multiculturalism: Successes and Failures*, ed. Stella Hryniuk (Winnipeg: St. John's College Press, 1992), 9. Robert Vineberg, in his history of the evolution of Canadian settlement programming, notes that a 6 June 1974 Cabinet decision decreed that "the department of Manpower and Immigration in essence would be dealing with the short term aspects of immigrant integration through the use of its existing services and that the Department of the Secretary of State would be looking after the longer term aspects of immigrant integration"; see Robert Vineberg, *Responding to Immigrants' Settlement Needs: The Canadian Experience* (The Netherlands: Springer, 2012), 28.

[150] Paul Bramadat, "Religious Diversity and International Migration: National and Global Dimensions," in *International Migration and the Governance of Religious Diversity*, ed. Paul Bramadat and Matthias Koenig (Montreal: McGill-Queen's University Press, 2009), 1–28.

[151] The first Canadian Conference on Multiculturalism was held in October 1973, the second in 1976, and the third in 1978.

[152] The Association for Canadian Studies appears to have picked up the Metropolis conferences in the last two years, so this venue may continue into the future.

[153] For an insider's perspective, see Griffith, *Policy Arrogance or Innocent Bias*.

MULTICULTURALISM IN THE 1990s: THE SMALLEST COMMON DENOMINATOR IN DEFINING CANADIAN NATIONAL IDENTITY

ELKE WINTER

INTRODUCTION[1]

Whereas in recent years, many Western immigrant-receiving societies experienced a retreat from multiculturalism (arguably less so in practice than in dominant discourses), in Canada, support for multiculturalism merely dipped in the early 1990s and climbed again in subsequent years.[2] As a normative principle and popular representation of national identity, multiculturalism became dominant not only among academics but also in government discourses and in the Canadian media. Indeed, as Rainer Bauböck has put it, "No other Western country has gone as far as Canada in adopting multiculturalism not only as a policy towards minorities but also as a basic feature of shared identity."[3]

This chapter unpacks the dominant discourse of multiculturalism as shared national identity and as a framework for society-building in the 1990s. It asks the following questions: What does *multiculturalism* mean? Who is included in the multicultural Canadian "we," and who is excluded? By doing so, the chapter dissects this discourse's constitutive segments. The empirical analysis identifies three types of perspectives – republican, liberal-pluralist, and liberal-multiculturalist – which respond to, reinforce, and contradict each other. Within this polyphony of voices, a vaguely defined, multicultural, pan-Canadian identity gains political

The Multiculturalism Question: Debating Identity in 21st-Century Canada, ed. Jack Jedwab. Kingston: School of Policy Studies, Queen's University. © 2014 The School of Policy Studies, Queen's University at Kingston. All rights reserved.

influence as the by-product of a shared opposition to Quebec's allegedly ethnically nationalist separatism. Toward the end of the 1990s, this definition of multiculturalism becomes the smallest common denominator for describing the Canadian national project within otherwise diverging or even contradictory views about what it means to be Canadian.[4]

The chapter is divided into six sections. I first remind the reader about the main characteristics of Canadian multiculturalism policy in the 1990s. I then briefly outline the theoretical and methodological framework of my study. In the sections making up the body of the chapter, I examine three types of majority discourse that were extracted from the media analysis. Finally, before I conclude, I discuss the relationships among these discourses, including the logical flow of arguments and the one representation that they all come to agree upon.

CANADIAN MULTICULTURALISM IN THE 1990S

In the 1990s, Canadian multiculturalism policy entered a third phase of policy orientation.[5] To recall, in the decade after its announcement, multicultural policy concentrated on symbolic matters but remained silent about political and economic inequalities. In the 1980s, the focus shifted from heritage issues (symbolic multiculturalism) to anti-racism, social participation, and equity issues (structural multiculturalism) to address the increasing concerns of Canada's visible minorities.[6] In the early 1990s, multiculturalism came under attack. Too much diversity, it was feared, would break up the country. The Reform Party, with its outspoken anti-immigration stance, emerged (in 1987) in Alberta. The Citizens' Forum on Canada's Future (known as the Spicer Commission) recommended the refocusing of multiculturalism policy so as to "welcome all Canadians to an evolving mainstream."[7] The Charlottetown referendum failed, arguably, because of the existence of too many diverse interest groups. As a consequence, multiculturalism policy became more and more defined by shared citizenship.[8] On the one hand, the emphasis on citizenship was welcomed for its commitment to civil society and as an inclusive expression for membership in the Canadian nation. On the other hand, the new policy guidelines were attacked for "diluting multiculturalism"[9] – dismantling the program financially (from $27 million in the early 1990s to $18.7 million in 1996–1997)[10] – and for shifting the remaining financial support from mono-ethnic associations to mainstream agencies serving a multi-ethnic clientele.[11]

While multiculturalism diminished in prominence in the first part of the 1990s, it regained political capital in the second half of the decade. Studying the policies of the time, Abu-Laban and Gabriel observe the "selling" of Canadian diversity and the commodification of multiculturalism for trade-enhancing purposes.[12] Furthermore, as I will argue below, the pluralist ideal supporting Canadian multiculturalism gained salience in comparison with Québécois separatism and supposedly ethnic nationalism as it both discredited the latter and allowed English Canada to shine in a brighter light at home and abroad. This was particularly the case against the backdrop of the 1995 Quebec referendum on independence. Finally, after disappointments with the myth of the American melting pot, international observers started looking to Canada for solutions to "managing diversity" in their own countries; Canadian scholars and political stakeholders too started casting Canada as a world leader in diversity management.[13]

These seemingly contradictory tendencies – of reduced institutional and financial support for multiculturalism policy and increased celebration of diversity and diversity management – were part of a wider trend of neo-liberalization that marked the 1990s. They are poignantly summarized by Karim: paradoxically, "as the bureaucratic target for anti-multiculturalism attacks has shrunk, Canada is increasingly described as a multicultural country in current dominant discourses."[14]

Part and parcel of the newly marketed Canadian diversity model was also the analytical separation among three types of minority groups: national minorities (such as Quebec), Aboriginal people, and ethnic groups of immigrant background; this analysis is an essential feature of Will Kymlicka's seminal work, *Multicultural Citizenship*, which appeared in 1995. National minorities and Aboriginal people are usually described as previously self-governing peoples who – through conquest or, as in the case of the latter, colonization and treaties of federation – have become incorporated into states of which they do not constitute the majority. The members of immigration-derived ethnic groups, by contrast, are said to have become members of society "individually" through more or less "voluntary" immigration.[15] While these distinctions have become widely accepted in academia, they matter less in public discourse and in the media representations analyzed below.

ANALYTICAL FRAMEWORK

The theoretical model used here examines how a pluralist "national we" is bounded by opposition to a real or imagined "them." It is particularly interested in whether and how this national "we" includes references to "others" alongside "us." It thereby traces a process by which one minority group is elevated by members of the dominant group and conditionally included in representations of a collective "we" by means of repressing, marginalizing, and excluding another.[16]

The unifying multiculturalism agenda of the 1990s was a project that was politically most significant in English-speaking central Canada, particularly in Canada's arguably most multicultural city. Hence, the empirical perspective chosen here is that of the national majority as it is represented in two mainstream English-language newspapers, the

Toronto edition of the *Globe and Mail* and the *Toronto Star*. The empirical
study consisted of 350 keyword-selected newspaper articles that appeared
between 1991 and 2001, out of which 123 op-ed pieces were submitted to
critical discourse analysis. The op-ed articles included columns, editorials,
letters to the editor, and comments. All articles were treated as intercon-
nected elements of a single media text about Canadian multiculturalism
and nationhood in the 1990s.[17] An individual analysis was written for each
selected newspaper article, focusing on the cultural/ideological "content"
of the multicultural project: Who and what constitute multiculturalism?
Who and what can or cannot be included?

Obviously, the spectrum of discourses identified here is not representative of all of Canada. Newspaper articles constitute only a small segment
of a country's dominant discourse; they vary regionally and follow a
corporate agenda. Nevertheless, the selected sample of newspaper texts
provides a window through which we can appreciate a multiplicity of
dominant interpretations of Canadian multiculturalism.

The analysis uncovered three major perspectives. Discourses classified as *republican* were found in roughly 40 percent of the articles.
They view both the accommodation of French-English dualism and the
extent of multiculturalism policy as being harmful to unified Canadian
nationhood. Discourses classified as *liberal-pluralist*, by contrast, view
a "pluralist compromise" as endemic to the Canadian societal project.
Identified in 40 percent of the articles, they argue in favour of the status
quo of current multicultural *and* multinational arrangements. In approximately 15 percent of the collected articles, Canada is portrayed as being
constituted through ethnic diversity that is related to (recent) immigration. This *liberal-multiculturalist* perspective was identified only in *Toronto
Star* articles. It claims that the current arrangements are insufficient and
that multiculturalism's role in Canadian identity must be extended. In
the following section, I will examine the three majority perspectives in
more detail.

A REPUBLICAN PERSPECTIVE ON MULTICULTURALISM

The type of discourse that is labelled *republican* oscillates between seemingly neutral Canadian patriotism and explicitly English Canadian nationalism. On the one hand, it seems to be "a better, finer, nobler thing to
love Canada – not the land or the people, but the idea – than to seek only
dumb contentment of huddling together with our own kind."[18] Here, a
deliberate attempt is made to abstract from the cultural characteristics of
(English) Canada, and the nation becomes merely the "largest act of em-
pathy of which we are yet capable."[19] On the other hand, these discourses
also uphold the conviction that "the glue that is holding Canada together
… is the culture and the values of English Canadians."[20] This ambiguity reminds us of the proximity in practice, if not in theory, between

a state-oriented, civic understanding of nationhood and a culturally motivated, ethnic interpretation. In both sub-currents of the republican perspective, national unity is viewed as the quintessential guarantor of a superior – "most tolerant, most liberal and least racist"[21] – form of society, which is "rooted neither in homogeneity nor in diversity, but in humanity."[22] The Canadian nation, supposedly the best possible approximation of universalism, thereby allows for individual emancipation: "We have created a country in which, more nearly so than anywhere else I know of, everyone can be whatever they want to be."[23]

The representation of Canadian nationhood as being primarily constituted through British or English Canadian culture and institutions produces fears about fragmentation and disintegration. The public recognition of ethnocultural diversity is seen as undermining social cohesion and ultimately leading to the disintegration of the nation, and this is considered to be detrimental to all members of society, the majority and minorities alike. Indeed, in the republican discourses investigated here, any type of "groupism" – whether it comes in the form of Québécois nationalism or the recognition of ethnic group identities through multiculturalism – is rejected. For the republican perspective, in its purest form, the "secessionists in Quebec ... do not represent the only danger" of national disintegration.[24] Rather, this perspective postulates "a broad coalition" among minority groups where Québécois "separatists" "make tacit common cause with the cries of interest groups, the demands of victims and the carping of the regions."[25] In sum, the republican perspective is equally opposed to special status for Quebec and to multiculturalism as an official policy and national ideology.

Within this representation of Canada, English Canadians are never viewed as different or located at the margins of the Canadian nation. On the contrary, in its ideal-typical form, the republican perspective constructs an opposition between "ideal citizens" – explicitly or implicitly identified as white, anglophone, British Canadians – and an undifferentiated, marginalized "rest." In fact, the centre of the Canadian majority, which does not participate in the "broad coalition against the very notion of common interest,"[26] consists of uncomplaining male WASPs: "everyone else is a victim."[27] Canada is here characterized by unmarked whiteness: "For about three decades, beginning with the accusations of having been unfair to *francophones*, and on down to today's charge of practicing 'systemic racism,' WASPs have [unjustifiably] been identified as the sole source of all of Canada's social and political ills."[28] Furthermore, the centre of the English Canadian nation is located in Ontario, which is said to be the only province that neither complains nor demands regional particularity.[29] The geographical, emotional, and irrational boundaries of regions are opposed to the rational, political delimitations of provinces – attributes that are said to reflect the character of the inhabitants.

In its ideal-typical form, the "Canadian we" identified in the republican perspective is thus highly ethnocentric and opposed to any sort of group-based pluralist arrangements. Nevertheless, in times of distress, this perspective accommodates strategic alliances between so-called ideal citizens ("us") and varying segments of the rest ("others" and "them"). Two variations can be observed: First, ethnic minorities' multicultural demands are rejected with reference to the "Canadian tradition," which includes francophones and Aboriginal people together with English Canadians (and white Europeans who assimilate into this culture). Ethnic minorities, by contrast, are identified as "them."

> Our multiculturalism may be turning into multinationalism. It hasn't happened yet.… But more and more Canadians care more passionately about events in their "home" country than in their "adopted" one.… A growing number of Canadians simply haven't been here long enough to have learned about Canada. As our ethnic communities expand in size and coherence, it becomes easier for individuals to live in the country while remaining outsiders, emotionally and psychically. *Most will become North Americans all right, or their children will, since the continental culture is so magnetic. But this isn't the same as their becoming Canadian in the sense of identifying with our history, our unique struggles and challenges.*[30]

Here, ethnic minorities are cast as outsiders through the construction of an opposition between those who "haven't been here long enough to have learned about Canada" and those who are "naturally" or have become "Canadian in the sense of identifying with our history, our unique struggles and challenges." Implicitly, Quebec and Aboriginal people are "contingent insiders" whose presence is included within "the Canadian tradition," even if the acknowledgement of their "unique struggles and challenges" remains at its margins. Specifically, dualism is perceived as a historical liability that cannot be avoided but must certainly not be extended to other groups who may "expand in size and coherence" and then make similar demands as francophones in Quebec.

Second, and more frequently, Québécois aspirations of independent nationhood are said to be realizable only at the expense of English Canada's open, tolerant, or even multicultural society, which then includes ethnic minorities and Aboriginal people along with English Canadians (and those accepting the primacy of Canadian nationhood). Particularly since the mid-1990s, ethnic minorities are regarded as conditional insiders since they appear less "deviant" when compared with an ethnically closed, French-speaking, "separatist" Quebec. Under these circumstances, and in a climate of international praise for Canadian multiculturalism, the republican perspective no longer opposes the notion of a multicultural society as such, but portrays it as being constituted through British culture and institutions.

Multiculturalism … is a unique, English Canadian invention. It exists nowhere else in the world, including in *Quebec*…. But this kind of Canada can only exist – outside of *Quebec* – within the template provided by the values and culture of English Canada. Also, by its sense of being heir to an historical continuum that stretches back to the Loyalists and their decision to come north to try to create a radically different kind of North America…. If those qualities, and sense of historical purpose, go, everything goes.[31]

While this vision of society seems more inclusive than the previously described English Canadian ethnocentrism, it remains a strongly patronizing perspective of a "multicultural we." English Canadian values and institutions constitute the multicultural society, which is then able to integrate limited expressions of other group-based identities. Furthermore, this vision of decorative multiculturalism derives much of its constitutive power from contrast: "Canada today is … composed of two quite different kinds of societies – an ethnic, European-style, nation in Quebec, and a 'rest of Canada' that is well on the way to becoming a multi-ethnic World Nation."[32] In some cases, by portraying francophone Quebec as the incarnation of anti-Canadianism, republican discourses construct a causal link between the "very nature of Canada – founded as an explicit partnership between two distinct peoples"[33] – and increasing national disintegration. The presence of Quebec is portrayed as the starting point for unavoidable fragmentation, which spreads "like a contagion" by shifting loyalties "to region and race."[34]

In sum, the construction of Canadianness in the discourses of the republican perspective comes closest to traditional representations of homogeneous nationhood. Three main strategies are employed to construct Britishness as irreplaceable and to position it at the centre of Canadian society.[35] First, English Canadian cultural particularity is downplayed so that Britishness becomes the condition of shared humanity; second, it is suggested that Britishness constitutes an open and possibly multicultural society; third, minorities are denied the society-constituting capacities that are attributed to English Canadians.

MULTICULTURALISM FROM A LIBERAL-PLURALIST PERSPECTIVE

The republican perspective competes with another type of discourse that can be defined as *liberal-pluralist*. This discourse celebrates limited amounts of ethnic diversity and calls for the maintenance of the status quo of pluralism in Canada. For this discourse, the "just balance" among Canadian nationhood, special status for Quebec, self-government rights for Aboriginal people, and multiculturalism has been established. The status quo refers to a situation where Quebec, de facto, enjoys more rights and recognition than ethnic groups, even though its status as a distinct society is not constitutionally recognized. Although the failure to include Quebec in the Canadian Constitution is regretted, no strong arguments are brought forth in favour of granting Quebec the political and economic autonomy it desires.

Rather than identifying a particular group or cultural quality (such as Britishness) as the guarantor of "unity in diversity," the liberal-pluralist perspective portrays compromise as Canada's essence. In principle, this compromise involves the *active* collaboration of different types of ethnic and/or national groups. In other words, the multicultural project of society is supposed to be constructed through multiple and normatively equal forms of community involvement. Built upon the stylization of compromise, integrated ethnic diversity is considered within this discourse as intrinsically Canadian, while the failure to achieve compromise is portrayed as undermining the very idea of Canadianness. As a consequence, attempts to unsettle current arrangements are viewed with suspicion.

Practically, however, the liberal-pluralist perspective reflects the power inequalities that still persist in Canadian society even though it strives to mitigate and downplay them. Quebec, Aboriginal people, and ethnic groups are represented as having less agency and being closer to irrational, ethnic forms of community than the English Canadian majority. Compared to the dominant representations in the republican perspective, the division between "us" and "others" within liberal-pluralist discourses is a much finer line. Because the promoted vision of Canada as a pluralist nation requires at least two parties (in compromise) to be situated within the (multi-)ethnic boundary, modestly "different" insiders ("others") enjoy a privileged position. Nevertheless, even within the liberal-pluralist perspective, English Canadians are never positioned as outsiders to the Canadian nation. They remain at the core of Canadianness, even though they are not imagined as being there alone.

This imagination of egalitarian pluralist compromise within Canada is created through diverse discursive strategies. The most important one is contrast. Elsewhere, I discuss how the imaginary of the multicultural nation is created through shifting opposition to assumed assimilationism (attributed to the United States) on the one hand and to assumed ethnocentrism (attributed to Quebec) on the other.[36] A second strategy of staging successful pluralism involves relegating ethnic conflict and inequality to the past. Thus, Canada's trajectory as a nation is often represented as an ongoing evolution of increasing diversity and tolerance. Usually, this evolution involves a transition from (sometimes "fractious, quarrelsome") dualism to relatively integrated, peaceful multiculturalism.[37]

Prior to the 1960s, we expected immigrants to assimilate; indeed, *we* tried to keep out any groups seen as incapable of assimilation. *Now* that means learning one or both official languages and adopting liberal democratic values; *once it also meant* becoming indistinguishable from native-born citizens in their style of speech, clothes, diet, political views, work habits, family size and leisure activities.... *We* repudiated this approach in 1971, when Canada became the first country to adopt a federal multiculturalism policy.[38]

The representation of Canadian diversity in the quotation above views pluralism as a linear evolution: past injustices have been rectified, and Canada is now travelling progressively toward more and more inclusiveness. Minorities' struggles and efforts in achieving equal rights without assimilation are downplayed. Indeed, within the discourses of the liberal-pluralist perspective, multicultural rights tend to be "given to *them* by an Invisible Self group," as Richard Day[39] claims. Minorities are still at the receiving end of social action, whereas unmarked Canadians – usually white and anglophone – have "had to continually adapt and innovate to meet the challenge of accommodating diversity while respecting individual rights and maintaining stable political institutions."[40] That these institutions are thoroughly British, Protestant, and male-dominated seems to be entirely forgotten.

Representations of Canada's proliferation of diversity (and diversity accommodation) also tend to neglect the fact that dualism has been enriched rather than supplemented by multiculturalism. While both original founding nations still enjoy substantial collective rights – far more than ethnic minorities – only Quebec's are cast as minority rights and carefully distinguished from those granted to Aboriginal people and immigrant minorities. Minority rights are here portrayed as static, "normal" categories outside the realm of negotiation and power relations. This strategy describes the simultaneous construction of diversity and its containment through classification.

Two strategic variations can be identified in the liberal-pluralist perspective. The first variation joins the republican discourse in cementing a multicultural alliance between English Canadians and ethnic groups by opposing it to Québécois ethnic nationalism and separatism. The second, and more frequent, variation situates the "French fact" and the recognition of Quebec closer to the centre than other forms of diversity and diversity accommodation. Here, representations of Quebec provide a frame for the integration of ethnocultural diversity. As I show elsewhere, this dualism provides a matrix into which, ideologically and discursively, multiculturalism is integrated as a "natural extension"[41] rather than a forced break with tradition. Quebec is thus located at the centre of Canadianness. Ethnic minorities (as well as English Canadians) are urged to respect this position – if only out of self-interest – since, within this logic, only a united Canada can assure their cultural protection.

What would *the world* have lost [if Quebec had separated]? The hope that different peoples with different religions, cultures and languages can find in each other not just tolerance, not even just respect, but *part of who they are*.

> For 350 years, aboriginal peoples, French Canadians, English Canadians
> and people from every quarter of the globe *have together made* a country that
> *at its finest moments* defines itself through its diversity. *Were it not for English*
> *or [sic] French together,* such moments would not have been imaginable *on*
> *the continent.* If Canada aspires to be a place where religions, cultures, lan-
> guages intersect, inform each other and live together, Quebec's presence is
> at the very heart of it all.[42]

In this quotation, pluralist compromise formally involves equally (in
historical chronology) "aboriginal peoples, French Canadians, English
Canadians and people from every quarter of the globe." At the same
time, the contributions of "English [and] French together" are especially
underlined. Their collaboration constitutes Canada and its uniqueness not
only "on the continent" (i.e., vis-à-vis the United States) but also in "the
world." This ambiguity is characteristic of the liberal-pluralist perspective, which is always concerned about striking a balance between unity
and diversity and, therefore, also reluctant to grant ethnic minorities full
equality in terms of structural group rights. While English Canadians'
group rights often remain unspecified in liberal-pluralist discourses, the
minority rights of Aboriginal people and, particularly, Quebec receive
more attention.

In the passage above, "Quebec's presence is at the very heart of it all."
This differs fundamentally from the republican point of view because in
the liberal-pluralist perspective, it is not English or French Canadians'
cultural properties that constitute Canadianness but the compromise
struck between them. Canada is here "constituted by the diversity of
people in its midst," and, among those, "the people of Quebec ... make
possible who we all are."[43] In these quotations, the ambiguities between
unity and diversity, as well as between individuals and groups, are
evident. Ultimately, these ambiguities are the reason why certain expressions of difference cannot be tolerated and why, in the liberal-pluralist
perspective, references to Quebec not only constitute Canadian pluralism
but also define its limits: while separatism fails to cherish the pluralist
compromise that constitutes Canadianness, ethnic nationalism is rejected
for advocating an "anti-liberal" culture of ethnic homogeneity, intolerance, and disrespect for individual rights.

In sum, within the liberal-pluralist perspective, dualism serves as a
symbol of both Canada's historical constitution as a nation and its potential death as a nation. The "dualist frame" that is constructed around
tolerable expressions of ethnocultural difference corresponds to what
Homi Bhabha has called "an attempt both to respond to and to control the
dynamic process of the articulation of cultural difference, administering
a *consensus* based on a norm that propagates cultural diversity."[44] This
dualist frame operates in two directions: it prescribes for ethnic groups
what they may and may not do (e.g., demand the status of minority

nations), and it informs Quebec about the limits on its rights to national self-government.

A LIBERAL-MULTICULTURALIST VIEW

In the sample of newspaper discourses analyzed, the republican and liberal-pluralist perspectives are dominant, with just over 40 percent of articles each. These discourses are spread evenly over the ten-year period from 1992 to 2001 and have been identified in both newspapers. While the two dominant perspectives are thus able to impose their logic on the discussion of nationhood and pluralism in the media and, presumably, considerable segments of the public space, they also keep each other at bay. This is why the emergence of a third perspective, toward the late 1990s, is important – even though, in the newspaper sample, it is not very significant in quantitative terms.

Roughly 15 percent of the newspaper articles in the sample pursue the goal of extending multiculturalism in Canada. These discourses, which can be defined as *liberal-multiculturalist*, oppose and reject both English Canadian monoculturalism and national dualism. They contend that the status quo of diversity accommodation in Canada is insufficient. While the vision of Canada as an egalitarian "unity in diversity" finds support in discourses that argue from a liberal-multiculturalist perspective, this ideal is portrayed as being not yet achieved. Rather, since immigrants – non-French, non-English "ethnic Canadians" of immigrant back-ground – and visible minorities are viewed as still being marginalized in the mainstream societies of English Canada and Quebec, more public recognition of immigration-induced ethnic diversity is demanded.[45] In fact, if the liberal-pluralist perspective fetishizes pluralist compromise as the essence of Canadianness, the liberal-multiculturalist perspective highlights ethnic diversity and its recognition in the public space. Here, liberal (and thus highly individualistic) "multiculturality" as such, rather than carefully manufactured agreements among groups, is represented as the essence of Canadian nationhood.

While voices for and from multicultural minorities in the mainstream press should not come as a surprise in an officially multicultural country, their presence seems to be a fairly recent phenomenon, at least if one judges from discussions in the academic literature. Thus, it seems telling that, in the sample of newspaper discourses, the liberal-multiculturalist perspective was identified only in articles in the *Toronto Star*. In the sample, the portrayed "us" claims to represent "immigrants and visible minorities in every sphere of Canadian society in every part of the country."[46] This "majority of Canadians" is said to not even want to hear about "nonsense political problems" such as "Quebec sovereignty and separation" because "our whole society is advancing toward a better and united Canada."[47] These discourses seem to reflect the confidence and social standing of a highly educated, multicultural, urban elite: "We want more educated and wealthy immigrants to come to Canada. We do not take anymore the 'wretched refuse' (to quote from the Statue of Liberty). Are they going to embrace wholeheartedly the British and French culture in Canada or would they want to maintain some of their culture and traditions? The 'wretched refuse' would have happily embraced biculturalism, lock, stock and barrel."[48]

Furthermore, it is argued that "if minorities become more accepted in Canadian society ... employment equity policies in the long run will become superfluous."[49] The newer immigrants no longer seem to need the support of their ethnic communities. Rather, they underline the importance of "let[ting] *each Canadian* speak the language of *his or her choice* and live and work in peace and tranquility with each other in *one new nation* made up of people with different cultures and backgrounds."[50] It is noteworthy that only very few discourses in the sample actually claim group rights.[51] Much more common are individualistic rejections of being treated as "second-class citizens": "In popular terminology ... newcomers are guests in the Canadian house and had better behave. This is obviously still true of refugees. But they constitute barely one-eighth of our annual intake of 200,000 immigrants. For most others, especially the well-educated and skilled in high-tech and information technology, *coming to Canada is a contract; they trade their talents for membership in a great nation.*"[52]

The quotation above underlines the trend toward an increasingly liberal conception of the multicultural project of society. The author rejects the idea that skilled immigrants are merely guests; however, he adopts a different standard when it comes to refugees. Hence, the quotation above also reminds us that the media sample is made up of majority discourses: while well-educated immigrants may "trade their talents for membership in a great nation," unskilled refugees remain "guests" and "had better behave." In the context of globalization, where states compete to attract the best brains in the world, the dividing line presented in the mainstream media is no longer one between established groups and newcomers, but rather between those who can and those who cannot "pay" for their membership in the nation. Although "evidence is mounting that unemployment levels among newer immigrants and Canadian-born visible minorities are very high,"[53] in the liberal-multiculturalist discourses of the sample, the notion of racism in Canada is largely avoided. As such, these discourses do not radically contradict the republican and liberal-pluralist perspectives. Rather, they respond to and reproduce those dominant discourses while adding a new dimension, which is best described as a constant push toward defining Canadianness in the multicultural terms of a highly diverse, urban, immigrant population.

In principle, the liberal-multiculturalist perspective insists that Canada was never constituted by a single group. It argues for the equality of ethnic minorities within the Canadian nation by emphasizing the contributions of ethnic minorities and immigrants. In some instances, one finds attempts to construct minority coalitions between ethnic minorities and francophone Québécois. In these cases, "the Quebec issue" is portrayed as "a wake-up call for all Canadians"[54] and as "just one of the ongoing unsettled questions about how we live together in this land called Canada."[55] Indeed, multicultural claims in Canada have long followed the logic that "ethnic minorities deserve rights too."[56]

Despite the attempts to construct parallels between French Canadians or Québécois on the one hand and immigrants' ethnic groups on the other, francophones' aspirations to power and recognition are viewed with suspicion. Therefore, in practice, liberal-multiculturalist discourses typically oppose – rather than celebrate (as a precedent) – minority rights for Quebec. Underlining the "ethnic" dimensions of Québécois nationalism, the liberal-multiculturalist perspective insists that Quebec's project of society is oppressive and prevents "Quebec's minority immigrants from contributing to their society with their rich cultural heritages."[57] Furthermore, "while sovereignists feel Quebec is not properly respected, their own treatment of minorities is not stellar."[58]

Overall, the liberal-multiculturalist perspective challenges the predominance of dualism in two ways: first, by claiming the same or similar rights for ethnic minorities as those claimed by and/or granted to Canada's "minority nations" and, second, by opposing the fragmenting, separatist overtones inherent in minority nationalism and demands for self-government rights. Elsewhere, I show how the rejection of separatism is used to support the representation of ethnic groups as being loyal to Canada.[59] By being better Canadians than Québécois separatists, ethnic groups are portrayed as having earned their place at the table. As a consequence, they can no longer be legitimately portrayed as outsiders. While the first strategy claims a similarity among diverse types of minorities, the second strategy constructs a difference between the integrative demands of immigrant minorities and the potentially destructive quarrels of the established groups: "The new diversified Canada is more generous, friendly, understanding and religiously and ethnically more tolerant than ... the Canada of the past."[60]

MULTICULTURALISM AS THE SMALLEST COMMON DENOMINATOR

The previous sections have shown that even within a relatively small and homogeneous sample of English-language newspaper discourses, there is no unified vision of the relationship between Canadian identity and multiculturalism. Although all three perspectives construct a "Canadian we" by contrasting the inclusion of second groups in the multicultural context with "deviant" third parties, they do so by adopting considerably different – even contradicting – premises. What the previous sections have *not* shown is the manner in which these discourses interact. This interaction can be interpreted in two ways. First, it constitutes a logical flow of claims-making and representation, where discourses contradict and respond to each other in a circular way until a new representation enters the public arena. Second, it exemplifies compromise – that is, the agreement on a particular representation of the multiculturalism–national identity nexus, even despite underlying ideological differences. Below, I address both points.

First, in the 1990s, republican, liberal-pluralist, and liberal-multiculturalist discourses contradict, reinforce, and respond to each other in a circular way. In the newspaper sample, the most important flow of arguments leads from discourses that define Canadianness in terms of British culture and institutions to discourses that view Canada as being historically constituted through dualist compromise (and not necessarily through English Canadian culture). From here, the flow leads to liberal-multiculturalist claims that Canada is mainly about ethnic diversity (and not merely about French-English dualism). Within the limits of the empirical study, the two dominant perspectives, republican and liberal-pluralist, hold each other at bay. The republican perspective simply reverses the image of a positively connoted extension of dualism. With roughly 42 percent each, the two perspectives are in balance: anti-pluralists oppose pro-pluralists.

On the one hand, the relatively small proportion of liberal-multiculturalist discourses (15.4 percent), identified in the *Toronto Star*, shifts the balance toward pro-pluralism – more precisely, toward immigration-related multiculturalism. On the other hand, this perspective alone is unable to change the dominant logic. As long as liberal-multiculturalist claims operate along the lines of "minorities deserve rights too (like Quebec)," ethnic minorities continue to carry the stigma of fragmenting Canada's collective identity and social cohesion. In fact, in reaction to demands for the extension of multiculturalism, republican discourses reproach ethnic Canadians for causing national disintegration, like Quebec. Associating ethnic groups closely with Quebec, they claim that multiculturalism multiplies the fragmentation that is said to have originated in Quebec francophones' quest for recognition. The liberal-multiculturalist perspective, in return, rejects this reproach, but it nevertheless views multiculturalism, as long as it operates within the logic of "immigrants are like French Canadians and the francophone population of Quebec," a villain by association. In other words, the flow of arguments is circular, with no side ultimately gaining the upper hand.

This situation changes in the second half of the 1990s. In English-speaking Canada, starting with the 1994 election of the Parti Québécois in Quebec, "deep diversity" is no longer associated merely with the idea of a "distinct society." Rather, framed as anti-liberal, oppressive, and separatist, Québécois ethnic nationalism comes to be perceived as putting the "survival of the nation" at stake. The "intolerable" nationalism of Quebec increases the need for strategic adaptations to the new political context within each perspective. The dualist compromise that previously united the dual majority weakens and thereby allows multiculturalism, almost as a by-product, to move from a discourse at the margins (supported mainly by the liberal-multiculturalist perspective) to a discourse invested with legitimacy at the centre (supported also by the liberal-pluralist and republican perspectives).

This brings me to my second point. The textual analysis presented above shows that, in the second half of the 1990s, all three ideological perspectives agree on one particular representation – namely, on positioning Quebec as an outsider ("them") to a fragile multicultural alliance between English Canadians and members of ethnic minorities. The "multicultural we" constituted in opposition to Québécois separatist and supposedly ethnic nationalism comes to be the smallest common denominator of otherwise conflicting perspectives on Canadian identity. This is the only representation that is shared by the republican, liberal-pluralist, and liberal-multiculturalist discourses; none of the other representations of insider-outsider constellations explored above can be found in all three discourses.

Constructing a contrast between a supposedly ethnically oppressive Quebec and a multicultural Canadian nation serves different purposes in different discourses: in the republican perspective, designating Québécois nationalism as separatist and ethnic serves to highlight the danger of fragmentation. It also helps to portray Canadian society as more tolerant and inclusive (than so-called ethnic nations) and to depict multiculturalism as a "unique English Canadian invention."[61]

In the liberal-pluralist perspective, Québécois deep diversity does not have negative connotations as such. However, separatism and ethnic nationalism are intolerable. Here, the opposition to Quebec's potentially separatist and ethnic nationalism serves to demonstrate the limits of pluralism and distinguish between acceptable and unacceptable expressions of ethnocultural difference. Separatism is deemed to be "wholly unCanadian."[62] Besides, distinguishing between potentially separatist minority nations and multiculturally integrating ethnic groups raises the public acceptance of a moderate, unifying multiculturalism.

From the liberal-multiculturalist perspective, opposing Québécois ethnic nationalism and separatism allows ethnic groups to be represented as the non-separatist "better Canadians" whose multicultural integration fosters unity in diversity. This representation stabilizes the precarious position of immigrants and other minorities as "conditional insiders." In the newspaper sample under investigation, liberal-multiculturalist discourses remain quantitatively marginal. They have to strategically align themselves with (at least) one of the more powerful perspectives.

This is shown by the fact that there are surprisingly few complaints about racism within the discourses that operate from a liberal-multiculturalist perspective. While this absence may be an unintended effect of the sampling method, it is more likely that radical multiculturalism was not allowed into the two mainstream newspapers' opinion pieces because it would not have resonated with their editorial stance. Similarly, liberal-multiculturalist claims that explicitly challenge both Québécois' and English Canadians' hegemonic status as Canada's ideal citizens remain marginal in the sample: attacks more often target Québécois minority rights than unacknowledged English Canadian majority rights. As a result, liberal-multiculturalist claims become acceptable even for the defendants of the other two dominant perspectives, republicanism and liberal-pluralism. As a consequence, otherwise divergent discourses on Canadian identity find themselves agreeing on at least one point: an opposition to a (real or imagined) Québécois "them."

CONCLUSION

In this chapter, I have explored the surprising success of multiculturalism as a dominant discourse of Canadian national identity in the 1990s. Drawing on the results of an analysis of English Canadian mainstream media, I have identified three perspectives that respond quite differently to the questions What does *multiculturalism* mean? Who is included in the multicultural Canadian "we," and who is excluded? The republican, liberal-pluralist, and liberal-multiculturalist perspectives propose distinct visions of the relationship between Canadian national identity and multiculturalism, but toward the end of the 1990s, they agree on a shared opposition to Quebec's allegedly ethnically nationalist separatism and an endorsement of multiculturalism as the quintessence of Canadian national identity. This smallest common denominator for describing the Canadian national project, however, remains vaguely defined and only papers over persisting contradictions among the three perspectives' ideological differences.

On the one hand, these findings add to our understanding of why, in the late 1990s, multiculturalism is much more popular in Canadian public discourses than it was in previous decades.[63] On the other hand, it would be false to assume that the collective rejection of real or assumed ethnically motivated separatism erases the fundamental differences among the republican, liberal-pluralist, and liberal-multiculturalist perspectives. On the contrary, this particular representation is not an ideal scenario in any of the three perspectives; rather, it describes a strategic adaptation of an ideological perspective to a particular socio-political context. The underlying differences among the three identified perspectives concerning the relationship between multiculturalism and Canadian national identity continue to persist. The common point of rejection can merely serve as a shared point of departure for new negotiations about the type of society Canadians want to live in.

In the first decade of the 21st century, these negotiations have taken a new turn. First, the wave of multinational conflict in Canada has receded somewhat. Between 2003 and 2012, the Liberal Party was in power in Quebec; since then, the Parti Québécois has governed the province, but only as a minority government. At the federal level, in 2006, after 12 years in power, the Liberals were replaced by the Conservative Party, who currently hold a majority government, while in the federal election of 2011, the Bloc Québécois was reduced to four seats. It seems fair to say that, at least for the moment, the threat of Quebec separating is largely gone.

Second, although Muslim immigration to Canada has been on the rise for decades, the attacks in New York and Washington on 11 September 2001 and the subsequent US-led "war on terror" have fundamentally changed the rules of the game. Muslims have become subjected to intense scrutiny almost everywhere in the Western world. Even in Canada, negotiations about multiculturalism are now marked by concerns about religious accommodation, gender equality, and national security.[64] In sum, with the threat of Québécois nationalism having declined, and fears about Muslim fundamentalism and terrorism dramatically changing insider-outsider representations, the coalition in favour of multiculturalism that dominated the 1990s seems to be breaking up in the first decade of the new century. As the *Globe and Mail* puts it, Canadians should "strike multiculturalism from the national vocabulary."[65]

In fact, over the past couple of years, the republican discourse has gained even more traction than it had during the 1990s, when the other two discourses still kept it at bay.[66] More research is necessary to decide whether the early 2000s mark the beginning of yet a new phase of Canadian multiculturalism. However, it seems obvious that there is a new-found consensus among politicians[67] and media representatives[68] in favour of a "thick" republican notion of citizenship, which includes Aboriginal people, English Canadians, and French Canadians unconditionally, admitting newcomers and second- or third-generation immigrants only on the condition that they at least partially give up their heritage cultures and assimilate to "our" values and ways of life. This new consensus stands in stark contrast to the ways in which multiculturalism was discussed in the 1990s.

NOTES

[1] I would like to acknowledge the research funding received from the Social Sciences and Humanities Research Council of Canada.

[2] For a discussion of popular support for multiculturalism and its impact on questions and policies of immigration, see Jeffrey Reitz in this volume (pp. 107–126).

[3] Rainer Bauböck, "If You Say Multiculturalism Is the Wrong Answer, Then What Was the Question You Asked?" *Canadian Diversity/Diversité canadienne* 4, no. 1 (2005):93.

[4] This chapter is a revised version of an argument that was first developed in my recent book, *Us, Them, and Others: Pluralism and National Identity in Diverse Societies* (Toronto: University of Toronto Press, 2011).

[5] See, for example, Audrey Kobayashi, "Multiculturalism: Representing a Canadian Institution," in *Place/Culture/Representation*, ed. James Duncan and David Ley (London, New York: Routledge, 1993).

[6] The category of *visible minorities* was established by the 1986 *Employment Equity Act*. It is an ambiguous construct. The criterion of "visibility" refers sometimes to skin colour (e.g., Blacks), sometimes to cultural belonging and/or religion (e.g., Arabs and South Asians), and sometimes to the nationality of origin (e.g., Chinese).

[7] Citizens' Forum on Canada's Future, *Report to the People and the Government of Canada* (Ottawa: Supply and Services, 1991).

[8] Denise Helly, "La nouvelle citoyenneté, active et responsable," in *Vivre la citoyenneté: Identité, appartenance et participation*, ed. Yves Boivert, Jacques Hamel, and Marc Molgat (Montreal: Liber, 2000).

[9] Bohdan S. Kordan, "Multiculturalism, Citizenship and the Canadian Nation: A Critique of the Proposed Design for Program Renewal," *Canadian Ethnic Studies* 29, no. 2 (1997):138.

[10] Yasmeen Abu-Laban and Christina Gabriel, *Selling Diversity: Immigration, Multiculturalism, Employment Equity, and Globalization* (Peterborough: Broadview Press, 2002), 15.

[11] Marie McAndrew, Denise Helly, and Caroline Tessier, "Pour un débat éclairé sur la politique canadienne du multiculturalisme: une analyse de la nature des organismes et des projets subventionnés (1983–2002)," *Politique et sociétés* 24, no. 1 (2005).

[12] Abu-Laban and Gabriel, *Selling Diversity*.

[13] Louise Fontaine, "Immigration and Citizenship in Canada and Belgium: Is the Canadian Model of Citizenship Useful for the European Union?" in *Migration, Citizenship and Ethno-National Identities in the European Union*, ed. Marco Martiniello (Aldershot: Avebury, 1995).

[14] Karim H. Karim, "The Multiculturalism Debate in Canadian Newspapers: The Harbinger of a Political Storm?" *Journal for International Migration and Integration (JIMI)* 3, no. 3 & 4 (2002):454.

[15] Will Kymlicka, *Multicultural Citizenship: A Liberal Theory of Minority Rights* (Oxford: Oxford University Press, 1995).

[16] This model is further explained in Winter, *Us, Them, and Others*.

[17] Günther Kress, "Text as the Punctuation of Semiosis: Pulling at Some of the Threads," in *Intertextuality and the Media: From Genre to Everyday Life*, ed. Ulrika Meinhof and Jonathan Smith (New York: Manchester University Press, 2000).

[18] *Globe and Mail*, "A Nation in Danger of Relativizing Itself to Death," 23 October 1995.

[19] Ibid.

[20] *Toronto Star*, "Canadian Society Owes a Debt to Vanishing WASPs," 7 March 1993.

[21] Ibid.

[22] *Globe and Mail*, "A Nation in Danger."

[23] *Toronto Star*, "Canadian Society Owes a Debt."

[24] *Globe and Mail*, "Canada, the Unfinished Country," 1 July 1996.

[25] Ibid.

[26] *Globe and Mail*, "Envy, Glue of Nationhood," 13 May 1994.

[27] *Toronto Star*, "Canadian Society Owes a Debt."

[28] Ibid.

[29] *Globe and Mail*, "The Provinces: A Region Called Ontario?" 5 June 1997.

[30] *Toronto Star*, "Is Multiculturalism Becoming Multinationalism?" 28 February 1993 (emphasis mine).

[31] *Toronto Star*, "Canadian Society Owes a Debt" (emphasis mine).

[32] *Toronto Star*, "Quebec, Rest of Canada March to Different Beats," 31 January 1993.

[33] *Globe and Mail*, "Envy, Glue of Nationhood."

[34] *Globe and Mail*, "On Being Canadian, Forever," 1 July 1997.

[35] It is interesting that republican discourses locate "Britishness," not "Englishness," at the core of Canada's national identity. For example, it is "the British connection" that binds Canada together; see *Globe and Mail*, "Brown of the Globe Got Canada Right: What Canada Was in the Beginning Serves It Well in the New Age," 1 July 1999.

[36] Elke Winter, "Neither 'America' nor 'Québec': Constructing the Canadian Multicultural Nation," *Nations and Nationalism* 13, no. 3 (2007).

[37] See, for example, *Globe and Mail*, "The Genius of Canada," 14 September 1994; *Globe and Mail*, "Brown of the Globe Got Canada Right"; and Elke Winter, "Les logiques du multiculturalisme dans les sociétés multi-nationales: une analyse des discours canadiens," *Revue Européenne des Migrations Internationales* 24, no. 3 (2008).

[38] *Globe and Mail*, "The Separatists in Search of Identity: Are Pro-secession Leaders Proposing, in Effect, to Create a Canada within Quebec?" 5 July 1999 (emphasis mine).

[39] Richard J.F. Day, *Multiculturalism and the History of Canadian Diversity* (Toronto: University of Toronto Press, 2000), 215–216.

[40] *Globe and Mail*, "Separatists in Search of Identity."

[41] *Globe and Mail*, "Brown of the Globe Got Canada Right." See also Winter, "Les logiques du multiculturalisme."

[42] *Toronto Star*, "Canada Must Restate Reasons for Remaining One Nation: Quebec's Continued Presence Is at the Very Heart of Our Multicultural Diversity," 18 December 1995 (emphasis mine).

[43] Ibid.

[44] Homi K. Bhabha, "The Third Space: Interview with Homi Bhabha," in *Identity: Community, Culture, Difference*, ed. Jonathan Rutherford (London: Lawrence & Wishart, 1990), 208 (emphasis in original).

[45] In the newspaper sample, demands for binationalism or multinationalism are rare. The absence of voices for and from Quebec in the collected empirical material (with few exceptions in the very early 1990s) confirms the existence of separate public spaces within Quebec and the rest of Canada; see Robert A. Hacket and Richard Gruneau, *The Missing News: Filters and Blind Spots in Canada's Press* (Ottawa: Canadian Centre for Policy Alternatives / Garamond Press, 2000).

[46] *Toronto Star*, "Siddiqui Is Right: Media Blind to New Face of Canada," 24 April 2001.

[47] Ibid.

48 *Toronto Star*, "Let's Make Multiculturalism Work," 23 January 1995.

49 Ibid.

50 *Toronto Star*, "Siddiqui Is Right" (emphasis mine).

51 See, for example, *Toronto Star*, "Redress for Ukrainian Canadians: A Modest Price for Justice," 4 November 1992; and *Toronto Star*, "An Injustice That Won't Die: Ottawa Won't Admit Ukrainian Internment Was a Criminal Act," 11 August 1995.

52 *Toronto Star*, "Immigrants Committed to Canada," 5 November 2000 (emphasis mine).

53 *Toronto Star*, "Budget Cuts Fray Cultural Diversity," 14 June 1998.

54 *Toronto Star*, "Alienation Haunts Canada," 16 October 1995.

55 *Toronto Star*, "Worthy Approach to Identity," 29 August 1995.

56 Winter, "Les logiques du multiculturalisme."

57 *Toronto Star*, "Siddiqui Is Right."

58 *Toronto Star*, "Worthy Approach to Identity."

59 Winter, "Les logiques du multiculturalisme."

60 *Toronto Star*, "Siddiqui Is Right."

61 *Toronto Star*, "Canadian Society Owes a Debt."

62 *Globe and Mail*, "Brown of the Globe Got Canada Right."

63 Karim, "The Multiculturalism Debate."

64 Karim H. Karim, "Press, Public Sphere, and Pluralism: Multiculturalism Debates in Canadian English-Language Newspapers," *Canadian Ethnic Studies/Études ethniques au Canada* 40, no. 1–2 (2008).

65 *Globe and Mail*, "Strike Multiculturalism from the National Vocabulary," 8 October 2010.

66 Winter, "Les logiques du multiculturalisme"; and Elke Winter, "Us, Them, and Others: Reflections on Canadian Multiculturalism and National Identity at the Turn of the 21st Century," *Canadian Review of Sociology/Revue canadienne de sociologie*, forthcoming 2014.

67 Elke Winter, "Becoming Canadian – Making Sense of Recent Changes to Citizenship Rules," *IRPP Study* No. 44 (January 2014), at http://www.irpp.org/en/research/diversity-immigration-and-integration/becoming-canadian/, accessed 17 January 2014.

68 Elke Winter and Marie-Michèle Sauvageau, "La citoyenneté canadienne dans la presse écrite anglo-canadienne et franco-québécoise: convergence ou divergence?" *Canadian Journal of Political Science/Revue canadienne de science politique* 45, no. 3 (2012).

ASSIMILATION BY STEALTH: WHY CANADA'S MULTICULTURAL POLICY IS REALLY A REPACKAGED INTEGRATION POLICY

Randall Hansen

Some years ago in Dublin, I heard an Irish joke told by an Irishman. (I should add that I am of Irish Catholic stock.) It went roughly like this: "We Irish have a very particular way of occupying other countries. We recognized long ago that if you march in, flash guns around, and speak foreign languages, you get people's backs up. What we do is infest. We come in, pat people on the back, buy a round of Guinness, and then we disappear to a cabin. Three weeks later, there are 40 Irishmen."

This, I wish to argue, is roughly how Canadians approach the assimilation of immigrants. All the while claiming that they are supporting immigrants' culture, they quietly do the opposite: they assimilate them, turning them rather quickly into the polite, kind, modest, and rather earnest people that make up the majority of this country's citizens. It is nothing short, to use another analogy, of a migratory coup.[1]

To begin with definitions, *integration* is here understood as a process through which the differences between migrants and the native-born in matters of educational achievement, income, and earnings disappear and migrants achieve economic outcomes that are, on average, the same as or better than the overall population. *Assimilation* is understood as a process through which the assumptions and attitudes of migrants about the norms of everyday life, the unreflective behaviour and reactions that govern interactions among people, and the hopes and expectations for

The Multiculturalism Question: Debating Identity in 21st-Century Canada, ed. Jack Jedwab. Kingston: School of Policy Studies, Queen's University. © 2014 The School of Policy Studies, Queen's University at Kingston. All rights reserved.

themselves and their children come to closely match those of their co-citizens. An assimilated individual – and assimilation works best at the second generation – talks, sounds, and seems like any other Canadian with his or her background. I see multiple examples every day in my classes at the University of Toronto.

The fact that Canada has an assimilation policy masquerading as a multicultural policy helps explain the 35-year trench warfare between the opponents and supporters of multiculturalism. For its supporters, multiculturalism removes barriers to, and encourages the integration of migrants into, Canadian society and the Canadian economy and polity. For its critics, multiculturalism "promotes ghettoization and balkanization, encouraging members of ethnic groups to look inward, and emphasizing differences between groups rather than their shared rights or identities as Canadian citizens."[2] As in real trenches, this war is a brutal one in which neither side gives any quarter, in which there are no victories or even much progress, and in which armistices are reached not because a clear victor has emerged but because both sides are exhausted.[3] This is so because, in normative and empirical terms, both sides have equal firepower, and because they have consistently shot past each other. The critics of multiculturalism are describing multiculturalism as it would be if that term corresponded to reality; the defenders are not describing multiculturalism at all. Rather, they are referring to the broader and far more important set of assimilationist policies into which the small, trivial, and over-theorized multicultural policies are nested.

If multiculturalism means anything other than integration and assimilation, it is that the migrant's culture is not merely passively tolerated; it is actively encouraged and fostered. What is more, when there are conflicts, as there inevitably will be, between the claims of a particular culture and the claims of Canadian culture (or, more to the point, Canadian law), particularistic cultural claims will win, and Canadian culture will lose. This is the conception of multiculturalism that British tabloid journalist Melanie Phillips had in mind when she wrote that "at the heart of multiculturalism lies a radical egalitarianism by which everyone's lifestyle and culture has equal validity and moral stature.... [Canada must not] allow religion to be used to incite hatred and violence.... But that can only happen if the shibboleth of multiculturalism is set aside."[4] It is the same conception that inspired *Guardian* journalist Hugo Young, Phillips's ideological opposite in every respect, to write that multiculturalism "can now be seen as a useful bible for any Muslim who insists that his religio-cultural priorities, including the defence of jihad against America, overrides his civic duties of loyalty, tolerance, justice and respect for democracy."[5] And it is the same conception of multiculturalism that underpinned essentially identical declarations by Trevor Phillips (the black British Labour party member appointed head of the Commission for Racial Equality), David Cameron (Conservative prime minister of Britain), and Angela Merkel (Christian Democratic chancellor of Germany) that multiculturalism is dead.

Canadian multiculturalism is not, and has never been, the stuff of Cameron's and Merkel's nightmares. This is partly a question of policy, partly of money. Starting with the latter, a fact that always surprises foreigners is the trivial amount of money devoted to the multiculturalism budget: $13.2 million in 2010–2011.[6] That is, as a French politician once said to me, "zero." It was this small, if not trivial, amount of money that supported the policies – funding for Ukrainian dances, a few foreign-language classes on Saturday afternoons – that attracted so much criticism. This was harmless stuff, and likely without much effect (as anyone who has struggled to convince a child of the merits of speaking a foreign language will know). But even this program now has an integrationist accent. During 2010–2011, the government provided funding for two "streams": the Inter-Action Projects Stream and the Inter-Action Events Stream. The former "provides funding for multi-year community development or engagement projects to promote integration," whereas the latter "provides funding for community-based events that foster one or more of the following: intercultural or interfaith understanding, civic memory and pride, and respect for core democratic values. The primary goal of this stream is to create concrete opportunities for interaction among cultural and faith communities."[7] With this budget and these aims, the program is as radical, transformative, and threatening as milk toast. It is a mark of the success of the Canadian government's propaganda efforts, and the naivety of sections of the Canadian professoriate and Canadian press, that so much causal effect is attributed to such a small program.

Where the federal government does spend a considerable amount of money – some $1.5 billion per year – is on settlement. The greatest amount of this money, which is granted to and spent by non-governmental organizations such as the United Way, goes to language training.[8] And language training is nothing less than a core element in the integration of immigrants.

It is not the only one. The fundamental institution for the assimilation of migrants into Canadian practices, attitudes, and social mores is – as it is in republican France and melting-pot America – the public school. The vast majority of immigrants attend, their parents want them to attend, and the government expects them to attend, Canadian public schools.[9] Where they do not, they sometimes attend faith-based schools, but equally often, their ambitious parents struggle to get them into private schools distinguished for decades as pillars of the white-Anglo establishment, such as Toronto's Upper Canada College or Havergal College. The importance of public schools, to old and new Canadians, was reflected in the debate that occurred during the 2007 Ontario provincial election on providing funding for faith schools beyond Roman Catholic ones. Encouraged by leaders of a few religious groups and by clearly overpaid polling firms, the centrist Progressive Conservative Party leader, John Tory, made it an electoral promise that provincial funding would be extended to all religious schools. It was a political and electoral disaster: there was a huge backlash from Ontario voters, and new immigrants to Canada showed little interest in the proposal.

The last piece of the puzzle is employment. The entire Canadian immigration system centres on work and getting new immigrants into it as quickly as possible. The selection system favours skill, either through a pure points system for education and experience or one that selects immigrants based on specific labour market needs (in engineering, mining, etc.).[10] Welfare rates are punitively low ($600 per month for a single person in the province of Ontario), access is difficult, and those running the program (revealingly called Ontario Works) do everything they can to get people on it back to work. In this context, the extensive public discussion about doctors driving taxis in Toronto overlooks an important fact: they are driving taxis rather than drawing welfare benefits because, as unpleasant as the job likely can be, it pays more than social assistance.

THE PUTATIVE SUCCESS OF MULTICULTURALISM

Commentators who wish to make a case in favour of multiculturalism's positive effects have no shortage of statistics to cite. They generally advance these arguments:

1. Multiculturalism in Canada is consistently popular: according to Environics, 85 percent of Canadians believe that multiculturalism is important to the country.[11]
2. Immigration in Canada is consistently popular. Canada is the only country in the Organisation for Economic Co-operation and Development (OECD) in which a majority of respondents consistently claim to want current or higher levels of immigration.
3. Immigrants naturalize in particularly high numbers in Canada: 79 percent in 2006.[12]
4. Immigrants are, with notable exceptions, more economically successful in Canada than they are in the United States.[13]

There is ample evidence to support these points. To be sure, there are well-documented problems associated with Canadian immigration policy, particularly in the area of declining employment levels, declining earnings, and a reduced sense of belonging among recent migrants.[14] These problems are real, and they should be addressed, although they will not admit of quick fixes. They are also, compared to the problems faced by many immigration countries, small beer. Canadian immigration policy generally works well: the country is popular among migrants (although many would go to the United States if they could); the children of immigrants, if not migrants themselves, do well in the labour market; and Canadians support immigration to an unusually high degree. These developments produce virtuous circles: as more immigrants come to Canada, as they concentrate in a few key ridings in Ontario, and as they naturalize in unusually high numbers compared with other countries, politicians have an interest in securing their votes.[15]

The question is how much any of this has to do with official multiculturalism; the answer is nothing, or at least very little. And this in turn leads to further definitional issues.

DEFINING MULTICULTURALISM

Much of the debate about multiculturalism in this country and abroad reflects the fact that the term means all things to all people. The most basic confusion is between multiculturalism as a sociological fact (that there are migrants from all corners of the globe living peacefully in the same country) and multiculturalism as a policy (which conceives of a particular way of incorporating migrants into a given society).[16] The two have nothing to do with each other. A highly diverse society can be consistent with both a robustly anti-assimilationist and a robustly assimilationist policy. That is, one can think that immigration is a "good thing," that immigrants should come from as many parts of the globe as possible, and that immigrants should fully assimilate to their new country's culture. Or one can think that immigration is a brilliant thing, that immigrants should come from everywhere, but that their own culture should be nourished and supported regardless of the effect on the receiving country's culture. And one can, of course, think that there should be very little immigration and that those who come should assimilate *or* that they should retain their own culture. Support for or opposition to multiculturalism as a policy is thus perfectly consistent with high or low levels of migration *and* with high or low levels of diversity.

Another basic distinction is between "thick" and "thin" multicultural policy. Thick multiculturalism implies that migrants integrate, if at all, through their own culture and that they privilege that culture over national laws, customs, and traditions. This conception of multiculturalism is, as argued, the *bête noir* of multicultural critics in Europe, and they have something of a point. Until a few commentators who could read pointed to terrible outcomes in employment, education, and (something that matters least) neighbourhood segregation, the Netherlands pursued a thick multicultural policy that subsidized foreign languages, separate faith schools, foreign radio and television programs, and so on.[17] Celebrated by academics around the world, multiculturalism in the Netherlands contributed to, or at least failed to prevent, lower educational achievement, higher unemployment, and worse earnings than those found among the same groups in neighbouring Germany, a country that had itself long been the *bête noir* of the left-leaning academic activists dominating immigration studies.[18] Similarly, Muslim public intellectual Tariq Ramadan, for a time the toast of London (although never of Paris) has said that Muslims will integrate into Europe but only on their own terms, which means no integration at all.[19]

Thin multiculturalism implies a right to one's culture insofar as the expression of it harms no one and is consistent with national laws and a human rights culture. Although it may shock some Torontonians, who think that they invented multiculturalism sometime after the Beatles era, you can find thin multicultural policy everywhere. French citizens from Africa wear dazzling, colourful ethnic dresses in Paris; Muslims attend mosques in Berlin; Italians operate restaurants in London; and Ukrainians tired of Edmonton's weather may organize dances and performances in Los Angeles. Thin multiculturalism exists everywhere because it is basic to liberal democracy and a respect for human rights. There are small differences in how liberal states approach such matters as religious dress in state institutions (which France largely bans, and Quebec at the time of writing is attempting to), but these differences rest at the margins.[20] No liberal democracy attacks freedom of religion or association in principle; there are, rather, differences of opinion on what these freedoms mean. Non-democracies, by contrast, are culturally homogenizing and constitutionally hostile to even thin multiculturalism. One of the most consistently persecuted groups in the world, and one that receives little attention in the West because of a particular obsession among human rights activists with our own inadequacies and those of Israel, is Christians in the Middle East. Similarly, there is no greater threat to religious minorities than the establishment of a theocracy, as the examples of Iran and Pakistan make abundantly clear.

Thin multiculturalism has its own downside: it has a tendency to privilege people's ethnic category over all other aspects of their identity – to regard them as primarily Indian, Chinese, or Jamaican and secondarily Canadian – and to tolerate a high degree of residential and personal segregation.[21] There is certainly something to this argument. For all of Toronto's much-trumpeted multiculturalism, the city and its suburbs are highly segregated, and many wealthy downtown neighbourhoods are as white now as they were 40 years ago. Those central neighbourhoods that have been transformed have been so through gentrification – that is, with wealthier white people moving in – rather than immigration. Different ethnic groups mix, to be sure, in the city's core, but they do the same thing in Amsterdam, Frankfurt, Miami, and Madrid. Canada and Toronto are somewhat unique in the range of people who come here, but this is a matter of selection rather than anything else. For all that, there is serious doubt that the state can do much about segregation; directing people's choice of friends or neighbourhoods is not a proper public policy matter.

MULTICULTURALISTS IN THEORY, ASSIMILATIONISTS IN PRACTICE

These distinctions might seem too sharply drawn, but think of the recent controversies over what is often termed "reasonable accommodation." In the sharia-law case in Ontario in 2005 (centring on the proposal to give sharia marriage tribunals legal standing), in the 2007 Ontario election furor over the Progressive Conservatives' proposal to extend funding to all faith schools, and in the most recent debates over requirements that women remove the burqa in voting booths and during citizenship ceremonies, a majority of Ontarians (in the first two) and Canadians generally (in the third) came down in favour of assimilationist positions: no sharia, no funding for faith schools beyond Roman Catholic ones, and no burqas in the voting booth. It would be difficult to convince an English-speaking Martian visiting Canada that these outcomes are evidence of a deep commitment to thick multiculturalism. A cynic might suggest that this is so because they all concern Islam, and in a post-9/11 context, anti-Islamic measures are good politics. There is certainly an undercurrent of anti-Islamic sentiment across the West, but denouncing these results as crude Islamophobia would be too quick: the faith-schools issue was about more than Islam; many Muslims opposed sharia and supported the burqa ban; and attitudes toward Muslims in Canada are, according to pollsters, generally positive.[22]

THE EFFECT OF MULTICULTURAL POLICIES ON MIGRANT INTEGRATION

Multiculturalism – strictly understood as the small range of programs supported by Canada's $13.2-million-per-year budget – plays almost no role in the country's relative success with immigration. The complex set of integration policies designed to help people learn English (or French) and to find a job probably contributes more to migrants' success, but there has been no systematic effort to evaluate these programs or their outcomes.[23] One of the largest comparative studies, which argues that Canadian settlement policies have had a positive impact, looks at political participation rather than labour market success.[24] This study bases its conclusions on Portuguese migrants in the United States and Canada; this is useful for comparative purposes, but Portuguese Canadians are by no means the educationally and economically most successful in the country.[25]

The most important factor in determining migrants' success, and therefore the success of the immigration policy under which they enter, is education. Among the factors explaining "variations in immigrant economic success, both cross-nationally and among urban areas," Jeffrey Reitz concludes, "the most important is education."[26] Educational levels are inherently relative: one is more or less educated than everyone else. The value added, therefore, of an immigrant's education depends on both the length and the quality of that education (whether the degree is from Berkeley or Brock) and the relative educational attainment of Canadians. Immigrants to Canada have traditionally earned more than immigrants, with similar educational levels, to the United States because Canadians have traditionally been less educated than Americans.[27] As Canadians' educational levels have increased, this gap has narrowed, and earnings among recent migrants have declined, although, in an international comparison, first- and above all second-generation immigrants do extremely well in Canada.[28]

What follows from this is that a successful immigration policy is one that selects migrants who have high educational levels, who value education for their children, and, equally important (for who does not in theory value education?), who are prepared to demand the extremely hard work required for educational success. Recent research on second-generation immigrants has confirmed this hypothesis.[29] The highest high school graduation and further education rates in Canada are to be found among Chinese and South Asians. These groups, in turn, have the highest employment levels and the highest earnings among ethnic minorities. "Second generation young adults who are Chinese and South Asian," writes Monica Boyd, "are the most likely of all groups to be attending school, to have university degrees or higher, to be working the fewest weeks, to be employed in high skill occupations and to earn the highest weekly wages."[30] Conversely, blacks and Latinos have the lowest high school and university education rates and, with Filipinos, the lowest wages. As is so often the case, social science research confirms what is perfectly obvious from everyday experience: ask any parent with a child in school in the Greater Toronto Area or in Greater Vancouver about Chinese Canadians' and Indo-Canadians' commitment to education. Similarly, it is perfectly obvious to everyone except academics studying them and activists lobbying for them that the relatively low economic achievements among former guest worker populations in Europe result from a lack of the same determination to use education, and to place an enormous amount of pressure on their children to use education, to achieve social mobility.

Canadian multiculturalism, then, is really a camouflaged integration policy, one focused above all on the school and the labour market but in which settlement programs play a role, although one that has not been properly quantified. The system works in large part because Canadian immigration policy works, and Canadian immigration policy works because immigrants to Canada work. That they work, how they work, and how much they make through work depends, in turn, on education. The great success of Canada's immigration policy has been admitting large numbers of individuals, particularly from South Asia and China, who see education as the key to their economic success. The rest, to quote an Oxford don in another context, is embellishment and detail.[31]

SO WHAT IS ALL THE FUSS ABOUT?

If Canadian immigration policy is chiefly an assimilation policy, and if multicultural policy is a small, if not trivial, part of it, one wonders why commentators devote so many column inches to it every year. Part of the answer concerns the way in which social science research is funded. Official multiculturalism is a government program, and, as such, the federal government has an interest in exaggerating its effects, not least because the program is not particularly expensive. Although there is a long-established and intellectually interesting radical critique of multiculturalism as an effort to cement rather than undermine white Anglo-French racial dominance, most government-sponsored studies of multiculturalism end with ringing endorsements of the policy. They do so partly because views on multiculturalism are taken as a proxy for views on immigration, and not entirely without reason: many critics of multiculturalism are critics of immigration. The result is that few "progressives" (and almost everyone in social science and humanities departments in Canada thinks of themselves as progressive) would want to associate themselves with such restrictionist views. But it also reflects the fact that government-sponsored research is hardly value-neutral. The fact that no one from the University of Calgary or the Fraser Institute, as well as no critical race scholar, is invited to review Canadian multiculturalism is hardly a coincidence. When governments commission reports, they choose people whose judgments they trust – in other words, people who will broadly agree with them.

To take an important case in point, the Department of Canadian Heritage recently commissioned six regional reports on emerging issues for multiculturalism in Canada. The cover of the consolidated publication has the suggestive tagline "Building a Stronger Canada" and is replete with smiling ethnic minorities surrounded by large Canadian flags. Had there been factories and more hard hats (there is one), the cover could have been published by the German Democratic Republic with the tagline "Building Socialism." The report's author and lead researcher, renowned scholar Will Kymlicka, tells us in the introduction that "the reports exhibit a remarkable degree of consistency in their underlying themes and concerns.... There appears to be a broad consensus across the country on the importance of a handful of issues that are crucial to the future of multiculturalism in Canada."[32]

As Canadian Heritage would hardly commission an official report from anyone known to be hostile to multiculturalism, this conclusion is to be expected. The enthusiasm has, however, regrettable consequences:

it encourages the report's author, like advocates of multiculturalism more broadly, to embellish the evidence. Thus, we are told that "uniquely among Western countries, second-generation immigrants in Canada actually outperform children of non-immigrant parents."[33] "Outperform" is pretty vague, but the source, without a page reference, is a 2006 OECD study. Support for this claim is to be found there in two figures – 2.1a and 2.1b – which show that, on average, immigrants to Canada do best, along with those to Hong Kong–China and Macao-China, in mathematics and reading.[34] There is no mention of Figure 2.1c, which shows that second-generation immigrants achieve poorer results in science than Canadians, whereas similar immigrants to Hong Kong–China achieve better results.[35] More important, the accompanying analysis shows that the conclusion over-interprets the two bars: "there is no significant performance difference," writes the OECD, "in mathematics between first-generation and native students in Australia, Canada, New Zealand and Macao-China."[36] For the second generation, "there are significant gaps in mathematics performance between the two groups in all countries, except in Australia, Canada and Macao-China."[37] In the case of reading, second-generation immigrants do better than natives, and notably better than the OECD average, in Canada and Hong Kong–China, and the differences are marginal in the case of Australia and Macao-China.[38]

So let us rephrase: uniquely, along with the Hong Kong Chinese and Macao Chinese, second-generation immigrants in Canada actually outperform children of non-immigrant parents, and the differences between Canada and Australia in second-generation immigrant performance are insignificant. The Chinese cases are excluded from the Kymlicka quotation by the "Western" designation, but that is something of an intellectual sleight of hand, one that in another context might be called Eurocentric. The important point is that neither Hong Kong nor Macao-China is renowned for its multicultural policies, and Australia turned away from official multiculturalism under former prime minister John Howard. We thus need to find another source of the successes in these countries and regions. What ties all four regions together is that they are dynamic economies that are highly attractive to educated migrants. What ties Canada and Australia together is the points system.

Thus, both statistical evidence and common sense support a simple conclusion: the immigrants to Canada who do well are skilled and/or exploit educational opportunities with determination. Settlement programs emphasizing English and assistance in job-seeking certainly cannot hurt, although I suspect that it is the most resourceful and motivated migrants who take the greatest advantage of them. Multicultural policies, strictly understood, do not and cannot have the profound impact attributed to them by their enthusiasts. This should come as no surprise. It would be a public policy miracle worth patenting if $13.2 million per year led to outstanding school achievement, job placement, and higher earnings.

Since other countries without official multiculturalism achieve similar results, the policy is clearly not doing the work claimed by its proponents.

The way in which enthusiasm for the "project of Canadian multiculturalism" – as one of my departmental colleagues called it in a breathtaking disavowal of critical academic distance – has refracted academic judgment can be seen in the enthusiastic reaction to a book by a Canadian expatriate at the University of California, Berkeley. In *Becoming a Citizen*, Irene Bloemraad compares broadly similar migrant communities – Portuguese and Vietnamese – in Boston and Toronto and concludes that, on the whole, Canadian settlement policies encourage more political participation. The excitement was palpable. Academic cheerleaders for official multiculturalism – and there is no shortage of them – cite the book generously at conferences on the topic. And Will Kymlicka, the aforementioned doyen of Canadian multiculturalism, introduces Bloemraad at some length in the government report cited above. Her study is the central anchor of his conclusion that "multiculturalism in Canada promotes integration and citizenship, both through its effect on attitudes, self-understanding and identity at the individual level and through its effect on institutions at the social level."[39]

Bloemraad's study is a fine one, and it does show that these and other communities in Canada naturalize and participate in politics more in this country than in the United States. But is this the result of policies that anyone from Europe would recognize as multicultural? It is not. As the author trenchantly argues, "Canadians underestimate contemporary Americans' tolerance for cultural diversity and overestimate their own support for substantive multiculturalism. In some ways the integrationist thrust of government-sponsored multiculturalism means that Canadians embrace more of a 'melting pot' approach to ethno-racial diversity than Americans. Canadian multicultural policy legitimizes and promotes symbolic ethnicity while also pushing for immigrants' incorporation into the social, economic, and political fabric of Canadian society. *This project has more similarities with old-fashioned assimilation than many Canadians might be ready to admit.*"[40]

A further factor explains the uniquely powerful appeal of multiculturalism for Canadian intellectuals and the Canadian public: identity. Along with a few other countries with permanent identity crises – Germany because of the Holocaust, Britain because of post-imperial decline – Canadians have for decades been obsessed with discovering the essence of who they are. Various candidates have been suggested, and they have all proved inadequate. The supposedly particularly Canadian cultural characteristics – being nice, polite, and reserved – are simply milder versions of English ones, shorn of the capacity for wit, irony, and private character assassination. Social programs, which university professors told us in the 1980s were the basis of our identity, do not work because (a) we can no longer afford them, and (b) even at their peak, they were terribly ungenerous compared with those in northern continental Europe.

Multiculturalism is a third effort, and it is particularly appealing because it seems to provide an endpoint to what otherwise might be the eternal Canadian quest: not being American. Successive governments have told Canadians that what makes them different from the United States is multiculturalism: the Americans are the melting pot, we are the mosaic. Canadians have, somewhat unremarkably, responded positively. Put another way, when we affirm multiculturalism, we affirm ourselves. This fact explains in part why Canadian nationalists, who hail almost exclusively from the left (a fact that mystifies German and Italian observers of this country), so consistently endorse multiculturalism. But it also explains why the concept attracts such warm support from across the country: we are, in effect, giving ourselves a pat on the back.

CONCLUSION

Canadian multicultural policy is really settlement policy; settlement policy is about integration; and it is nested in a Canadian public school system and a labour market that encourages assimilation. Critics of this thesis might object that Canada does not assimilate because migrants are not asked to abandon their religion, languages (at home), or culture. Such extreme demands are, however, not assimilation as most people understand it; they are *forced* assimilation, what some excitable individuals would call cultural genocide. No liberal democracy has ever pursued such a policy against immigrants,[41] a point often ignored by political theorists of multiculturalism who, in matters of history, travel light.

Much of the multicultural critique of old-style assimilation is based on the claim that the pre-1960s period was particularly hostile to group rights and that only a post-liberal, multicultural paradigm can sustain them. It became accepted only in the 1970s, Kymlicka writes, "that immigrants should be free to maintain some of their old customs regarding food, dress, religion, and recreation, and to associate with each other to maintain these practices. This is no longer seen as unpatriotic, 'un-American,' or 'un-Australian.'"[42] This historical reading is clearly wrong. A German in New York in the 1890s could have lived in "Little Germany" (today's Alphabet City), joined a German band, drunk German beer, and sent his children to a German school. He could have taken books out of the *Freie Bibliothek und Lesehalle* on Second Avenue and passed under an inscription – still there – reading *Einigkeit macht stark* ("strength through unity") as he entered the German American shooting club. Irish Americans lived similarly in Hell's Kitchen. In the 1920s, during the height of the Americanization movement, Italians operated restaurants, worshipped in Catholic churches, and played bocce. The examples are endless.

Indeed, the one thing that these and other new immigrants enjoyed was cultural expression; their economic, social, and political position was far worse. They crowded, at least in the early years after their arrival, into poor neighbourhoods, were shut out of jobs ("no dogs or Irish"), and found themselves beholden for patronage to Tammany Hall. The same is obviously true to a greater extent for African Americans, who suffered severe and institutionalized forms of exclusion. Indeed, culture, in the form of music, churches, and distinctive food, was the one thing they had. The most salient change since the 1960s has not been, *pace* Kymlicka, the adding of a new right to old cultural practices but, rather, the extension of liberal, individual rights (to housing, to the vote, to competition for jobs on a meritocratic basis) that had been denied to vast swathes of the population.

Properly understood, assimilation is a process, rather than an endpoint,[43] in which migrants to a new country gradually and naturally acquire and reproduce the basic norms, expectations, and understandings governing political and social life. And those norms, expectations, and understandings will gradually and naturally evolve under the influence of new immigrants. Gradual assimilation is an entirely reasonable expectation, empirically and normatively, and it occurs for the most part in our schools.

Does this mean that the debate between the supporters and opponents of multiculturalism, outlined above, has been for naught? Not quite so. The failure of either side to marshal much evidence in favour of its case is itself informative. The many critics who view multiculturalism as divisive and likely to lead to segregation, political radicalism, minority illiberalism, and even anti-migrant prejudice have found precious little evidence to support their case. At the same time, migrants' demonstrable success in Canada has nothing to do with multiculturalism and everything to do with the way we select migrants and the way they educate themselves. Since migrants themselves are doing most of the metaphorical and literal work that contributes to their success, Canada's benign experience does not justify the "Hallelujah Chorus" taken on the international conference circuit by the mostly white, mostly male social scientists attending these events. But that is another matter. The essential point is that the defenders and critics of multiculturalism share more in common than they realize: they are both wrong.

NOTES

[1] This chapter reflects on Canada's policy toward permanent, wanted migrants; it does not consider the very large number of temporary migrants who enter Canada each year.

[2] Will Kymlicka, *The Current State of Multiculturalism in Canada and Research Themes on Canadian Multiculturalism 2008–2010* (Ottawa: Citizenship and Immigration Canada, 2010), 7.

³ Although the first two characteristics apply more or less accurately to World War I, the second does not: the Germans were thoroughly defeated.

⁴ Melanie Phillips, "The Country That Hates Itself," *Daily Mail* (London), 16 June 2006. My attention was drawn to this quotation in Michael Adams, *Unlikely Utopia: The Surprising Triumph of Canadian Pluralism* (Toronto: Viking, 2007).

⁵ Hugo Young, "A Corrosive National Danger in Our Multicultural Model," *Guardian* (Manchester), 6 November 2001. This quotation also comes from Adams, *Unlikely Utopia*.

⁶ Citizenship and Immigration Canada, "Annual Report on the Operation of the *Canadian Multiculturalism Act* 2010–2011, Part Three: The Multiculturalism Program 2010–2011," at http://www.cic.gc.ca/english/resources/publications/multi-report2011/part3.asp#a1, accessed 29 August 2012.

⁷ Ibid.

⁸ Citizenship and Immigration Canada, Evaluation Division, *Evaluation of the Strategic Plan for Settlement and Language Training under the Canada-Ontario Immigration Agreement (COIA)* (Ottawa: Citizenship and Immigration Canada, December 2011), at http://www.cic.gc.ca/english/resources/evaluation/2012-coia/sec01.asp#ftn04, accessed 29 August 2012.

⁹ Irene Bloemraad, *Becoming a Citizen: Incorporating Immigrants and Refugees in the United States and Canada* (Berkeley: University of California Press, 2006), 142.

¹⁰ For a review of the system since it was set up in the 1960s, see Triadafilos Triadafilopoulos, *Becoming Multicultural: Immigration and the Politics of Membership in Canada and Germany* (Vancouver: UBC Press, 2012), ch. 4.

¹¹ Adams, *Unlikely Utopia*, 20.

¹² Garnett Picot and Feng Hou, *Divergent Trends in Citizenship Rates among Immigrants in Canada and the United States*, Analytical Studies Branch Research Paper Series (Ottawa: Statistics Canada, October 2011), at http://www.statcan.gc.ca/pub/11f0019m/2011338/part-partie1-eng.htm#h2_1, accessed 29 August 2012.

¹³ Jeffrey G. Reitz, "Immigrant Employment Success in Canada, Part I: Individual and Contextual Causes," *Journal of International Migration & Integration* 8 (2007):31.

¹⁴ See Jeffrey G. Reitz and Rupa Banerjee, "Racial Inequality, Social Cohesion, and Policy Issues in Canada," in *Belonging? Diversity, Recognition and Shared Citizenship in Canada*, ed. Keith Banting, Thomas J. Courchene, and F. Leslie Seidle (Montreal: Institute for Research on Public Policy, 2007), 489–545.

¹⁵ I owe this point to Phil Triadafilopoulos.

¹⁶ A conversation with Christian Joppke of the University of Berne some years ago clarified this distinction.

¹⁷ Ruud Koopmans, "Good Intentions Sometimes Make Bad Policy: A Comparison of Dutch and German Integration Policies," in *The Challenge of Diversity: European Social Democracy Facing Migration, Integration, and Multiculturalism*, ed. René Cuperus, Karl A. Duffek, and Johannes Kandel (Innsbruck: StudienVerlag, 2003), 163–168.

¹⁸ For the worst example of this sort of scholarship, see Joyce Marie Mushaben, *The Changing Faces of Citizenship: Integration and Mobilization among Ethnic Minorities in Germany* (Oxford: Berghahn, 2008).

¹⁹ Paul Berman, "Who's Afraid of Tariq Ramadan? The Islamist, the Journalist and the Defense of Liberalism," *New Republic*, 4 June 2007, 37–63.

²⁰ See "Welcome to the Multiculturalism Policy Index," at http://www.queensu.ca/mcp/, accessed 1 September 2012; for a discussion, see Keith

Banting and Will Kymlicka, "Is There Really a Backlash against Multicultural Policies? New Evidence from the Multicultural Policy Index," rev. ed., July 2012, at http://cesem.ku.dk/papers/Banting_and_Kymlicka__Backlash__CEP__ revised_July_2012.pdf/, accessed 1 September 2012.

[21] Neil Bissoondath, "Seeing the Individual in Society: A Flawed Mosaic Held by Adhesive," *National Post*, 24 July 1999, B5.

[22] See Adams, *Unlikely Utopia*, ch. 3.

[23] Reitz, "Immigrant Employment Success in Canada," 15; also interview with a Citizenship and Immigration Canada official, 21 August 2012.

[24] Bloemraad, *Becoming a Citizen*.

[25] Citizenship and Immigration Canada, "The Current State of Multiculturalism in Canada and Research Themes on Canadian Multiculturalism 2008–2010, Section 1: The Current State of Multiculturalism in Canada – The New Evidence on Multiculturalism and Integration," at http://www.cic.gc.ca/english/resources/publications/multi-state/section1.asp, accessed 29 August 2012.

[26] Reitz, "Immigrant Employment Success in Canada," 36.

[27] Ibid., 15.

[28] Ibid.

[29] Monica Boyd, "Variations in Socioeconomic Outcomes of Second Generation Young Adults," *Canadian Diversity* (Spring 2008):20–24.

[30] Ibid., 23.

[31] Peter Pulzer, *Political Representation and Elections: Parties and Voting in Great Britain* (New York: Praeger, 1967), 98.

[32] Will Kymlicka, *The Current State of Multiculturalism in Canada and Research Themes on Canadian Multiculturalism 2008–2010* (Ottawa: Citizenship and Immigration Canada, 2010), 4.

[33] Ibid., 8.

[34] Organisation for Economic Co-operation and Development, *Where Immigrant Students Succeed: A Comparative Review of Performance and Engagement in PISA 2003* (Paris: OECD Programme for International Student Assessment, 2006), 33, 34.

[35] Ibid., 35.

[36] Ibid., 30.

[37] Ibid., 32.

[38] Ibid., 34.

[39] Kymlicka, *Current State of Multiculturalism*, 11.

[40] Bloemraad, *Becoming a Citizen*, 141 (emphasis mine).

[41] Both Canada and the United States pursued such a policy, in different ways and with varying degrees of brutality, against North American Indians.

[42] Will Kymlicka, *Multicultural Citizenship* (Oxford: Oxford University Press, 1996), 14.

[43] On this, see Rogers Brubaker, "The Return of Assimilation? Changing Perspectives on Immigration and Its Sequels in France, Germany, and the United States," *Ethnic and Racial Studies* 24, no. 4 (2001):531–548.

OUR MULTICULTURALISM: REFLECTIONS IN THE KEY OF RAWLS

PHIL RYAN

The most influential critiques of Canadian multiculturalism are marred by serious weaknesses.[1] "Multicultiphobic" critique blames multiculturalism for phenomena that existed long before multiculturalism itself, such as the identification with their homeland that many immigrants continue to cherish. It indulges in "once upon a time" thinking, which fosters nostalgia for a time that never was, a time when Canadians were united by a shared identity and sense of history.

This certainly does not mean that all criticism of multiculturalism is mistaken. Nor does a critique of multicultiphobic discourse constitute an uncritical hymn of praise to multiculturalism. The point is simply that multicultiphobia is a problem that Canadians need to outgrow. Why? What is the problem with multicultiphobia? There is a sort of Gresham's Law that operates in society: bad debates drive out good ones, weak critiques eclipse strong ones.[2] Think, for example, of all the questions that are obscured by the assertion that "they" must embrace "our" values. Or think of the range of complex social phenomena that vanish from awareness when someone claims that because of multiculturalism, immigrants are choosing to live in "ethnic ghettos." This Gresham's Law of debates is no small matter. At its best, a society steers itself over time through open debates. Bad debates gum up the steering mechanism, allowing society to drift and decisions to be subject to unacknowledged influences or uninformed knee-jerk reactions.

Bad debate drives out good because, among other reasons, bad is more exciting: it offers simple heroes and villains. Multicultiphobia is attractive

The Multiculturalism Question: Debating Identity in 21st-Century Canada, ed. Jack Jedwab. Kingston: School of Policy Studies, Queen's University. © 2014 The School of Policy Studies, Queen's University at Kingston. All rights reserved.

for another reason: it protects *amour propre* by transforming difficult questions about our society as a whole into complaints about *them*, about immigrants, immigrants led astray by multiculturalism. It provides a further psychic bonus: even while shunning serious debate, the multicultiphobic critic can sneer at the "politically correct" who are stifling any debate around multiculturalism. These psychic benefits of multicultiphobia are unwittingly acknowledged in a recent polemic against multiculturalism. Sun Media columnist Salim Mansur cites, with approval, French conservative Pascal Bruckner's claim that multiculturalism has become "the tool of guilt peddlers" and "instills relativism and doubt in a serene conscience sure that it is in the right."[3] If one really cherishes a serene certainty that one is right, a multicultiphobia that deflects uncomfortable questions about the justice of our society is most useful.

By deflecting debate, by taking concerns about our society as a whole and interpreting them as problems of one policy alone, multicultiphobia leads to a *misdiagnosis* on various questions. One of the most pervasive misdiagnoses attributes to multiculturalism what are, in fact, aspects of liberal modernity itself. When critics complain, for example, of multiculturalism's destruction of "shared values" and its alleged promotion of relativism,[4] are they not simply bemoaning a characteristic feature of modernity, the evaporation of "basic convictions that were culturally sanctioned and did not need to be argued for"?[5]

Which brings us to Rawls. John Rawls was a theorist who grappled with the challenges of liberal modernity. Given his status as perhaps the most influential liberal philosopher of recent decades, and given the controversy over the relation between multiculturalism and liberal values,[6] a Rawlsian assessment of our multiculturalism may lead us to ask fruitful questions about that multiculturalism and its prospects. This chapter will begin by examining Rawls's thoughts on pluralism. I will then summarize his vision of "justice as fairness," which will be used to reflect upon our multiculturalism. I conclude with some Rawlsian speculations on the prospects of that multiculturalism.

RAWLS ON PLURALISM

In a 1998 interview, Bernard Prusak asked Rawls why his recent writing had paid so much attention to religion, given that the index of *A Theory of Justice* did not even mention it. Rawls answered,

> The basic explanation is that I'm concerned about the survival, historically, of constitutional democracy. I live in a country where 90 or 95 percent of the people profess to be religious.... So the question is: In a constitutional democracy, how can religious and secular doctrines of all kinds get on together and cooperate in running a reasonably just and effective government? What

assumptions would you have to make about religious and secular doctrines, and the political sphere, for these to work together?[7]

What might it mean, exactly, for various doctrines, and those who hold them, to "get on together and cooperate"? We might answer by way of contrast.

Consider the musings of Katherine Harris, Republican candidate for the US Senate, who warned voters in 2006 that

> if you're not electing Christians then in essence you are going to legislate sin. They can legislate sin. They can say that abortion is alright. They can vote to sustain gay marriage. And that will take western civilization, indeed other nations because people look to our country as one nation as under God and whenever we legislate sin and we say abortion is permissible and we say gay unions are permissible, then average citizens who are not Christians, because they don't know better, we are leading them astray and it's wrong.[8]

However mangled her syntax, Harris's position is clear. Conservative fundamentalists, though, have no monopoly on intolerance. At the height of the "political correctness" debates, literary theorist Stanley Fish declared that "it makes perfect sense to desire the silencing of beliefs inimical to yours, because if you do not so desire, it would be an indication that you did not believe in your beliefs."[9]

So for people holding a range of doctrines, to "get on together and cooperate" requires, at a minimum, that they *not* think like Harris or Fish. But what prevents people from thinking this way, from thinking that "true" belief must silence others, or that those who think differently are "sinful" and "don't know better"? This question became central to Rawls's thought after the early 1970s.

Modern societies, argued Rawls, display an *ineradicable* pluralism of "reasonable comprehensive doctrines."[10] This key claim requires some unpacking. A comprehensive doctrine "includes conceptions of what is of value in human life, and ideals of personal character, as well as ideals of friendship and of familial and associational relationships, and much else that is to inform our conduct, and in the limit to our life as a whole."[11] A religious belief system can thus be comprehensive, but so too can other outlooks: stoicism, utilitarianism, Kantianism, even a focus on "self-actualization." In each case, everything depends on the degree of seriousness with which a doctrine is lived. Thus, we can say that a comprehensive doctrine is a set of ideas that has the *potential* to shape the most important domains of one's life.[12]

"Reasonable," for its part, does heavy duty in Rawls. Reasonable persons, first, "are ready to propose, or to acknowledge when proposed by others … fair terms of cooperation." Terms are fair when they benefit others as well as ourselves. Hence, fair terms "specify an idea of reciprocity."[13] Related to this, reasonableness involves a willingness to consider another's point of view with seriousness, and recognition that other people may have very good reasons for seeing things differently, even on life's most vital questions.[14]

Although Rawls did not address multiculturalism directly, reasonableness, in his sense, has a strong claim to be *the* core multicultural virtue. Its spirit of reciprocity counters the "we were here first" mentality that lies behind much resistance to cultural pluralism. And the recognition that others may have good reasons for their beliefs and practices resists facile judgments of cultural superiority or inferiority. Yet this recognition entails no judgment – positive, negative, or neutral – on those beliefs and practices. Nor does it entail that any *particular* belief or practice is in fact justifiable. Reasonableness is thus an inducement to understanding others, rather than an undiscriminating acceptance of difference.

A "reasonable comprehensive doctrine," then, is one that allows its adherents to be reasonable. It does not claim, to give an extreme contrast, that competing belief systems are expressions of "satanic power."[15] Nor does it hold that any particular secular ethical maxim, such as "maximize happiness in society," is so self-evidently correct that only fools can reject it. For Rawls, a key marker of the reasonableness of a comprehensive doctrine is its respect for freedom of conscience.[16] He argued that "except for certain kinds of fundamentalism, all the main historical religions admit of such an account [of free faith] and thus may be seen as reasonable comprehensive doctrines."[17] This is too optimistic: it might be better to say that these religions have the *potential* to be reasonable, but also the clear potential to be otherwise.[18]

The foregoing explicates Rawls's claim that modern societies have an ineradicable pluralism of "reasonable comprehensive doctrines." This condition of "reasonable pluralism" has important implications: it "limits what is practicably possible here and now, whatever may have been the case in other historical ages when, it is often said, people within a domestic society were united (though perhaps they never really have been) in affirming one comprehensive doctrine."[19] In particular, "a continuing shared adherence to one comprehensive doctrine can be maintained only by the oppressive use of state power, with all its official crimes and the inevitable brutality and cruelties, followed by the corruption of religion, philosophy, and science."[20]

Given the reality of reasonable pluralism, how – to return to Rawls's question – do we "get on together and cooperate"? Rawls answered that a "well-ordered" democracy is viable on the basis of an "overlapping consensus" in which citizens with a wide range of outlooks endorse core political values such as democracy and freedom of conscience *on the basis of* their various comprehensive doctrines.[21] Rawls's ideal is thus that Muslims find reasons to support democratic values within Islam itself, Christians find them within Christianity, and so on. Democratic "concepts, principles, and virtues," then, are "theorems, as it were, of their comprehensive views."[22] One of the implications of the overlapping consensus is that believers accept the need for *restraint* in the political sphere: they do not seek to use political power to impose policies based on their own comprehensive doctrines: policies should be based on "plain truths now widely accepted, or available, to citizens in general."[23]

Now, one might give a very different account of how we "get on together and cooperate." I noted in *Multicultiphobia* that each of us has multiple dimensions to our identity. A person might be a believer of a particular type, a citizen, a parent, a sitar player, a plumber, and so on. Respect for democratic goods might then be based on a certain hierarchy in those identity dimensions, one in which supportive elements outweigh any unreasonable beliefs people might hold. In this case, people might affirm democratic values *in spite of*, rather than because of, their comprehensive doctrines. But Rawls could answer that such a condition is not stable: rearrange the hierarchy of identity, and commitment to democratic goods could weaken. And, in truth, rearrangement of identity does happen for various reasons.[24] Much better, then, to have democratic goods supported by an overlapping consensus, rather than in tension with some people's deepest beliefs.

But is an overlapping consensus possible? Rawls believed that it was, arguing, "A reasonable and effective political conception may bend comprehensive doctrines toward itself, shaping them if need be from unreasonable to reasonable."[25] Indeed, substantial "bending" did take place in the 20th century. An influential example of this was Vatican II's "Declaration on Religious Freedom." Before that, Rome's official position had been that Catholics should support religious freedom when in a minority, but not otherwise! This stance was defended with the claim that "it is contrary to reason that error and truth should have equal rights," as Pope Leo XIII bluntly put matters.[26] But Vatican II declared that "no one is to be forced to act in a manner contrary to his own beliefs, whether privately or publicly, whether alone or in association with others, within due limits."[27] Reflecting Rawls's view that support for freedom of conscience could be grounded in a particular comprehensive doctrine, the declaration devoted a section to arguing that "this doctrine of freedom has roots in divine revelation."[28] The case of Vatican II certainly contributed to Rawls's optimistic hope for an overlapping consensus.[29]

As we have seen, in the last decades of his life, Rawls grappled with issues bypassed in his *A Theory of Justice*.[30] Rawls's development on the matter of pluralism led him to find new arguments for the essentials of his earlier theory, rather than abandon them. Let us very briefly review those essentials.

JUSTICE AS FAIRNESS

Imagine that we come together to choose the basic principles of justice for a society. Oddly, though, we are ignorant of "the particular circumstances" of the society, such as its level of development.[31] In this "original position," each of us is a *trustee*, representing the interests of a person who will live in that society.[32] Yet we know nothing about the specific person we represent: whether male or female, rich or poor, unbeliever or believer of some sort, and so on. From behind this "veil of ignorance," Rawls claims, we will choose two principles of justice.

(a) Each person has the same indefeasible claim to a fully adequate scheme of equal basic liberties, which scheme is compatible with the same scheme of liberties for all; and

(b) Social and economic inequalities are to satisfy two conditions: first, they are to be attached to offices and positions open to all under conditions of fair equality of opportunity; and second, they are to be to the greatest benefit of the least-advantaged members of society (the difference principle).[33]

These principles chosen within the original position would be fair ones, *by definition*, as the interests of all affected parties had been freely represented in a situation of equality. Hence, Rawls termed his original position device, together with the principles derived from it, "justice as fairness."

Now, the objection is often raised that it is absurd to expect a Christian, for example, to pretend that she is not a Christian in order to derive principles of justice. Theologian Stanley Hauerwas, for example, complains that with Rawls's approach, "alienation from self becomes the fundamental moral virtue."[34] But Rawls repeatedly stressed that he was not presenting a full vision of justice, but a "political conception" that specifies only the core principles of a pluralist polity.[35] Given that, "Putting people's comprehensive doctrines behind the veil of ignorance" makes perfect sense in order to identify principles "that can be the focus of an overlapping consensus."[36]

Rawls also noted that the original position is just one member of a family of thought experiments.[37] Discussion of specific constitutional provisions, as opposed to general principles of justice, requires that the veil of ignorance be lifted somewhat, allowing us to know "the relevant general facts about their society." A discussion of specific laws requires that the veil be lifted still further. But we still assume that we each represent individuals about whom we know nothing specific. The underlying idea is that at each stage, the trustees have enough information to clarify an issue, but not enough to locate the *particular* interests of the individuals they represent. Thus, the full original position is not an all-purpose tool for clarifying all political issues. Rather, "the flexibility of the idea of the original position is shown at each step of the procedure by its being modifiable to fit the subject in question."[38]

JUSTICE AS FAIRNESS, AND MULTICULTURALISM

We can use Rawls's central ideas to reflect upon various aspects of our multiculturalism. Rawls noted that his theory of "justice as fairness" has two central components: the original position device and the principles he derived from it; he also maintained that one might reject either of these components, while accepting the other.[39] In the same way, one may reject my application of Rawls's vision without rejecting the idea of using that vision as a useful device for reflecting on multiculturalism and other political issues.

Justice as fairness, first, can endorse one of the underlying intuitions of Canadian multiculturalism, Trudeau's 1971 observation that Canada has "no official culture," *if* by culture we mean a way of life shaped by a comprehensive doctrine.[40] Yet justice as fairness does aim at the development of an overarching *political* culture. It is clear that for Rawls, the stability of a just society depends on its shaping people's outlook over time, deepening their shared commitment to justice and to public deliberation. A just multiculturalism thus requires a multi-level conception of culture.[41] Perhaps some fears concerning multiculturalism would have been forestalled had this been made clearer at the outset.

The Rawlsian value of "fair equality of opportunity"[42] would certainly support many multicultural policies that promote integration, such as provisions against workplace discrimination. But substantial information would be required to address the more specific question of which anti-discrimination measures would best advance equality of opportunity. On employment equity measures, for example, a Rawlsian would ask whether they had been crafted with an eye to the difference principle. That is, are they developed so that the burden of adjustment does not fall on more vulnerable sectors of society?

Let us now consider a broad issue that has fuelled much discomfort with multiculturalism: our society's response to various problematic practices, often related to religious traditions. Rawls recognizes, first, the "permanent fact of life" of *unreasonable* comprehensive doctrines, doctrines that "reject one or more democratic freedoms." These must be *contained*, "like war and disease – so that they do not overturn political justice."[43] But he has little to say concerning just how this is to be done. The main point on which a Rawlsian would insist is that any religious regulation must be applied consistently to both mainstream and minority religions, to long-standing Canadian religious groups as much as to those of immigrants.[44]

But there are also doctrines that are "reasonable," in that their followers do not seek a monopoly of state powers or wish to limit the rights of those who hold other doctrines, yet are nonetheless troubling. The current-day Catholic Church, for example, accepts religious pluralism, but also has a sexist power structure and is a source of homophobic discourse. Should a just society accept discriminatory rules and practices that are *internal* to religious groups?[45] One might very much doubt whether those rules and practices would have been chosen within the religious group itself had its members been reflecting from behind a veil of ignorance, not knowing whether they represented women or men, clergy or laity, and so on. But these groups were not formed in this way, and today they are what they are, and they present us with a tension between equality and the freedoms of religion and association, *so long as* membership in a religious group truly is an exercise of one's freedom.

Here, again, the pure original position cannot give sufficient guidance: the veil of ignorance must be lifted substantially before we can assess how truly voluntary is membership in any particular religious group. This can obviously vary: the believer in a pluralist milieu has a less costly exit option than someone whose family and friends all belong to the same religious group. So long as membership is reasonably voluntary, Rawls's position is relatively tame, reflecting more or less the status quo in liberal democracies: society should not impose internal equality – for example, by ordering that the Catholic Church ordain women.[46] But neither is a religious group a rights-free zone: laws against various forms of abuse, for example, apply inside the group.[47] And just as liberal democracies can "bend" comprehensive doctrines in the direction of reasonableness, it is natural for those who cherish equality to wish to bend them in that respect as well.

But what of cases where exit (or even dissent) is very costly? Again, much detail is required before one can determine whether the threat of shunning, for example, substantially limits freedom.[48] Society cannot ban shunning. But governments can avoid doing anything to exacerbate the problem, such as partnering with, or delegating functions to, religious groups whose members' freedom is substantially limited. At the same time, tailoring practices to the circumstances of each religious community could well increase alienation. It will often be wiser, then, to avoid certain practices across the board, even when they pose risks for the members of some communities only.

The fact that the broad Rawlsian approach does not resolve questions such as this does not count against it: the pure original position is not intended for use in judging specific policies. But the underlying intuition – that we are to reflect on a policy by considering how it might be viewed from a wide variety of social locations, rather than unreasonably insisting on judging it only from where we happen to be ourselves – is always applicable. If this can be done through real social deliberation, rather than through the always limited efforts of our thought experiments, so much the better.

Up to this point, we have considered multiculturalism as a policy. A Rawlsian approach can also shed light on a related matter: the cultural demands that should be placed upon newcomers. Much Canadian discourse betrays a deep confusion: are certain immigrant practices opposed merely because they differ from "the way we do things here," or because they are thought to violate fundamental norms? These two types of opposition are often run together: the town council of Hérouxville lumps "stoning women to death" together with vegetarianism and kosher or halal diets in its rejected practices, while the city of Gatineau warns immigrants against honour killings and "cooking smelly foods."[49] Hoping to protect our "values," these media-savvy declarations instead trivialize fundamental human rights.

The "public-private" model, according to which an immigrant's culture should be sustained only in the privacy of one's home, betrays a similar confusion.[50] If a "private" cultural practice is unjust – providing insufficient nutrition to daughters, for example[51] – society need not be squeamish about trying to eradicate it. If it does not violate justice, society must have good reasons for not wishing to tolerate it in public; the fact that it differs from mainstream practices is not enough.

A Rawlsian approach can help us distinguish between current practices that have no greater claim to validity than the fact that this is "the way we do things here," and others with a claim to universal validity, and thus it can help distinguish between those points upon which we can be flexible and those around which we should be intransigent. Imagine that someone says, for example, that "their culture" endorses a subordinate role for women. We can answer that "their" culture does this only because subordination itself has barred women from having an equal voice in determining just what their culture should be. Thus, those who justify inequality by invoking cultural values are defending an oppression that "takes advantage of a silence which it prevents from being broken," to borrow from Rousseau.[52] In opposition to this, we can assert that parties deliberating behind a suitably tailored veil of ignorance, not knowing whether they represented males or females, would never endorse sexist institutions or cultural practices. One insight that emerges from this analysis is that the practices and norms we should consider most fundamental may not be of long standing, or even fully shared by Canadians today.[53] In fact, variations on the original position can be used to assess elements, not only of cultures brought to Canada, but of existing culture as well.

Now, this places great demands on all of us. A Rawlsian approach to multiculturalism would reject the view that "in a multicultural society, respecting people equally includes respecting their cultural commitments."[54] *Any* cultural commitment may be subject to critical scrutiny.[55] This applies to the commitments of native-born Canadians as much as to those of immigrants. Truly accepting this in practice requires of

Canadians a courageous and generous spirit. While we all like to think of ourselves as "reasonable," true Rawlsian reasonableness may in truth be in short supply.

PROSPECTS FOR OUR MULTICULTURALISM

Rawls believed that his political philosophy was "realistically Utopian."[56] Its utopian quality is evident enough. And its realism? Rawls held that the "first principles and precepts" of justice as fairness are "workable and applicable to ongoing political and social arrangements."[57] This may be so, but Rawls did not address the question of how we "get there from here." Rather, he simply claimed that, if we *did* get "there," we would have a good chance of staying there: he believed that his just society would be a stable equilibrium.[58] He assumed that "if we grow up under a framework of reasonable and just political and social institutions, we shall affirm those institutions when we in our turn come of age, and they will endure over time."[59] A just society, in short, should be able to produce the "moral sentiments" required to sustain itself.[60]

And our multiculturalism? Can we believe that it is stable in the same way, that it generates the moral sentiments it needs to survive? I do not think so, primarily because, unlike Rawls's "well-ordered society," our multiculturalism is not a social whole, but a subset of policies, beliefs, and sentiments.[61] Its health thus depends on a multitude of broader trends. I wish to note here some causes for concern, factors toward which a specifically Rawlsian approach to multiculturalism directs our attention.

Economic Inequality

Up to this point, I have generally bypassed a key element of Rawls's vision, his difference principle, according to which a society should accept only those inequalities that benefit its least-advantaged members. Rather than review the controversy over the principle here, we can simply note that for Rawls, the regulation of inequality is a matter of fundamental justice and also vital to the stability of a just society.[62]

In Canada, the era of official multiculturalism has also been an era of intensified inequality. How might economic polarization affect multiculturalism's prospects? Some effects are obvious: to the degree that particular ethnic groups tend to be overrepresented at different points in our economic hierarchy, increasing polarization can impede integration into various life spheres, such as residence, education, and the workplace.[63] But we can also speculate on other, more subtle consequences.

Recall that Rawlsian reasonableness is not a "live and let live" philosophy of mutual indifference. It involves a commitment to understanding others' points of view, the reasons why they differ from us on important matters. It seems clear that this must be grounded in a sense of identification with one's fellow citizens, a sense that we are all "in this together." Is this sense vulnerable to growing inequality? Adam Smith once wrote that the rich seek "marks of opulence which nobody can possess but themselves."[64] Much later, Thorstein Veblen chronicled the great inventiveness with which human beings seek to put their superiority on display, arguing that this thirst for "invidious distinction" is a fundamental motive of economic activity.[65] In recent decades, we have seen many wealthy Americans increasingly disengage from the institutions of the larger society, retreating to gated communities, private education, even private law enforcement. It thus seems likely that increasing economic distance among citizens will increase psychic and "institutional" distance as well. Ongoing economic polarization would thus be incompatible with the sort of identification among citizens that Rawlsian reasonableness requires.

Unreasonable Comprehensive Doctrines

An overlapping consensus supporting democratic political values is an essential requirement for Rawls's "well-ordered society." Another is that *unreasonable* comprehensive doctrines "do not gain enough currency."[66] For many Canadians, the only unreasonable doctrine to worry about is either Islam or something closely related: in September 2011, the prime minister declared "Islamicism" to be the greatest threat to our national security. Indeed, one of the recurring media criticisms of multiculturalism is that it disarms us in the face of the Islamist threat: since "multiculturalists" supposedly believe that "all cultures are equal," it follows that "there is nothing specific and precious about the West to begin with, thus no sacrifice is meaningful in its defence."[67]

But a security threat should not be confused with a threat to democracy itself, although in a couple of scenarios, the two might fuse. One possibility is that a radical group expands its political influence to the point that it threatens to take power under the existing rules of the game and then suspend those rules. This does not appear to be a serious possibility anywhere in the Western world. The other scenario, frequently seen in history, occurs when a security threat leads to widespread support for the limitation or even suspension of democratic freedoms. This is hardly inconceivable in Canada today and suggests that Canadian democracy may be threatened less by "Islamists" than by the reaction against them.

But let us consider other comprehensive doctrines that might be cause for concern. It is clear that many Americans today are uncomfortable with the norms of pluralist democracy. While Rick Santorum and Rick Perry both failed in their quest for the Republican presidential nomination, it is worrisome that their intolerant strain of Christian political rhetoric garnered substantial support.[68] Marci McDonald's controversial *The Armageddon Factor* argues that this intolerant brand of Christianity is becoming more influential in Canada and enjoys some support within the federal cabinet.[69] It is not easy to distinguish the policy impact of "theo-cons" from that of secular social conservatives, but some policies, such as the government's extreme position on Israel and Palestine and its de-funding of aid organizations linked to the Catholic and mainstream Protestant churches, indicate a shift in the political influence of various religious groups. As we have seen in the United States, fundamentalist influence can wax and wane over time, yet come to represent a permanent factor in the political landscape.

Shifting demographics might play a role here. Mainstream Protestant denominations that have supported political and religious pluralism are in decline: between the 1991 and 2001 censuses, Anglican and United church membership dropped by nearly 8 percent,[70] and an internal Anglican Church report claims that "at the present rate of decline ... only one Anglican would be left in Canada by 2061."[71] Meanwhile, other Christian groups, some of which are less supportive of the overlapping consensus, are projected to continue growing.[72]

Rawls believed that liberal democracy had been able to "bend" some religious doctrines toward support for pluralism and freedom of conscience. Some "unbending" has clearly taken place in the United States, and it appears to be occurring here. How might this affect our multi-culturalism? Rawls once noted that, before the "successful and peaceful practice of toleration in societies with liberal institutions there was no way of knowing of that possibility"; it was hence quite natural to believe that intolerance was "a condition of social order and stability."[73] But no insight is acquired once and for all. If it is lost, people can develop an exaggerated notion of the sort of unity a society needs in order to thrive. I believe that those among multiculturalism's critics who pine for a united Canada that never was suffer from precisely this mistake.

And there is a broader consequence of the weakening of the overlapping consensus, to which we now turn.

Politics and Reasonableness

Recall what the overlapping consensus *does*: when support for pluralism is grounded within a comprehensive doctrine, the believer need suffer no psychic division when embracing pluralist democracy, and restraint in politics is seen as *morally* right, not merely a tactical ruse. But to those who do not accept the overlapping consensus, to refrain from seeking to impose their comprehensive doctrines through politics is an illegitimate self-muzzling: separation of church and state becomes nothing more than a "lie we have been told," as Republican Katherine Harris has put it.[74]

When politics is seen as a struggle to impose a comprehensive doctrine upon the nation, it is natural to demonize one's opponents, who now stand in the way, not merely of one's preferred policies, but of Truth itself.

Thus, Democrats stand accused of fighting a "long war on Christianity in America,"[75] and Republican contender Rick Perry accuses Obama of waging "war on religion."[76]

However many Conservative supporters see politics this way, the ongoing challenge of sustaining a majority government makes it unlikely that we will hear *public* rhetoric of this sort from Canadian politicians. More generally, though, the demonizing style of politics has crossed the border: environmentalists are recast as pawns of foreign interests; concern over the war in Afghanistan is equated to appeasement of Hitler.[77] Should the opposition parties judge that this particular fire can be fought only by fire, Canadian politics could be changed for a long time to come. We may be entering an age in which politics "betrays the marks of warfare."[78] There is no easy road back: as Robert Hughes once observed, "Polarization is addictive. It is the crack of politics."[79]

To be reasonable includes a willingness to understand the views of those who differ from us. A polarized politics of demonization is the antithesis of reasonableness. Now, I have suggested that reasonableness may be the core multicultural virtue. Is it possible, then, that the fate of multiculturalism, as well as the overall quality of Canadian society and discourse, hinges on the survival of reasonableness? We do not know because a certain reasonable spirit has tempered Canadian politics for so long that it is hard to know what life would be like in its absence.[80] Perhaps we are about to find out.

A reasonable society, Rawls once commented, is nothing spectacular: "It is very much a part of our ordinary human world, not a world we think of much virtue, until we find ourselves without it."[81] Or, as a Canadian philosopher once put it, "Don't it always seem to go, that you don't know what you've got till it's gone."

NOTES

[1] Phil Ryan, *Multicultiphobia* (Toronto: University of Toronto Press, 2010).

[2] The original Gresham's Law holds that "bad money drives out good." Thus, if a government issues adulterated coins, pure ones will vanish from the market as people hoard them or melt them down.

[3] Pascal Bruckner, *The Tyranny of Guilt: An Essay on Western Masochism* (Princeton, NJ: Princeton University Press, 2010), quoted in Salim Mansur, *The Muddle of Multiculturalism: A Liberal Critique* (Halifax: Atlantic Institute for Market Studies, 2010), 20.

[4] The link between multiculturalism and relativism is not at all clear. Consider the following argument: "The moral claim of people like myself is every bit as legitimate as that of other groups. Surely our value judgment is just as good as that of others. Surely our cultural identification is as meaningful as any other." Many people would label this an example of corrosive multiculturalist relativism. But the statement was made by Richard Ogmundson, hardly a supporter of multiculturalism, which he denounces as "a form of cultural genocide"; see "On

the Right to Be a Canadian," in *20 Years of Multiculturalism: Successes and Failures*, ed. Stella Hryniuk (Winnipeg: St. John's College Press, 1992), 47–48.

[5] Jürgen Habermas, *The Theory of Communicative Action II: Lifeworld and System*, trans. Thomas McCarthy (Boston: Beacon Press, 1987), 353.

[6] Will Kymlicka's *Multicultural Citizenship* (Oxford: Clarendon, 1995) presents an influential articulation of liberal multiculturalism. Brian Barry's *Culture and Equality* (Cambridge, MA: Harvard University Press, 2001) asserts the fundamental incompatibility of liberalism and multiculturalism.

[7] John Rawls, interview by Bernard Prusak, *Commonweal*, 25 September 1998.

[8] Katherine Harris, interview, *Florida Baptist Witness*, 22 August 2006, at http://www.gofbw.com/News.asp?ID=6298, accessed 4 November 2011.

[9] Stanley Fish, *There's No Such Thing as Free Speech* (New York: Oxford, 1994), 118.

[10] John Rawls, *Political Liberalism* (New York: Columbia University Press, 1996), xviii.

[11] Ibid.

[12] By contrast, one would be hard pressed to forge a whole form of life on the basis of a passion for stamp-collecting, for example. An interesting question is whether multiculturalism might be a comprehensive doctrine, whether its commitments are broad enough to shape an entire life, at least for some people. I personally doubt this.

[13] John Rawls, *Justice as Fairness: A Restatement*, ed. Erin Kelly (Cambridge, MA: Belknap Press, 2001), 6.

[14] Rawls, *Political Liberalism*, 54–58.

[15] Fundamentalist preacher Albert Mohler applies the term to all non-Christian belief systems, offering Islam, Buddhism, Hinduism, and dialectical materialism as examples; quoted in David Roach, "Mohler, on 'O'Reilly Factor,' Discusses Islam, Demonic Power," *Baptist Press*, 20 March 2006.

[16] Rawls, *Justice as Fairness*, 191.

[17] Rawls, *Political Liberalism*, 170.

[18] "The sacred texts of Judaism, Christianity, and Islam all contain strains of tolerance and intolerance" (Ryan, *Multicultiphobia*, 195). In all three cases today, we can see that some groups have chosen to accentuate the tolerant strains, others the intolerant ones.

[19] John Rawls, *The Law of Peoples* (Cambridge, MA: Harvard University Press, 1999), 12. The caveat mentioned only in passing ("perhaps they never really have been") points to an important gap in the conservative critique of multiculturalism. These critics never specify just *when* society enjoyed the organic unity for which they pine. In the case of European societies and their colonial offspring, do we not have to go back *at least* to the Reformation? And is even that far enough? Historian Marc Bloch's portrayal of feudal Europe notes that Christianity "n'avait qu'incomplètement pénétré les masses ... leur vie religieuse se nourrissait d'une multitude de croyances et de pratiques"; see *La Société Féodale* (Paris: Albin Michel, 1989), 129.

[20] Rawls, *Justice as Fairness*, 34.

[21] Rawls, *Political Liberalism*, 39. Rawls's full definition of a "well-ordered society" can be found in *Justice as Fairness*, sec. 3.

[22] Rawls, *Justice as Fairness*, 33.

[23] Rawls, *Political Liberalism*, 61, 225.

[24] Philosopher Charles Taylor notes that our identity is forged through ongoing interaction with others; see "The Politics of Recognition," in *Multiculturalism: Examining the Politics of Recognition*, ed. Amy Gutmann (Princeton, NJ: Princeton University Press, 1994), 34. A rearrangement in one's identity hierarchy can thus be *imposed* upon people to some extent. Islamophobia or anti-Semitism, for example, can easily lead its victims to magnify the importance of their religious identities; see Amin Maalouf, *Les Identités Meurtrières* (Paris: Grasset, 1998), 20.

[25] Rawls, *Political Liberalism*, 246.

[26] Leo XIII, *Libertas Praestantissimum*, 20 June 1888, para. 34, at http://www.vatican.va/holy_father/leo_xiii/encyclicals/documents/hf_l-xiii_enc_20061888_libertas_en.html, accessed 18 January 2012.

[27] Second Vatican Council, *Declaration on Religious Freedom*, 7 December 1965, para. 2, at http://www.vatican.va/archive/hist_councils/ii_vatican_council/documents/vat-ii_decl_19651207_dignitatis-humanae_en.html, accessed 19 May 2012.

[28] Ibid., para. 9.

[29] Indeed, although Rawls may have coined the term "overlapping consensus," the underlying idea was articulated earlier by Catholic philosopher Jacques Maritain, *Man and the State* (Chicago: University of Chicago Press, 1951), 108ff. The passage was later cited by Rawls in "The Idea of Public Reason Revisited," *University of Chicago Law Review* 64, no. 3 (Summer 1997):774.

[30] Victoria Camps suggests that this "second Rawls" emerged precisely in response to communitarian and multiculturalist critiques of his earlier work; see "El segundo Rawls, más cerca de Hegel," *Daimon, Revista de Filosofia* 15 (1997):64. It is not surprising, then, that philosopher Brian Barry's critique of multiculturalism, although drawing on the earlier Rawls, declares that "Rawls has by now abandoned most of the ideas that made *A Theory of Justice* worthwhile"; see *Culture and Equality* (Cambridge, MA: Harvard University Press, 2001), 331.

[31] Rawls, *A Theory of Justice* (Cambridge, MA: Belknap Press, 1971), 137.

[32] Rawls, *Justice as Fairness*, 85.

[33] Ibid., 42. I am bypassing various important aspects of Rawls's theory, such as his general defence of these principles and his arguments concerning their order of priority. On the latter, see Rawls, *Theory of Justice*, 42–43.

[34] Stanley Hauerwas, *Truthfulness and Tragedy* (Notre Dame, IN: University of Notre Dame Press, 1977), 218.

[35] Rawls, *Justice as Fairness*, 11.

[36] Rawls, *Political Liberalism*, 25.

[37] Rawls, *Justice as Fairness*, 197–198.

[38] Rawls, *Law of Peoples*, 86.

[39] Rawls, *Theory of Justice*, 15.

[40] Pierre Elliott Trudeau, speech to the House of Commons, 8 October 1971, at http://www.canadahistory.com/sections/documents/Primeministers/trudeau/docs-onmulticulturalism.htm, accessed 22 May 2012. What Trudeau might have actually meant by the phrase is unclear.

[41] See also Ryan, *Multicultiphobia*, 146.

[42] *Fair* equality of opportunity is contrasted with a purely formal or legal equality. Thus, for Rawls, its pursuit requires instituting ongoing measures, such as public education and redistributive taxation, to limit inherited advantages.

[43] Rawls, *Political Liberalism*, 64.

[44] On this, see Ryan, *Multicultiphobia*, 193–194.

[45] The Catholic Church's position on gay rights certainly straddles the internal-external divide. I take it as a given that society has a legitimate interest in regulating discriminatory practices that affect non-members, and I focus here on internal practices because their regulation raises more complex issues.

[46] The US Supreme Court has only recently recognized a "'ministerial' exception" from workplace discrimination laws. Its scope is unclear, but the spirit seems captured by Justice Alito's concurring opinion that the exception "should apply to any 'employee' who leads a religious organization, conducts worship services or important religious ceremonies or rituals, or serves as a messenger or teacher of its faith." See *Hosanna-Tabor Evangelical Lutheran Church and School v. Equal Employment Opportunity Commission et al.* at http://www.supremecourt. gov/opinions/11pdf/10-553.pdf, accessed 2 July 2012. The Canadian exception is far more sweeping. Section 20 of Quebec's *Charter of Human Rights and Freedoms*, for example, states, "A distinction, exclusion or preference based on the aptitudes or qualifications required in good faith for an employment, or justified by the charitable, philanthropic, religious, political or educational nature of a nonprofit institution or of an institution devoted exclusively to the well-being of an ethnic group, is deemed non-discriminatory" (at http://www.learnquebec.ca/en/content/curriculum/bal/cit_com/rights/qcrights.html, accessed 22 May 2012).

[47] There is no social space, Rawls insists, "exempt from justice"; see *Justice as Fairness*, 166.

[48] Bhikhu Parekh notes a case in which a British court "took the view that although acute social pressure did not amount to duress for a white British girl, it did so for her Asian counterpart" and granted her request to annul her marriage. Parekh comments, "Since ostracism by the family virtually amounts to social death and hence to duress in Asian society but not in white British society, the differential treatment of the Asian and white girls does not offend against the principle of equality"; see *Rethinking Multiculturalism* (Cambridge, MA: Harvard University Press, 2000), 248.

[49] Ingrid Peritz, "Gatineau's Values Guide for Immigrants Stirs Controversy," *Globe and Mail*, 5 December 2011.

[50] As Neil Bissoondath put it, "one should do everything one can to fit in with the society at large. It does not mean that at home you should change your habits or change your way of living." "Interview by Aruna Srivastava," in *Other Solitudes: Canadian Multicultural Fictions*, ed. Linda Hutcheon and Marion Richmond (Toronto: Oxford University Press, 1990), 316.

[51] Hanna Papanek, "To Each Less Than She Needs, from Each More Than She Can Do: Allocations, Entitlements, and Value," in *Persistent Inequalities*, ed. Irene Tinker (New York: Oxford University Press, 1990).

[52] Jean Jacques Rousseau, *The Social Contract* (New York: Washington Square, 1967), 106.

[53] As recently as 1982, Member of Parliament Margaret Mitchell's House of Commons statement on domestic violence was greeted by a "chorus of laughter." See Mary Hynes, "Words, Not Wife Beating Prompted Laughter: MP," *Globe and Mail*, 14 May 1982.

[54] David Miller, "Liberalism, Equal Opportunities and Cultural Commitments," in *Multiculturalism Reconsidered*, ed. Paul Kelly (Cambridge: Polity Press, 2002), 48.

[55] A critic might say that this claim reflects liberalism's notorious individualism and neglects how profoundly culture shapes us. Not at all. I assume only that we are able to gain some psychic distance from at least some of the aspects of the reality in which we are immersed, not that we can float above that reality as a whole and judge it dispassionately.

[56] Rawls, *Law of Peoples*, 11.

[57] Ibid., 13.

[58] This does not mean that "the institutions and practices of the well-ordered society do not alter," but rather that there is stability in "the basic structure and the moral conduct of individuals"; see Rawls, *Theory of Justice*, 457.

[59] Rawls, *Law of Peoples*, 7.

[60] Rawls, *Theory of Justice*, 458.

[61] I leave aside the vexing problem that we seem unable to agree on just which policies, beliefs, and sentiments constitute multiculturalism.

[62] Rawls, *Justice as Fairness*, sec. 37.

[63] Ryan, *Multicultiphobia*, 179–180.

[64] Adam Smith, *The Wealth of Nations* (New York: Modern Library, 1937), 172.

[65] Thorstein Veblen, *The Theory of the Leisure Class* (New York: Dover, 1994).

[66] Rawls, *Political Liberalism*, 39.

[67] Salim Mansur, "Let the Dismantling Begin," *Ottawa Sun*, 15 March 2008.

[68] Among many other symptoms of American discomfort with pluralism is a July 2007 Gallup poll that found that only 45 percent of respondents could imagine voting for an atheist presidential candidate *of their own party*. See Jeffrey Jones, "Some Americans Reluctant to Vote for Mormon, 72-Year-Old Presidential Candidates," Gallup News Service, 20 February 2007.

[69] Marci McDonald, *The Armageddon Factor* (Toronto: Random House Canada, 2010).

[70] Statistics Canada, "Overview: Canada Still Predominantly Roman Catholic and Protestant," n.d., at http://www12.statcan.ca/english/census01/Products/Analytic/companion/rel/canada.cfm, accessed 24 May 2012.

[71] Michael Valpy, "Anglican Church Facing the Threat of Extinction," *Globe and Mail*, 8 February 2010.

[72] Statistics Canada, Demography Division, *Projections of the Diversity of the Canadian Population, 2006 to 2031* (Ottawa: Statistics Canada, 2010), at http://www.statcan.gc.ca/pub/91-551-x/91-551-x2010001-eng.pdf, accessed 9 March 2010.

[73] Rawls, *Political Liberalism*, xxvii.

[74] Harris, interview, *Florida Baptist Witness*. In addition, Republican presidential contender Rick Santorum is so appalled by John F. Kennedy's acceptance of the separation of church and state that he even denied, in a 2002 speech to members of ultra-conservative Opus Dei in Rome, that Kennedy was a Catholic president. See David Alandete, "Opus Dei Santorum," *El País* (Madrid), 25 March 2012.

[75] Mike Allen, "GOP Congressman Calls Democrats Anti-Christian," *Washington Post*, 21 June 2005. The remark was made by a Republican Congressman in response to a motion to ban coercive religious proselytizing taking place at the Air Force Academy, where cadets are being warned that they "will burn in the fires of hell" if they do not accept Christ and Jewish students are told that the Holocaust was "just punishment." The issue was also the subject of an earlier editorial in that paper; see "'Team Jesus Christ,'" *Washington Post*, 4 June 2005.

[76] Catalina Camia, "Perry Slams Obama's 'War on Religion' in New Ad," *USA Today*, 7 December 2011.

[77] Stephen Harper gave notice of this political style in his 2003 Civitas speech: the Liberals, he alleged, manifested "obvious glumness at the fall of Baghdad." As to the "Left," it hopes that "we actually lose" the war on terrorism and is consumed with "deep resentments, even hatreds, of the norms of free and democratic western civilization." See "Rediscovering the Right Agenda," *Citizens Centre Report* 30, no. 10 (June 2003):72–77.

[78] Rawls, *Justice as Fairness*, 118. When politics is warfare, every issue is a battlefield. For example, the already cited screed by Salim Mansur demonizes multiculturalism and its supporters. Multiculturalism is "an insidious assault on freedom in the West." Its supporters are among those who "loathe openness and freedom." "The enemies of open society," he warns, "are vast in number [and are] like tidal waves relentlessly beating down on dykes that, if not regularly attended, would break and be washed away." See *Muddle of Multiculturalism*, 19, 23. In the wake of the Norway massacre, it is surely legitimate to demand of opponents of multiculturalism that they present their arguments without stooping to such violent rhetoric.

[79] Robert Hughes, *Culture of Complaint* (New York: Oxford University Press, 1993), 28.

[80] Should someone object that politics has always involved bellicose posturing, we can note that Canadian politics has generally involved much *more* than that: politicians have been willing to exchange views in a reasonably rational fashion at the committee level, decision-making has been open to the influence of expert opinion, and so on.

[81] Rawls, *Political Liberalism*, 54.

MULTICULTURALISM POLICIES AND POPULAR MULTICULTURALISM IN THE DEVELOPMENT OF CANADIAN IMMIGRATION [1]

JEFFREY G. REITZ

In assessing the impact of multiculturalism in Canada, two aspects should be distinguished. One is the impact of distinctive multiculturalism policies announced and implemented by governments and the allegedly positive or negative impacts these policies may have on minority group members and their communities. The other is the impact of popular support for multiculturalism, as the idea is understood by the general public. Impacts of public opinion may extend beyond support for multicultural policies to encompass all policies related to immigration, including preferences for numbers of immigrants as well as policies and programs providing all manner of assistance for immigrants to integrate into society. These two aspects of the impact of multiculturalism are quite different, as are their dynamics. They are not necessarily equally significant.

Multiculturalism policies are a compelling topic. For one thing, the distinctive underlying principles, primarily the recognition and support for minority cultures, are important philosophical questions in a liberal democracy. Many regard them as fundamental for Canadian political culture and, in fact, for Western political culture generally. Some argue that recognition and support for minority cultures reinforce equality and in this way help integrate minorities into the mainstream.[2] Those on the left worry that recognition and support for minorities leads to

The Multiculturalism Question: Debating Identity in 21st-Century Canada, ed. Jack Jedwab. Kingston: School of Policy Studies, Queen's University. © 2014 The School of Policy Studies, Queen's University at Kingston. All rights reserved.

increased marginality, exacerbating minority disadvantage.[3] Those on the right counter that such recognition is a form of reverse discrimination, disadvantaging the mainstream. Are there reasonable limits to the accommodation of various cultures, and, if so, what are they?

The following discussion argues that in the Canadian case, evidence suggests that the most important impacts actually arise from widespread popular support for multiculturalism as a symbol that is formally undefined, but that stands in a general way for progressive views on ethnocultural and racial diversity. Popular multiculturalism is an important social and political fact in Canada, but its impact depends on what it means to most people. This is an empirical question, of course, and one cannot assume a declaration of support for any particular set of principles. The celebration of multicultural Canada as a popular ideal is not a mandate for governments to undertake any particular efforts in support of minority cultures; nor do governments see it that way. Instead, in the general population, support for multiculturalism seems to be an expression of goodwill toward the entire subject of diversity and immigration. Popular multiculturalism creates a positive political environment for the development of Canada's expansionist immigration policy and helps immigrants integrate into the economy and society. In short, *support for multiculturalism represents social capital playing an important role in the development of Canadian immigration*. It constitutes a resource that enables policy-makers to develop programs to assist immigrant integration and to address emerging problems affecting immigrants.

The effect of popular multiculturalism as social capital in the development of Canadian immigration is important. Canadians seek relatively high levels of immigration, and they welcome immigrants. Since 1990, well over 5 million new immigrants have been admitted, mostly members of visible minorities. Toronto alone welcomes nearly 100,000 new immigrants each year. Immigration is a key part of Canada's overall nation-building strategy. So there is a lot at stake here. Compared to other countries, we have more to gain from bringing immigrants into the mainstream – and more to lose if we fail.

The relative success that Canada has had in integrating immigrants owes much to their careful selection and to efforts to support their integration into the mainstream: instruction in an official language, settlement services, and assistance in acquiring citizenship. Direct effects of the distinctively multicultural component of policy on these outcomes, positive or negative, appear to be quite limited, if not entirely negligible.

To understand the role of popular multiculturalism, we must consider how public opinion, as a form of social capital, influences the direction of immigration policy-making. Does the positive environment created by popular support for multiculturalism improve the quality of policy-making in the area of immigration by providing scope for more open and frank public discussion, or does it restrict that discussion? Does it improve or reduce public accountability for immigration policy? In addition, understanding the impact of Canadian multiculturalism as social capital sheds light on the applicability of multiculturalism in other countries.

The following discussion reviews evidence on both aspects of the impact of multiculturalism in Canada. It first considers the distinctive impacts of Canadian multiculturalism policy; it then compares the Canadian immigration experience with that of other countries not espousing multicultural policies, especially the United States. The conclusion it reaches, based on the available evidence, is that the impact of multiculturalism policy per se has been small to non-existent. The discussion then turns to a consideration of public support for multiculturalism in Canada and its implications for policy-making. The evidence suggests that this impact may be much larger and more significant than the first, particularly with respect to the expansionist immigration policy and support for the integration of immigrants, including language learning and citizenship acquisition.

IMPACT OF CANADIAN MULTICULTURALISM POLICIES ON IMMIGRANT INTEGRATION

The debate over multiculturalism policy evokes divergent and strongly argued views. In the minds of the critics of multiculturalism, almost anything that goes wrong in minority communities can be blamed on multiculturalism. They argue that recognizing and celebrating diversity not only encourages minorities to maintain anti-democratic or sexist cultures and extraneous political agendas in Canada; it also exempts them from criticism based on mainstream values. Incompetence is excused, crimes are condoned, and terrorist threats are ignored – all because multiculturalism makes people fear that criticism of minority groups, or even individual group members, will attract accusations of racism. Negative features of minority cultures flourish. In this vein, former British Columbia premier Ujjal Dosanjh blames multiculturalism for helping promote Sikh extremism; in his view, multiculturalism has been distorted and used to make the claim that "anything anyone believes – no matter how ridiculous and outrageous it might be, is okay and acceptable in the name of diversity."[4]

On the other side, almost anything that goes right in minority communities can be, and has been, credited to multiculturalism. Its proponents claim that by recognizing and supporting minority cultures, multiculturalism promotes social inclusion and helps integrate minorities into the mainstream. Whether it is minority businesses being successful, minority kids doing well in school, or even Ujjal Dosanjh becoming the first South Asian–immigrant premier of British Columbia – all of these are possible because multiculturalism encourages a sense of belonging among minorities and the confidence to realize their full potential in a diverse society. Citing such positive experiences, Canadian philosopher Will Kymlicka, internationally renowned theoretician of multiculturalism and its recognition of minority cultures, announced in his 1998 book, *Finding Our Way: Rethinking Ethnocultural Relations in Canada,* "The multiculturalism program is working."[5]

The international context has influenced this Canadian debate only slightly. The initial international reception of Canada's multiculturalism, adopted as policy in 1971, was quite warm. A multiculturalism policy was adopted in 1978 by Australia and in the 1980s and 1990s by a number of European countries, including the United Kingdom and the Netherlands. In 1997, an international consensus was proclaimed by American sociologist Nathan Glazer in his book *We Are All Multiculturalists Now.*[6] But if there was an international consensus, it was upended by the terrorist attacks of 11 September 2001, the war on terrorism, and various related events, including the 2004 Madrid bombing, the murder of filmmaker Theo van Gogh in the Netherlands, more bombings in London, and widespread disturbances in Maghreb communities in France. Suspicion focused on Muslim immigrants generally, fuelled by criticism of Islamic attitudes toward women, as symbolized by head scarves and veils. Doubts were raised about the whole idea of support for minority cultures. US and British academic critics, including Brian Barry, Samuel Huntington, and Amartya Sen,[7] added weight to the backlash. In 2007, a column in *The Economist* said of multiculturalism that "almost everyone now agrees it has failed."[8] Francis Fukuyama even blamed Canada for exporting an ideology promoting violence.[9]

Through all this, the Canadian public and their governments have stuck with multiculturalism. They think multiculturalism is basically a good idea. But does multiculturalism really "work" in Canada?

It is generally acknowledged that on a comparative basis and up until now, Canada's immigration program has been a success story. Canada takes large numbers of immigrants, and despite problems related to employment and evidence of racial barriers, compared to other countries there appears to be a relatively smooth integration of immigrants into the mainstream. Immigrants have not only contributed significantly to the development of the economy, they have also become an integral part of the Canadian community, and their social and cultural contributions are frequently celebrated.

Can any part of Canada's success be attributed to its embrace of multiculturalism and the key principles underlying the policy? To examine this issue empirically, we need a definition of what Canadian multiculturalism policy actually is. The initial policy, as introduced by Prime Minister Pierre Trudeau in 1971,[10] stated that the main objective was to assure "the cultural freedom" of Canadians. It offered "assistance" to cultural groups who demonstrated a need and expressed a desire to contribute to

Canada, promising help for immigrants to overcome inequality, engage with other groups, and learn an official language.

What is distinctively multicultural in this Canadian policy is the promise of assistance to cultural groups. In fact, recognition of and support for minority ethnic cultures are the hallmarks of Canadian multiculturalism. Without these, the other features would appear to be reflective of conventional settlement programs and measures to encourage equal opportunity. A country that adopted only a program of mainstream language instruction for immigrants would not be considered to have a multiculturalism policy. The same applies to equal opportunity provisions. Canada had equal opportunity policies for many years, and these cannot be considered multicultural in their orientation. For example, fair employment-practices legislation was introduced at the provincial level over the period 1951 (in Ontario) to 1964 (in Quebec) and at the federal level, including in the *Canadian Bill of Rights* in 1960 and the *Canadian Charter of Rights and Freedoms*, in 1982.[11]

Elaborations of Canadian multicultural policy have retained the original emphasis on recognition of and support for minority cultures. For example, the inclusion of multiculturalism in the Charter focuses on the right to maintain cultural heritage.[12] The *Canadian Multiculturalism Act* of 1988 adds the obligation for the government to report annually to Parliament, but again without changing the essential thrust. The same is true of multicultural policies adopted at provincial and municipal levels of government, in many community organizations, and in school curricula.

Some other possible multicultural policies are not well established in Canada. Kymlicka points this out, identifying 13 policies and programs "often discussed under the rubric of 'multiculturalism' in the public debate."[13] Some are essentially cultural-support policies, including funding for ethnic cultural festivals and ethnic studies programs, heritage-language courses in schools, and revisions of educational curricula to give greater recognition to the historical and cultural contributions of minorities. Others are human rights guarantees that predate multiculturalism. Kymlicka also lists affirmative action programs, but while these are multicultural in the sense that they emphasize the rights of groups, they lack wide application or support in Canada. Affirmative action exists as formal policy in the *Employment Equity Act* adopted in 1986, but this applies only to federally regulated employers, who represent less than 10 percent of workers. And although visible minorities are included in the act as a target group, policy enforcement has been directed at equality for women. Elsewhere, employment equity has been rejected. It was enacted briefly by the New Democrats in Ontario, but resoundingly repealed and rejected by a Conservative government as a racial quota, and it has not been discussed seriously since, in Ontario or in any other province.

It is noteworthy that policies aimed directly at integrating immigrants, such as instruction in the language of the host society, settlement services, assistance finding work, and promotion of citizenship acquisition, are not normally included as part of multiculturalism. None of these are included on Kymlicka's list, and for good reason. They are policies that one might expect to find in a jurisdiction promoting a *melting pot* (i.e., American) philosophy and rapid assimilation for immigrants. As noted earlier, in the original Trudeau formulation of multiculturalism, efforts such as promoting instruction in an official language was included, thus emphasizing that multiculturalism is not opposed to integration of immigrants into the mainstream. But they are not in themselves distinctively multicultural policies.

An important empirical focus for assessments of the impact of multiculturalism in Canada is comparing immigrant integration in Canada with that in countries without a multiculturalism policy. For example, Will Kymlicka's statement that "multiculturalism is working" in Canada is based on observations that he believes show that "immigrant groups integrate more quickly and more effectively today than they did before the adoption of multiculturalism policy, and they do so more successfully in Canada than in any other country that does not have such a policy."[14] He adds, "Whether we examine the trends within Canada since 1971, or compare Canada with other countries, the conclusion is the same: multiculturalism is working."[15] Although in his 2007 book, *Multicultural Odysseys*, in which he surveys international experiences with multiculturalism, Kymlicka observes less confidently that "we cannot simply declare [Canadian] multiculturalism to be either a 'success' or a 'failure,'"[16] in more recent writings, he again states that multicultural policies in Canada are having "a positive effect."[17] He goes so far as to claim, "Canadian multiculturalism has enhanced the political participation, equal opportunity and social acceptance of immigrants."[18]

Of course, in making cross-national comparisons of immigrant integration, the effect of factors other than multiculturalism policies must be recognized. These include the characteristics of immigrants themselves and immigrant settlement policies. This is particularly important for the case of Canada because Canada's immigrant selection system, which is designed to pick those with the best chances for successful integration, is as well known as its multiculturalism policy. Furthermore, Canada makes important investments in direct immigrant-integration policies, which, as we have seen, are not an integral part of multiculturalism. To attribute all differences between Canada and other countries to multiculturalism is unwarranted.

The most obvious point of international comparisons is with the United States, since Canadian multiculturalism is frequently contrasted with the American melting pot, which in reality is merely laissez-faire. Simply stated, the US government has no policies related to recognition of or support for minority cultures.

Although it is common to observe that immigration is a far more divisive issue in the United States than in Canada, and that immigrants in the US are less integrated and have lower incomes, on average, than those in Canada, this is influenced by the fact that the many immigrants to the US from Mexico have, on average, quite low levels of education. Canada does not have a comparable immigration stream, largely due to its geographic isolation from relatively poor countries such as Mexico. When "fair" comparisons are made between Canada and the US – i.e., focusing on similar groups of immigrants, such as highly educated immigrants from China, India, or the Caribbean – any differences that result from Canadian multiculturalism are quite small. My own study of this question, co-authored with Raymond Breton, concluded that

> comparison of the Canadian mosaic and the American melting pot reveals that the differences between them are not overwhelming.... The differences appear to be limited to specific aspects of relations among ethnic groups in the two countries, and these differences do not add up to major differences between them in the overall pattern of relations. Furthermore, where there are differences, they are much more likely to characterize the attitudes of the majority group toward minorities rather than either their behaviour or the experiences of the minorities themselves.[19]

Rates of economic and social integration for comparable immigrants are virtually identical in the two countries. Nearly all other indicators of immigrant integration, including residential patterns, social equality, economic opportunity, and mobility, show no consistent or pronounced differences between the two countries.

Consider the question of economic opportunity. Comparisons of economic success for Canada's immigrants with similar populations in the United States show little or no difference. Apart from the Mexicans, the US has many immigrants from sources similar to those most prominent in Canada – namely, Chinese, South Asian, Southeast Asian, and Afro-Caribbean. Immigrants from these areas, and taking account of education and other personal human-capital attributes, show no consistent differences between the two countries.[20]

The lack of Canadian-US differences in economic outcomes specifically for the case of Black immigrants has attracted some attention from US researchers. Attewell, Kasinitz, and Dunn compare the earnings of Blacks in Canada and the United States, based on 2001 Canadian census data and a pooled sample from the US Census Bureau's Annual Social and Economic Survey for the years 2001–2006. They find that Blacks generally have lower incomes in the US than in Canada but that this difference disappears when the focus is on Black immigrants specifically: "Canada and the US are not so different in terms of the mechanisms generating racial income inequality."[21] It is worth quoting their conclusion at length.

Disaggregating by generation and by controlling for differences in education and region and number of earners in the household, the pattern of racial inequality in the US and Canada converges. For example, after controls, the black-white income gap for the third generation is very close in the US (18 percent) and in Canada (17 percent) and the black-white wage gaps are similar. So Canada and the US are not so different in terms of the mechanisms generating racial income inequality.[22]

They find this interesting given that the different historical and institutional contexts affecting race relations in the two countries might have been expected to produce more negative outcomes in the United States. They make no mention of a positive impact of multiculturalism in Canada.

As evidence of better economic outcomes for immigrants in Canada, Kymlicka points to the children of immigrants. He cites the 2006 study by the Organisation for Economic Co-operation and Development (OECD) of the educational performance of the children of immigrants and minorities across 17 OECD nations, based on tests of academic achievement, and notes that those in Canada "outperform" those in "any other Western democracy," even after the economic background of the immigrants is taken into account.[23] However, in the OECD findings, the country that is a close second in the rankings of the 17 countries is the United States, and third is Australia. In fact, the key finding is that the traditional countries of immigration – with or without multiculturalism policies – outperform European countries, which generally lack institutional experience in integrating immigrants.[24]

Furthermore, in its examination of policies to assist the children of immigrants, the OECD study emphasizes the importance of policies to ensure instruction in the mainstream languages. This implies efforts supporting the mainstream culture rather than minority cultures, pointing away from issues of multiculturalism. The OECD study nowhere mentions multiculturalism and expresses skepticism on some related issues, such as the importance of minority-language learning for general academic achievement.[25] Kymlicka creates a different impression when he states that "the massive OECD study that established Canada's comparative advantage in educating immigrant students emphasized that a crucial factor in this success was the presence of policies to address issues of cultural and linguistic diversity in the school population, policies that, in the Canadian context, have emerged under the rubric of multiculturalism."[26] However, these are policies of provincial governments that focus on support for mainstream-language learning. If they are stronger because of some link to the "rubric" of multiculturalism, I argue that it is rooted not in a philosophical commitment to support for minority cultures, but in the broad public support for efforts to assist immigrants, which is part of the social capital effects of multiculturalism to which I return later.

Shifting to the broader differences in overall educational, occupational, and income success for the children of immigrants in Canada, the United States, and Australia, specifically comparing Chinese, South Asians, and (for the US and Canada) Blacks shows very similar results.[27] Second-generation Asian success is common to all three countries. Immigrant offspring in all three countries experience "consistent upward inter-generational mobility,"[28] and, in fact, the rates of intergenerational mobility for the children of immigrants in the US are higher than in Canada or Australia. Any effects of multiculturalism in these patterns are so small as to be negligible.

Higher rates of inter-group marriage in Canada are sometimes cited as indicating greater inclusiveness, but recent studies reveal this difference to be more a result of demographics and opportunity than of preferences possibly arising from multiculturalism. Evidence of higher rates of citizenship acquisition for immigrants in Canada than the United States indicates that Canadian government funding of ethnic community organizations is important, as Irene Bloemraad shows in her excellent study.[29] However, her evidence suggests that government funding plays a role because of programs directed at encouraging citizenship acquisition and that while multiculturalism policies seem to provide the impetus for such funding in the case of Canada, there is nothing about multiculturalism's principle of support for ethnic cultures that is essential to such support for citizenship acquisition.[30] As mentioned above, this is an activity one might expect in any country that seeks immigrants and encourages their integration into the mainstream; it does not reflect an emphasis on minority cultural recognition or support.

Some useful research compares countries with and without multicultural policies, but the few existing studies show little effect either way. One of these shows that multiculturalism policies in 21 countries bear little relation to the strength of the welfare state.[31] While this undermines critics' claims of divisiveness, it does not support proponents' claims of enhanced cohesion; rather, it indicates that multiculturalism has little effect one way or the other.

Another way to ferret out the effects of multicultural recognition of and support for minority cultures might be to compare Quebec with the rest of Canada as Quebec policy does not embrace multiculturalism by name and is symbolically different. In Quebec, ambivalence toward multiculturalism has resulted in a provincial policy of *interculturalism*. More specifically, the re-emergence of national identity in Quebec during the 1960s raised issues of culture and language, eliminating traditional assimilationism as an option. When multiculturalism was chosen as a Canadian policy instead of biculturalism to accommodate immigrant groups, many Quebecers believed that their interests had been downgraded. While a debate has arisen about whether there is a significant difference between multiculturalism and interculturalism, Quebec policy prioritizes support for the French language and culture over the language and culture of any immigrant group. Even so, results from Statistics Canada's 2002 Ethnic Diversity Survey suggest that Quebec's use of a different word makes no practical difference to immigrant integration. Apparently, governments can support diversity without mentioning multiculturalism.

One could ask what might happen if multiculturalism actually had the effect of reinforcing minority cultures. How would processes of integration be affected? Research based on the Ethnic Diversity Survey indicates that residence in enclaves helps immigrants feel at home, but tends to isolate them. In other words, persistent diversity both promotes and slows the process of integration, depending on different aspects of that process.[32] The processes in particular religious communities, such as those of Muslims, Hindus, and Sikhs, are little different and are mainly related to visible-minority status rather than religious beliefs.[33] In fact, among visible minorities, the religious groups with the lowest levels of successful integration are the Protestants (many of whom are Black).

Overall, the evidence points to the conclusion that any direct impact of the Canadian policy to recognize and support minority cultures through a policy of multiculturalism on the integration of immigrants in Canada is quite small, possibly diverse, and most likely negligible. This is an important conclusion for both sides in the debate over multicultural-ism's recognition of and support for minority cultures. Both positions are refuted by the evidence. The effects, whether positive or negative, are simply very small. However, this does not mean that the multicultural policy is a failure – far from it. Politically, multiculturalism is successful in Canada; it enjoys widespread support and has emerged as a feature of the national identity. The next section explores the effects of this popular multiculturalism.

POPULAR MULTICULTURALISM AS SOCIAL CAPITAL SUPPORTING IMMIGRATION

Simply stated, multiculturalism is popular in Canada. In the public debate, the pro side won long ago. Most Canadians think that multiculturalism is a good idea. The policy received all-party approval from the moment it was introduced, and successive opinion polls have shown that it is backed by solid majorities. Many see it as part of the national identity. Pollster Michael Adams[34] asked Canadians in 1985 what made them most proud about Canada and found multiculturalism on the list at tenth. When he asked again in 2006, it had climbed to second place. In November 2010, the Environics Institute's Focus Canada survey asked respondents, "How important is the following for the Canadian identity?" One of the 13 items included was multiculturalism. Fully 86 percent of respondents thought that multiculturalism was either very important or at least somewhat important to the national identity. Compared to other important national symbols, multiculturalism was behind national parks, health care, the flag, and the *Canadian Charter of Rights and Freedoms*, all rated as very or somewhat important by over 90 percent; at about the same level as the national anthem, Canadian literature and music, and the Royal Canadian Mounted Police, between 80 and 89 percent; but ahead of hockey and bilingualism, the national capital, the Canadian Broadcasting Corporation, and the Queen, which were rated as very or somewhat important by less than 80 percent.[35] Multiculturalism seems well established as a distinctive feature representing the country.

What do most Canadians mean by *multiculturalism*? And what behaviour follows from support for that concept, however defined?

It seems likely that the meaning of multiculturalism has evolved significantly over time. As mentioned above, its initial significance was in the context of policy to accommodate Canada's English-French linguistic duality. The enduring presence of two national groups, neither of which could expect to assimilate the other, required the acceptance and institutionalization of diversity in Canadian society to prevent its dissolution. After that time, as Breton suggests, multiculturalism had a singular place in the entire process of nation-building for Canada following World War II.[36] The declining position of Britain and the rise of the United States created a shifting political environment for Canada, and new symbols of national identity were a response. As the policy developed, Canadian multiculturalism became viewed by many as a proud point of distinction from the neighbouring Americans and their melting pot policy. Reflecting on public opinion, Canadian pollster Michael Adams describes multiculturalism as "a national aspiration at the very core of Canadian idealism."[37] Using the US as the point of reference, he asserts, "It's the Canadian Dream."[38]

Interestingly, popular multiculturalism in Canada does not reflect an unusually strong sentiment favouring recognition of and support for minority cultures, the most distinctive tenet of multicultural policies. In fact, public opinion data show that it would be a mistake to assume that support for multiculturalism translates into any particular set of ideas about minority cultural recognition. Despite support for multiculturalism, for most Canadians, the priority is for immigrants to integrate fully into the mainstream of society. They are concerned that too many immigrants are not adopting Canadian values, and they worry about the implications.

In the 2010 Focus Canada survey,[39] respondents were asked whether they agreed that "Ethnic groups should try as much as possible to blend into Canadian society and not form a separate community." Nationally, an overwhelming 80.0 percent agreed, with 51.3 percent agreeing "strongly." The percentage was even higher in Quebec, at 90.4 percent, but it was also strong in the rest of Canada, at 76.6 percent. In addition, a clear majority of Canadians – 68.4 percent – agreed that "there are too many immigrants coming into this country who are not adopting Canadian values," with 40.3 percent saying they "strongly" agreed.

In recent years, the social and cultural integration of Muslim immigrants have been a focus of concern. Accordingly, the Focus Canada survey asked, "Do you think most Muslims coming to our country today want to adopt Canadian customs and way of life or do you think they want to be distinct from the larger Canadian society?" A majority, 55.3 percent, thought that Muslims "want to be distinct," while only 27.9 percent thought they want to adopt Canadian customs (3.3 percent thought they want to do both; 13.4 percent did not express an opinion). Another question asked about a potential ban on the wearing of head scarves in public places, including schools; respondents were about equally divided on whether such a ban was a good or bad idea: a slightly greater proportion thought it was a good idea, 47.6 percent, compared to 43.9 percent who thought the opposite.[40]

Generally, concern about the cultural integration of immigrants does not vary markedly by region. However, controversies regarding Muslims are particularly notable in Quebec, and this is reflected in the Focus Canada results. In Quebec, 60.4 percent thought that Muslims want to be distinct from the larger Canadian society, compared to 53.7 percent who thought this way in the rest of Canada. And in Quebec, 66.0 percent thought that banning head scarves worn by Muslim women in public places was a good idea, compared to 41.5 percent in the rest of Canada.

In public opinion, support for cultural retention among Canadians is not necessarily greater than in the United States, an indication that support for minority cultures is not a distinctive feature of popular multiculturalism in Canada. A survey conducted by Decima Research in 1989 showed that substantial majorities of both Canadians and Americans supported the idea of immigrant "blending" and that without multiculturalism, Americans supported immigrant cultural retention more often than Canadians.[41] Respondents were asked, "What do you think is better for Canada, for new immigrants to be encouraged to maintain their distinct culture and ways, or to change their distinct culture and ways to blend into the larger society?" Only 34 percent of Canadians favoured the maintenance of "distinct cultures and ways." Meanwhile, a parallel survey showed that the percentage of Americans favouring the maintenance of "distinct cultures and ways" was higher, at 47 percent, although still not a majority.

The Canadian emphasis on immigrant integration found by the Decima survey goes back at least to the 1970s, when the multicultural policy was introduced. For example, a national survey conducted in 1976,[42] when the majority of immigrants were of European background, showed that although most Canadians accepted the idea of minorities retaining their culture, the emphasis was on maintaining culture that did not affect mainstream society in a significant way.[43] From the 1970s to the present time, however, Canadians have definitely favoured the idea of immigrants becoming an integral part of mainstream society.

While the two viewpoints – support for multiculturalism and support for immigrant blending – are different, they are, of course, not necessarily contradictory. In principle, they may even be consistent since multiculturalism in Canada was always intended to accomplish the goal of integrating minorities into the mainstream. Nevertheless, the issue has caused confusion. A *National Post* article about a November 2010 Angus Reid poll[44] reported that more than half, 54 percent, thought Canada should be a melting pot rather than a mosaic. The article argued that the public had repudiated multiculturalism, even though the poll found that a majority, 55 percent, thought multiculturalism was good for Canada, while only 30 percent thought it was bad. The author suggests that Canadians are confused and "have no idea" what multiculturalism actually is.[45] In effect, Canadians do not see multiculturalism as favouring support for minority cultures.

In interpreting such poll results, care should be taken to consider the actual meaning of the questions. First of all, the questions do not provide respondents with a definition of either multiculturalism or terms such as melting pot, mosaic, blending, separate communities, and so on. Respondents are simply asked to select from the choices presented and are free to apply any meaning to any of them. Second, and more significant, when questions present respondents with a binary choice between opposites such as melting pot versus mosaic, or blending versus separate communities, supporters of multiculturalism may have difficulty because it is precisely this binary choice that multiculturalism is intended to overcome: it offers the potential for both integration and cultural maintenance. So faced with what might be viewed as a philosophically inappropriate request to choose between them, many come down on the side of blending. Such a response does not necessarily imply a demand for complete immigrant assimilation or a repudiation of multiculturalism (although for some it may mean this). Third, note that the desire for immigrant blending refers to the outcomes that people would like to see; support for multiculturalism influences the criteria people bring to the assessment of whether immigrant integration is working. The criteria may be less exacting for supporters of multiculturalism than for others. In sum, support for multiculturalism may be consistent with an emphasis on blending if the latter is understood to include a degree of minority-cultural maintenance. What is clear is that Canadians support *both* multiculturalism *and* immigrant integration into mainstream society.

What, then, does multiculturalism mean? In Canadian public opinion data, the link between support for multiculturalism and support for high levels of immigration is very strong. In addition, support for immigration is widely distributed across the country. Data from the 2010 Focus Canada survey show majority support in every major region, with somewhat higher support in Eastern Canada (62.5 percent), Quebec (61.8 percent), and the Prairies (62.8 percent) than in Ontario (53.5 percent), Alberta (54.4 percent), and British Columbia (57.4 percent). The data also show that a majority favours immigration in the major cities with very high immigration (Toronto, 60.3 percent; Montreal, 62.7 percent; Vancouver, 56.4 percent).[46]

Further, the data indicate that support for multiculturalism reinforces support for immigration. Those respondents who cite the importance of multiculturalism are significantly more likely to support immigration. Of those who think that multiculturalism is "very important" to the national identity (more than a majority, 56.4 percent), 67.7 percent support existing levels of immigration, compared to 49.6 percent among the smaller group who find it "somewhat important," and only 41.8 percent among the even smaller group (11.8 percent) who find it unimportant. The correlation analysis shows the positive relation between support for multiculturalism and support for immigration (r = 0.33).

In short, findings from public opinion and other survey research suggest that for most Canadians, support for multiculturalism is an expression of support for the idea of Canada as a country committed to immigration and its benefits. Those who endorse multiculturalism also tend to support high levels of immigration. They are likely to view multiculturalism as an expression of their welcoming approach toward immigrants, which they believe distinguishes them from their American neighbours. At the same time, most Canadians give priority to the integration of immigrants into mainstream society, and, in this respect, they do not differ substantially from Americans. In other words, popular multiculturalism is a pro-immigration ideology.

Further analysis helps clarify the relationship among support for multiculturalism, support for immigration, and attitudes to immigrant cultures. The results suggest that multiculturalism bolsters support for immigration by fostering a more open or flexible standard for assessing immigrant integration, leading to immigrants more often being seen as meeting that standard.[47] When all the immigrant-specific social items are considered, including both multiculturalism and the perceptions of immigrants, all have smaller coefficients representing unique effects. This indicates that their impacts are interrelated. Multiculturalism appears to moderate the impact of the desire for blending and to alleviate concerns about whether it is occurring.

Support for multiculturalism is also related to attitudes toward the United States and, in this way, is linked to questions of Canadian national identity. Regarding multiculturalism, Canadian discourse makes frequent reference to a presumed contrast between the Canadian cultural mosaic and the American melting pot, and Canadian pride in multiculturalism may be reinforced by its role in defining Canadian identity vis-à-vis the

American. Could national pride play a role in support for multiculturalism, thereby reinforcing a pro-immigration point of view? This appears
to be the case since supporters of multiculturalism are more likely to
express a general preference for the Canadian lifestyle over the American.

Multiculturalists more often prefer the Canadian quality of life. Of
those who state that multiculturalism is "very important" to the national identity, the proportion preferring Canadian to American life is
95.4 percent, whereas for those who think that multiculturalism is not at
all important, the figure drops to 83.1 percent.[48] Those who support gun
control and a ban on capital punishment also tend to prefer the Canadian
quality of life. These patterns have implications for immigration attitudes
since the survey results show a small but significant relationship between
pride in the Canadian quality of life and support for immigration.[49]

This analysis provides a number of insights into the relationship among
general social attitudes, multiculturalism, and support for immigration.
To some extent, social attitudes influence perceptions of immigration.
At the same time, some social items have significant effects on their
own. Those who believe that the crime rate is decreasing, those who
support same-sex marriage, and those who prefer Canadian lifestyles
over American ones are more likely to support immigration, regardless
of their immigration-specific beliefs. These effects are something of a
surprise. It may be that these items reflect a general level of comfort with
social change and personal security, leading to an easier acceptance of
immigration and its impact on Canadian society.

Overall, popular multiculturalism in Canada is strongly associated
with welcoming immigrants as part of the Canadian identity and is
included in what it means to be Canadian. Whether this affects actual
behaviour toward immigrants in the community is an interesting (albeit
unanswered) question, but the evidence suggests that it definitely supports immigration policy.[50] Perhaps surprisingly, however, multiculturalism's official recognition of and support for minority cultures does not
appear to be salient in the popular version of multiculturalism.

UNDERSTANDING THE IMPACT OF MULTICULTURALISM
ON IMMIGRATION IN CANADA

The preceding review of social science evidence suggests that multiculturalism has significance for Canada's immigration program mainly
because of the role that popular multiculturalism plays in supporting
policies on immigration and immigrant integration.

While recognition of and support for minority cultures seem key to
the philosophical justification of multiculturalism, however, any directly
related policies appear to have little effect "on the ground," either positive or negative. Moreover, although Canada and the United States are
widely perceived to be different (multiculturalism versus the melting

pot), any differences between the two countries in the integration of similar groups of immigrants are quite small; they are probably the result of Canadian programs supporting language learning, citizenship acquisition, and other requirements for participation in the mainstream culture, not to programs recognizing and supporting minority cultures. This is not surprising given the small size of the cultural-support aspect of the multiculturalism program, which represents only a few million dollars a year.

The most significant fact about immigration in Canada, compared to other countries, is the scale of national commitment to immigration, the extent of public support, and the success of immigrants in integrating into society.[51] Multiculturalism plays a part in this, but not mainly because of any unusual level of Canadian public commitment to the idea of recognizing and supporting minority cultures or the importance of this principle in helping immigrants to integrate. Rather, for most Canadians, celebrating multiculturalism as a national ideal reflects their enthusiasm for immigration and its cultural and economic benefits. It is in this way that Canada's multiculturalism plays a role in the national immigration experience and its comparative success.

It is important to underscore that while popular multiculturalism reinforces support for immigration as a national project, evidence indicates that it does not materially influence barriers to the social and economic integration of immigrant minorities in the community. Although support for immigration is comparatively high in Canada, this reflects not only openness to diversity but also a strong belief in the economic benefits of immigration. The evidence reviewed here suggests that the prevalence of discrimination in employment against Blacks and other visible minorities, for example, occurs in Canada to roughly the same extent as it does in other countries, such as the United States, that have no multicultural policies, but perhaps different traditions supporting diversity.

If the impact of popular multiculturalism is primarily as social capital supporting immigration policy, then it would be useful to know more about the underlying processes. Obviously, this support is helpful to policy-makers. For one thing, the impact on public support for immigration provides a strong incentive to maintain the multicultural themes in popular discourse. For another, if resources are required to address certain problems of immigration, support for multiculturalism may make such resource allocations less controversial.

At the same time, support for multiculturalism may shield immigration policy from necessary criticism. What is "necessary" is a political judgment, but consider the question of immigration levels. It was once a basic feature of immigration policy in Canada to adjust immigration levels in response to labour market demand, an idea affecting thinking about such levels in most countries. However, in recent years, Canadians have not routinely made labour-market adjustments. Beginning with the recession of the early 1990s, immigration levels have been kept at a constant level, even when unemployment rates are high. Some may be reluctant to suggest reducing those levels if maintaining high immigration is seen as a national duty. Or it may be that higher levels of immigration should be considered, but are rejected based on the belief that once established, such increases may be difficult to reverse. The point is that the multiculturalism basis for immigration policy may render some aspects of the policy difficult to review in public debate if they are perceived to carry implications for national identity.

The role of multiculturalism as social capital in support of immigration may be difficult to transfer to other countries, and, in any case, the key Canadian contribution is support for large-scale skilled immigration. Questions about the transferability of multiculturalism to other countries are often based on the principle of the recognition of minority groups and their cultures. However, this aspect has had little actual impact in the Canadian case. Other countries seeking to find best practices in the development of immigrant integration strategies might as well look to language training, support for citizenship, and other settlement policies pursued in Canada and other countries. Furthermore, if the role of popular multiculturalism in Canada reflects unique features of Canadian history – the French-English divide and the relationship of Canada to the United States – the establishment of multiculturalism in other countries seems unlikely. In the end, Canada's experience with immigration may have meaning only for those willing to undertake a program of carefully planned mass immigration as a strategy of national development as this is a distinguishing feature of Canadian policy and the basis for Canada's success.

NOTES

[1] This chapter draws from my two previous papers, "Getting Past 'Yes' or 'No': Our Debate over Multiculturalism Needs More Nuance," *Literary Review of Canada* (July/August 2010); and "Pro-immigration Canada: Social and Economic Roots of Popular Views," *IRPP Study* No. 20 (Montreal: Institute for Research on Public Policy, October 2011).

[2] Will Kymlicka, *Multicultural Citizenship: A Liberal Theory of Minority Rights* (Oxford: Oxford University Press, 1995).

[3] Neil Bissoondath, *Selling Illusions: The Cult of Multiculturalism in Canada*, rev. ed. (Toronto: Penguin, 2002); Robert Putnam, "E Pluribus Unum: Diversity and Community in the Twenty-First Century – The 2006 Johan Skytte Prize Lecture," *Scandinavian Political Studies* 30, no. 2 (2007):137–174.

[4] *Globe and Mail*, "'Distorted' Multiculturalism to Blame for Rise in Sikh Extremism, Dosanjh Says," 21 April 2010.

[5] Will Kymlicka, *Finding Our Way: Rethinking Ethnocultural Relations in Canada* (Toronto: Oxford University Press, 1998), 22.

[6] Nathan Glazer, *We Are All Multiculturalists Now* (Cambridge, MA: Harvard University Press, 1997).

[7] See Brian Barry, *Culture and Equality: An Egalitarian Critique of Multiculturalism* (Cambridge, MA: Harvard University Press, 2001); Samuel Huntington, *Who We Are: Challenges to America's National Identity* (New York: Simon and Schuster, 2004); Amartya Sen, "Two Confusions, and Counting," *Globe and Mail*, 6 August 2006; Amartya Sen, "The Uses and Abuses of Multiculturalism: Chile and Liberty," *New Republic*, 27 February 2006; and Arthur Schlesinger, *The Disuniting of America: Reflections on a Multicultural Society* (New York: W.W. Norton, 1992).

[8] Bagehot, "In Praise of Multiculturalism: Almost Everyone Now Agrees That It Has Failed – Has It Really?" *Economist*, 14 June 2007.

[9] Frances Fukuyama, "Identity and Migration," *Prospect* (25 February 2007).

[10] Canada, Parliament, House of Commons, *Debates*, 28th Parliament, 3rd Session, 1970–1972, vol. 8 (Ottawa: Queen's Printer, October 1971), 8545–8546.

[11] See Ronald Manzer, *Public Policies and Political Development in Canada* (Toronto: University of Toronto Press, 1985).

[12] Section 27 states, "This Charter shall be interpreted in a manner consistent with the preservation and enhancement of the multicultural heritage of Canadians." See *Canadian Charter of Rights and Freedoms*, Part I of the *Constitution Act, 1982*, at http://laws.justice.gc.ca/eng/Const/Const_index.html, accessed 13 January 2014.

[13] Kymlicka, *Finding Our Way*, 42.

[14] Ibid., 8.

[15] Ibid., 22.

[16] Will Kymlicka, *Multicultural Odysseys: Navigating the New International Politics of Diversity* (New York: Oxford University Press, 2007), 165.

[17] Will Kymlicka, "Multiculturalism in Normative Theory and in Social Science," *Ethnicities* 11, no. 1 (2011):8.

[18] Ibid.

[19] See Jeffrey G. Reitz and Raymond Breton, *The Illusion of Difference: Realities of Ethnicity in Canada and the United States* (Toronto: C.D. Howe Institute, 1994), 125.

[20] Reitz and Breton review earnings analyses for these immigrant groups and replicate them in a direct comparison of immigrant earnings in 1980–1981 census data for Black and Chinese immigrants in the two countries; see ibid., 101–124.

[21] Paul Attewell, Philip Kasinitz, and Kathleen Dunn, "Black Canadians and Black Americans: Racial Income Inequality in Comparative Perspective," *Ethnic and Racial Studies* 33, no. 3 (2010):15.

[22] Ibid., 14–15.

[23] See Will Kymlicka, "Testing the Liberal Multiculturalist Hypothesis: Normative Theories and Social Science Evidence," *Canadian Journal of Political Science* 43, no. 2 (2010):257–271.

[24] Organisation for Economic Co-operation and Development, *Where Immigrant Students Succeed: A Comparative Review of Performance and Engagement in PISA 2003* (Paris: OECD, 2006), 67; also 200–201, Table 3.5.

[25] Ibid., 145–146.

[26] Kymlicka, "Testing the Liberal Multiculturalist Hypothesis," 262.

[27] See Jeffrey G. Reitz, Heather Zhang, and Naoko Shiva Hawkins, "Comparisons of the Success of Racial Minority Immigrant Offspring in the United States, Canada and Australia," *Social Science Research* 40 (2011):1051–1066.

[28] Ibid., 1064.

[29] See Irene Bloemraad, *Becoming a Citizen: Incorporating Immigrants and Refugees in the United States and Canada* (Berkeley: University of California Press, 2007).

[30] Summarizing her findings, Bloemraad states that "the [ethnic] community's ability and interest in promoting political integration [i.e., citizenship] relies heavily on symbolic and material support of government as provided by policies such as multiculturalism and newcomer settlement"; see ibid., 232, also 171ff for the presentation of the findings themselves.

[31] See Keith Banting, Will Kymlicka, Richard Johnston, and Stuart Soroka, "Do Multiculturalism Policies Erode the Welfare State? An Empirical Analysis," in *Multiculturalism and the Welfare State: Recognition and Redistribution in Advanced Democracies*, ed. Keith Banting and Will Kymlicka (Oxford: Oxford University Press, 2006), 49–91.

[32] Jeffrey G. Reitz, "Assessing Multiculturalism as a Behavioural Theory," in *Multiculturalism and Social Cohesion: Potentials and Challenges of Diversity*, ed. Jeffrey G. Reitz, Raymond Breton, Karen Kisiel Dion, and Kenneth L. Dion (New York: Springer, 2009), 1–45.

[33] Jeffrey G. Reitz, Rupa Banerjee, Mai Phan, and Jordan Thompson, "Race, Religion, and the Social Integration of New Immigrant Minorities in Canada," *International Migration Review* 43, no. 4 (Winter 2009):695–726.

[34] See Michael Adams, *Unlikely Utopia: The Surprising Triumph of Canadian Pluralism* (Toronto: Viking Canada, 2007).

[35] See the analysis of the Focus Canada survey in Jeffrey G. Reitz, "Pro-immigration Canada: Social and Economic Roots of Popular Views," *IRPP Study* No. 20 (Montreal: Institute for Research on Public Policy, October 2011).

[36] Raymond Breton, "Multiculturalism and Canadian Nation-Building," in *The Politics of Gender, Ethnicity and Language in Canada*, ed. Alan C. Cairns and Cynthia Williams (Toronto: University of Toronto Press, 1986), 27–66.

[37] Adams, *Unlikely Utopia*, 41.

[38] Ibid.

[39] See Reitz, "Pro-immigration Canada," 15.

[40] Ibid, 15–16.

[41] See Reitz and Breton, *Illusion of Difference*, 27–28.

[42] John W. Berry, Rudolf Kalin, and Donald M. Taylor, *Multiculturalism and Ethnic Attitudes in Canada* (Ottawa: Supply and Services Canada, 1977).

[43] See the summary and discussion by Jeffrey G. Reitz, "Immigrants, Their Descendants and the Cohesion of Canada," in *Cultural Boundaries and the Cohesion of Canada*, ed. Raymond Breton, Jeffrey G. Reitz, and Victor Valentine (Montreal: Institute for Research on Public Policy, 1980), 383–384.

[44] Angus Reid Global, "Canadians Endorse Multiculturalism, but Pick Melting Pot over Mosaic," poll released 8 November 2010, at http://www.angusreidglobal.com/polls/43492/canadians-endorse-multiculturalism-but-pick-melting-pot-over-mosaic/, accessed 13 January 2014.

[45] *National Post*, "Multiculturalism Gets a Swift Kick," 13 November 2010.

[46] See Reitz, "Pro-immigration Canada," 11.

[47] See ibid, 17.

[48] Reitz, "Pro-immigration Canada," 18.

[49] Ibid.

[50] Data from public opinion surveys show that immigration is seen as an important economic strategy as well. In fact, multiculturalism and belief in the economic benefits of immigration are the twin pillars of popular support for immigration; see Reitz, "Pro-immigration Canada."

[51] German Marshall Fund of the United States, "Transatlantic Trends: Immigration" ([Washington, DC?]: German Marshall Fund of the United States, 2010), at http://www.gmfus.org/wp-content/blogs.dir/1/files_mf//galleries/ct_publication_attachments/TTImmigration_2010_final.pdf, accessed 30 June 2012.

(NEVER) COMING OUT TO BE MET? LIBERAL MULTICULTURALISM AND ITS RADICAL OTHERS

Richard J.F. Day

INTRODUCTION

In the name of intellectual honesty, I feel compelled to admit that I have very little that is new to add to the debates on liberal multiculturalism. My work over the past ten years, in both theory and practice, has tended more toward the exploration of alternatives to this, and other, discourses of the dominant order than it has toward trying to change them. This situation has come about mostly because of my own shifting interests and ethico-political commitments, but has also been encouraged by the multiculturalists themselves, who have done an excellent job of avoiding anything I have ever had to say about the topic. Of course, I am hardly the only person to suffer this fate, and it is not in the name of my own wounded sensibilities that I draw attention to it. Rather, it seems that the proponents of liberal multiculturalism have been remarkably adept at ignoring almost *everyone* who challenges their paradigm from outside its own carefully circumscribed space of enunciation.

I have had enough life experience to understand that people who live in different worlds find it extremely difficult to speak to one another, to actually have a conversation. This is the case in everything from bad marriages, to radical subcultures, to suburban cul-de-sacs, and it is no less true among academic intellectuals – even when they happen to work in the same building. Because of the banality of incommensurability, I have to admit that if philosophy were all that was at stake here, I would simply let sleeping state theorists, and their theories, lie.

The reason, perhaps, that I am willing to have one more tilt at this wind-powered turbine of a discourse is that despite its pretensions to unbiased universality, liberal multiculturalism is, as Charles Taylor has famously and ominously intoned, a "fighting creed."[1] And not only that, it is a relatively triumphant creed, one that has won many more battles than, say, anti-racisms, non-liberal feminisms, indigenisms, marxisms, anarchisms – to name just a few of the spectres that continue to haunt the so-called politics of recognition. As a key component of the state-capitalist system, liberal multiculturalism can afford to ignore its enemies, in a way that its enemies cannot afford to ignore it. Thus, on this point – and probably no other – I would have to (slyly and ironically) agree with Will Kymlicka:[2] those who speak of the demise of multiculturalism are greatly underestimating the importance of this discourse to the maintenance of the dominant global order. If multiculturalism, or something very much like it, did not exist, the system of states and corporations would very quickly be forced to invent it.

Thus, in one sense, liberal multiculturalism is working very well. As a way of limiting dissent, marketing identity-based commodities and services, perpetuating the power of established racial-national hierarchies, and preserving the current distribution of geographical territories to particular nations and states, it has no equal, or perhaps no competitors at all. Yes, there are still bothersome "ethnic nationalisms" and "separatisms," but anyone with a view to history can see that such events are intrinsic to the system of nation-states itself. This is an evolving, necessarily antagonistic field, one in which there is endless struggle over the allocation of identities to territories and the articulation of territorial identities with other political, economic, cultural, and social systems.

Within the tradition of liberal-statist capitalism, multiculturalism has been successful primarily because of its ability to extend the fantasy of state identification beyond the limits set for it by the likes of Hegel and Herder – that is, beyond the margins of a particular *Volk*. By showing how it is possible to articulate several national identifications with a single state apparatus linked to a global capitalist system, multiculturalism has arguably allowed this system to de-simulate in a more ordered and less brutal way than might otherwise have been the case. It would seem as though Hegel was right: most people, most of the time, really *do* want to be part of a relatively homogeneous culture that defends and advances itself with the help of all of the powers available to the (post-)modern state form. If this is so, then the world may one day contain one state or pseudo-state apparatus per territory per articulable identity – a limit that, of course, given the infinite vicissitudes of identification, can be approached only asymptotically – but a limit nonetheless, in the mathematical sense, and one toward which liberal multiculturalism is helping the system to tend.

Where multiculturalism has failed, however – and once again I feel compelled to invoke Hegel – is in its mandate of contributing to the main-tenance of a free and open public sphere that takes in all comers. While it may be favourably inclined toward institutions such as the working-class-affordable World Café at Toronto's Harbourfront Centre, liberal multiculturalism continues to exclude far too many people, in far too many ways, from its conversations. I am speaking here, of course, of those who seek to push this ideology beyond its comfort zone as "liberal phil-osophy and policy," to consider its roots in, and ongoing linkages with, colonialism, racism, nationalism, statism, heteronormativity, patriarchy, and of course neo-liberal capitalism. In his book *Multicultural Nationalism*, Gerald Kernerman notes that there exists not only a "Canadian school" of liberal multiculturalism, composed of theorists like Taylor, Kymlicka, Carrens, Chambers, Ignatieff, and Webber, but also a large body of work that attempts to enter into debates with the liberals.[3]

The outcome of these many decades of critical work is dismal if measured solely in terms of the difference it has made to the theory and policy of multiculturalism. In the essay cited above on the "rise and fall" of multiculturalism, Kymlicka discusses the various points of view from which one might address and assess the downward trajectory of Canadian-style multiculturalism, from "the populist right" to "the social-democratic left."[4] He then goes on to acknowledge, perhaps for the first time in public, that "there are also political perspectives on multicultural-ism beyond the populist right and the social-democratic left" and even begins to engage with some of these perspectives.

> For example, the radical left has traditionally viewed multiculturalism as a state-led reformist project that seeks to contain the transformative potential of subaltern political movements and thereby forecloses the possibility of a more radical critique of the capitalist nation-state (Day 2000; Žižek 1997).[5]

This was the start of a response that many people had been waiting for. But it was not destined to amount to much. Kymlicka continues,

> The French republican tradition, in both its right and left strands, has also generally opposed multiculturalism as an obstacle to its vision of equality and emancipation. However, since the radical left and the republicans were never in favour of multiculturalism their opposition does not explain the rise and fall narrative. This narrative presupposes that former supporters of multiculturalism have now lost faith in it, and I believe that it is predomin-antly amongst the social democrats that one can see this sort of rise and fall.[6]

Having deftly put aside the critiques of two male, Euro-identified theorists in the present because they have never agreed with him in the past, Kymlicka feels justified to, once again, move on to make his usual argument. If Kymlicka had dealt with the Euro-identified "radical left" in previous articles, if he had responded to indigenists and anti-racist feminists in other articles – that is, when not discussing the "rise and fall narrative" – this move would be less disingenuous. But, as we will see, there is simply *no time* that is right for Kymlicka – and most other liberal-multiculturalist theorists – to engage with their radical critics.

The problem this poses for liberal multiculturalism, on its own ground, is that as long as it ignores so many people who want to join the conversation over which it presides, its drive for universality cannot be achieved by consensual means – it can be sustained only through relations of force. While some individuals obviously do choose to become a citizen of a particular nation-state – e.g., through elite immigration schemes – most of us find ourselves subject to these formations by accidents of birth, by acts of conquest, or because we are fleeing war, oppression, economic inequality, genocide, etc. And once we find ourselves within a territory claimed by a particular state, we cannot resist our inclusion in the hegemonic national formation without becoming "terrorists," "traitors," or "separatists," particularly under today's increasingly (in)security-conscious regimes. Multiculturalism, then, necessarily enacts itself as liberal, statist, capitalist colonialism. And each article, each book, each talk, each PhD thesis that ignores this fact simply reinforces it.

In this chapter, then, I am going to sift through some of the critiques of liberal multiculturalism that have come from Outside over the past 40 years, with the aim of synthesizing, categorizing, and generally rendering them into a form that (I hope) should be comprehensible to liberal philosophers. That is, I am going to *immanentize* the radical critiques of liberal multiculturalism so that it will be as difficult as possible, for anyone guided by intellectual honesty and theoretical rigour, to ignore them. No Deleuze or Guattari theory cards will be required to play this game; nor does one need to purchase a copy of *A Merely Semi-Lethal Introduction to the Thought of Jacques Lacan* to gain entry to the room in which it is played. Liberals will be given good, old-fashioned, *liberal* reasons to pay attention to those who oppose them.

Although there are many ways in which one might proceed with the task at hand, I am going to deploy the central paradigm used by multiculturalist theory. That is, I will base my discussion on the ascription of particular rights to particular identities – "national minorities" and "immigrants" – based on what liberals see as being the valid claims that each of them might make against a state apparatus. I will then run this up against the positions actually being taken by some of the people who would be included in these groups, from the liberal-multiculturalist perspective, but see themselves differently, and have quite different expectations, than the view that state theory provides. I will also address the expectations that multiculturalism has for the identification that is currently hegemonic within a given space – what I like to call the "State

People" – whose positions are also more differentiated and complex than liberal theory lets on.

Along the way, I will attempt to prove, using a relatively social scientific method, my claim that liberal multiculturalism tends to ignore those Others who are, one might say, a little more differentiated than is comfortable for the theory of differential citizenship. The chapter will end with a discussion of some of the intellectual and political effects of this liberal fear of, and subsequent indifference toward, those who might be called its Real Others. Because of my own limits and interests, and in humble acknowledgement of their global relevance, I will focus on the Canadian case and will place a particular emphasis on the work of Will Kymlicka. Let us turn, then, to a short exposition of Kymlicka's liberal-multiculturalist theory of differentiated citizenship.

WHO GETS WHAT IN (KYMLICKA'S) (CANADIAN) LIBERAL MULTICULTURALISM?

In this section, I have no intention of running through the many debates that liberals have amongst themselves with regard to the (for them) very vexing question of the kinds of gifts that the state should give to various groups based on their "ethnocultural identity." I feel that I have done my bit in this regard, most substantially in my book *Multiculturalism and the History of Canadian Diversity*. This is where I would direct those who desire more background work on, and more detailed textual exegesis of, multiculturalist theory and practice than is on display here.

The ideas of crafty high theorists, I find, often come across most clearly in interviews and popular texts. With this in mind, I am going to rely on the introduction to Kymlicka's *Finding Our Way*[7] as a "way" into his – and the Canadian state's[8] – basic ideas about "differentiated citizenship."

The identifications that matter, for this text and for liberal multiculturalism in general, are pretty straightforward. First of all, there are the "national minorities," which, in the Canadian case, are the Québécois and Aboriginal people.[9] In Kymlicka's view, each of these identity groups deserves some form of "self government," as "founding partners" within a "multination state."[10] (I will have much more to say on this formulation later. For now, since I am trying to produce an immanent reading, I am simply letting it stand.) There are also the "immigrant groups," which Kymlicka finds difficult to differentiate from the "ethnic groups," and therefore elects to use the terms interchangeably.[11] These types are to be handled differently from the national minorities.

Historically, immigrant/ethnic groups have sought and achieved social and political integration in Canada – not self-government – although they have also wanted some accommodation of their ethnocultural distinctiveness.[12]

So, then, we have self-government within the Canadian state for national minorities and integration within the Canadian state for immigrant/ ethnic groups. But what of the "non-Aboriginal, non-Québécois majority,"[13] who are, one might assume, much more stalwartly identified with the Canadian state? They, apparently – and problematically – are not as up to date on liberal-multiculturalist theory and practice as they could be.

> If there is no way to paper over these differences [between the non-Aboriginal, non-Québécois majority and the Others], the only way to keep Canada together may be to persuade English-speaking Canadians to accept a multination model of federalism.[14]

Just as the non-Anglo minorities need to be taught how to be properly Anglo – that is, statist, capitalist, and colonial – the Anglos themselves also have some lessons to learn. They must become more "tolerant" and flexible – that is, they must give up some of their privilege as the State People. But there are, of course, "limits of tolerance"[15] that must also be respected. It is here, I would suggest, that liberal multiculturalism most clearly reveals itself, despite its willingness to give gifts, as a fighting creed. Some Others are simply too different to be tolerated. I will now move on to a discussion of who some of these Others are and what they have to say – for themselves.

CRITICS COMING OUT TO BE MET: LIBERAL MULTICULTURALISM AND THE "IMMIGRANT/ETHNIC GROUPS"

The system just described is, in a condensed form, what I have called the fundamental fantasy of liberal multiculturalism. As I have shown in *Multiculturalism and the History of Canadian Diversity*, radical rejection of this fantasy in fact predates its explication as theory. Even before the signing into law of the *Canadian Multiculturalism Act* in 1988, an academic literature had already emerged that focused on an "ideology critique" of the discourse on Canadian diversity.

> In this approach, multiculturalism as an achieved social ideal is confronted with an analysis of unequal relations of power between various racial and ethnic groups and found to be a "false" representation. The classic text here is *The Vertical Mosaic*, in which John Porter began to take apart Canadian multiculturalism before it had even been put together: "Segregation in social structure, to which the concept of the mosaic or multiculturalism must ultimately lead, can become an important aspect of social control by the charter group" (Porter 1965: 73–4). Karl Peter, writing after the official adoption of multiculturalism in a bilingual framework, called multiculturalism a "myth … based on high-sounding liberal ideals, not on the empirical

reality of Canadian society" (Peter 1981: 65). Peter ended this piece with a call for a "true multiculturalism" which would be "put into the service of revitalizing and reconstructing a Canada for the twenty-first century – a Canada that is built by all for the benefit of all" (66). Kogila Moodley has very subtly and sharply attacked the "superficial nature" and "depoliticization" of Canadian multiculturalism policy (Moodley 1983: 324), which "trivializes, neutralizes and absorbs social and economic inequalities" (326). She also makes reference to a "true multiculturalism" which, in her case, "presupposes official multilingualism" (324). The "multiculturalism as ideology" debate [was] still going strong into the 1990s, with Laverne Lewycky trying to move beyond false consciousness and into a Mannheimian conception of ideology and utopia (Lewycky 1992).[16]

A closely related tradition is that of Canadian anti-racist feminism, which has been challenging hegemonic articulations of race, nation, state, gender, and capitalism since at least the time of Moodley's article. Himani Bannerji's essay "On the Dark Side of the Nation: Politics of Multiculturalism and the State of 'Canada'" is a classic in this field. In this piece, Bannerji argues that multicultural ethnicities are "officially constructed identities"[17] arising out of individual and group acceptance of a "machinery of state that has us impaled against its spikes."[18] Bannerji goes on to point out that

> on the one hand, by our sheer presence we [non-White peoples] provide a central part of the distinct pluralist unity of Canadian nationhood; on the other hand, this centrality is dependent on our "difference," which denotes the power of definition that "Canadians" have over "others." In the ideology of multicultural nationhood, however, this difference is read in a power-neutral manner rather than as organized through class, gender and race.[19]

Over the past 20 years, many other writers have made significant contributions to the field of intersectional critique of liberal multiculturalism, bringing out many ways in which this apparently "power-neutral" (i.e., universalistic) discourse in fact harbours Euro-colonial particularisms, hierarchies, and oppressions. Bakan and Stasiulis, in their *Negotiating Citizenship*,[20] succeed in removing the blinders from liberal theory and policy regarding "who gets in," what they are allowed to do when they get here, and how easily they can be put out again. They show that the current Canadian immigration system, despite being "points-based," still retains links between admissibility and country of origin, race, class, and gender. This means that not all immigrants – or even all "national minorities" – face the same conditions, a situation that has been well documented at least since the publication of John Porter's *The Vertical Mosaic* and that has been continuously updated since then in work carried out by researchers such as Peter Li; Tania Das Gupta; Frances Henry, Carol

Tator, and Tim Rees; and Grace-Edward Galabuzi.[21] The point here is that not all immigrants to Canada are treated in the same way, and therefore it is theoretically and politically suspect to allocate rights to them as if they faced the same conditions.

Also important for my purposes is that Bakan and Stasiulis highlight the fact that there are "ever increasing numbers of *non*-citizens who are working and residing in migrant receiving states."[22] The fact that economic and political refugees have not exactly "chosen" to leave their home and tried to find a new one has long vexed the multiculturalist idea that immigrants do not deserve the same rights as national minorities since multiculturalists tend to see immigrants as "having uprooted themselves" voluntarily.[23] The increasing numbers of migrant workers in Canada, whose precarity is built in by law, constitutes a further differentiation that liberal-multiculturalist theory is going to have a hard time justifying. There is an obvious concern that a system that is all about "citizenship rights" leaves non-citizens completely out of the picture. These hyper-marginalized subjects are intentionally exposed to the worst forms of state domination and capitalist exploitation – they are, one might say, differentiated right out of the system of rights.

That the Canadian immigration system is deeply structured by a racialized hierarchy is not some sort of aberration. As Sherene Razack's edited collection, *Race, Space, and the Law*, argues, Canada is a "White Settler society," a

> society established by Europeans on non-European soil. Its origins lie in the dispossession and near extermination of Indigenous populations by the conquering Europeans. As it evolves, a White settler society continues to be structured by a racial hierarchy.... A quintessential feature of White settler mythologies is ... the disavowal of conquest, genocide, slavery, and the exploitation of the labour of peoples of colour. In North America, it is still the case that European conquest and colonization are often denied, largely through the fantasy that North America was peacefully settled and not colonized.[24]

In the introduction to the collection, Razack shows this denial operating in the discourse of Michael Ignatieff, a prominent liberal-multicultural theorist and politician, as he refers to "centuries of collaboration between newcomers and aboriginal nations" and declares that "each has a fair claim to the land" and that "it must be shared."[25]

Ignatieff, of course, presents a relatively easy target. Other multicultural theorists are more subtle. They acknowledge the "fact of conquest," only to rapidly deny it so that it can be deployed as a tool of differentiation that preserves the Euro-colonial state. This move is evident, for example, in Kymlicka's *Finding Our Way*.

First comes the acknowledgement of conquest.

> They [Aboriginal peoples and French Canadians] formed complete and functioning societies, long settled on their own territories, with their own institutions operating in their own languages, prior to being incorporated into British North America.[26]

Followed by its partial erasure.

> Although this incorporation was involuntary, the result of colonization and conquest, efforts have been made to turn it into a more voluntary federation of peoples through the signing of treaties with Aboriginal peoples and the negotiation of Confederation with French Canadians.[27]

And then its transformation into an apparently consensual system, articulated with the Euro-Canadian state form.

> Aboriginal peoples and the Québécois are not simply demanding a general decentralization of power, to promote administrative efficiency or local democracy. Rather they are demanding recognition as distinct peoples and as founding partners in the Canadian state who have maintained the right to govern themselves and their land *in certain areas*.[28]

In these passages, we are witness to the discursive transformation of angry colonized peoples into happy denizens of the Canadian state. In order to achieve this effect, "Aboriginal peoples" and "Québécois/French Canadians" must be both *pasteurized* and *homogenized*. To achieve the first effect, Kymlicka assumes the position of the one who knows what the Other thinks, and wants, and ascribes to the Other a position that his theory can easily handle. To achieve the second effect, he assumes that *all* of the Others of a particular type want what he says they want. Obviously, it is absolutely crucial to the achievement and maintenance of this kind of "knowledge" that the Others are never allowed to speak for themselves. With these voices out of the conversation, it becomes relatively easy to eradicate Otherness at the very point that one appears to be "recognizing" it. Thus is the strong potion of Indigenous and Québécois resistance turned into safe, white milk that can be bought at the liberal-multiculturalist supermarket.

As Yasmin Jiwani has put it, citing Teun van Dijk, "denials of racism [and colonialism and all other modes of oppression] are the stock in trade of racist [and colonialist and all other modes of oppressive] discourse."[29] In *Discourses of Denial*, Jiwani shows how colonial, racist violence permeates everyday and every-night life for racialized girls and women in Canada. She seeks to draw attention to "the ways in which racialized differences are inferiorized and racialized people 'put in their place' through the discursive economy of violence that culminates in the denial, dismissal, trivialization, erasure, and exoticization of their lived realities."[30]

This, I would contend, is exactly what liberal-multiculturalist theory does when it carries out its processes of homogenization and pasteurization of the Other. People are firmly put in their place in a hierarchy controlled by the White liberal state and justified by White liberal state theorists. The Canadian Settler state, and its allies, cannot seem to hear, and therefore cannot understand, that for many people, colonialism is not a thing of the past. The White Folks didn't just "win" when they "conquered," so that now the Québécois and Indigenous peoples will be happy with whatever the Euro-colonial state thinks they deserve. And those who come after the White folks are not content to submit to White Anglo rule either since they cannot understand what was so special about those immigrants who happened to arrive at a particular time, from a particular place, that allowed them to become the State People. Not only is liberal multiculturalism a fighting creed; it is, right now, involved in a multi-front war.

"ABORIGINAL PEOPLE" VERSUS "INDIGENOUS PEOPLES"

Nowhere is the violent nature of the policies and theories of the Canadian state more evident than in relations between mainstream Settlers and Indigenous peoples. This is, of course, the opposite of the harmonious history of coexistence that is claimed to be the case by liberal multiculturalism. One might well wonder how – or whether – both claims could be true. I think they can, and not only because they are both simply truth claims rather than truths. Because of their nature as claims, they are discursive products, and because they emerge out of different discursive contexts, they are not subject to the rules of contradiction that govern other systems, such as those of mathematics or formal logic.

One sign of this incommensurability is that where liberal multiculturalists often talk about "Aboriginal people," I am using the term "Indigenous peoples." The plural, or its lack, here is very important since to view all of those who have been living on Turtle Island since the beginning of time as one "people" is to ignore vast differences among the many discrete, self-ascribed, and other-accepted nations that are being referenced. This ignorance, of course, is very important for liberal-multiculturalist discourse as it is necessary for the intellectual-political process of homogenization to be carried out effectively. As difficult as it is to appear to speak for one people with whom one is not identified at all, it would be even more difficult to appear to speak for many.

There is much more to this than homogenization, however, and it involves, not surprisingly, what I have called pasteurization. Although it is not my place or my intention to criticize any Indigenous person for the way in which he or she relates to Canadian colonialism, I think the distinction between aboriginality and indigeneity, as enunciated by Taiaiake Alfred and Jeff Corntassel, is extremely important if one wants to begin to understand Settler-Indigenous relations outside the frame of liberal theory and practice.

> In Canada today, many Indigenous people have embraced the Canadian government's label of "aboriginal", along with the concomitant and limited notion of postcolonial justice framed within the institutional construct of the state. In fact, this identity is purely a state construction that is instrumental to the state's attempt to gradually subsume Indigenous existences into its own constitutional system and body politic since Canadian independence from Great Britain – a process that started in the mid-twentieth century and culminated with the emergence of a Canadian constitution in 1982. Far from reflecting any true history or honest reconciliation with the past or present agreements and treaties that form an authentic basis for Indigenous–state relations in the Canadian context, "aboriginalism" is a legal, political and cultural discourse designed to serve an agenda of silent surrender to an inherently unjust relation at the root of the colonial state itself.[31]

Alfred and Corntassel contrast aboriginality with indigenousness, or indigeneity, defined as follows:

> Indigenousness is an identity constructed, shaped and lived in the politicized context of contemporary colonialism. The communities, clans, nations and tribes we call *Indigenous peoples* are just that: Indigenous to the lands they inhabit, in contrast to and in contention with the colonial societies and states that have spread out from Europe and other centres of empire. It is this oppositional, place-based existence, along with the consciousness of being in struggle against the dispossessing and demeaning fact of colonization by foreign peoples, that fundamentally distinguishes Indigenous peoples from other peoples of the world.[32]

Unlike aboriginalism, which, as multiculturalism hopes, is relatively on board with the liberal-state-capitalist game plan, indigenism is in contention with almost all aspects of the dominant order. As Alfred has put it elsewhere, indigenism shares a number of ideas and practices with anarchism in positing – and positively valuing – modes of social organization in which there is "no absolute authority, no coercive enforcement of decisions, no hierarchy, and no separate ruling entity."[33] Indigenism is thus inherently non-capitalist, non-statist, and against the attempted domination of nature. As such, there is no place in the liberal-multiculturalist framework for indigenists and, therefore, no place for those Indigenous individuals and communities who identify in this way.

THE EXALTED SUBJECTS OF ENGLISH AND FRENCH CANADA

So far, the discussion has dealt with those identities that are seen as most problematic within the ethnocultural-political hierarchies that structure the dominant order presided over by the Canadian state – i.e., those who are racialized as non-White. The importance of this racial divide to the preservation of the system might imply that those who signify as White have no problems at all. I have shown elsewhere that this is not the case, that in fact there is a clear hierarchy, even among those racialized as White, that runs from northwestern Europe to southeastern Europe.[34] For present purposes, however, and in keeping with the liberal-multiculturalist paradigm of differentiated citizenship rights as described above, I will focus on two identities: the French Canadian/Québécois and the non-Aboriginal, non-Québécois majority, also known as English Canadians.

This latter identity constitutes what Sunera Thobani has called the "exalted subject" of Canadian nationalism: the proper normative citizen, who is "universally deemed the legitimate heir to the rights and entitlements proffered by the state."[35] Thobani notes that this subject embodies the "quintessential characteristics of the nation," personifying "its values, ethics and civilizational mores,"[36] and thus does not have to "integrate" or in any other way validate its entitlement to the gifts of citizenship. However, even the exalted Anglo-Canadian can find himself tossed out of the mainstream by professing intellectual and political identifications that defy the quintessential characteristics of the proper citizen. Here I am thinking of political radicals of all stripes, figures such as Alex Hundert of the Toronto 19 or the many European and American radicals who have been recently denied entry to Canada based on nothing more than their usually non-violent political beliefs.[37] Again, English Canadians are not a homogeneous group, nor are we a pasteurized group. There is plenty of dissent out there, dissent that is not based on racism and nativism, but on solidarity with Indigenous people and people of colour and our own struggles against Canadian colonialism.

Next to the exalted subject of English Canada, in terms of the racialized hierarchy, come the "French Canadians." Again, terminology is important in a way that can tend to elude the liberal multiculturalists. Given the recent upsurge in the popularity of sovereigntist parties and politicians, it is not at all clear that everyone in Quebec sees themselves as some kind of Canadian. Like indigenists, those who identify as Québécois have not fallen into a post-colonial stupor – they remember the past and have their own plans for the future. They have come very close to voting their province out of the country and may well succeed in doing so at some point in the future. As with all of the other "groups" conjured up in the liberal-multiculturalist fantasy world, it is theoretically disingenuous and politically ridiculous to try to homogenize and pasteurize even the most *pure laine* of the citizens – and non-citizens – of the province/nation of

Quebec. This is so not only because of the well-known "differences" of language and culture but also because of the specificities of Québécois racism and colonialism. While they remember so much else, the Québécois, like the English Canadians, do have a tendency to forget certain aspects of their own history as colonizers and as a relatively successful State People who claim pride of place over other immigrants to the territories over which they claim control. There is far, far more "difference" at work here than a simple ascription of "national minority" status can account for.

AND, ONCE AGAIN, THE LIBERAL MULTICULTURALISTS

In the previous sections, I hope to have established that the differentiated citizenship categories deployed by liberal multiculturalism can be brought into existence only with the help of a homogenization and pasteurization of what are, from other points of view, complexly contested spaces of identification. I have also tried to show that there are many people, located in the interstices and on the margins of the liberal-multicultural system of categorization, who have advanced radical critiques of various aspects of this discourse. The task now is to provide some evidence to back up my claim that liberal multiculturalists have tended to ignore both these identities and their critiques. My inclination, as something of a social scientist, was to go about this empirically rather than philosophically. That is, I set out to look for "hard data" from the texts of liberal-multiculturalist theory that might support or disprove my hypothesis.

To this end, I examined the works of several key multiculturalist theorists for references to their more high-profile critics, beginning with Will Kymlicka's *Multicultural Citizenship*. Of course, none of us is prescient, so I adjusted my list to correspond to the state of critique at the time of writing. In 1995, there had been about a quarter-century of progressive (i.e., non-nativist and non-racist) literature critical of Canadian multiculturalism as state policy from writers such as Ken Adachi, Howard Adams, Himani Bannerji, Neil Bissoondath, Howard Cardinal, Evelyn Kallen, Kogila Moodley, Karl Peter, and Pierre Vallières,[38] to name just a few. Table 1 below summarizes the results of my search through Kymlicka's text, using primarily the bibliography and index, to see how many of these authors he had engaged with.

Of course, this list is somewhat subjective. It is in fact drawn from my PhD thesis, but for that very reason, I would argue, it gives an overview of writers who were important, in the late 1990s, to at least one of the "radicals" whom the liberal multiculturalists feel they can safely ignore.

As influential as Will Kymlicka's work has been, it is surely unfair to tar all liberal multiculturalists with the same brush. One can imagine that other prominent thinkers, such as Charles Taylor, would fare better in this kind of test. With that in mind, I did the same experiment on Taylor's extremely famous essay, "The Politics of Recognition."[39] Kant, Hegel, Rawls, Mead, Mill, and Rousseau all figure prominently in this

TABLE 1
Will Kymlicka's *Multicultural Citizenship*

Author	Present in Bibliography?	Number and Nature of References
Adachi	No	0
Adams	No	0
Bannerji	No	0
Bissoondath	No	0
Cardinal	No	0
Kallen	Yes, one article	Page 202, note 26; no discussion
Moodley	No	0
Peter	No	0
Vallières	No	0

Source: Author's compilation.

work, and even such a darling of postmodern literary criticism as Bakhtin is cited. But none of the critics of Canadian multiculturalism – on my list or not – or critics of any other brand of multiculturalism – make even a one-note appearance.

Kymlicka and Taylor have been influential, no doubt, but a skeptical reader might well question the inference that they can stand for the entire discourse of liberal multiculturalism. Surely one must also consider those who have written with, and around, these major figures. And, just as surely, one would expect the conversation to be wider. So I turned to a collection edited by Kymlicka, entitled *The Rights of Minority Cultures*.[40] This book contains chapters by Kymlicka and 17 others, including Bhikhu Parekh, whose work definitely skirts, if not outright exceeds, the limits of liberal political theory. In this text, then, there appears at least one person who is not entirely, and always, a safe interlocutor. The "Guide to Further Reading" mentions Boldt, Long, and Little Bear's *The Quest for Justice: Aboriginal Peoples and Aboriginal Rights*[41] as well as some of the early work of Jim Tully,[42] who, like Parekh, is not always on side and is indeed increasingly friendly with some of the more radical critics of the Canadian school. There is no centralized list of references for this book, but a scan of the apparently thorough index of names produced only a handful of references to the Evelyn Kallen piece already mentioned,[43] all from the same chapter. Otherwise, the landscape is characteristically flat.

Of course, these texts have been around for quite a while now, so, to be fair, I should take on some more recent works. Hence, I now turn to Will Kymlicka's *Multicultural Odysseys*[44] using an updated list of critics drawn from a previous section of this chapter. This book was easier to deal with using my methodology, since it is available in a full-text version – I can say with confidence that I have indeed done an exhaustive search.

TABLE 2
Will Kymlicka's *Multicultural Odysseys*

Author	Present in Bibliography?	Number and Nature of References
Abu-Laban, Yasmeen	No	1 – a misleading reference in the main text, on p. 104 (see below for discussion)
Alfred, Taiaiake		1 – a footnote citing Alfred's first book, published in 1995 (see below for discussion)
Bannerji, Himani	No	0
Coulthard, Glen	No	0
Day, Richard J.F.	No	0
Galabuzi, Grace-Edward	No	0
Jiwani, Yasmin	No	0
Mackey, Eva	No	0
Razack, Sherene	No	0
Smith, Andrea	No	0
Thobani, Sunera	No	0

Source: Author's compilation.

As is easily seen from Table 2 above, the most recent book on multiculturalism by Will Kymlicka continues to evade any substantive engagement – or any engagement at all – with the critical work that has been done by indigenists, anti-racist feminists, and those involved in settler-colonial studies. And when these critics *are* mentioned, it is in a politically – and theoretically – dubious way. The reference to the work of Yasmeen Abu-Laban is a good example. Kymlicka writes, "As Yasmeen Abu-Laban notes, Canada is widely seen around the world as a country where multiculturalism 'exists' (Abu-Laban 2002: 460) – where multiculturalism is a well-established practice, not just a rhetoric."[45] This quote implies that Abu-Laban is on side with the view of the Canadian school. Yet if one returns to the primary text and reads around the single quoted word – "exists" – one sees the following:

> Canada has also come to be seen by outsiders as "the 'place' where multiculturalism 'exists'" (Hinz, 1996, pp. viii–ix). In large part this is because over the last decade, the Canadian experience with multiculturalism has been refracted primarily through the widely read work of some political philosophers – particularly Charles Taylor and Will Kymlicka – to thinking about all Western industrialized countries (Day, 2000, p. 210).[46]

Doing the scholarly detective work pays off in an interesting way here. In order to buttress his – and the Canadian state's – rhetorical claim that "Canada is multiculturalism/multiculturalism is Canada," Kymlicka ends up citing someone who is citing someone who is in fact *challenging* and subtly *mocking* that claim as mere rhetoric, as something invented – by Kymlicka himself. This convoluted yet productive misreading is even more curious when one notes that it is clear, from Abu-Laban's positioning in various texts controlled by Kymlicka, that he sees her as one of the few viable interlocutors among the legion of critics of liberal multiculturalism.

The note referring to Tai Alfred's *Peace, Power, Righteousness* is similarly tangential: "On the adoption of the rhetoric of nationhood by Indigenous peoples, see ... Alfred 1995."[47] It is certainly true that Alfred talks about Indigenous nationhood, but he has always done so in the context of an anti-statist, non-capitalist, decolonizing paradigm and is deeply critical of anything the Canadian state might offer as a gift of recognition. None of this makes it into the discussion, however.

The same sort of thing happens with the work of Slavoj Žižek, whose 1997 article is cited, once again, for pointing out that multiculturalism works well with global neo-liberalism by providing a zero-reference point, a black hole around which identities of all kinds can orbit. In response, Kymlicka points out that multiculturalism "didn't emerge out of neo-liberalism but out of social democracy."[48] The idea that neo-liberalism and social democracy lie at opposite ends of a political spectrum might have held up during the 1980s, when figures like Reagan and Thatcher dominated the scene. By the time of the appearance of Clinton and Blair, however, it was well established that the Third Way was quite capable of making these ends meet. Once again, it seems that Kymlicka treats his radical Others with much less theoretical care than he bestows upon his liberal counterparts.

I could continue in this way for quite some time by adding more writers, more books, more time periods, by starting to include PhD theses, etc. But I will stop here in the hope that I have done an adequate job of showing that the most influential theorists of the Canadian school of multiculturalism – and those who congregate around them – have a marked tendency to ignore their radical critics and that when they do not ignore them, they are very likely to dismiss them through a cursory (mis)reading.

The skeptical liberal theorist who constitutes my imaginary audience might very well, at this point, say, "So what? This is a free country; we can talk with those we like and ignore those we dislike." As individuals in a purely individualistic society, that would surely be true. But one of the hallmarks of liberal multiculturalism is its partial acknowledgement that (some) collectivities do matter. And all forms of liberalism have long understood that some sort of relationship between the individual and the community must be struck in any human society. Thus, Kymlicka himself acknowledges that "liberals have no automatic right to impose their views on non-liberal national minorities."[49] He goes on to declare, in an echo of Charles Taylor's philosophical position, that "they [liberals] do have the right, and indeed the responsibility, to identify what those views actually are. *Relations between national groups should be determined by dialogue.*"[50] No matter what they might think about the "right" relation between the individual and the communal, for all liberals, as Amy Gutmann points out, "it is the neutrality of the public sphere ... that protects our freedom and equality as citizens."[51] Or, as Charles Taylor puts it, harking back to the glory days of the French Revolution, "In a functioning republic, the citizens do care very much what others think."[52]

On the liberals' own terms, then, their consistent ignorance of what the views of their radical critics "actually are" marks a failure of responsibility, a sign of dysfunction. More damning than that, by refusing to acknowledge the existence of these radical views, liberals cannot take them into account in their own formulations – they are excluded from the public sphere; they are not in dialogue. This amounts to a tacit assumption that liberals do indeed have a right to impose their views on *some* of their Others. By entering into dialogue only with homogenized and pasteurized theoretical-political simulacra, liberal multiculturalists are advancing a theory that is, on its own ground, illiberal – and, therefore, should not be tolerated.

CONCLUSION

As I confessed at the outset of this chapter, I really have nothing new to say with regard to these debates. At the end of *Multiculturalism and the History of Canadian Diversity*, I pointed to the possibilities of what I then called "multiculturalism as radical imaginary."[53] My work since that time has been devoted, one might say, to doing my best to explore, in both theory and practice, what this might mean. As I like to point out, I have nothing but failures to show for my efforts, but with sufficient passage of time, most of these failures have transformed themselves into intellectual, spiritual, personal, and political compost. I am happy to have had every one of them since after a sufficient time for recovery, they energize me to move on to new things.

As is surely obvious, I am hinting that Canadian/global liberal-statist multiculturalism might also strive to learn from its failures, first by accepting them as such and then by sufficiently transforming its underlying assumptions and modalities – that is, by submitting to its own becoming in a way that has so far eluded it. To this end, and again trying hard to remain immanent, I would suggest that in order to be true to its own pretensions as at least a quasi-universal ground for engagement across difference, liberal multiculturalism must press itself to become able to work on a host of axes other than those of race and ethnicity – axes that, as

I have shown, it mostly ignores precisely because it knows, in its heart of hearts, that it cannot respond to them without shattering its own identity.

Another way to think about this is to recall the founding schism out of which Canadian liberal multiculturalism emerged – i.e., the famous "separation of language and culture" carried out at the time of the Royal Commission on Bilingualism and Biculturalism in the 1960s. Not only were language and culture separated from each other at this point, but both had been always, already, separated from economy, polity, society – that is, from all other aspects of human identity. This is why indigenists, for example, have never been able to get on board with multiculturalism. They understand and revere the deep links among *all* of these elements of what makes us who and how we are. Thus, it is as ridiculous to think that a longhouse Haudenosaunee could be happy stocking the shelves at Walmart as it is to think that a Québécoise could feel content while surrounded by street signs in English.

If multiculturalism is really going to start "working," then, if it is going to last long enough to live up to its promise, its proponents will have to learn to operate on all possible axes of oppression – they cannot limit themselves to the safe terrain of "ethnocultural difference." And they will have to stop shying away from engagement with their radical Others, stop hiding behind their status as purveyors of a dominant ideology. They will have to make themselves vulnerable, in a way that is, indeed, very difficult and frightening for those who inhabit mainstream subject positions within the Euro-colonial system of states and corporations. As difficult as it may be, in order to be true to their own professed ethico-political commitments, the proponents of liberal multiculturalism must more authentically come out to be met on the open field of political and philosophical debate.

NOTES

[1] Charles Taylor, "The Politics of Recognition," in *Multiculturalism: Examining the Politics of Recognition*, ed. Amy Gutmann (Princeton, NJ: Princeton University Press, 1994), 62.

[2] Will Kymlicka, *The Rise and Fall of Multiculturalism? New Debates on Inclusion and Accommodation in Diverse Societies* (Oxford: Blackwell, 2010).

[3] Gerald Kernerman, *Multicultural Nationalism: Civilizing Difference, Constituting Community* (Vancouver: UBC Press, 2005). For an excellent discussion of both sides of this "debate," see the introduction to Rita Dhamoon, *Identity/Difference Politics: How Difference Is Produced, and Why It Matters* (Vancouver: UBC Press, 2009).

[4] Kymlicka, *Rise and Fall of Multiculturalism?*, 98.

[5] Ibid. Kymlicka is referring to Richard J.F. Day, *Multiculturalism and the History of Canadian Diversity* (Toronto: University of Toronto Press, 2000); and to Slavoj Žižek, "Multiculturalism, or, the Cultural Logic of Multinational Capitalism," *New Left Review* I, no. 225 (September–October 1997):28–51.

[6] Ibid.

[7] Will Kymlicka, *Finding Our Way: Rethinking Ethnocultural Relations in Canada* (Don Mills, ON: Oxford University Press, 1998).

[8] At the time I am writing this, Canada is under the control of the Harper regime, which is about as racist and anti-multiculturalist as any regime in the history of the country. But it is quietly, stealthily so, echoing the polite racism that is so common in both English Canada and Quebec – which is not to say that other kinds of racism are not also being practised.

[9] Kymlicka seems to use *Québécois* and *French Canadian* interchangeably. I would tend to think that there is a difference here, based on one's desire to submit to Anglo domination.

[10] Kymlicka, *Finding Our Way*, 6, 10.

[11] Ibid., 7.

[12] Ibid., 7–8.

[13] Ibid., 10.

[14] Ibid., 11.

[15] Ibid., 8.

[16] The main quote is from Day, *Multiculturalism and the History of Canadian Diversity*, 30–31. The other works cited are John Porter, *The Vertical Mosaic: An Analysis of Social Class and Power in Canada* (Toronto: University of Toronto Press, 1965); Karl Peter, "The Myth of Multiculturalism and Other Political Fables," in *Ethnicity, Power, and Politics in Canada*, ed. Jorgen Dahlie and Tissa Fernando (Toronto: Methuen, 1981); Kogila Moodley, "Canadian Multiculturalism as Ideology," *Ethnic and Racial Studies* 6, no. 3 (1983):320–331; Laverne M. Lewycky, "Multiculturalism in the 1990s and into the 21st Century: Beyond Ideology and Utopia," in *Deconstructing a Nation: Immigration, Multiculturalism and Racism in '90s Canada*, ed. Vic Satzewich (Halifax: Fernwood, 1992).

[17] Himani Bannerji, "On the Dark Side of the Nation: Politics of Multiculturalism and the State of 'Canada,'" *Journal of Canadian Studies* 31, no. 33 (1996):105.

[18] Ibid., 104.

[19] Ibid.

[20] Abbie Bakan and Daiva Stasiulis, *Negotiating Citizenship: Migrant Women in Canada and the Global System* (Toronto: University of Toronto Press, 1995).

[21] Peter Li, *Ethnic Inequality in a Class Society* (Toronto: Wall and Thompson, 1988); Tania Das Gupta, "Political Economy of Gender, Race and Class: Looking at South Asian Immigrant Women in Canada," in *Canadian Ethnic Studies* 26, no. 1 (1994):59–73; Frances Henry, Carol Tator, and Tim Rees, *The Colour of Democracy: Racism in Canadian Society* (Toronto: Harcourt Brace, 2000); and Grace-Edward Galabuzi, *Canada's Economic Apartheid: The Social Exclusion of Racialized Groups in the New Century* (Toronto: Canadian Scholars' Press, 2006).

[22] Bakan and Stasiulis, *Negotiating Citizenship*, 2 (emphasis mine).

[23] Will Kymlicka, *Multicultural Citizenship: A Liberal Theory of Minority Rights* (Oxford: Clarendon, 1995), 114. It is interesting that Kymlicka expects immigrants to "become members of the national societies which already exist in their new country." If the English and French had followed this rule, we would be living in a much different – and much better – place.

[24] Sherene Razack, ed., *Race, Space, and the Law: Unmapping a White Settler Society* (Toronto: Between the Lines, 2002), 1–2.

[25] Ibid., 2.

[26] Kymlicka, *Finding Our Way*, 6.

27 Ibid. I do not want to interrupt the flow of my argument, but it must be noted that the fact that the Québécois are also colonizers is effaced here. This formulation also begs the interesting question of how liberal multiculturalists would respond should Canada be invaded by the United States once again, but this time without the Haudenosaunee warriors protecting us, as they surely would not. Apparently this would be fine provided that efforts were later undertaken to make our involuntary incorporation more voluntary – say, for example, by allowing Tim Hortons unlimited access to the US market?

28 Ibid. (emphasis mine).

29 Yasmin Jiwani, *Discourses of Denial: Mediations of Race, Gender, and Violence* (Vancouver: UBC Press, 2006), xi.

30 Ibid., 205.

31 Taiaiake Alfred and Jeff Corntassel, "Being Indigenous: Resurgences against Contemporary Colonialism," in *Government and Opposition* 40, no. 4 (2005):598.

32 Ibid., 597.

33 Taiaiake Alfred, *Peace, Power, Righteousness: An Indigenous Manifesto* (Don Mills, ON: Oxford University Press, 1999), 56. On the further development of these links between anarchism and indigenism, see *Affinities: A Journal of Radical Theory, Culture, and Action* 5, no. 1 (2011).

34 Day, *Multiculturalism and the History of Canadian Diversity.*

35 Sunera Thobani, *Exalted Subjects: Studies in the Making of Race and Nation in Canada* (Toronto: University of Toronto Press, 2007), 4.

36 Ibid., 3.

37 I am afraid that protection of those I am talking about is going to have to trump the academic will-to-know here. There is no need to give the Canadian Security Intelligence Service any more information than they already have on the people they are targeting. To the reader who doubts that this is going on, and has been increasingly the case under the Harper regime, I suggest that you invite a reasonably well-known radical to the country and see what happens when he or she applies for a visa or tries to cross the border.

38 Ken Adachi, *The Enemy That Never Was: A History of the Japanese Canadians* (Toronto: McClelland and Stewart, 1976); Howard Adams, *Prison of Grass: Canada from a Native Point of View* (Saskatoon: Fifth House Publishers, 1989); Himani Bannerji, ed., *Returning the Gaze* (Toronto: Sister Vision Press, 1993); Neil Bissoondath, *Selling Illusions: The Cult of Multiculturalism in Canada* (Toronto: Penguin, 1994); Howard Cardinal, *The Unjust Society* (Edmonton: M.G. Hurtig, 1969); Evelyn Kallen, "Multiculturalism: Ideology, Policy, and Reality," *Journal of Canadian Studies* 17, no. 1 (1982):51–63; Moodley, "Canadian Multiculturalism as Ideology"; Peter, "The Myth of Multiculturalism and Other Political Fables"; and Pierre Vallières, *White Niggers of America* (Toronto: McClelland & Stewart, 1969).

39 Charles Taylor, "The Politics of Recognition," in *Multiculturalism and "The Politics of Recognition,"* ed. A. Gutmann (Princeton, NJ: Princeton University Press, 1992).

40 Will Kymlicka, ed., *The Rights of Minority Cultures* (Oxford: Oxford University Press, 1995).

41 Menno Boldt, J. Anthony Long, and Leroy Little Bear, *The Quest for Justice: Aboriginal Peoples and Aboriginal Rights* (Toronto: University of Toronto Press, 1985).

42 James Tully, *Strange Multiplicity: Constitutionalism in an Age of Diversity* (Cambridge: Cambridge University Press, 1995).

[43] Kallen, "Multiculturalism: Ideology, Policy, and Reality."

[44] Will Kymlicka, *Multicultural Odysseys: Navigating the New International Politics of Diversity* (New York: Oxford University Press, 2007).

[45] Ibid., 107. The quote is from Yasmeen Abu-Laban, "Liberalism, Multiculturalism and the Problem of Essentialism," *Citizenship Studies* 6, no. 4 (2002):460.

[46] Abu-Laban, "Liberalism, Multiculturalism," 460. The quotes are from Evelyn J. Hinz, "What Is Multiculturalism? A 'Cognitive' Introduction," *Mosaic* 29, no. 3 (September 1996):vii–xiii; and Day, *Multiculturalism and the History of Canadian Diversity*.

[47] Kymlicka, *Multicultural Odysseys*, 286. Kymlicka is referring to Taiaiake Alfred, *Heeding the Voices of Our Ancestors* (Oxford: Oxford University Press, 1995).

[48] Ibid., 130.

[49] Kymlicka, *Multicultural Citizenship*, 171.

[50] Ibid. (emphasis mine).

[51] Amy Gutmann, ed., *Multiculturalism: Examining the Politics of Recognition* (Princeton, NJ: Princeton University Press, 1994), 4.

[52] Taylor, "The Politics of Recognition," 46.

[53] Day, *Multiculturalism and the History of Canadian Diversity*, 222–227.

REFORM BY STEALTH: THE HARPER CONSERVATIVES AND CANADIAN MULTICULTURALISM

YASMEEN ABU-LABAN[1]

It's a real honour for me to take to this august podium of the Empire Club. This is a club whose history goes back over a century, 109 years.... And it's a club that keeps alive a real part of our identity and our history. And that has a particular resonance for me as the Minister for Citizenship, Immigration and Multiculturalism, because it was really the genius of what many call a British liberal imperialism that led to Canada's approach toward pluralism, toward accommodating differences, and openness toward the world.[2]

Canada's federal policy of multiculturalism, first articulated in 1971, entered its fifth decade of existence under the leadership of Prime Minister Stephen Harper's Conservative Party. As a growing body of cross-national research has informed us, Canada stands out from other Western countries not only for having an explicit policy of multiculturalism, but also for having multiculturalism entrenched in the Constitution, maintaining relatively high levels of permanent immigration, delivering social services (like education and health) in ways that are sensitive to the diversity of the population and inclusion, and having a relatively open pathway to citizenship acquisition.[3] Moreover, government leaders in Canada have not made headlines through negative pronouncements about multiculturalism, as German Chancellor Angela Merkel did in 2010, when she claimed that it had "utterly failed."[4]

While Canadian politicians do not always create a media spectacle, however, it is important to think about what they are saying about

The Multiculturalism Question: Debating Identity in 21st-Century Canada, ed. Jack Jedwab. Kingston: School of Policy Studies, Queen's University. © 2014 The School of Policy Studies, Queen's University at Kingston. All rights reserved.

multiculturalism because it can attune us to differences over time. From the vantage point of the history of Canada's multiculturalism policy, Jason Kenney's embrace of the "imperial bond" historically fostered by the Empire Club of Canada, and, in particular, his embrace of British imperialism and empire as being central to the project of multiculturalism, are striking.

In this chapter, I will posit that since the Harper Conservatives came to power in 2006, there has been a systematic remaking of select symbols and discourses relating to "Canadian identity" and "Canadian history," which, as suggested in Jason Kenney's speech to the Empire Club, resurrect elements of Canada's colonial links with Britain. At its core, this trajectory has involved a multiculturalism agenda that I call "reform by stealth." Reform by stealth captures the fact that both Stephen Harper and Jason Kenney were first elected to Parliament as members of the Reform Party. Additionally, while the now defunct Reform Party once sought the elimination of multiculturalism, the Conservatives are using reform by stealth to signal that rather than directly attacking multiculturalism policy, they are reformulating it in ways that are sensitive to the platform once advanced by the Reform Party. Reform by stealth involves very publicly reconfiguring other policies associated with multiculturalism (particularly, but not exclusively, immigration and citizenship) as well as redirecting certain priorities and funding with implications for multiculturalism. Reform by stealth undoubtedly takes a considerable amount of strategizing and political maneuvering vis-à-vis minorities – perhaps even the same kind of "genius" that gives rise to Kenney's open and unabashed admiration of "British liberal imperialism." Not surprisingly, the reform-by-stealth agenda shares with imperialism (British or otherwise) the tendency to include minorities only on the terms of those in power.

To better understand what is distinct in reform by stealth, this chapter considers the evolution of multiculturalism over time. Canadian multiculturalism is a framework that has and may still serve as an inclusionary one for ethnic minorities – that is, non-French, non-British, and non-Aboriginal Canadians – to pursue claims for state recognition and resources.[5] But multiculturalism is not static, nor are policies closely associated with the evolution of multiculturalism – like immigration and citizenship. As such, the content and meaning of multiculturalism are also shaped by state actors, by social actors with unequal power, and by shifting political circumstances.

Since its inception, multiculturalism has been mainly a symbolic policy, and while symbolism should not be discounted in meeting real and legitimate interests,[6] the policy clearly has not always been effective in ameliorating material inequities stemming from race, class, or gender, amongst other forms of social inequality.[7] As this chapter will argue, this long-standing inadequacy in dealing with social inequality has been exacerbated by the reform-by-stealth agenda pursued by the Harper

Conservatives, which chips away at multicultural symbolism and (re-) entrenches social inequality.

In order to substantiate this argument, this chapter takes a twofold approach. First, I will outline how multiculturalism has been advanced in Canada and discuss major points in its evolution that stem from shifting state and popular forces as well as political circumstances. Second, I address in more detail the reform-by-stealth agenda pursued by the Harper Conservatives and by Minister Kenney. In the concluding section, I give some closer consideration to why reform by stealth has been successful at this juncture.

THE EVOLUTION OF MULTICULTURALISM AND ITS CHALLENGERS AND CHALLENGES

Canada stands out from a handful of countries in having adopted an explicit or official policy of multiculturalism; in fact, even the term *multiculturalism* was coined in Canada. In contrast to the image presented by Jason Kenney's Empire Club speech of multiculturalism flowing naturally from imperialism and empire, in fact multiculturalism was not handed down from the powerful, and the climate that produced multiculturalism was its opposite. The broader (international) context that influenced the development of multiculturalism stemmed from, amongst other things, the human rights revolution, the American civil rights movement, and movements for decolonization in the developing world.[8]

While the forms of decolonization that emerged in the 1960s included both a general assertion of Canadian independence from Britain (through, for example, the adoption of the maple leaf flag) as well as efforts by Indigenous peoples for self-rule and self-government, it was the resurgence of nationalism in Quebec that was an especially salient form of decolonization for the federal government. The growing strength of the national movement led to the formation in 1963 of the Royal Commission on Bilingualism and Biculturalism (B and B Commission), and, in this domestic context of weakening legitimacy attached to the presentation of Canada as only British and renewed pressures to give recognition to French Canada, Canadians who were of neither French nor British origin objected to the depiction of Canada as composed of only two cultures.[9] The policy of multiculturalism came about as a result of the struggles and demands of non-British, non-French, non-Aboriginal minorities[10] – not least because the pressure they applied led to the publication of the B and B Commission's fourth volume, *The Cultural Contribution of the Other Ethnic Groups.*[11] In many ways, this volume speaks to the geographically diverse waves of immigration, historically favoured from Europe, that accompanied Canada's formation and evolution as a settler colony, and it laid a basis in the years that followed for greater consideration of the (social) histories of ethnic minorities.

In response to the findings of the B and B Commission, the government of Pierre Elliott Trudeau announced a policy of multiculturalism, to be applied within a framework of (English and French) bilingualism. In the words of Trudeau in 1971, "although there are two official languages, there is no official culture, nor does any ethnic group take precedence over any other."[12] This quote is often used to indicate the challenge to Quebec's constitutional claim of being a founding nation (and, in fact, multiculturalism was never a policy that held much attraction for Aboriginal people or francophones in and outside Quebec, who have pursued their claims in relation to the Canadian state through other legal, policy, and discursive mechanisms).[13] However, Trudeau's statement also reflected a challenge to the hegemony of Anglo conformity that had shaped Canada's historical evolution as a settler colony. As such, multiculturalism provided a more inclusionary discourse for ethnic minorities.

In its first decade of existence, the federal multiculturalism policy was consolidated primarily as a policy supporting the folkloric expression of culture,[14] a feature that has fed the critique of the policy for masking racism and other forms of inequality. However, because multiculturalism was advanced as a feature of the unfolding Canadian welfare state, whereby minority ethnic groups could legitimately claim resources in the name of Canadian citizenship, its content could and did shift.[15] Thus, whereas the 1970s version of multiculturalism as "song and dance" did not have combatting racism and fostering equity as its central mission,[16] by the early 1980s, multiculturalism had shifted to emphasize greater attention to anti-racism, in large part because of the experiences and demands of growing numbers of visible minorities.[17]

Reflecting on the fact that multiculturalism has carried the potential to be an inclusionary framework advancing the goals of minorities, we can see that in many ways, the decade of the 1980s marks the high point of multiculturalism for direct support given by the Canadian state to minorities to organize and pursue claims as well as for an anti-racist equity agenda.[18] Many developments spoke to the growth of the scope of multiculturalism, as well as the organizational strength of minority ethnic groups. For example, the entrenchment of multiculturalism in section 27 of the 1982 *Canadian Charter of Rights and Freedoms* was both significant and possible because minority groups were able to mobilize. Likewise, the passage of employment equity legislation in 1986 and the *Canadian Multiculturalism Act* in 1988 were the result of such mobilization.[19] The *Canadian Multiculturalism Act* served to solidify the basis upon which multiculturalism was founded, and its status was further augmented in 1989, when the Progressive Conservatives under Prime Minister Brian Mulroney created a new Department of Multiculturalism and Citizenship. Multiculturalism also enjoyed support across all major federal political parties of the day (the Liberals, the New Democrats, and the Progressive

Conservatives), and most provinces and many municipalities adopted their own versions of multiculturalism.

Despite these evident ways in which multiculturalism expanded in the period of the 1980s, by the decade's end, new challenges and challengers were beginning to emerge. The two most salient for the trajectory of the policy concerned, first, the breakdown of the national partisan consensus governing the policy and a reframing of multiculturalism as weakening national unity; the second was the broad embrace of neo-liberalism. Each will be discussed in turn, before considering evident forms of continued, and even growing, racialized exclusion.

Partisan Consensus

The patriation of the Constitution and adoption of the Charter without Quebec's consent in 1982 spawned a new round of constitutional negotiations in the 1980s and 1990s. While, since its foundation, multiculturalism was subject to critique by many academics on the left for "co-opting" the interests of minorities, and by many Quebec academics for covering over Quebec's specific national and constitutional claims (as a founding people and as a "distinct society"), the argument that multiculturalism actually threatened Canadian national unity was not a relevant one in debates until the late 1980s and 1990s. In the context of constitutional discussions, as well as anxiety over growing numbers of non-white immigrants, the idea that multiculturalism endangered national unity by weakening Canadian identity became much more central.[20] The new dominance of the national unity debate was symbolically apparent in the 1997 publication of a collection of contrasting positions from politicians, academics, and activists in a book tellingly entitled *The Battle over Multiculturalism: Does It Help or Hinder Canadian Unity?*[21]

A key contributor to the critique of multiculturalism on grounds of national unity was the Reform Party, which was formed in 1987. It is relevant to consider key elements of the party's platform because even if now defunct, the party aided in introducing new themes into partisan discussions of multiculturalism and immigration, and it is a key part of the lineage of the Harper Conservatives. The Reform Party has been described in the literature as ushering in a clear "race discourse,"[22] not least because in its earliest platforms, it explicitly objected to the current immigration policy for changing "the ethnic makeup" of Canada.[23] Although the party's criticisms of immigration were, over time, increasingly couched in code words as opposed to direct references to Canada's demographics, on multiculturalism and the role of the state it was explicit. A 1990 resolution adopted as official party policy held that it was "the responsibility of the state to promote, preserve and enhance the national culture" and that "ethnic cultures" should "integrate into the national culture."[24] On multiculturalism, the Reform Party sought to abolish not only the separate multiculturalism department but also "the concept of multiculturalism and hyphenated Canadianism."[25] Additionally, the Reform Party sought the return of "traditional" symbols like the Royal Canadian Mounted Police (RCMP) Stetson.[26] This was in direct reference to a highly publicized 1990 change to the uniform code that allowed orthodox Sikh men wearing turbans to forfeit the Stetson when they joined the RCMP.

Neo-liberalism

While the Reform Party never formed a national government, themes relating to immigration, Canadian identity, and Canadian symbols had a reverberating impact on the Progressive Conservative government headed briefly by Kim Campbell. For example, in 1993, it disbanded the Department of Multiculturalism and Citizenship and integrated the Multiculturalism Program into the Department of Canadian Heritage, a process continued under the Liberal governments of Jean Chrétien and Paul Martin. The positioning of multiculturalism under the umbrella of Canadian Heritage symbolized a shift in the policy to stress, in a very broad sense, belonging and attachment to Canada among all people.

The clear embrace by the Jean Chrétien Liberals of neo-liberalism, with its emphasis on limiting social spending, put pressure on Canada's multiculturalism policy through the 1990s and 2000s. Cuts to funding, along with new terms for community funding and the removal of core funding, made it difficult for groups to mobilize as they once had.[27] In this neo-liberal context, the rationale for multiculturalism shifted from supporting equity to supporting Canada's global competitiveness and promoting business links abroad.[28] As a consequence, the 1990s and 2000s were characterized by a much weakened equity agenda compared to the 1980s.[29]

Minority Mobilization and Racialized Inequality

Lacking the stronger national voice they had when aided by core federal government funding, minorities have been less able to collectively mobilize and pursue claims despite developments that have exacerbated racialized inequality.[30] One major development concerns the fact that the climate in the years since September 11, 2001 has led to renewed policy emphases on – and justifications for – security, surveillance, and even torture. They have been especially felt by those who are (or are perceived to be) Muslim and/or Arab and have dramatically exposed the fault lines of Canadian multiculturalism.[31] In this way, the global war on terrorism and a "clash of civilizations" discourse have had both international and domestic implications.

A clear way to see these domestic implications is in the views of Canadians. For example, in a 2011 survey conducted near the tenth anniversary of 9/11, a majority (56 percent) agreed with the statement, "There is an irreconcilable conflict between Western societies and Muslim societies," and a full 39 percent of the respondents agreed that "Airport personnel should be allowed to do extra checks on passengers who appear to be of Muslim background."[32] Jedwab[33] uses a March 2012 survey to show that "some 43% of Canadians strongly agree that they have heard negative comments about Muslims over the past year compared with 31% in the case of Aboriginals and 25% in the case of Jews." This is of concern not least because exposure to negative and/or racist comments can impact the views and attitudes of individuals toward specific groups.[34]

In addition to the fallout from 9/11, which may be seen to especially target those who are (or are seen to be) Arab and/or Muslim, there is also evidence of more generalized and growing racialized and gendered forms of inequality amongst immigrants and minorities.[35] In particular, it has been clear for some time that incoming immigrants (even if selected since 1967 for their high skills) have not had the same success in the labour market since the 1990s as they had in the 1970s and 1980s.[36] More specifically, many immigrant women are fettered by chains of care in which work is both very demanding and poorly remunerated.[37] As Galabuzi[38] summarizes, the current socio-economic status of racialized (visible-minority) groups is characterized by:

- a double-digit income gap
- chronic higher-than-average levels of unemployment
- segregated labour market participation
- deepening levels of poverty
- differential access to housing and segregated neighbourhood selection
- disproportionate contact with the criminal justice system
- higher health risks
- post-9/11 legislative and administrative measures that limit the free movement of racialized groups, especially members of Muslim, Arab, and Asian communities
- lack of representation in political institutions

This broader racialization of inequality may be seen to have been further aggravated by the increasing use of temporary migrant workers, who are denied Canadian citizenship. In fact, since 2006 – the year the Harper Conservatives came to power – the number of temporary entrants to Canada has actually exceeded the number of those who are selected for permanent residence.[39] Indeed, the growing diversity and array of programs to facilitate temporary entry has led to a plethora of rules and practices governing issues relating to security of presence, employment for spouses, and social services, including settlement services, suggesting that Canada is fostering inequality through policy.[40] This inequality is not only between citizens and non-citizens who reside in Canada but also amongst non-citizens who reside in Canada.

It is notable that support for multiculturalism has continued despite these signs of inequality, despite the older constitutional debates over national unity, and despite neo-liberal (and, increasingly, on the grounds of austerity) rationales for cutting spending. Thus, for example, Elke Winter[41] notes how in the period 1992–2001, newspaper coverage in the *Toronto Star* and the *Globe and Mail* presented Quebec, as well as the United States, as negative counterpoints in discourses emphasizing (English-speaking) Canada's purported civic (non-ethnic) and multicultural (non–melting pot) ethos. (Despite English-language print media frames, it remains debated whether there are significant differences between Canada and Quebec and between Canada and the United States on matters of pluralism.)

The relevance of multiculturalism policy for the construction of identity in Canada, as well as the positive association of the discourse, can also be seen in recent surveys. Thus, for example, an April 2012 survey conducted by the Association for Canadian Studies found that when asked their "opinion of Canadian Multicultural Policy," the majority of Canadians had a very positive or somewhat positive attitude (58 percent); a somewhat negative or negative opinion was held by 35 percent.[42] Support was strikingly strong amongst younger cohorts, with some 74 percent of young adults (aged 18–24) holding positive views toward the policy.[43] Additionally, in a June 2010 poll, the word *multiculturalism* (by itself) generated very positive or positive responses from 73 percent of respondents across Canada, including 71 percent of those from Quebec.[44] Evidence of such continued general public support for multiculturalism is relevant when considering why the Harper Conservatives have chosen to reform, rather than eliminate, multiculturalism.

REFORM BY STEALTH: MULTICULTURALISM SINCE 2006

With its support base in western Canada, the Reform Party faced severe challenges in becoming a national party. In 2000, it became the Canadian Alliance (2000–2003), and eventually both the Canadian Alliance and the Progressive Conservatives disbanded and merged into the Conservative Party of Canada, led by Stephen Harper. Winning two minority governments (2006 and 2008) and a majority in 2011, the Harper Conservatives have steered a course distinct from the Reform Party in that they have never mobilized any overt race discourse (which even Reform muted over time), and they have never overtly attacked multiculturalism or sought its elimination as policy or discourse. Indeed, either move would be extremely difficult politically because multiculturalism enjoys public support and its entrenchment in the Charter makes constitutional changes difficult. As well, not directly attacking multiculturalism has given the Conservatives a way to distance themselves from the lingering image of the Reform Party as racist and is therefore a way to better appeal to voters, some of whom might be minorities.

What the Harper Conservatives have done is to reformulate multiculturalism, especially through related policies toward immigration and citizenship. They have effected this in part by moving multiculturalism from the Department of Canadian Heritage into the Department of Citizenship and Immigration. Bearing in mind that the Reform Party's position to disband the earlier multiculturalism department was actually enacted by both Progressive Conservative and Liberal governments, this move has been a distinct bureaucratic change for multiculturalism and thus carries symbolic significance. First, it suggests that multiculturalism is associated with immigrants and new Canadians. Second, it bureaucratically decouples it from official bilingualism because responsibility for official languages is retained in the Department of Canadian Heritage; this can be seen as further marginalizing multiculturalism because official languages have always had greater resources and stature. Another way in which the Harper Conservatives have reformulated multiculturalism is by creating programs that deal with historical redress.

These developments have been accompanied by the Harper Conservatives providing a more monarchical content for "Canadian identity" and militarized "Canadian history" than their Liberal or Progressive Conservative predecessors. More specifically, the content echoes the Reform Party's rejection of "hyphenated Canadianism," assertion of a strong role for the state in articulating a singular "national culture," a "tough" approach to immigration,[45] and emphasis on select "tradition." Reform by stealth, then, chips away at multicultural symbolism by using other policies to go around it rather than directly attacking or eliminating it.

The construction of a singular (as distinct from hyphenated) "Canadian identity" has reflected a strong emphasis on British traditions, with implications for ideas of both ancestry and history. For instance, commenting on the oath required of the foreign-born to become Canadian citizens, Jason Kenney has observed,

> The oath that citizens take to Canada's Queen commits them to a tradition that stretches back to the *Bill of Rights* (1960), the *British North America Act* (1867), the *Quebec Act* (1774), the *Royal Proclamation* (1763), and further still to *Magna Carta* (1215) – reaffirmed by the *Charter of Rights and Freedoms* in 1982. By means of the oath, they join a millennium-old civic tradition, one that we inherited from our founders and ancestors, and will pass on to our descendants.[46]

In Kenney's words, new immigrants to Canada are joining a civic tradition dating back 1,000 years to England's charter, *Magna Carta*. This is a position that not only ignores the influence of Indigenous traditions (e.g., the Iroquois Confederacy) on such Canadian constitutional principles as federalism and the relevance of the French civil law tradition in Quebec, but also refracts British history as Canada's history. Curiously, boiling Canada's civic essence down to *Magna Carta* also echoes Samuel Huntington's refraction of British history when he posited that this charter was the essence of "the West."[47]

In addition, under the Conservatives, a form of militarized patriotism is relevant to the playing out of immigration and citizenship, with consequences for multicultural symbolism. As will be traced further, this militarized patriotism comes out most strongly in the form of military history (and a singular national narrative), effectively trumping social history (and multiple narratives) in official presentations.

These elements of reform by stealth relating to a singular Canadian identity and a singular Canadian history have operated with a seeming paradox that should be dealt with up front, and that is the willingness of the Harper Conservatives to redress select historical injustices in which select minorities were denied equality and the rule of law. The 1988 redress for the internment of Japanese Canadians during World War II was a battle hard fought by minority Canadians[48] and viewed as an exceptional response by the government of the day. When Progressive Conservative Prime Minister Brian Mulroney eventually apologized, extended a modicum of individual compensation, and funded what would become the Canadian Race Relations Foundation, it was on the grounds that it would be the last request entertained.[49] In the 1990s, mirroring Prime Minister Pierre Elliott Trudeau's classic refusal, successive Liberal governments also rejected the quests of groups seeking redress and compensation for past injustices.[50] This was most obvious when Chinese Canadians turned to the courts in an effort to have their claims heard regarding the head tax (a policy that worked historically to discourage the settlement of female spouses and children of this collectivity).

In contrast, in the lead-up to and during the 2006 election, Stephen Harper promised that his government would deal with redress for the head tax.[51] On 22 June 2006, Harper made good on this promise and issued an apology to all Chinese Canadians as well as compensation ($20,000) to each person who had paid the head tax (or their surviving spouse). Edwards and Calhoun suggest that the rhetoric of this apology makes it an "exemplar of collective apology."[52] This is because it positioned Canada to close the past, heal in the present, and, in the words of Prime Minister Harper, nourish "an unwavering commitment to build a better future for all Canadians."[53] This is relevant because as Matt James[54] has convincingly shown, what actually constitutes an apology (as opposed to a quasi-apology or non-apology) is highly contested, and, moreover, both in Canada and around the world, the novelty of the political apology renders it subject to considerable equivocation.

It indicated the significance of redress politics for the Harper Conservatives that on the same day as they gave the apology for the head tax, they also announced that the federal government was committing $10 million to a new National Historical Recognition Program and $24 million to the Community Historical Recognition Program (CHRP).[55] The latter, which ran 2008–2013 under the auspices of multiculturalism, sought to "help commemorate and educate Canadians about the historical experiences and contributions of communities affected by wartime measures and immigration restrictions."[56]

While specifically ruling out the possibility of any apology, the CHRP nonetheless had by 2009–2010 distributed some $3.5 million to support 18 projects, which included a documentary film on Chinese Canadians and their successful redress for the head tax; a memorial wall, time capsule, and booklet on Italian Canadian internment during World War II; a monument at Halifax's Pier 21 to commemorate the ship *MS St. Louis* and the Jewish refugees fleeing Nazi persecution in 1930 who were denied entry to Canada and were turned back, to their deaths; as well as a book about the 1914 ship *Komagata Maru* and the denial of entry of immigrants from India and their subsequent fate, which for many included death.[57]

Such projects are a good reflection of the fact that the CHRP limited consideration to wartime measures and immigration restrictions as well as the fact that the main participants have been the Canadian Chinese, Ukrainian, Italian, Jewish, and South Asian communities.[58] Funding such educational and commemorative projects on traumatic experiences that have shaped the lives of diverse groups in Canada may be seen as positive, but this should not preclude paying attention to the larger dynamics of the CHRP. As Matt James argues, the overall approach can be critiqued as one of what he aptly dubs "neoliberal heritage redress."[59] For James, neo-liberal heritage redress joins forces with neo-liberal multiculturalism in placing restrictive conditions on both the possibility and the use of state funding, thereby allowing the government to pick select groups to be rewarded as well as severely limiting contemporary claims for social justice, equity, and anti-racism.[60]

Another concern that can be levelled at this example of reform by stealth is that redress and even apology do not necessarily alleviate the sidelining of patterned and even structural racialized inequality and may even contribute to it. Although neo-liberal heritage redress under the rubric of multiculturalism stands separate bureaucratically from redress efforts that the Harper Conservatives have engaged in vis-à-vis Aboriginal people, it is worth considering how the centrality of Canada's colonial past and present in Indigenous narratives clashes with the way Stephen Harper himself has depicted Canadian history. On the heels of a 2008 apology to survivors of the residential school system, and at the same time that the Truth and Reconciliation Commission was undertaking its work, Harper proclaimed in 2009 – to the chagrin of many First Nations leaders – that Canada was a fitting host for the upcoming G20 meeting because, amongst other things, it had "no history of colonialism."[61] While the Prime Minister's Office claimed that First Nations leaders had taken the statement out of context, in point of fact, the 2008 apology also did not use the term *colonialism*. This leads Henderson and Wakeham to suggest that the residential school "apology enables a strategic isolation and containment of residential schools as a discrete historical problem of educational malpractice rather than one devastating prong of an overarching and multifaceted system of colonial oppression that persists in the present."[62]

Despite the disavowal of colonialism, Stephen Harper is, like Jason Kenney, very forthright in expressing Canada's ties and shared experience with Britain in glowing superlatives that effectively trump the historical experiences of minorities – whether of trauma or contribution. Thus, in 2006, the same year that he issued the apology for the head tax, Stephen Harper spoke at a London business gathering and averred, "At the heart of our relationship is the golden circle of the Crown which links us all together with the majestic past that takes us back to the Tudors, the Plantagenets, the Magna Carta, habeas corpus, petition of rights and English common law."[63] Notably, in his tract *It's the Regime, Stupid! A Report from the Cowboy West on Why Stephen Harper Matters*,[64] Barry Cooper portrays Stephen Harper as uniquely poised to defend "the regime" as defined by what is purportedly best and most distinctive about Canada's settled ways of doing things.

Given Harper's close personal and political association with what has been dubbed the "Calgary School" of political scientists like Barry Cooper,[65] it is worth noting what Ian McKay and Jamie Swift take to be especially salient from the tracts associated with the Calgary School in rebranding Canada as a "warrior nation." They summarize David Bercuson and Barry Cooper's 1994 work, *Derailed: The Betrayal of the National Dream*, by saying that Canada should move "from a nation of 'whiners' associated with a 'thoroughly undignified and suffocatingly maternal' political order into a nation of virtuous warriors." The welfare state epitomizes a maternal political order and should be jettisoned in favour of a nation where "individuals contend for prizes, honours, and recognition of their superiority."[66]

For McKay and Swift, the valorization of virtuous (male) warriors is especially seen in the Harper government's citizenship guide, first released in 2009 (and most recently reissued in 2012). Aimed at helping immigrants selected for permanent residence prepare for the citizenship test, the guide, entitled *Discover Canada: The Rights and Responsibilities of Citizenship*, makes heavy use of a particular rendition of military history. As a consequence, McKay and Swift assert, "Warriors are *the* significant

Canadians – no one else is in the running. Of thirty images on 'Canada's History' twenty depict plainly military events or figures," in contrast to none that appeared in the Liberals' guide of 2005.[67] Moreover, war is made to look romantic: "No blood, refugees or bombed out cities are in sight.... Even better we have acquired a whole new cast of Canadian heroes, fighting for the Empire long before Canada took shape in 1867."[68]

To be sure, one position holds that the 2009 guide produced by the Harper Conservatives is not essentially different from those produced by successive Liberal, Progressive Conservative, and Conservative govern-ments between 1947 and 2008, which have also stressed themes relating to Canadian history, Canada's international role, and civic participation.[69] In addition, the new guide, with its emphasis on "taking responsibility for oneself and one's family" – since "getting a job, taking care of one's family and working hard in keeping with one's abilities are important Canadian values"[70] – clearly embraces the valorization of the neo-liberal citizen found in guides produced by the previous federal Liberal govern-ment.[71] However, the position that there is no difference is misleading because it ignores the fact that there has been a growing international policy convergence in liberal-democratic countries toward reforming citizenship tests and that, in the case of the Conservative guide since 2009, these changes have been part of a more generalized effort to control and manage the immigration, refugee, and citizenship systems.[72] Moreover, it also neglects the fact that the repackaging of the guide (and the emphasis on military victories, as opposed to traditional post–World War II tropes like peacekeeping) was not only presented as a significant change by the Conservative government but was also explicitly linked to multicultural-ism and the production of a singular civic-historical memory for both potential and actual Canadian citizens. Hence, Jason Kenney asserts,

> Our commitment to multiculturalism is emphasized throughout the broad continuum of immigration and citizenship. I am pleased to reflect this in *Discover Canada: The Rights and Responsibilities of Citizenship.* This new study guide is proving extremely popular, with 112,000 printed copies distributed and over 470,000 internet visits. *I believe that* Discover Canada, *by placing increased emphasis on Canada's values, history and symbols, will promote civic memory and pride among newcomers and citizens alike.*[73]

When viewed in the light of a more generalized strategy to assert a singular historical narrative stressing "civic memory and pride" through military success, it makes sense that certain projects have been funded outside the rubric of multiculturalism. For example, in 2012, the federal government committed over $28 million to support the bicentennial of the War of 1812, making it the largest commemoration of this war ever.[74] In October 2012, the Conservative government announced a plan to transform the Canadian Museum of Civilization in Gatineau, Quebec, into a new Canadian Museum of History. Amongst others, the Canadian Association of University Teachers (CAUT), the national body representing academic staff in universities and colleges in Canada, protested this plan. CAUT did so on the grounds that the plan threatened the way the Canadian Museum of Civilization currently reflects the attention given by Canadian historians to social history.[75] Social history, often contrasted with military, intellectual, or diplomatic history, draws attention to the experiences and narratives of diverse collectivities that have been traditionally marginalized – such as women, workers, children, minorities, immigrants, and Indigenous peoples.

In terms of the new citizenship guide, it is also worth noting that one leading expert consulted in its production was military historian Jack Granatstein, whose bestselling book, *Who Killed Canadian History?*, sought to assert the importance of history for a nation. In it, Granatstein blames "the decimation of our history"[76] on social historians dealing with, amongst others, themes of labour, gender, and ethnicity as well as ethnic communities "conned by Canada's multiculturalism policy into demanding an offence-free education for all."[77] In keeping with Granatstein's argument for "a history that puts Canada firmly in the context of Western civilization," but is not "airbrushed with all the warts removed,"[78] *Discover Canada* issues a series of regrets about the treatment of some groups without detracting from a strong narrative of pride in military victories, pride in the (former) British Empire as well as pride in certain Canadian traditions and institutions. As a result, the abrogation of principles of equal treatment, due process, and the rule of law experienced by collectivities are treated as blips on an otherwise exemplary record. Hence, of World War I:

> Regrettably, from 1914 to 1920, Ottawa interned over 8,000 former Austro-Hungarian subjects, mainly Ukrainian men, as "enemy aliens" in 24 labour camps across Canada, even though Britain advised against the policy.[79]

And of World War II:

> Regrettably, the state of war and public opinion in B.C. led to the forcible relocation of Canadians of Japanese origin by the federal government and the sale of their property without compensation. This occurred even though the military and the RCMP told Ottawa that they posed little danger to Canada. The Government of Canada apologized in 1988 for wartime wrongs and compensated the victims.[80]

Not only does *Discover Canada* engage a containment of acts of racialized exception to the far distant past (when Canada's treatment of Maher Arar, the dual Canadian-Syrian citizen rendered to torture in Syria in 2002, might suggest otherwise), it also injects contemporary gendered and racialized stereotypes evident in the post-9/11 framing of Muslims. As Sherene Razack has argued, central to media and political discourses in Canada, and in the war on terror, is the construction of the dangerous and barbaric Muslim male (whose torture and death may place him outside the rule of law in a state of exception) and the oppressed Muslim female in need of rescue by Western law.[81] In this regard, discourses around gender equality have frequently been appropriated into a clash-of-civilizations framing of us and them. Hence, in *Discover Canada*, immigrants to Canada seeking citizenship will encounter a construction of the barbaric "other" who contrasts with the civilized Canadian "us." To quote:

> In Canada, men and women are equal under the law. Canada's openness and generosity do not extend to barbaric cultural practices that tolerate spousal abuse, "honour killings," female genital mutilation, forced marriage or other gender-based violence. Those guilty of these crimes are severely punished under Canada's criminal laws.[82]

Taking racialized and gendered differentiation still further, while also drawing on ideals of gender equality, Jason Kenney announced in December 2011 that those covering their face during a citizenship ceremony would not be eligible for Canadian citizenship. This was clearly aimed at forcing women wearing the niqab (a head and face cover worn by a very small minority of Muslim women) to remove it should they wish to become Canadian. As well, in 2012, the Department of Citizenship and Immigration announced in an operational bulletin that a member of the Canadian Forces (preferably a veteran of the war in Afghanistan) should play a prominent role in all citizenship ceremonies.[83] Hence, the salience of a singular Canadian identity and militarized patriotism extends from what immigrants are taught, to the ceremony relating to the extension of citizenship, and even to what immigrants may wear.

Since so few Muslim women wear the niqab, the ban will likely not exclude many from citizenship. However, what needs to be stressed is that the new guide, *Discover Canada*, is already making it more difficult for a significant number of immigrants to acquire citizenship because it now involves changes to the citizenship test that are not neutral. There is a new emphasis on testing the ability to speak English or French before the exam, more questions are required to be correct than in the past, and both of these changes are proving to make it more difficult for immigrants to pass the test, especially those arriving from non-English-speaking countries. The failure rates have not only increased but gone up dramatically for some groups. Thus, for example, nearly half of all immigrants from Afghanistan failed the test in 2011 (compared to only 21 percent in 2009, before the Harper changes), and over 41 percent of immigrants from Vietnam failed the test in 2011 (compared to less than 15 percent before the Harper changes).[84] By way of contrast, 98 percent of immigrants from the United States, Australia, and the United Kingdom passed the test in 2011.[85]

In contrast to the focus on the past, contemporary efforts to foster anti-racism (and related themes of equity and social justice) are not on prominent display in the reform-by-stealth agenda for multiculturalism, either in projects that are funded or in discourse. In fact, rather than talking about anti-racism, Jason Kenney has tended to talk more about bridge-building aimed at immigrant or second-generation employment and integration. This is exemplified in the Somali-Jewish Canadian Mentorship Project, which in Kenney's view provides "young Canadians of Somali origin, typically refugees or their children, with an opportunity to find internships in Jewish-owned businesses and professions so they can meet and interact with people from other communities, while pursuing new opportunities for economic integration."[86] Notably, while Kenney presents this project as a model for "similar cross-cultural projects,"[87] the retreat of anti-racism is at best about fostering conditions for individual success rather than addressing persistent structural inequalities. In combination with the advance of a colonial British and militarized, singular Canadian identity, reform by stealth may be seen, then, to re-entrench growing forms of racialized (as well as gendered) inequality, while simultaneously undermining the symbolism associated with multiculturalism as policy.

CONCLUSION

To sum up, as this chapter has argued, the Harper Conservatives have adopted a strategy that does not directly question or attack multiculturalism policy. Since 2006, new programs have been created to commemorate certain past wrongs, but comparatively less attention has been paid to contemporary injustices as well as anti-racism. In addition, there is an emphasis on a singular (as opposed to hyphenated) Canadian identity in conjunction with the advancement of a militarized patriotism. These developments have consequences for multicultural symbolism, and they help to (re-)entrench racialized as well as gendered forms of inequality.

Given the shift evident under the Harper Conservatives, it could be asked why they seem to have been so successful in putting forward an agenda of reform by stealth. Several developments relating to contemporary politics and the dynamic between state and social actors may be seen to feed into a relative quiescence in relation to this agenda. First, and critically, long before the Conservatives came to power, the equity agenda was weakened by neo-liberal policy shifts that impacted the demobilization of ethnic minority groups through the removal of core funding. In the period of its development, multiculturalism was often referred to as a "social movement," and there was even talk about non-Aboriginal, non-French, and non-British Canadians serving as a "third force" in Canadian politics. Lacking geographical concentration and power, the image of a third force may have been overstated. Still, as noted, there were ways in which minority groups could assume a national voice and lobby for such things as the *Canadian Multiculturalism Act* in the late 1980s. In the aftermath of neo-liberal funding cuts, there is no cohesive national voice that brings together groups to offer a shared vision or response to reform by stealth.

Second, for the Harper Conservatives, it has become insidiously easy to cease to fund and even engage with organizations that they do not agree with politically.[88] This has been evident in the removal of grants and the refusal by Jason Kenney to even meet with the Canadian Arab Federation (CAF). Given that the CAF is the national umbrella organization of Arab Canadians and has long engaged with the federal government in issues related to multiculturalism, this is a striking development.[89] More broadly, the Harper Conservatives, and Jason Kenney in particular, have shown a tendency to bypass national minority organizations in favour of individual minorities, and specific groups, who may support the Conservative Party's vision. Indeed, precisely because of such cultivated electoral inroads with some minorities, in the lead-up to the 2011 election, *Maclean's* magazine dubbed Jason Kenney "Harper's Secret Weapon."[90]

Third, the role of Quebec may contribute to the shifting dynamics that have allowed for reform by stealth. On the one hand, for many Indigenous people and francophones, a stress on Canada's ties to the British Empire is likely to be alienating. On the other hand, the Harper government may have already concluded that beyond giving recognition to Quebec as a "nation within a united Canada," their electoral success will not and cannot depend on Quebec. This approach may seemingly "work" now insofar as Quebec sovereignty has not been a major issue on the national agenda over the course of the 2000s, as it was in the 1990s. Even with the 2012 election of Pauline Marois as Parti Québécois (PQ) premier of the province (with a minority government), it is doubtful that the dynamic will shift soon to what it was in the wake of the constitutional turmoil of the 1990s, when issues of recognition and symbolism were particularly prominent.

Moreover, in Quebec, the heated debate on reasonable accommodation of religious minorities – while impacting all religious minorities – has been particularly concerned with Muslims. That it shows no signs of abating may be seen by the fact that in 2011, the city of Gatineau issued a Statement of Values directed at immigrants. The Gatineau statement was remarkably similar (in tone, content, and targeting of Muslims) to one issued in 2007 by the hamlet of Hérouxville, which helped lead to the formation of a provincial commission on reasonable accommodation.[91] The debate spawned in 2013 by the minority PQ government's proposed Charter of Values, which would ban public servants from wearing religious symbols, also indicates the continued saliency of debates over religion in the context of Quebec.

Notwithstanding the fact that Prime Minister Harper has indicated that such a charter would face federal challenge on constitutional grounds,[92] in point of fact, in many other ways, the Harper Conservatives have sought to mesh with the more exclusionary elements represented in Quebec's debate. Thus, for example, in advance of a 2007 by-election in the province, when debates over reasonable accommodation were central, Stephen Harper challenged the voting rights of women who wear the niqab.[93] Likewise, Jason Kenney's rather sudden decision to ban the extension of citizenship to women wearing the niqab may be seen to parallel the 2010 Quebec ban on extending government services or government employment to women wearing the niqab. In this sense, a realignment may be happening between Quebec, which has been the most proactive of provincial governments in challenging religious symbols,[94] and the federal government. In this way, and in contrast to the 1990s debates, which pitted the federal government against Quebec, a distinct " triad"[95] may be seen in which the federal government and Quebec find common ground in "othering" Muslims.

Fourth, not only has multiculturalism policy never appealed much to Quebec or to Aboriginal people, but the larger international climate, especially after September 11, 2001, has not been conducive to the development or enhancement of multiculturalism policy. It is a very different climate than in the 1960s, and it is also a different climate than in the 1990s. The securitization of immigration and intensified surveillance of particular diasporic communities, coupled with weakening welfare states and economic recession, have made many European governments overtly hostile to multiculturalism. As well, anxiety regarding stigmatized groups is evident in Canada, too, with discussions of "ethnic enclaves" belying a new fear of the "homegrown terrorist" who is lurking behind multiculturalism's generosity. The time is not propitious for multiculturalism policy or symbols, let alone a more radical multiculturalism aimed at empowering minorities or challenging inequalities.

Finally, and returning to my starting point, multiculturalism was malleable from the start. It emerged as an important framework for advancing the goals of minorities, but it is not static. This also suggests, however, that the reform of multiculturalism by stealth might also shift because multiculturalism rests on the ongoing interface between state and social actors. The glimmers of challenge to the more obvious forms of minority political disempowerment may be seen in new (coalitional) activities such as the Voices-Voix campaign, begun in 2010. This has brought together human rights–oriented civil society groups (such as Amnesty International Canada) to challenge the perceived silencing of Canadian civil society through actual or threatened cuts to funding, and other forms of control, by the federal government. Notably, the treatment of the Canadian Arab Federation by Jason Kenney and the Harper Conservatives forms one of many examples that Voices-Voix seeks to challenge.[96]

The glimmers of a direct challenge to a singular (military) history of Canada, as well as to a singular Canadian identity, may be seen in the rather remarkable, concerted response of a number of historians and other scholars in publishing, in 2011, the *People's Citizenship Guide: A Response to Conservative Canada*.[97] This collection serves to popularize social history and express the plural stories of a different Canada than the one advanced in *Discover Canada*. Like *Discover Canada*, the *People's Citizenship Guide* ends with questions. But these questions are very different. Among them are the following:

What is settler-colonialism and why did European Empires seek to conquest North America?

Who are some of the people living and working in Canada who are excluded from citizenship? How do laws make distinctions between who is a "citizen" and who is not?

Rebellion, civil disobedience and dissent have been crucial factors in the expansion of individual and collective rights. What were some of these challenges to state authority? How have social movements and contentious politics helped to shape citizenship rights?

Why do symbols of militarism and royalty – Mounties, soldiers and Queens – appear in many recent representations of the Canadian nation?[98]

Campaigns such as Voices-Voix and the questions posed in the *People's Citizenship Guide* reflect the fact that the divide-and-conquer strategies pursued by the Harper Conservatives are subject to challenge – just as the divide-and-conquer strategies of the British Empire, so admired by Jason Kenney, were in the period of decolonization. As a consequence, the fate of multiculturalism and an equity agenda is far from being completely settled, despite reform by stealth.

NOTES

[1] For helpful comments and suggestions on an earlier draft of this chapter, I thank Matt James and Jack Jedwab. My thanks to Stephanie Stone for copy editing, and my thanks to Valerie Jarus for her work in the publication process on this chapter.

[2] Jason Kenney, "Speaking Notes for the Honourable Jason Kenney, P.C., M.P. Minister of Citizenship, Immigration and Multiculturalism: Address to the Empire Club" (Toronto, 25 May 2012), at http://www.cic.gc.ca/english/department/media/speeches/2012/2012-05-25.asp, accessed 20 August 2012.

[3] Yasmeen Abu-Laban, "North American and European Immigration Policies: Divergence or Convergence?" *European View* 5 (Spring 2007):9–14.

[4] Matthew Weaver, "Angela Merkel: German Multiculturalism Has 'Utterly Failed,'" *The Guardian*, 17 October 2010, at http://www.guardian.co.uk/world/2010/oct/17/angela-merkel-german-multiculturalism-failed, accessed 26 October 2012.

[5] Yasmeen Abu-Laban and Daiva Stasiulis, "Ethnic Pluralism under Siege: Popular and Partisan Opposition to Multiculturalism," *Canadian Public Policy* 18, no. 4 (1992):365–386.

[6] Raymond Breton, "The Production and Allocation of Symbolic Resources: An Analysis of the Linguistic and Ethnocultural Fields in Canada," *Canadian Review of Sociology* 21, no. 2 (1984):123–144.

[7] Abu-Laban and Stasiulis, "Ethnic Pluralism under Siege"; Grace-Edward Galabuzi, "Hegemonies, Continuities, and Discontinuities of Multiculturalism and the Anglo-Franco Conformity Order," in *Home and Native Land: Unsettling Multiculturalism in Canada*, ed. May Chazan, Lisa Helps, Anna Stanley, and Sonali Thakkar (Toronto: Between the Lines, 2011), 58–82; Nandita Sharma, "Canadian Multiculturalism and Its Nationalisms," in *Home and Native Land: Unsettling Multiculturalism in Canada*, ed. May Chazan, Lisa Helps, Anna Stanley, and Sonali Thakkar (Toronto: Between the Lines, 2011), 84–101.

[8] Will Kymlicka, "Ethnocultural Diversity in a Liberal State: Making Sense of the Canadian Model(s)," in *Belonging? Diversity, Recognition and Shared Citizenship in Canada*, ed. Keith Banting, Thomas J. Courchene, and F. Leslie Seidle (Montreal: Institute for Research on Public Policy, 2007), 39–86.

[9] Raymond Breton, "Multiculturalism and Canadian Nation Building," in *The Politics of Gender, Ethnicity and Language in Canada*, ed. Alan Cairns and Cynthia Williams (Toronto: University of Toronto Press / Royal Commission on the Economic Union and Development Prospects for Canada, 1986), 44; Abu-Laban and Stasiulis, "Ethnic Pluralism under Siege," 365–366.

[10] Breton, "Production and Allocation of Symbolic Resources"; Daiva K. Stasiulis, "The Symbolic Mosaic Reaffirmed: Multiculturalism Policy," in *How Ottawa Spends 1988/89: The Conservatives Heading into the Stretch*, ed. Katherine A. Graham (Ottawa: Carleton University Press, 1988), 81–112.

[11] Canada, Royal Commission on Bilingualism and Biculturalism, *Report of the Royal Commission on Bilingualism and Biculturalism – Book IV: The Cultural Contribution of the Other Ethnic Groups* (Ottawa: Information Canada, 1970).

[12] Canada, Parliament, House of Commons, *Debates*, 28th Parliament, 3rd Session, 1970–1972, vol. 8 (Ottawa: Queen's Printer, 8 October 1971), 8545.

[13] Abu-Laban and Stasiulis, "Ethnic Pluralism under Siege."

[14] Yasmeen Abu-Laban, "The Politics of Race and Ethnicity: Multiculturalism as a Contested Arena," in *Canadian Politics*, 2nd ed., ed. James P. Bickerton and Alain-G. Gagnon (Peterborough: Broadview Press, 1994), 244–247.

[15] Ibid.; Yasmeen Abu-Laban and Christina Gabriel, *Selling Diversity: Immigration, Multiculturalism, Employment Equity and Globalization* (Peterborough: Broadview Press, 2002).

[16] Abu-Laban, "Politics of Race and Ethnicity," 248.

[17] Stasiulis, "Symbolic Mosaic Reaffirmed," 90.

[18] Abu-Laban and Gabriel, *Selling Diversity*; Audrey Kobayashi, "Ethnocultural Political Mobilization, Multiculturalism, and Human Rights in Canada," in *Group Politics and Social Movements in Canada*, ed. Miriam Smith (Peterborough: Broadview Press, 2008), 131–157.

[19] Stasiulis, "Symbolic Mosaic Reaffirmed," 90–92; Abu-Laban, "Politics of Race and Ethnicity," 251.

[20] Abu-Laban and Stasiulis, "Ethnic Pluralism under Siege."

[21] Andrew Cardozo and Louis Musto, eds., *The Battle over Multiculturalism: Does It Help or Hinder Canadian Unity?* (Ottawa: Pearson-Shoyama Institute, 1997).

[22] Della Kirkham, "The Reform Party of Canada: A Discourse on Race, Ethnicity and Equality," in *Racism & Social Inequality in Canada: Concepts, Controversies & Strategies of Resistance*, ed. Vic Satzewich (Toronto: Thompson Educational Publishing, 1998), 243–267.

[23] Reform Party of Canada, *Principles and Policies*, 1990.

[24] Carol Johnson, Steve Patten, and Hans-Georg Betz, "Identitarian Politics and Populism in Canada and the Antipodes," in *Movements of Exclusion: Radical Right-Wing Populism in the Western World*, ed. Jens Rydgren (Hauppauge, NY: Nova Science, 2005), 89.

[25] Reform Party of Canada, "Blue Sheet," 1993, 6.

[26] Ibid.

[27] Yasmeen Abu-Laban, "On the Borderlines of Human and Citizen: The Liminal State of Arab Canadians," in *Targeted Transnationals: The State, the Media, and Arab Canadians*, ed. Jenna Hennebry and Bessma Momani (Vancouver: UBC Press, 2013), 68–85.

[28] Abu-Laban and Gabriel, *Selling Diversity*.

[29] Kobayashi, "Ethnocultural Political Mobilization."

[30] Abu-Laban, "On the Borderlines of Human and Citizen."

[31] Ibid.

[32] Jack Jedwab, "Canadian Opinion Ten Years after 9-11," 11 September 2011, at http://www.acs-aec.ca/en/search/?table=polls&ssection=0022&date=&title=&keywords=&action=search, accessed 27 January 2014.

[33] Jack Jedwab, "Exposure to Group Prejudice and Its Impact on Attitudes to Aboriginals, Muslims and Jews in Canada" (PowerPoint presentation based on a Leger Marketing survey conducted for the Association for Canadian Studies between 17 and 19 March 2012), 2012.

[34] Ibid.

[35] Galabuzi, "Hegemonies, Continuities, and Discontinuities of Multiculturalism"; Sharma, "Canadian Multiculturalism and Its Nationalisms."

[36] Daniel Hiebert, "Winning, Losing, and Still Playing the Game: The Political Economy of Immigration in Canada," *Tijdschrift voor Economische en Sociale Geografie* 97, no. 1 (2006):38–48.

[37] Janine Brodie, "Putting Gender Back In: Women and Social Policy Reform in Canada," in *Gendering the Nation-State: Canadian and Comparative Perspectives*, ed. Yasmeen Abu-Laban (Vancouver: UBC Press, 2008), 165–184.

[38] Galabuzi, "Hegemonies, Continuities, and Discontinuities of Multiculturalism," 80.

[39] Deepa Rajkumar, Laurel Berkowitiz, Leah F. Vosko, Valerie Preston, and Robert Latham, "At the Temporary-Permanent Divide: How Canada Produces Temporariness and Makes Citizens through its Security, Work and Settlement Policies," *Citizenship Studies* 16, no. 3–4 (June 2012):484.

[40] Ibid., 483–510.

[41] Elke Winter, *Us, Them, and Others: Pluralism and National Identity in Diverse Societies* (Toronto: University of Toronto Press, 2011).

[42] Association for Canadian Studies, "Younger Canadians Believe Multicultural-ism Works; Older Canadians, Not So Sure," 4 April 2012, at http://www.acs-aec.ca/en/social-research/multiculturalism-diversity/, accessed 13 September 2012.

[43] Ibid.

[44] Association for Canadian Studies, "Canadians Preferred Rhetoric: What Words and Phrases Resonate Most with Canadians?," 2 July 2010, at http://www.acs-aec.ca/en/social-research/canadian-history-knowledge/#?limit=10&start=10&csort=&order=, accessed 31 January 2014.

[45] It is beyond the scope of this chapter to address in detail all elements of im-migration policy and its evolution under the Harper Conservatives. However, while immigration numbers remained consistent under the Liberal governments of the 1990s and 2000s, the Harper Conservatives may be seen to have mobilized themes of security, control, and fraud into immigration and refugee policy. These emphases are in keeping with some of the more coded language of the Reform Party on immigration as the party's policy platforms evolved. See Kirkham, "Reform Party of Canada."

[46] Jason Kenney, "Foreword by the Minister," in *Annual Report on the Operation of the Canadian Multiculturalism Act 2007–2008* (Ottawa: Citizenship and Im-migration Canada, 2009), iii.

[47] Samuel P. Huntington, "The West Unique, Not Universal," *Foreign Affairs* 75, no. 6 (November/December 1996):28–46.

[48] Kobayashi, "Ethnocultural Political Mobilization."

[49] Hector Mackenzie, "Does History Mean Always Having to Say You're Sorry?" *Canadian Issues* (Winter 2010):48.

[50] Ibid.

[51] Jason A. Edwards and Lindsay R. Calhoun, "Redress for Old Wounds: Ca-nadian Prime Minister Stephen Harper's Apology for the Chinese Head Tax," *Chinese Journal of Communication* 4, no. 1 (2011):78.

[52] Ibid., 86.

[53] Ibid., 83.

[54] Matt James, "Wrestling with the Past: Apologies, Quasi-Apologies, and Non-Apologies in Canada," in *The Age of Apology: Facing Up to the Past,* ed. Mark Gibney, Rhoda E. Howard-Hassmann, Jean-Marc Coicaud, and Niklaus Steiner (Philadelphia: University of Pennsylvania Press, 2007), 137–153.

[55] Canadian Heritage, *Annual Report on the Operation of the Canadian Multicul-turalism Act 2006–2007* (Gatineau: Canadian Heritage, 2008).

[56] Citizenship and Immigration Canada, *Annual Report on the Operation of the Canadian Multiculturalism Act 2009–2010* (Ottawa: Citizenship and Immigration Canada, 2011), 17.

[57] Ibid.

[58] Matt James, "Neoliberal Heritage Redress," in *Reconciling Canada: Critical Perspectives on the Culture of Redress,* ed. Jennifer Henderson and Pauline Wakeham (Toronto: University of Toronto Press, 2013), 31–46.

[59] Ibid.

[60] Ibid.

[61] Jorge Barrera, "Prime Minister Needs to Apologize for Colonialism Denial: Native Groups," CanWest News Service, 30 September 2009, at http://ctvnewslondon.ca/SmokeSignals/news/HarperApologize.pdf, accessed 16 September 2012.

[62] Jennifer Henderson and Pauline Wakeham, "Colonial Reckoning, National Reconciliation? Aboriginal Peoples and the Culture of Redress in Canada," *English Studies in Canada* 35, no. 1 (March 2009):2.

[63] Quoted in Ian McKay and Jamie Swift, *Warrior Nation: Rebranding Canada in an Age of Anxiety* (Toronto: Between the Lines, 2012), 11.

[64] Barry Cooper, *It's the Regime, Stupid! A Report from the Cowboy West on Why Stephen Harper Matters* (Toronto: Key Porter, 2009).

[65] Marci McDonald, "The Man behind Stephen Harper," *The Walrus* (October 2004).

[66] David Jay Bercuson and Barry Cooper, *Derailed: The Betrayal of the National Dream* (Toronto: Key Porter, 1994), quoted in McKay and Swift, *Warrior Nation*, 13.

[67] McKay and Swift, *Warrior Nation*, 55; Citizenship and Immigration Canada, *Discover Canada: The Rights and Responsibilities of Citizenship* (Ottawa: Citizenship and Immigration Canada, 2012).

[68] Ibid., 15.

[69] Adam Chapnick, "A 'Conservative' National Story? The Evolution of Citizenship and Immigration Canada's *Discover Canada*," *American Review of Canadian Studies* 41, no. 1 (March 2011):20–36.

[70] Citizenship and Immigration Canada, *Discover Canada*, 9.

[71] Shauna Wilton, "Projecting Gender and Nation: Literature for Immigrants in Canada and Sweden," in *Gendering the Nation-State: Canadian and Comparative Perspectives*, ed. Yasmeen Abu-Laban (Vancouver: UBC Press, 2008), 60–75.

[72] Mireille Paquet, "Beyond Appearances: Citizenship Tests in Canada and the UK," *Journal of International Migration and Integration* 13 (May 2012):243–249.

[73] Jason Kenney, "Foreword: Minister of Citizenship, Immigration and Multiculturalism," in Citizenship and Immigration Canada, *Annual Report 2009–2010*, 5 (emphasis mine).

[74] Daniel Schwartz, "War of 1812 Reinterpreted over the Centuries: Comparing Commemorations 100, 150 and 200 Years after the War," CBC News, 15 June 2012, at http://www.cbc.ca/news/canada/war-of-1812-reinterpreted-over-the-centuries-1.1266067, accessed 6 December 2013.

[75] Don Butler, "Museum of Civilization Changes a Mistake, University Teachers Association Says," *Ottawa Citizen*, 17 October 2012, at http://www.ottawa citizen.com/travel/Museum+Civilization+changes+mistake+university+teachers/7405788/story.html, accessed 20 October 2012.

[76] J.L. Granatstein, *Who Killed Canadian History?* (Toronto: HarperCollins, 1998; repr. 2007), 173.

[77] Ibid., 174.

[78] Ibid., 110.

[79] Citizenship and Immigration Canada, *Discover Canada*, 21.

[80] Ibid., 23.

[81] Sherene H. Razack, *Casting Out: The Eviction of Muslims from Western Law & Politics* (Toronto: University of Toronto Press, 2008).

[82] Citizenship and Immigration Canada, *Discover Canada*, 9.

[83] Joe Friesen, "Ottawa Pumps Up Military Role in Citizenship Ceremonies," *Globe and Mail*, 24 August 2012, at http://m.theglobeandmail.com/news/politics/ottawa-pumps-up-military-role-in-citizenship-ceremonies/article2083103/?service=mobile, accessed 19 September 2012.

[84] Carys Mills, "How Applicants Are Stumbling on the Final Step to Becoming Canadians," *Globe and Mail*, 29 June 2012, at http://www.theglobeandmail.com/news/national/how-applicants-are-stumbling-on-the-final-step-to-becoming-canadians/article4382633/, accessed 20 October 2012.

[85] Ibid.

[86] Jason Kenney, "Foreword by the Minister," in *Annual Report on the Operation of the* Canadian Multiculturalism Act *2008–2009* (Ottawa: Citizenship and Immigration Canada, 2009), iii.

[87] Ibid.

[88] Voices-Voix, "Documenting the Silencing of Canadian Voices," at http://voices-voix.ca/en/facts, accessed 15 September 2012.

[89] Abu-Laban, "On the Borderlines of Human and Citizen."

[90] Paul Wells, "Jason Kenney: Harper's Secret Weapon," *Maclean's*, 29 November 2010, at http://www2.macleans.ca/2010/11/29/harper's-secret-weapon/, accessed 15 September 2012.

[91] Daiva Stasiulis, "Worrier Nation: Quebec's Value Codes for Immigrants," *Politikon* 40, no. 1 (2013):183-209.

[92] Michael Woods, "Quebec Values Charter Won't Pass, Harper Predicts, but Government Will 'Take Whatever Action Necessary' If It Does" *National Post*, 16 September 2013, at http://news.nationalpost.com/2013/09/16/quebec-values-charter-wont-pass-harper-predicts-but-government-will-take-whatever-action-necessary-if-it-does/, accessed 26 January 2014.

[93] Abu-Laban, "On the Borderlines of Human and Citizen."

[94] Stasiulis, "Worrier Nation."

[95] Winter, *Us, Them, and Others.*

[96] See Voices-Voix, "Documenting the Silencing of Canadian Voices."

[97] Esyllt Jones and Adele Perry, eds., *People's Citizenship Guide: A Response to Conservative Canada* (Winnipeg: Arbeiter Ring, 2011).

[98] Ibid., 73–74.

NATIONALISM, PLURALISM, AND THE DEMOCRATIC GOVERNANCE OF DIVERSITY

GENEVIÈVE NOOTENS

There has been much concern, in the last decade or so, about the kinds of claims allowed by liberal (pluralist) regimes of accommodation and integration. Such concerns, of course, have been influenced by prejudices against specific communities following the events of 11 September 2001, but they also reveal a more fundamental uneasiness concerning faith-based claims. In some countries, moreover, they seem to reflect a populist reaction to the impact of migration and globalization on welfare, the job market, and social stratification.

Quebec and Canada are no exceptions. Recall that when the Consultation Commission on Accommodation Practices Related to Cultural Differences (the Bouchard-Taylor Commission) held its hearings in 2007, many people expressed concerns about the protection of secularism and gender equality, which were largely identified as two basic values of *société québécoise*.[1] But such reactions are not unique to Quebec; very similar concerns have been expressed in English Canada about faith-based multiculturalism.[2] And, actually, some academics had already warned about an upcoming backlash against multicultural policies in English Canada.[3]

Once prejudices and ignorance are put aside, though, we are still left with the issue of distinguishing between claims that are legitimate and should be accommodated – either because they conform to basic principles

The Multiculturalism Question: Debating Identity in 21st-Century Canada, ed. Jack Jedwab. Kingston: School of Policy Studies, Queen's University. © 2014 The School of Policy Studies, Queen's University at Kingston. All rights reserved.

of liberal-democratic life, such as freedom of conscience and of faith, or because even if they could coexist uneasily with such principles, they are instrumental to integration[4] – and those that are not. At this level, it is important to recall that pluralism is not to be equated with relativism. As Daniel Weinstock has explained, "Moral pluralism is the view that moral values, norms, ideals, duties and virtues cannot be reduced to any one foundational consideration, but that they are rather irreducibly diverse."[5] Moral pluralism posits, first and foremost, that human beings are agents in a world characterized by heterogeneous moral experience. Relativism, on the other hand, embodies the claim "that the truth of moral judgments is relative to the conventions of the social group (or even to the individual whim) of the person issuing the judgment, and that these conventions or whims are not themselves subject to any further criterion of adequacy."[6] In the former case, there are moral constraints on what can count as a moral value, whereas in the latter case, there are no such constraints.[7]

Multiculturalism and interculturalism are both regimes of pluralism grounded in a threefold concern for respect for diversity, commitment to liberal rights and values, and integration into a civic identity and common public culture. It seems to be no easy thing to point to any significant difference between them.[8] For example, whereas interculturalism is sometimes interpreted as a will to assert a hierarchy to the benefit of French-speaking Québécois, it is clearly and deeply committed to the protection of basic liberal rights and freedoms. And while multiculturalism is charged with not being concerned about integration into a common civic culture, Kymlicka has argued that in Canada, immigrants are actually much more likely to participate in the political process; that the "ethnic penalty" in translating skills into jobs is the lowest in Canada of all Western societies; and that there seems to be a high level of mutual identification among immigrants and native-born Canadians, the latter viewing diversity as a key part of their Canadian identity.[9]

Yet interculturalism presents itself as a peculiar model of integration, and, very often, multiculturalism acts as a foil to explain its peculiarities; for example, interculturalism is said to stress integration, while multiculturalism is associated with "fragmentation." And when rightists in Quebec charge the province's "elites" with speaking out for multiculturalism, they actually suggest that Quebecers should doubt their patriotism. But why is this so? It has to do, of course, with the fact that when the Canadian policy of multiculturalism was established, it was seen, in Quebec, as an attempt by the federal government to downplay the significance of the *nation québécoise* as one of the founding peoples of Canada and to make it just one amongst the many cultures or ethnic groups to which Canadians of whatever origins belong. Recall that the first wave of this multiculturalism policy was shaped by the concerns and interests of white ethnic groups (Ukrainians, Poles, Hungarians, Germans, Dutch, and Italians) who feared that their status in Canada was threatened by the growing call, in the 1960s, to emphasize the French-English duality in the context of the emergence of Quebec nationalism.[10]

The main difference and tension between interculturalism and multiculturalism actually seems to rest with the issue of the clash of majority and minority nationalisms in Canada. As Labelle and Rocher have argued, the two models clash on a core dimension, one of "the explicit identification of the society in which the recognition of pluralism unfolds and the conditions related to it."[11] Interculturalism and multiculturalism are committed to the same basic principles, but they are founded on different views, experiences, and representations of the state and sub-state units composing the Canadian federation, of their legitimate claims and how they should be assessed, and of the impact of public policies on this status and claims. Hence, and once again, it is not that multiculturalism does not care about integration or that interculturalism asserts a hierarchy benefiting the Quebec French-speaking majority. The point is that as regimes of pluralism, they have developed along distinctive, related, and conflicting pathways. Multiculturalism began as a concern to recognize the contribution of white ethnic groups to the making of Canada;[12] interculturalism was developed as a model of integration for, and by, a minority nation concerned with the survival and flourishing of its own distinctive culture and language within a huge anglophone environment. In other words, multiculturalism and interculturalism relate to different – although not mutually exclusive – national identities.

This chapter will focus on such a "clash." More precisely, I am interested in clarifying the nature and impact of the power relationships that are rooted in it. Hence, I will not propose a detailed comparison of the models or the public policies they sustain.[13] The fact that they are embedded in related, different, and sometimes conflicting political and historical pathways impacts upon how the basic principles to which both are committed are represented and embodied.

A CASE OF CONFLICTING NATIONALISMS

The way in which Quebec has faced the challenges posed by the integration of ethnocultural diversity can be properly understood only if one takes a number of facts into account. The province, as a minority nation within the Canadian federation, has to deal with a majority nationalism conveyed by the central state. It must also deal with the challenges and prejudices commonly faced by minority nations. These include non- or mis-recognition by the majority, the necessity to protect its autonomy, the dominance of the majority in institutions and the Constitution, and a prejudice that some public policies designed to protect specific political and cultural institutions are illiberal (or, at the very least, less liberal than similar ones enacted by the majority) – for example, the protection of a common public language.

Several factors explain these challenges and prejudices. A significant one is that there has been a long-standing assumption, shared by dominant groups and consolidated states, that minority nationalism is illiberal (or less liberal than the nationalism of the majority or dominant group) or even non-modern. However, significant work on minority nationalism has demonstrated the falseness of this assumption. Minority nations are not necessarily less liberal, democratic, or modern than dominant groups or consolidated states.[14] Most often, the dominant group succeeds in presenting its values and cultural features as universal or "natural," but this capacity to diffuse its culture and own view of the state is a contingent historical result, not a fact of it being more democratic than minorities. The capacity to mark out minorities as minorities depends upon this capacity of the dominant group to present its values and principles as universal.

A second, and related, significant element in explaining the situation faced by minority nations is the equally long-standing assumption that the state is ethnoculturally neutral and, hence, that minorities are not endangered as long as the basic individual rights of their members are protected. Yet Kymlicka has shown such an assumption to be a myth. All liberal-democratic states are grounded in the diffusion of a majority culture and an overarching national identity as a means to subsume the national and ethnocultural differences among groups within the state, with the aim of contributing to state consolidation and stability.[15] Such an undertaking has gone hand in hand with the repression of ethnocultural diversity or its "benign neglect."[16] Canada is no exception to this. For example, James Bickerton stresses that there have been successive, and overlapping, forms of Canadian nationalism "that correspond to different majority orientations toward the nationhood claims of Québécois and Aboriginal minorities."[17]

This element in turn points to a third, also related, element: liberal-democratic states have long associated nationalism with minorities and their contention with the powers of central states; yet central states also project a powerful nationalism, one that is imbued with a legitimacy denied to minority nationalism. This is the phenomenon of majority nationalism. It is associated with policies of nation-building and articulated through the state. Such policies are usually meant to give citizens a language, a culture, and a common identity. Majority nationalism does not necessarily entail the transfer of the majority group's cultural characteristics to the nation projected by the state, but it "nonetheless consists in the articulation of a national community that usually has its core within the majority group and/or within the representations of the state's national identity as that group sees it (notably through the elites)."[18]

But is not that a wrong view of liberal-democracies since they basically relate legitimacy to individual consent and the protection of individual rights? It is true that liberal-democratic theory relates legitimacy to individual consent and rights, which, from its point of view, are key conditions for the proper exercise of political authority within a polity. However, the real story is much more complicated. For one thing, the modern representation of the body politic depends very much on the idea of the nation, and liberal-democratic states are no exception to this. Popular sovereignty in its modern guise is closely related to the idea of the nation: it is the people as a nation who rules and who is the beholder of ultimate sovereignty within the state. This is not a merely theoretical concept. It was developed in very empirical, concrete contexts in which representations of the body politic were changing and the power of the people (which was to include, eventually, ordinary people, the "commons") was asserted and won. (Let us think of the French Revolution, of the British "Glorious Revolution," of the American Revolution, for instance.) And the idea of the nation was also used as a tool to consolidate states, to mobilize citizens and sustain their identification with the polity by "building" the nation. Such processes are well documented.[19] So it is not only that the development of liberal democracy and the rights of peoples – as nations – have been closely intertwined since the 18th century; it is also that nation-building has accompanied, and reinforced, state-building. Processes of socialization, such as state-run education systems with "national" curricula and institutions in which people intermingle and cooperate, developed and sustain feelings of solidarity as well as the sense of a common history and fate. As the nation came to be identified as the rightful, and indivisible, holder of popular sovereignty, states benefited from consolidating as nations. Such policies can be implemented at the expense of national minorities without necessarily violating individual rights; for example, intra-state units may be delineated so that national minorities cannot form a local majority.[20]

One consequence of this is that one usually assumes, for example, that belonging to one state-wide community mitigates the impact of majority mechanisms since such belonging ensures solidarity even when some are in a minority on specific decisions. Yet the situation of minority nations obviously contradicts such assumptions. Even territorially concentrated minority nations in federal systems constantly risk being in a minority for decisions that pertain to competences belonging to the federal government or mechanisms depending upon a majority of provinces. But what is so special about the claims of minority nations? Unlike other types of claims to recognition, they invariably involve claims to self-rule – and those claims do not have to be framed in the language of identity politics. Nationality claims have a special status since, as Keating stresses, they carry with them "a more or less explicit assertion of the right to self-determination."[21] They are based on the claim "that the nation is historically constituted as a self-governing community; and that its people see themselves as a nation and wish to determine their future as a collectivity."[22] Self-determination "is part of the normative content of nationality itself."[23] Hence, recognizing national pluralism means recognizing that minority nations possess "a constituent power of their own."[24]

Self-rule does not, of course, imply outright secession; however, it implies equal participation by constituent powers in deciding the credentials of the association in the commonwealth. In the case of Quebec, for example, this principle was infringed upon by the 1982 patriation of the Constitution. When minority nations' self-rule is subordinated to the decisions of the majority within the state, and participation presented as a mere wilful devolution from the state to sub-state entities, minority nations are actually denied equal participation in the commonwealth. It is not that unity, stability, and co-operation within a larger polity are not valuable social goals. However, when such requirements subject minority nations solely on numerical grounds – namely, because they are in a minority – this cannot be justified from the point of view of liberal-democratic theory. In other words, at the level of the justification of norms – which assists us in evaluating the fairness of actual practices and institutions – liberal-democratic theory cannot subject minority nations' right to self-determination to the historically contingent domination of the majority or dominant group in the consolidation process.

Thus, dominant representations of political communities as national states conceal significant exclusions and asymmetries – amongst other things, what self-rule consists of. Acknowledging these forms of domination provides sufficient reason to embody some form of recognition of the right to self-rule in principles, norms, and institutions. Therefore, one can sustain an argument for the recognition of minority nations' claims to self-rule by stressing these asymmetries in power relationships that mark out majorities and minorities. One need *not* anchor such recognition in an argument debating group rights versus individual rights or in an essentialized conception of group identities. The commitment to self-rule is all the more important in plurinational federations like Canada since the legitimacy of such regimes depends not only upon their compatibility with liberal-democratic values, but also upon the respect of the normative ideal of reconciling shared rule with self-rule.

INTERCULTURALISM, LIBERAL-DEMOCRATIC THEORY, AND THE RIGHTS OF PEOPLES

From my point of view, it is largely because of this clash of nationalisms that Quebec's national identity and institutions – including the framework of integration developed since the late 1960s – have sometimes been depicted, implicitly or explicitly, as being illiberal – or, at the very least, as less liberal than those developed in English Canada – or even, sometimes, as racist. Multiculturalism is seen as emphasizing pluralism and diversity, while interculturalism is seen as emphasizing integration to the benefit of the French-speaking majority. But the fact that multicultural policy does not (yet) go along with the need for the majority to assert itself as such – as a majority – does not mean that the majority does not *act* as a majority. It merely means that it does not need to assert this status because it goes without saying. Its values are assumed to be shared, or shareable, by every citizen and would-be citizen of Canada. In other words, it goes without saying that immigrants, in English Canada, are to integrate into the majority culture and institutions, including English as the common public language – even though they may wish to retain some cultural traditions of their own. This is because majorities are inclined to see their values as being universal and to assume that for people to integrate into them is natural, normal, and even beneficial.

Quebec's situation is quite different, not because it is less committed to liberal-democratic values than the rest of Canada, but because its political status as a minority compels the design of public institutions to explicitly assert the embodiment of norms, principles, and mechanisms whose legitimacy would not be challenged if Quebec were a sovereign state. It is only in the case of minority nations that what Bouchard calls the "precedence" of the majority culture is seen as a kind of "accommodation" that minorities grant to the majority (which is itself a minority). For majority nations, precedence goes without saying. For example, the choice of an official language is not usually challenged and, in the case of majority nations, is actually obfuscated as a meaningful expression of nationalism. But the legitimacy of such a choice and the means by which minority nations need to implement it are very often challenged.[25] Hence, as Keating rightly stresses, "any status quo embodies a power structure, which allocates influence and resources in more or less unequal ways, and to subject the minorities to the test of universal norms while exempting the majority itself is a violation of universal values."[26]

One can, therefore, ground the assertion of national pluralism in the recognition that minority nations possess a constituent power of their own – a power that is conceded to majorities but often denied to minorities for reasons that I have explained – and the explicit assertion of the reality of power asymmetries that mark out majorities and minorities. But if this is sound – and if, for example, liberal-democratic theory really is dependent upon nationalism – why then has liberalism been so reluctant to recognize the rights of peoples? There are several historical, political, and philosophical reasons for this, but, basically, it is because the debate has often been framed as pitting individual against collective rights and requiring a stand to be taken on which has precedence. But this can only lead to a dead end. It is not because it is difficult to explain how those different "rights" are connected and should relate to each other that we should renounce fine-line thinking and end up deciding that only a hierarchization can clear up the matter – in which case, of course, we will stand for individual rights. The fact is that the basic unit of democratic theory is actually a *group* of people deciding together on their common public life.[27] To say so does not amount to asserting, for example, that the interests of the community – whatever this may mean – justify infringing upon the basic rights of individuals. It is merely to recognize that it is as a body politic that some people decide together how they are to organize and manage their relationships in the public sphere.

Moreover, significant works of liberal political philosophy in the last three decades clearly contradict the assumption that talking about the rights of peoples implies hierarchizing rights to the benefit of collective ones. Let me give but two examples, the works of Will Kymlicka and Michel Seymour. Kymlicka's work is built on the assumption that cultural belonging – belonging to a societal culture – is a primary good since it is the framework within which individuals may make autonomous choices about their life plans – about, actually, what a good life is and how it should be led. On this basis, Kymlicka justifies three types of rights for individuals as members of minorities (national minorities, ethnic groups, new social movements).

As for Seymour, he proposes a liberal theory of the collective rights of peoples whose core idea rests upon an analogy between peoples' institutional identity as national societal cultures and individuals' institutional identity as citizens. In both cases, it is toleration of the different ways that they (peoples or individuals) conceive of themselves that grounds the recognition of their institutional identity. In much the same way that being recognized as a citizen does not depend upon one's specific religious beliefs, it is not because of specific values, beliefs, ends, or projects that national societal cultures are recognized, but because of core goods relating to a common public language, common public institutions, and common public history. Peoples are the subject of collective rights because they have a public institutional "personality" that is embodied in the public sphere through features that *seem* to be collective – a common public language, for example. And there is no hierarchy of individual and collective rights: both are equally significant as both peoples and individuals are autonomous sources of valid moral claims. The collective rights of peoples ensure that they can sustain, develop, and manage their own institutions, and those institutions frame individuals' range of options for a good life.[28]

Thus, we shall neither underestimate the importance of majority nationalism as a prism through which minority nations' claims and models of integration are interpreted nor fear the impact of the recognition of pluralism, whether as ethnocultural diversity or as national plurality within a state. The advent of a pluralist perspective in several fields of political philosophy[29] has accompanied a wider trend to debates about the monist nature of a battery of political, legal, and social representations – one of which is the sovereign territorial nation-state. The most significant works in this trend are surely the critique of the dominant statist historiography,[30] a series of works on minority nationalism,[31] groundbreaking work on the politics of recognition,[32] the critique of modern constitutionalism,[33] and the critique of the naturalization of the sovereign territorial state. These works challenge dominant views of the organization and justification of the legal-political order, and they make explicit the power relationships that have structured them – and, hence, that also impact upon how the moral universe of agents is structured. For example, Tully's critique of modern constitutionalism shows how it has been used to impose on First Nations a normative and legal order to which they are estranged and that has made them into objects, rather than agents, of public policy.[34] None of these works defends "fragmentation" or relativism; rather, they challenge the monism of dominant representations and question how the interests and views of dominant groups have structured policies and been imposed upon "minorities."

Nor do they imply that all claims to recognition are equivalent and should be accommodated. As I have said, nationality claims involve claims to self-rule – this is part of the normative content of nationality. This does not mean that any claim to self-rule in any circumstances would be acceptable. Yet if one is well aware of the inequalities embedded in dominant (state) nationalism and the consequences of this for minority nations – including, very often, the assessment of claims by two sets of standards depending on whether one is in a majority or in a minority – the following rule should prevail: in order to object to self-rule, one would have to demonstrate that self-rule by a specific minority nation would produce undemocratic consequences that do not in any way parallel the undemocratic consequences, for this minority nation, of being subjected to a majority nation. Many people have feared that the recognition of minority nations is actually a slippery slope to secession; but there are significant issues of fairness that are to be taken into account, and one should also not underestimate the threats to stability that may follow from denials of recognition.

As to ethnocultural diversity, all claims are not equivalent to one another or necessarily worthy of recognition and accommodation. They are to be assessed, even if this exercise is sometimes difficult and does not necessarily lead to straightforward, unequivocal "answers." As I have stressed, pluralism is not skeptical about the existence of moral values. Recognizing the complexity of the moral universe, the under-determinacy of moral principles, and the different ways in which human beings as moral agents relate to such a universe does not imply renouncing moral judgment or the building of a common world, of a "we" that is public. To paraphrase Taylor, the assumption of the equal value of cultures is but a starting point; it does not mean that all cultures have a *right* to equal value.[35]

In some cases – for example, in Jacques Beauchemin's work[36] – I suspect that the charges against pluralism are actually grounded in an unwillingness – or at least an incapacity – to distinguish relativism from the relativization of the modern ideal of the nation-state. But this amounts to defending a static ideal and neglecting the changing character of political communities, including the empirical processes of democratization. The latter largely depends on contentious politics, in the course of which social and symbolic boundaries are challenged and renegotiated. Hence, representations of the nature of political communities and of the governing relationships also change.

Liberalism is an inclusive ideal endowed with powerful philosophical and political resources. In many cases of claims to recognition and accommodation, we can build on these resources to assess these claims – although the basic principles may be interpreted differently and do not lead to straightforward answers, as I have said. Let me take, for example, one case that was widely discussed in Quebec, the one of the kirpan.[37] Although in the ruling the Court referred to "Canadian values based on multiculturalism," the decision is justified on the ground of protection of freedom of religion – which is an individual right – and respect for minorities. The right to wear the kirpan was granted to an individual, not a group, after a careful analysis of its nature, the possible risks it could raise, and the impact of infringing upon it. Hence, it is no different from the case in which an employee of a Montreal store was granted the right not to work on Sundays because, as a Catholic, she considered it to be contrary to the principles of her faith.[38] Recall that in other cases, infringing upon religious freedom was considered justified under section 1 of the *Canadian Charter of Rights and Freedoms*, such as in the case of those parents who, as Jehovah's Witnesses, refused medical treatment for their minor child, alleging that it infringed upon their freedom of religion.[39]

However, since liberalism is closely related to the development of the modern territorial state – which has been consolidated in part thanks to nation-building – it has yet to redefine its relationship to that political form of the polity and to grant a full place to claims – such as those of minority nations – that challenge international society as it has developed since the 18th century. Works such as Kymlicka's and Seymour's contribute to such a reflection. And interculturalism, indeed, seems very close to Seymour's liberal theory of the collective rights of people. It places equal emphasis on the commitment to liberal rights and democracy, the development of a common public culture, integration, and the common responsibility of citizens to its realization; and it stresses equally the significance of Quebec's historical journey and the changing character of its culture(s).[40]

In other words, interculturalism is consistent with the liberal conception of the right of peoples to self-determination because it emphasizes the participation of every citizen in public institutions in which principles, orientations, norms, and public policies are debated within the framework of liberal-democratic rights – the representation of the people as institutional agent. It is definitely a liberal-pluralist regime that is able to deal with ethnocultural diversity. In the context of the Canadian federation, its main difficulty in being recognized as such rests mainly with the sometimes tense relations between the two conflicting national pathways.

NOTES

[1] Similar concerns came to the fore once again in 2009–2010, although accommodation of faith-based claims was not the only target of critics.

[2] Will Kymlicka, "The Evolving Canadian Experiment with Multiculturalism" (paper presented at the *Symposium international sur l'interculturalisme: Dialogue Québec-Europe*, Montreal, 25–27 May 2011), at http://www.symposium-interculturalisme.com/pdf/actes/Chap1_4KYMLICKA.pdf, accessed 17 December 2013.

[3] Some commentators even think that the cross-party consensus on multiculturalism actually hides its failure; see ibid. In Europe, there is clearly such a backlash, although there, multiculturalism is most often used to describe cultural diversity rather than coherent public policies aiming at integrating immigrants. Academics criticize multiculturalism, arguing that it actually undermines the pursuit of justice – see, e.g., Brian Barry, *Culture and Equality* (Cambridge, MA: Harvard University Press, 2001) – or that it continues racist and colonial policies. For a discussion of these standpoints, see Duncan Ivison, "The Moralism of Multiculturalism," *Journal of Applied Philosophy* 22, no. 2 (2005):171–184.

[4] For example, some people hold that the hijab should not be worn in public institutions such as schools because it is a religious symbol or may be interpreted as a symbol of the subjugation of women (or both). Nonetheless, it seems far preferable in the long run to tolerate it in schools than to have young women withdrawn from these institutions, where they are socialized to common liberal-democratic values.

[5] Daniel Weinstock, "Moral Pluralism," in *Routledge Encyclopedia of Philosophy*, vol. 6, ed. Edward Craig (London: Routledge, 1998), 529. Tenets of moral pluralism disagree as to the plural sources of moral value, yet they share the view "that morality has developed to protect and promote basic interests related to human wellbeing and flourishing, but that since there is no unique form that human wellbeing must take, there can consequently not be a theory of morality unified around one supreme value" (ibid.). See also Veit Bader and Ewald R. Engelen, "Taking Pluralism Seriously: Arguing for an Institutional Turn in Political Philosophy," *Philosophy and Social Criticism* 29, no. 4 (2003):379.

[6] Weinstock, "Moral Pluralism," 530.

[7] Ibid.

[8] See, e.g., Gérard Bouchard, "What Is Interculturalism?" *McGill Law Journal* 56, no. 2 (2011):395–468.

[9] Kymlicka, "Evolving Canadian Experiment with Multiculturalism," 5–6. He has warned against the idea that multiculturalism fares relatively well in English Canada because English Canadians are uniquely tolerant and open-minded. He believes that the comparative success of multiculturalism in English Canada is due primarily to lucky timing (ibid.). Actually, Quebec does not seem less tolerant than English Canada; see, e.g., Gérard Bouchard, *L'interculturalisme: Un point de vue québécois* (Montreal: Boréal, 2012), 266–267. In addition, a recent study

by Statistics Canada revealed that in 2010, there were, proportionally, twice as many hate crimes committed in Ontario (5.7 per 100,000) as in Quebec (2.7 per 100,000); Statistics Canada, "Police-Reported Hate Crime in Canada, 2010," at http://www.statcan.gc.ca/pub/85-002-x/2012001/article/11635-eng.htm, accessed 3 February 2014.

[10] Kymlicka, "Evolving Canadian Experiment with Multiculturalism," 9. These groups feared that the talk about duality, the two founding nations, and bilingualism and biculturalism would leave them marginalized. So they mobilized to make sure "that the accommodation of Quebec not be done at their expense, and that any strengthening of linguistic duality therefore be accompanied by recognition of ethnic diversity" (ibid.).

[11] Micheline Labelle and François Rocher, "Les limites indépassables de l'interculturalisme en contexte canadien" (paper presented at the *Symposium international sur l'interculturalisme: Dialogue Québec-Europe*, Montreal, 25–27 May 2011), 10, at http://www.symposium-interculturalisme.com/pdf/actes/Chap8_1Labelle et Rocher.pdf, accessed 17 December 2013 (translation mine).

[12] Kymlicka, "Evolving Canadian Experiment with Multiculturalism."

[13] Recall that interculturalism had no official definition before the Bouchard-Taylor Commission was established in 2007 and that no official governmental policy on interculturalism per se has yet been enacted. However, the commission stressed that the analysis of the way Quebec has dealt with ethnocultural diversity since the 1960s reveals a broad framework of continuity operating on the recognition that Quebec is a nation. For a detailed description of interculturalism, see, amongst others, Gérard Bouchard and Charles Taylor, *Building the Future: A Time for Reconciliation* (Quebec: Consultation Commission on Accommodation Practices Related to Cultural Differences, 2008); Bouchard, "What Is Interculturalism?"; and François Rocher, Micheline Labelle, Ann-Marie Field, and Jean-Claude Icart, "Le concept d'interculturalisme en contexte québécois: généalogie d'un néologisme," report presented to the Bouchard-Taylor Commission (Chaire de recherche en immigration, ethnicité et citoyenneté, Université de Québec à Montréal: Montreal/Ottawa, 2007).

[14] See, e.g., Michael Keating, *Plurinational Democracy: Stateless Nations in a Post-Sovereignty Era* (Oxford: Oxford University Press, 2001); Jocelyn Maclure and Alain-G. Gagnon, eds., *Repères en mutation: Identité et citoyenneté dans le Québec contemporain* (Montreal: Québec Amérique, 2001); Alain-G. Gagnon and James Tully, eds., *Multinational Democracies* (Cambridge: Cambridge University Press, 2001); and Alain-G. Gagnon, Monserrat Guibernau, and François Rocher, eds., *The Conditions of Diversity in Multinational Democracies* (Montreal: IRPP, 2003).

[15] Will Kymlicka, "Nation-Building and Minority Rights: Comparing West and East," *Journal of Ethnic and Migration Studies* 26, no. 2 (2000):183–212; and André Lecours and Geneviève Nootens, "Understanding Majority Nationalism," in *Contemporary Majority Nationalism*, ed. Alain-G. Gagnon, André Lecours, and Geneviève Nootens (Montreal and Kingston: McGill-Queen's University Press), 3–18.

[16] Kymlicka, "Nation-Building and Minority Rights."

[17] James Bickerton, "Janus Faces, Rock, and Hard Places: Majority Nationalism in Canada," in *Contemporary Majority Nationalism*, ed. Alain-G. Gagnon, André Lecours, and Geneviève Nootens (Montreal and Kingston: McGill-Queen's University Press), 147. One of these forms relates to an orientation "that rests on

a pluralistic but uninational concept of Canada embodied in the core ideas of bilingualism, multiculturalism, a strong central government, and a constitutionally entrenched *Charter of Rights and Freedoms*" (ibid.). Another form embraces various forms of political asymmetry, and a third form defends equally the idea of one inclusive nation and distinct minority nations (ibid.).

[18] Lecours and Nootens, "Understanding Majority Nationalism," 11.

[19] As to the implicit dependency of liberal-democratic theory on nationalism, see, e.g., Margaret Canovan, *Nationhood and Political Theory* (Cheltenham, UK: Edward Elgar, 1996).

[20] Will Kymlicka and Christine Straehle, "Cosmopolitanism, Nation-States and Minority Nationalism: A Critical Review of Recent Literature," *European Journal of Philosophy* 7, no. 1 (1999):65–88.

[21] Keating, *Plurinational Democracy*, 3.

[22] Ibid.

[23] Ibid., 4.

[24] Ibid., 161. Hence, such recognition raises issues that are different from those concerning the integration of immigrants or equal rights for women. See Geneviève Nootens, "Nations, Sovereignty, and Democratic Legitimacy: On the Boundaries of Political Communities," in *After the Nation? Critical Reflections on Postnationalism*, ed. Keith Breen and Shane O'Neill (London: Palgrave Macmillan, 2010), 196–213.

[25] Lecours and Nootens, "Understanding Majority Nationalism," 3. Indeed, official language is a good example of the existence of two sets of standards for minority nations. The enactment of an official language for the overarching citizenry is deemed legitimate because of its properties as a tool for national integration. But when a territorially concentrated minority nation wishes to enact its own language as the official one on its territory, it is often depicted as being illiberal, backward, discriminating, or even racist.

[26] Keating, *Plurinational Democracy*, 2.

[27] The idea of the nation is a way of representing such a *universitas* as a body politic.

[28] Michel Seymour, *De la tolérance à la reconnaissance: Une théorie libérale des droits collectifs* (Montréal: Boréal, 2008). He argues that the object of collective rights are institutional (participatory) goods that have a collective (identity) dimension. A participatory good is a good whose production and consumption are collective; it must be beneficial for individuals and cannot run counter to their interests. The collective right *par excellence* is the right to self-determination, but it is an internal right. Secession is only a remedial right.

[29] See Daniel Weinstock, "Le défi du pluralism," *Lekton* III, no. 2/IV, no. 1 (1993):7–28.

[30] See, e.g., Keating, *Plurinational Democracy*.

[31] See Gagnon and Tully, *Multinational Democracies*; Gagnon, Guibernau, and Rocher, *Conditions of Diversity in Multinational Democracies*; and Stephen Tierney, *Constitutional Law and National Pluralism* (Oxford: Oxford University Press, 2004).

[32] Charles Taylor, "The Politics of Recognition," in *Multiculturalism: Examining the Politics of Recognition*, ed. Amy Gutmann (Princeton, NJ: Princeton University Press, 1994).

[33] James Tully, *Strange Multiplicity: Constitutionalism in an Age of Diversity* (Cambridge: Cambridge University Press, 1995).

[34] On the last point, see Martin Papillon, "Towards Postcolonial Federalism? The Challenges of Aboriginal Self-Determination in the Canadian Context," in *Contemporary Canadian Federalism: Foundations, Traditions, Institutions*, ed. Alain-G. Gagnon (Toronto: University of Toronto Press, 2009), 408.

[35] Taylor, "Politics of Recognition."

[36] From Beauchemin's point of view, claims to recognition divide and make it difficult to frame a political project that embodies some idea of social responsibility and solidarity that may mobilize people. He argues that pluralism supports a representation of society as fragmented and divided and that interculturalism implies that the majority group renounces its own identity and its own history as a French-speaking nation. All claims that do not conform to the ideal of the nation-state are *a priori* to be rejected. See Jacques Beauchemin, *La société des identités* (Montreal: Éditions Athéna / Chaire MCD, 2004). A significant paradox ensues since if this is the case, then it is also a justification of majority nationalism and cannot support the recognition of Quebec as a nation and constituent power within the Canadian state.

[37] In a unanimous ruling in 2006, the Supreme Court of Canada granted a young Sikh from Montreal the right to wear his kirpan at school. The court ruled that the decision of the school board prohibiting him from doing so infringed significantly upon his freedom of religion since it actually deprived him of the right to attend public school. Such an infringement was not considered justified for the purpose of section 1 of the *Canadian Charter of Rights and Freedoms*. See *Multani v. Commission scolaire Marguerite-Bourgeoys*, 2006 SCC 6, [2006] 1 SCR 256.

[38] *Smart c. Eaton*, T.D.P.Q. MONTRÉAL, 1993 CanLII 1039 (QC TDP).

[39] This is a very good description of the fact that liberal rights belong to a wider moral conception, to which are related the choices that one may make thanks to these rights. These choices are assessed on two grounds – namely, their proper meaning and whether they embody acceptable forms of autonomy.

[40] All citizens accept that their culture may be transformed through their interactions, and such interactions give rise to a new culture, nurtured by all the others; see Bouchard and Taylor, *Building the Future*.

WHAT IS REALLY AT STAKE IN THE MULTICULTURALISM/ INTERCULTURALISM DEBATE

DANIEL WEINSTOCK

Much ink has been spilled in recent years in trying to determine whether there exists a substantive difference between *multiculturalism* and *interculturalism* and, to the extent that a difference does exist, whether one or the other can claim superiority as both a theoretical and a policy response to the fact of ethnocultural and religious diversity in modern societies, especially those that have in the last century or so been marked by significant immigration.

This debate has occurred in a context in which there has been both philosophical and, more important, political questioning of the approach that countries such as Canada, Australia, and the United Kingdom have taken to addressing the challenges and the opportunities presented by the significant immigration that has occurred in these countries and of the philosophical vision that has underpinned this approach. Criticisms have come both from the political right, among observers and politicians who think that a more aggressive model of integration is required in order to avoid immigration giving rise to a "fifth column" of domestic enemies, and from the political left, among those who fear that the lack of a common identity, which too generous a policy of cultural accommodation might give rise to, risks eroding the psychological and emotional basis of support for the redistributive policies of the welfare state.

In this context, interculturalism might be seen both, on its merits, as a better way of integrating immigrants and, strategically, as a way

The Multiculturalism Question: Debating Identity in 21st Century Canada, ed. Jack Jedwab.Kingston: School of Policy Studies, Queen's University. © 2014 The School of Policy Studies, Queen's University at Kingston. All rights reserved.

of responding to the concerns that have been voiced by both left- and right-wing critics of multiculturalism without having to throw the baby out with the bathwater.

The context that I have just briefly described is exacerbated in Quebec. Not only have Quebec politicians echoed the concerns voiced around the world, including English Canada, concerning the potentially pernicious effects of multiculturalism, but they have also voiced suspicion about Canadian multiculturalism being part of an attempt by federalist politicians to drown out the distinctiveness of Quebec's claim to national distinctiveness in an ocean of ethnocultural and religious diversities of all kinds. It is no surprise that in this context, prominent Quebec politicians have gone out of their way to state that multiculturalism is not a Quebec value. Nor is it a surprise that theorists and politicians who may have been sympathetic to multiculturalism have felt the need to hide that fact and to rally instead around the banner of interculturalism in order to be able to speak out in favour of values and policies of openness and accommodation to ethnocultural diversity that might not even get a hearing were they too closely associated with a reviled concept.

My intention in this chapter is to obtain a clearer sense of what the stakes are in the multiculturalism/interculturalism debate. The argument that I will be developing is that interculturalist critics of multiculturalism have been mistaken in their characterization of the relationship between the two models of diversity management. On the one hand, I will argue that multiculturalism, far from constituting a distinct political philosophy or ideology, is best thought of as resulting from the application of core liberal principles to circumstances of cultural diversity. On the other, I will argue that interculturalism is best thought of not as a policy-relevant set of principles. Rather, it puts forward an attractive vision of the kind of society that might (or might not) emerge from a society ordered by just principles (including multicultural principles) given the presence of the right mix of sociological characteristics.

INTRODUCTION

What is the putative distinction between multiculturalism and interculturalism? This is a difficult question to answer. Both terms are moving targets and are defined in slightly different ways by different theorists. What is more, sets of policies that have been identified as "multicultural" in different jurisdictions have often been quite different.

Defenders of interculturalism have made out the key philosophical differences in the following way.[1] Multiculturalism, in their view, has not taken seriously enough the demands of social cohesion. Multiculturalist theorists have on this account been right to insist on the fact that the assimilationist model that characterized many countries touched by immigration (and by other forms of internal diversity, such as linguistic and national diversity) until at least the immediate post–World War II period did an injustice to minority cultural groups by making the more or less complete renunciation of their patrimonial cultures into a condition of full citizenship and by enacting policies, especially in the area of education, that have sought to enforce that condition. They have been right to assert that we should not think of the state as "belonging" to the majority group within society.[2] They have been right to assert that the identities of such groups should be not only tolerated but "recognized."[3] And they have been correct in thinking that this requires more than just abstract pronouncements about the equal worth of all cultures, but rather active policies through which multicultural citizens are given space to continue to live according to the strictures and rites of their patrimonial cultures at the same time as they take on aspects of the culture of the society to which they have migrated. What is most controversial in the context of recent Quebec politics, multiculturalism rightly requires of states that, within reasonable limits, they structure workplaces, public institutions, and "public space" more broadly so as to accommodate the practices of minority cultural groups. They must, to use the term that has been at the centre of heated debate in Quebec for almost a decade now, practice "reasonable accommodation."

Where multiculturalism goes wrong according to interculturalists is to ignore the risks for social cohesion that the policies and principles that I have just mooted represent. According to interculturalist theorists, if multiculturalist principles, which provide citizens of diverse cultural provenances with ample opportunities to "opt out," are not balanced by principles that incite them to "opt in," then ghettoization of an unattractive and potentially politically costly kind might ensue. To rehearse two concerns that I have briefly alluded to above, and that have been widely discussed, the lack of a shared identity might make it more difficult to generate the psychological basis of support for the redistributive policies of the welfare state, and it might also create enclaves of people who, though formally citizens, identify to a greater degree with foreign governments and foreign causes than they do with domestic ones, to the point where they might in extreme circumstances be tempted to commit acts of violence when tensions arise between the country in which they live and the country with which their allegiance still lies. Above and beyond these instrumental concerns, interculturalists have claimed that a "purely multicultural" society – that is, one in which people live peacefully and solidaristically beside one another, but without forging a shared identity – is, all things being equal, less attractive than one in which they exit their enclaves to engage in interactions of various kinds with their fellow citizens.

Interculturalists claim to have forged a position that allows for the strengths of both the multiculturalist and the assimilationist views to be combined, while rejecting the disadvantages linked to both of these positions, at least in their orthodox variants. Interculturalism shares with the assimilationist perspective an emphasis on the importance of shared identity, but it rejects the thought that such an identity is best arrived at through the coercive imposition of the identity of the majority culture. Rather, it hypothesizes that such an identity can come about through the non-coercive interactions of citizens. It therefore shares with multiculturalism the idea that recognition and respect for cultural differences are non-negotiable imperatives in a society marked by ethnocultural and religious diversity. But for the interculturalist, these moral attitudes are starting points for respectful dialogue and interaction.

I put to one side the question of whether the interculturalist critique of multiculturalism is or is not a caricature of the latter position. Nasar Meer and Tariq Modood have, for example, shown that canonical texts in the multicultural literature, like those of Charles Taylor and of Bhikhu Parekh, place dialogue at the core of their theories of multiculturalism.[4] What I want to suggest is that the kinds of policy goals that are put forth by multiculturalists (as construed in the foregoing portrayal), and those that are argued for by interculturalists, are not the same *kinds* of goals. While multiculturalist policy objectives are, in my view, best construed as requirements of liberal justice, the interculturalist is with respect to the policy objectives that she recommends caught on the horns of an unattractive dilemma. Either she cleaves to the strictures of a broadly liberal-democratic political ethos, or she is forced to resort to a kind of perfectionism that might end up being perfectionistic and coercive in ways that are not dissimilar to the ways in which the assimilationist is. Let me develop this point in two stages. First, I will substantiate the view that those multicultural policies that have been at the centre of the greatest discussion and controversy in many parts of the world, and in particular in Quebec in recent years, are best thought of as straightforward demands for liberal justice. Second, I will describe the dilemma that I foist upon interculturalism and suggest that the best move for the defenders of that position is to join forces, *from the point of view of policy*, with multiculturalists.

MULTICULTURAL POLICIES AS DEMANDS FOR LIBERAL JUSTICE

Will Kymlicka has in a recent paper argued that multiculturalism in Canada and in other countries marked by a variety of patterns of diversity has revolved around three "reversals" in policy and in basic philosophy. These reversals have had to do with the selection and treatment of immigrants, with the treatment of sub-state nationalisms, and with the perspective taken on Indigenous groups. In all three cases, Kymlicka argues, states such as Canada and Australia have moved from an assimilationist perspective to one that is more accommodating of diversity. The way in which that shift has occurred obviously depends upon the particularities of these three very different kinds of cases. Recognizing national groups, be they Aboriginal or based on prior colonial settlement, as in the case of the Québécois, means recognizing a long history of occupation of a territory as well as settled institutions and practices. A similar attitude toward recent immigrants will have quite different policy implications.[5]

In all three of these cases, what might be termed "multicultural restraint" is a direct implication of principles of liberal-democratic justice. Kymlicka himself has provided the canonical case for multicultural restraint in the case of multi-nation states.[6] Why should larger entities not seek to impose their institutional forms and laws upon constituent national groups (or, as Kymlicka calls them, "societal cultures")? The argument can be developed in two ways, one that is grounded in the quintessential liberal value of liberty, the other in the value of equality. These arguments are almost too well known to rehearse: are there reasons grounded in liberty for the state to prescind from imposing its own laws and institutions upon sub-state national groups and accept constitutional strictures that protect those institutions from the potential steamroller that unadulterated majoritarianism would represent?

One reason is that for the members of those groups, the liberty to pursue an autonomously constructed conception of the good life requires membership in a "societal culture." Members of the majority societal culture do not have to take any particular steps to ensure that their culture with its attendant institutional infrastructure will survive, but members of minority cultures do need to take such steps in order to achieve the same result. The liberty-based argument thus dovetails into an argument based on the consideration of equality. It seems unfair that people not be positioned equally with respect to the important good of membership in a societal culture simply because of the contingent fact that they happen to belong to a smaller rather than a larger societal culture. Providing members of smaller, sub-state nations with some degree of institutional independence and self-determination seems to be a way of levelling the playing field, rather than providing them with a benefit unavailable to others.

The case for accommodation of cultural differences born of the diversification of societies like Canada through immigration can similarly be made either through a liberty or through an equality lens. Though it is a mistake to conflate religious accommodation with management of immigration at the conceptual level, there can be no doubt at the empirical level that one of the main results of immigration, and especially of immigration policies that have departed from earlier policies, which basically favoured the immigration of white European Christians, has been to increase the religious diversity of a society such as Canada. It is thus no surprise that the question of religious accommodation has loomed large in recent debates, both in Canada and in a host of other countries.

Here again, the case for accommodation is an outgrowth of core liberal commitments. Either because they ascribe intrinsic importance to the goods that flow from religious belonging, or because they recognize the importance that religion has in the lives of people of faith, or more pragmatically because they are cognizant of the bloodshed and suffering that have resulted from the failure to protect religious freedoms, most modern constitutions contain robust protections of religious liberty.

In the Canadian constitutional context, this liberty is not without limits. Section 1 of the *Canadian Charter of Rights and Freedoms* opens up the possibility of religious liberty being abridged when such an abridgment can be shown to serve a legitimate policy goal and that the abridgement is as parsimonious as possible. So laws that limit religious freedom, even in the pursuit of a legitimate legislative objective, must avoid being overly broad in their restriction of religious freedom. Where the exercise of religious liberty by a member of a minority (or of a majority) religious group does not demonstrably impede the attainment of a legitimate goal, that exercise must be accommodated.[7]

As in the case of minority nationalism, the liberal case for accommodating cultural differences that arise paradigmatically (but not exclusively) as a result of immigration can also be made through an equality lens. A seemingly "neutral" law, such as one that prescribes that the day of religious worship of the majority religious group be chosen as a mandatory day of rest and of cessation or limitation of economic activity, weighs disproportionately on members of minority religious groups. What is more, members of such groups are antecedently much more likely to be victims of discrimination and stigmatization than are members of the religious majority. Laws that weigh more heavily upon them than upon members of the majority thus compound disadvantages that they may already be suffering as members of religious minorities.

The case for reversing the previous policy of aiming at assimilation for Aboriginal nations can also be justified on impeccably liberal grounds. That case can be grounded in considerations similar to those that Kymlicka has developed more generally for sub-state national groups. As Kymlicka has pointed out, it can also be grounded in a concern for respecting treaties. And, more controversially,[8] it can be grounded in an imperative to repair or compensate for historical injustice.

To the extent that multiculturalism points to the requirement that members of minority cultural groups be provided with institutional space within which to express their cultural identities, that requirement is a straightforward implication of principles of liberal justice.

Now, some might argue that I have rigged the argument here by presenting a minimalist version of multiculturalism, one that would not be recognized by many of its principal exponents. First, it could be argued, multiculturalism is not just about the state getting out of the way in order to allow people to express their cultural identities. Rather, it is also about the state actively *supporting* such minority groups in a context in which an unbridled marketplace of cultural identities would inevitably lead to the erosion of some smaller and more vulnerable groups.[9] Second, and in a related context, some might argue that multiculturalism in its full-blooded form is not simply about accommodation. Rather, it is also about celebration and recognition.[10]

Let me begin by considering this second potential objection to the minimalist conception of multiculturalism that I have just described. In this view, a multicultural society is one in which a warmer relationship obtains between the state and the cultural groups that are present in civil society, one that can be characterized by using notions such as respect and recognition.

Respect and recognition denote attitudes and dispositions rather than state policies. In order to determine whether the claim according to which multiculturalism requires something akin to recognition or respect, it is important that we determine how this requirement can be "cashed out" in policy terms. One way in which respect and recognition might denote a requirement that goes above and beyond the kinds of accommodations that, as we have seen, are direct implications of multiculturalism in contexts of cultural diversity would be to claim that it is not sufficient that states allow members of minority cultural groups to express their identities; they must also provide these groups with support sufficient to buttress them against the vagaries of the cultural marketplace. It is one thing, in this view, for the state simply to step out of the way and allow its citizens to live their lives according to the precepts and strictures of the cultures with which they identify. It is quite another to provide groups with tools with which to increase the likelihood that when the state does step aside, there will still be communities robust enough to take advantage of the institutional space thus provided.

If this is the way in which to understand the stronger requirement of recognition and respect, then it essentially reduces to the first of the objections described above. An appropriate response to this line of argument would begin by pointing out that it is not true that the kind of requirements that can be derived from liberal principles merely require abstention, or "benign neglect," on the part of the state. Most obviously, the accommodation of minority nations' institutions requires a proper constitutional framework that clearly delineates spheres of jurisdiction. Such a constitutional framework is a positive achievement. Compensatory justice for historical wrongs requires the setting up of appropriate institutional mechanisms for adjudication and the formulation of just settlements. And in the Canadian context, at least, courts have adopted a fairly capacious understanding of religious freedom, one that requires not only that individuals be able to act as they see fit in accordance with their beliefs, but also that believers' communities be given some degree of latitude in the articulation of the requirements of faith.

So the rights to accommodation that follow from liberal principles are not purely "negative." They require not only abstention on the part of the state, but also the setting up of institutions and the recognition of the institutions and rules of cultural groups. But, and here we come to the second aspect of the response that can be made to the defenders of a more robust multiculturalism, it is one thing for multicultural policies to make it easier for individuals who are antecedently disposed to want to live their lives in at least partial accord with their patrimonial cultures that they be able to do so without too much difficulty. The centripetal force of majority cultures is very great, and so there can be some circumstances in which individuals will succumb to it not wholeheartedly, but rather for lack of a feasible alternative. When the state supports minority cultures – for example, by providing funding to ethnocultural organizations or by allowing such accommodations to have circumscribed decision-making powers over some aspects of community life – then it increases the ability of individuals to act in accordance with desires that they already have, but that may in a less generous political context appear unrealizable.

But it is quite another thing for the state to tolerate practices through which minority groups ensure their viability by denying members' exit rights or by making these rights difficult or very costly to exercise. When the state allows this to happen – for example, by enforcing collective property-rights regimes that require individuals who wish to leave a community to accept destitution as a condition of exit – then it has gone beyond the perfectly acceptable practice of levelling the playing field by removing obstacles to individuals being able to act on intentions and de-sires that they already have and has entered the much more dubious area of protecting groups against the autonomous agency of their members.[11]

Thus, to respond to the first criticism of the pared-down multicultur-alism that, I have argued, is a requirement of liberal-democratic first principles, the claim is that defenders of a more robust multiculturalism either fail to appreciate the positive institutional implications of what I have been describing here as a more "minimal" multiculturalism, or they would have it act in ways that would appear to be deeply problematic, something that would involve their complicity in propping up structures of authority that seek to preserve the viability of a minority community by preventing its members from exercising their autonomous agency.

There may be other ways in which to understand the second of the objections mooted above. It could be that defenders of a respect- or recognition-centred conception of multiculturalism would have the state express these attitudes toward the minority cultural communities in their midst through symbolic affirmation – for example, through the inclusion of the symbols of minority cultural communities in official settings, or by prescinding from too overt a display of the symbols of the cultural majority, with the aim of ensuring that all citizens are made to feel as if they are full-fledged members of the community, regardless of their status as members of minority or of majority ethnocultural or religious groups.

Again, I would argue that liberal first principles generate robust and plausible conclusions with respect to what might be termed the "symbolic" activity of the state. Clearly, there are institutional functions and locations that are sufficiently central to the identity of the state that considerations of equal citizenship require that the state evince neutrality in the symbols it makes use of. To revert to a much-discussed example in the Quebec context: it is one thing for the seat of the Speaker of the National Assembly to be dominated by a crucifix; it is quite another for public and institutional spaces less central to the identity of the state to bear reminders of the dominant role that the Catholic Church has played in Quebec history. A non-Catholic can reasonably consider that the presence of the former is incompatible with her being treated as an equal citizen by the state. No such implication is reasonably drawn from non-neutral symbolism in other contexts.

The idea that I want to put forward is that the language of equal citizenship provides us with a way in which to generate principles to govern the symbolic activity of the state. Neutrality is required of the state when the failure to act neutrally would be incompatible with the principle of equal citizenship. It also, however, allows the state to define plausible limits to the requirement of neutrality in the symbolic domain. While citizens of diverse cultural origins have a right to be treated as equal citizens, they do not have a right to be immunized from the natural cultural bias that might be the natural concomitant of the particular history that the community that they are now a part of has undergone.

The main conclusion of this discussion is that multiculturalism is, at least according to one of its most influential and important philosophical accounts, best construed as a distinct ideology or theory. Rather, it results from applying bedrock liberal-democratic principles to social conditions of cultural diversity. This does not in and of itself constitute a defence of multiculturalism. But it does increase the burden of argument that has to be taken on by those who would reject it.

INTERCULTURALISM EMERGES FROM A SOCIETY ORDERED BY JUST PRINCIPLES

In a paper entitled "Multicultural States and Intercultural Citizens," Will Kymlicka makes the following observation: while states such as Canada and Australia have engaged in the "reversals" described above, abandoning assimilationist policies and practices in favour of ones that seek to accommodate immigrant groups, religious minorities, and minority, sub-state national groups, this process has not been matched by a concomitant increase in the degree to which citizens evince interest in the other cultures that surround them. In Kymlicka's words, "the *state* has made itself accessible to all citizens, and affirms the important contribution that each group makes to the larger society. But from the point of view of individuals, the presence of other groups is rarely experienced as enriching."[12] Kymlicka points out the paradox that as states become more accommodating of cultural difference, the need for individuals to engage with others, and to develop skills for intercultural exchange and communication, might actually lessen as citizens are enabled by state multiculturalism to avoid contact with others to greater degrees than had previously been the case.

Kymlicka's characterization of the ideal of the intercultural citizen does not, in my view, capture the distinctiveness of the intercultural position. In Kymlicka's view, the intercultural citizen is one who would develop skills and dispositions for intercultural exchange as a path for personal enrichment and flourishing. Interculturalists would argue that what matters is not that citizens in an intercultural dispensation learn to appreciate those from whom they differ culturally, but rather that they engage in dialogue and shared practices that might over time give rise to a shared identity. However, the important point for present purposes is the relative vagueness of the prescriptions that in Kymlicka's view flow from the observation that a gulf is beginning to appear between the multiculturalism of the state and the relative lack of interest that citizens of multicultural states display in engaging with members of other cultures, whether for the purposes of personal enrichment or for that of the uncoerced, dialogical creation of a shared identity. "We should," he writes, "encourage individuals to have the ability and desire to seek out interactions with the members of other groups, to have curiosity about the larger world, and to learn about the habits and beliefs of other peoples."[13]

As a policy prescription, this is quite vague and indistinct. Presumably, it points to a requirement that our educational institutions ought to try to meet. It is, however, quite unclear that this is an educational goal that clearly distinguishes interculturalism from multiculturalism. Indeed, more minimal multiculturalists of the kind that I have been describing would happily endorse such an educational agenda. Indeed, multiculturalists of the kind that I have described would have their own reasons to sign off on such an educational agenda. Indeed, to the extent that multicultural theorists are concerned with people being able to exercise their rights of exit, it would seem that one empirical condition of their being able to do so is by being educated in contexts that allow them to acquire a full appreciation of the cultural possibilities that exist for them in the society to which they belong, rather than being trapped by a strictly monocultural education.

The problem is that the ideal of the intercultural citizen is one that, in a sense, lies beyond the plausible reach of policy, at least of policy that seeks to remain within broadly liberal-democratic bounds. What interculturalists have done is not so much describe a plausible policy goal as formulated a wish as to the kind of society that citizens will create with one another once multiculturalist policy goals have been achieved.[14] Creating space in which different cultural groups can affirm their distinctive practices and identities rather than being forced into an assimilationist straightjacket can give rise to a number of social states of affairs. It can give rise to a society of cultures living side by side peacefully but with only limited interaction. Or it can generate a society in which citizens of different groups engage passionately and intensely with one another across ethnocultural lines. It can give rise to just about any intermediate point between these two extremes.

Let us accept for the sake of the present argument that social states of affairs that lie closer to the latter extreme are to be preferred to those that lie closer to the former, either because of the intrinsic merits of this kind of society or because of the instrumental benefits that flow from it. Once the state has implemented the kinds of multicultural policies that, as we have seen, are requirements of a liberal-democratic political morality applied to circumstances of ethnocultural and religious diversity, what further policies can it enact in order to nudge the society it governs closer to the interculturalist ideal? Clearly, as we have seen, it can tailor educational policy to attempt to reach this result, though we should maintain a healthy skepticism about what might be termed "educational voluntarism," the idea that educational institutions can orient the ways in which students will take up the messages conveyed to them by pedagogical initiatives aimed at creating a specific set of dispositions and that the main way in which schools reach this objective is through the explicit, rather than through what has been called the "hidden," curriculum.[15]

But, educational policy with all of its limitations notwithstanding, the question of whether a society that has enacted multicultural policies of the kind required by liberal first principles comes to resemble an interculturalist utopia of uncoerced communication and interaction or a more fragmented, ghettoized society of the kind that interculturalists fear lies well beyond the reach of public policy (unless policy is of a perfectionist, coercive kind that, as we shall see in a moment, risks being counterproductive even if it were possible) remains. Indeed, the disposition of members of diverse cultural groups to engage in the kind of dialogue that interculturalists hope will give rise to a shared identity depends upon a wide range of factors. For example, the history of relations among groups may have a significant impact on the willingness of members of groups to interact. One could well understand members of groups that have been subjected to stigmatization and injustice before the adoption of multicultural policies feeling distrustful of the members of the majority cultural groups with whom they are now expected to engage in dialogue. Geographical considerations may also loom large: it may be easier for the breaking down of cultural walls required for patterns of exchange and dialogue to emerge to occur in dense urban areas than in places where groups are more geographically spread out. The extent of cultural and linguistic differences among groups may also affect their ability and willingness to engage in intercultural communication. In other words, once the state has established just relations among members of different cultural groups, there may be very little it can do to steer a society ordered by just institutions and principles in one direction rather than another. The direction it ends up taking will result from patterns of sociological facts more than it will from policy.

I have been assuming in making this argument that policy-making in the kind of society I have been envisaging occurs within a broadly liberal framework. By this I mean that it largely avoids coercive paternalism and wholesale limitations on individual liberties. Perhaps this assumption is unwarranted, however. Indeed, perhaps it involves me in a form of vicious circularity. Why assume that liberal constraints on the pursuit of perfectionist ends should obtain? Powerful arguments have been formulated by legal and political philosophers in recent years to the effect that the liberal stricture according to which states should remain neutral with respect to controversial conceptions of the good have prevented them from achieving desirable policy ends, especially, but not exclusively, in the area of public health. Why should we not countenance a little bit of paternalism, be it of the "libertarian"[16] or "coercive"[17] variety, if doing so will allow us to reduce smoking-related deaths, obesity, and the like?

This is not the place to wade into the complex debates that have opposed defenders of the position according to which states ought to remain neutral among controversial conceptions of the good and perfectionists who believe that, within limits, the state ought to be able to override individual preferences in order to achieve desirable ends.[18] The point I want to make is that in the present case, one in which the policy objective to be achieved would be to inculcate dispositions for intercultural dialogue and interaction among members of a culturally diverse society, paternalism may very well be counterproductive. When paternalistic policies seek to change individual behaviour – for example, by making it harder for people to smoke or eat unhealthy foods – the emphasis is on changing what people do. Public health objectives are more robustly met when people stop wanting to eat fatty foods or lose the addiction to nicotine. But they can also be met without, as it were, a change of heart.

This is resolutely not the case where the dispositions to engage in cultural dialogue are concerned. As we have known since John Locke wrote his famous *Letter on Toleration*, legislation can coerce and thereby alter behaviour, but it cannot change people's hearts. If what is required to achieve the kind of society that interculturalists admire is not just that people behave toward one another in certain ways, but also that they feel disposed to engage in dialogue and interaction possessed of certain attitudes, then it is unlikely that even coercive paternalism will achieve its end. Indeed, one can imagine it being downright counterproductive – people may feel more ill-disposed toward groups that they have been forced to interact with than they might otherwise. Imagine, for example, the resentment that might arise were a state intent upon breaking down institutional obstacles to intercultural interaction in order to prohibit religious or cultural groups from educating children in religiously or culturally homogeneous schools. Children and their parents would by virtue of such a policy be thrown into a situation in which they were forced to interact across cultural lines. But it is unlikely that the circumstances under which they were led to interacting would be propitious from the point of view of giving rise to the kind of social relation that interculturalists hope for.

CONCLUSION

I conclude from these admittedly brief remarks that although interculturalists may be correct in claiming that multicultural policies are only a prolegomenon to the development of harmonious intercultural relations, and of the emergence of the kind of shared identity that they think might come about as a result of uncoerced intercultural exchanges, they are wrong to the extent that they think that the achievement of this kind of society lies within the reach of policy. Policies that cleave to broadly liberal strictures – for example, educational policies of the kind that have been adopted in Quebec through the new course on Ethics and Religious Cultures – may be of dubious efficacy in achieving intercultural objectives given the other forces of socialization to which children are subjected (including the "hidden curriculum" present in schools).[19] Perfectionist policies that may be effective in changing behaviour are beside the point when what is required is changing people's minds and hearts.

Where does this leave us? I will conclude with some largely impressionistic observations that lead me not to share the pessimism evinced by Kymlicka. Kymlicka observes, for example, that the transformations that have occurred at the level of policy in Canada have not given rise to a concomitant shift in individual attitudes. French and English Canadians, in his view, are no more interested in learning about one another than they were in the bad old days of "whites only" immigration policy and of assimilationist attitudes toward minority nations. And, in general, he fears that multicultural policies at the level of the state may actually inhibit the development of the requisite attitudes on the part of citizens because they are people with the ability to live a culturally isolated life if that is what they want.

My own experience of a city like Montreal – which is at the heart of the debates about diversity management that have occurred in Quebec in recent years – belies this pessimistic assessment. The geographical boundaries that used to separate English- and French-speaking communities quite rigidly are beginning to erode. Children of immigrants are, like urban youth all over the world, forging an urban culture that draws in a syncretic manner on the French culture they encounter in public schools, on North American and increasingly global Anglophone culture, and on their own patrimonial traditions. Multicultural *mélange* and the creation of the kind of intercultural identities that interculturalists hope for at the level of the nation-state are developing in a chaotic manner in Montreal and in immigrant cities around the world. Indeed, in my view, the challenge that immigrant societies will have to face squarely in years to come has to do with the growing gulf between densely populated urban centres on the one hand and suburban and rural areas on the other.

NOTES

[1] Here I draw heavily on Nasar Meer and Tariq Modood, "How Does Interculturalism Contrast with Multiculturalism?" *Journal of Intercultural Studies* 33, no. 2 (2012):175–196. For the most systematic statement of the position in the Quebec context, see Gérard Bouchard, *L'interculturalisme: Un point de vue québécois* (Montreal: Boréal, 2012).

[2] For a very radical formulation of this position, see Joseph Raz, "Multiculturalism," *Ratio Juris* 11, no. 3 (1998):193–205.

[3] Charles Taylor, "The Politics of Recognition," in *Multiculturalism: Examining the Politics of Recognition*, ed. Amy Gutmann (Princeton, NJ: Princeton University Press, 1994); Anna Elisabetta Galeotti, *Toleration as Recognition* (Cambridge: Cambridge University Press, 2002).

[4] Meer and Modood, "How Does Interculturalism Contrast with Multiculturalism?"

[5] Will Kymlicka, "Canadian Multiculturalism in Historical and Comparative Perspective: Is Canada Unique?" *Constitutional Forum* 13, no. 1 & 2 (2003):1–8.

[6] Will Kymlicka, *Multicultural Citizenship* (Oxford: Oxford University Press, 1995).

[7] For the most thorough and systematic account of religious freedom in the Canadian constitutional context, see Louis-Philippe Lampron, *La hiérarchie des droits: Convictions religieuses et droits fondamentaux au Canada* (Brussels: Peter Lang, 2012).

[8] Jeremy Waldron, "Superseding Historical Injustice," *Ethics* 103, no. 1 (1992):4–28; Nahshon Perez, *Freedom from Past Injustices: A Critical Evaluation of Claims for Inter-generational Reparations* (Edinburgh: Edinburgh University Press, 2012).

[9] I have explored this more ambitious conception of multiculturalism and its philosophical rationale. See Daniel Weinstock, "Le paradoxe du multiculturalisme libéral," in *Le multiculturalisme a-t-il un avenir?*, ed. Sophie Guérard de Latour (Paris: Hermann, 2013).

[10] See Galeotti, *Toleration as Recognition*.

[11] This is a variant of Will Kymlicka's much-discussed distinction between external protections and internal restrictions. See Kymlicka, *Multicultural Citizenship*.

[12] Will Kymlicka, "Multicultural States and Intercultural Citizens," *Theory and Research in Education* 1, no. 2 (2003):156.

[13] Ibid., 158.

[14] I have discussed this point at greater length in relation to the work of Gérard Bouchard; see Daniel Weinstock, "Interculturalism and Multiculturalism in Canada and Quebec: Situating the Debate," in *Liberal Multiculturalism and the Fair Terms of Integration*, ed. Peter Balint and Sophie Guérard de Latour (Palgrave-Macmillan, 2013).

[15] See Daniel Weinstock, "The Problem of Civic Education in Multicultural Societies," in *The Politics of Belonging: Nationalism, Liberalism, and Pluralism*, ed. Alain Dieckhoff (Lanham, MD: Lexington Books, 2004).

[16] Richard H. Thaler and Cass R. Sunstein, *Nudge: Improving Decisions about Health, Wealth, and Happiness* (London: Penguin Books, 2009).

[17] Sarah Conly, *Against Autonomy: Justifying Coercive Paternalism* (Cambridge: Cambridge University Press, 2013).

[18] I have contributed to this debate; see Daniel Weinstock, "Neutralizing Perfection," *Dialogue: Canadian Philosophical Review* 38, no. 1 (1999):45–62.

[19] This is not to say that courses such as this are not justified in virtue of the informational content they place at the disposal of students. All things being equal, it is better that our children know more rather than less about the religious cultures that surround them even if this knowledge does not smoothly translate into a desire to engage in intercultural dialogue and thereby to forge a new, inclusive shared identity.

MULTICULTURALISM, LANGUAGE, AND IMMIGRANT INTEGRATION

EVE HAQUE

In late 2012, Statistics Canada released the final portion of its 2011 census data, focusing on language use across the country: both official and non-official languages, including Indigenous languages. As always in Canada, discussions about language issues tend to be of great interest to the broader public, and this was reflected in the wide coverage generated by the census data and the attendant analyses they generated, particularly in the mainstream media. However, discussions about language also become a proxy for a host of other discussions, including anxieties, about the state of the nation and national belonging. This is particularly notable given that the data suggest an increase in non-official-language mother tongues and their use in homes across the nation.

Some of the reported data included the fact that about one-fifth of the Canadian population (6.6 million people) spoke a language other than French or English at home in 2011, with a vast majority of these languages being "immigrant" languages. Only about 213,000 people reported speaking an Indigenous language at home, and 25,000 reported using a sign language.[1] Despite the increasing presence of immigrant languages in Canada, the official languages remained strong, with 58 percent reporting English as a mother tongue, 22 percent reporting French as a mother tongue (66 percent reported English as a home language, and 21 percent reported French to be a home language), and 98 percent of Canadians stating that they were able to conduct a conversation in either English or French (English and French are also spoken on a regular basis at home by 94 percent of the population).[2]

The Multiculturalism Question: Debating Identity in 21st-Century Canada, ed. Jack Jedwab. Kingston: School of Policy Studies, Queen's University. © 2014 The School of Policy Studies, Queen's University at Kingston. All rights reserved.

These general facts about the state of official and non-official languages generated a lot of coverage in the media, and the analyses of the relationship between official and non-official languages were inevitably couched in terms of multiculturalism. This was particularly visible in the print media and exemplified in such headlines as "Is Multiculturalism Stifling Bilingualism," "Over 200 Languages Spoken in Multicultural Canada: Census," and, in the context of Quebec, "Allophones on the Cusp of Outnumbering Francophones in Canada."

Given the interactive nature of online print media, the hundreds of comments generated by stories on the language census data also served as a direct entry into the opinions of the broader public on language issues and reflected how media-circulated discourses about language are interpreted and taken up by the general reading public. Reading through hundreds of comments in the national online print media, it is clear that for a majority of the comment writers, relatively banal facts of the language census data can inflame extensive ethnicized and racialized anxieties about multiculturalism and the integration of "multicultural others," presumably indexed through their perceived official language(s) proficiency and use of non-official languages.

In this chapter, I want to examine how these concerns about non-official languages have become a naturalized site for articulating a host of anxieties about multiculturalism and the integration of racialized "immigrants" in Canada. Specifically, I want to trace how language and culture have, in the present, come to be an acceptable proxy for the articulation of exclusions and commentary about multiculturalism and immigration, even as articulating these exclusions overtly in terms of race and ethnicity is seen to be unacceptable in the public sphere. Tracing this shift requires first an examination of the assumptions about language that are embedded in these present-day discourses, then a careful historicization of language policy and immigration in Canada, with a particular focus on the Royal Commission on Bilingualism and Biculturalism (1963–1970), as it is out of this commission that the dual-white-settler foundations of the nation are affirmed through the *Official Languages Act* (1969) and, as a response, multiculturalism first emerges as policy (1971). I argue that it is the affirmation of Canada as a dual-white-settler nation, and the consolidation of immigrants as multicultural others in the terrain of language and culture in an era when paradigmatic changes to immigration policy were taking place, that underlies the naturalization of these contemporary exclusionary discourses through the proxy of language.

CONTEMPORARY DISCOURSES

Online print media provide a direct window into the opinions of the broader public on language issues in Canada because of the immediate interactivity readers have through the online comments sections of newspaper articles. This was very much the case for articles published on the language census results as these newspaper articles generated hundreds of comments, particularly in national newspapers such as the *Globe and Mail* and the *National Post*. Although the online commentary covers the full spectrum of opinions on languages in Canada, some dominant threads of concern can be traced. These overlapping threads include the links made among non-official languages, multiculturalism, immigration, and integration.

One discernible theme is the identification of non-official languages as a problematic outcome of multiculturalism and thereby also a threat to official languages; this is emblematized in comments such as this one.[3]

> Comment 1: Whilst around the world people are craving to learn English, in Canada a native English speaker must constantly dumb themselves down to speak broken English with New Canadians who have been told to "keep their cultures." The solution: government services in English or French ONLY. And kill Multiculturalism while there is still a semblance of a nation left. Or, be prepared to speak Mandarin, Tagalog, Punjabi, Farsi … if you want a job.

As well, embedded in these comments is the idea that immigration, specifically immigration from the Global South, serves to overwhelm the viability of official languages, cultures, and dual-settler harmony.

> Comment 1: The current government's toughening of language require-ments is long overdue. And we also need to reassess two sacred cows of that pockmarked P.O.S., Pierre Trudeau: third world mass immigration and multiculturalism. Throwing the doors open to immigrants from cultures with values 180 degrees out of sync of ours was a disaster. And allowing ethnic enclaves – something big U.S. cities experienced, with disastrous results – was the inevitable result of Turdeau's [*sic*] multiculti experiment.

> Comment 2: I think it would be worth embracing our own culture instead of being swallowed by immigrating cultures. I think it is sickening to see all that fighting between "French" and "English" speakers, because at the end of the day they are fighting for the same exact thing – to preserve their cultural identity.

As an extension of anxieties about the threats posed by multiculturalism and immigration, non-official-language use is also frequently cited as a barrier to integration.

> Comment 1: People coming to Canada to live should take every opportun-ity to build their English or French language skills if either is not their first language. I work with people whose ability to advance is directly related

to their inability to speak English properly. By continuing to focus on their native tongue and by not becoming totally fluent in the primary language of this region, they are failing their own futures. My forebears all came to this country not speaking a word of English and all worked very hard to develop their English language skills to integrate. Their children, grandchildren and great-grandchildren are all successful Canadians. I am grateful that they didn't try to hold on (too much) to the languages they brought with them.

Comment 2: The Toronto subway is like a tower of Babel. Two people talking right in front of you in a different language is rude. Two bank tellers the other day talking in front of me in some Indian language. I complained to the manager. Speak English or French in public. Do what you want at home. Can't speak the language don't complain you can't find good work. I won't hire anyone who cannot communicate properly.

Finally, online comments also served to reaffirm the naturalized dual-white-settler foundations of Canadian society.

Comment 1: There's more to this than numbers. English and French are the founding languages. Yes, though it's not politically correct to mention history before 1971, Canada was FOUNDED. There's a reason English and French are the official languages.

Comment 2: Canada's official languages are French and English. This is not a negotiable point. Language is a corner stone of culture. I feel quite strongly that people who come to Canada should come with the language skills needed to thrive in our society. Why? Because English and French are what defines Canada as Canada. If they don't have the language skills, then they simply shouldn't be here. At some point what [sic] have to ask that people coming here show the respect Canada deserves.

These comments are all premised on a number of naturalized assumptions about the relationships among language, culture, immigration, and integration into the nation. First, there is an assumption that a shift from non-official-language to official-language proficiency is inevitable and desirable, as well as an index of functional progress measured through generational socio-economic mobility and unidirectional integration into an unpacked notion of "Canadianness." This is related to the common idea that lack of official-language skills is jeopardizing the socio-economic integration of immigrants, with integration primarily defined narrowly and instrumentally as integration into the labour market.

Critical here is the conflation of language and culture so that concerns about non-official languages become concerns about racialized immigrants and that English and French come to stand in for the founding cultural groups. This underscores the idea that Canada was "founded" by the English and French, thereby erasing a viable Indigenous presence and offering a truncated view of Canadian history as one of equivalence between the English and French as dual-white-settler founders of the nation. Acknowledgement, if at all, of Indigenous peoples is at best as homogenized past presence and a pathologized present, and this gives rise to the contemporary discourse of the inevitable decline of Indigenous languages, captured best in headlines such as "Aboriginal Languages in Deep Trouble."

What remains unexamined in these comments is the question of who is considered to be "Canadian" and neo-liberal assumptions about integration as the sole responsibility and, in the case of a perceived lack of integration, the pathology of immigrants. As well, these discourses are deeply embedded in assumptions about the primacy of a monolingual norm, or at best an aspirational official bilingual norm, which in turn serves to denigrate non-official languages and erase the human capacity and global pre-eminence of multilingualism. The interesting question is, how did this understanding of language, immigration, and integration, commonly collapsed under the rubric of multiculturalism, come to be naturalized to the point that it has become banal commentary whenever the question of language in Canada is invoked? A careful historicization of language policy and immigration can begin to unpack these discursive relations.

THE EMERGENCE OF LANGUAGE POLICY IN CANADA

Although a genealogy of language policies in Canada should ostensibly begin at Indigenous contact with European peoples in the territories that now constitute the Canadian nation-state, policies on language or policies that have had direct implications for language use in Canada can be traced back to the pre-Confederation era, most notably to the *Treaty of Paris* in 1763, which put an end to the Seven Years' War between England and France and made Canada a British colony. Written in French, the treaty explicitly guaranteed no linguistic rights for the inhabitants of the colonies, but it did clearly guarantee freedom of religion, which was significant given that the French inhabitants were mostly Catholic. The *Royal Proclamation* of 1763, written and retaining its legal force in English, not only declared that all civil and criminal cases would now be judged in accordance with English law but also put in place a test oath for Anglicanism for employees of the state, something that in effect excluded most French Canadians from government and related jobs. However, in 1774, the *Quebec Act* was passed, allowing for the reinstatement of French civil law, a repeal of the test oath, and recognition of the Catholic faith, thereby allowing French Canadians to move into the civil service.

In 1791, the *Constitutional Act* was passed, dividing Canada into Upper and Lower Canada. The act mentioned language only in sections 24 and

29, which concerned the administering of oaths for voters or members of the legislative assembly in either English or French. In Lower Canada, the *Constitutional Act* resulted in conflicts over the selection of the speaker for the assembly and wrangling over which language(s) the minutes and legislative documents would be recorded in, although, in practice, legislative bilingualism became the norm. In Upper Canada, English law was established, and English became the de facto language of the legislature. After the Rebellions of 1837, Lord Durham wrote his famous Durham Report (1839), which provided the basis for the *Act of Union*; Durham advocated the union of both Upper and Lower Canada and the assimilation of the French Canadians.

The *Act of Union* was passed in 1840; it joined Upper and Lower Canada and created a single legislative assembly. Although section 41 declared English to be the sole language of Parliament, francophone members agitated to have it abrogated, and, in 1848, section 41 was finally repealed to reinstate the previous de facto bilingualism. Canada came into being on 1 July 1867 with the confederation of the four provinces – Ontario, Quebec, Nova Scotia, and New Brunswick – but would remain a British colony until 1931. The *Constitution Act*, or *British North America Act*, also came into force on 1 July 1867 and included two sections with implications for language rights. The first was section 133, which guaranteed the right to use English and French in the Parliament of Canada and the federal courts. Section 93 protected the educational rights of religious minorities – that is, rights that could be dated back to before 1867. This section meant that francophones could use these religious rights to protect the French Catholic schools, and this would provide a framework for future language protections for official-language minorities.

Since Confederation, at the provincial level, there have been many notable language-policy issues, including, among others, the Laurier-Greenway compromise of 1896 in Manitoba and Ontario's notorious Regulation 17, passed in 1912. Federally, however, a policy of non-intervention meant that outside the legislative sphere and the judicial system, there was little intervention by the federal government to expand bilingualism.[4] This does not mean that there was no desire to expand bilingualism; from as early as 1904, Henri Bourassa, founder of *Le Devoir*, began to press for bilingualism in federal institutions: "The basis of Confederation is the duality of races, the duality of languages, guaranteed by the equality of rights."[5] Bourassa's statements would foreshadow André Laurendeau's editorials in *Le Devoir* many decades later, in the early 1960s. In Quebec, this was the post–Quiet Revolution era, with the independence movement gaining momentum and giving rise to new types of political groups, which used a variety of means to advocate for a range of sovereignty and separatist options. At this time, concerns about the Anglo-centric linguistic practices of the federal government were being raised, and it was in this era that calls for an inquiry began to emerge, including in various editorials by Laurendeau in *Le Devoir*.[6]

It was Laurendeau's editorial of 20 January 1962 that would be the most explicit in demanding a royal commission of inquiry into bilingualism, in turn sparking other calls for a commission. Although Prime Minister Diefenbaker rejected all calls for an inquiry, when the Liberals were elected with a minority government in 1963, the establishment of the royal commission became one of Prime Minister Pearson's first acts. In his Speech from the Throne on 16 May 1963, Pearson declared that he would be establishing a commission to examine how "the basic partnership of English speaking and French speaking people" could be "truly equal" and "how the fundamentally bicultural character of Canada may best be assured."[7] Pearson's speech anticipated the terms of reference, and on 19 July 1963, the creation of the royal commission was announced as well as the appointment of ten commissioners, including André Laurendeau and Davidson Dunton as co-chairs. It is through this commission that contemporary anxieties about multiculturalism and integration come to be naturalized as concerns about non-official languages.

ROYAL COMMISSION ON BILINGUALISM AND BICULTURALISM

The Royal Commission on Bilingualism and Biculturalism (RCBB) was critical for transforming the terrain upon which national belonging would be articulated in the modern Canadian nation-state. The post–World War II historical context was ripe for the shift from a strict discussion of "races" to one of culture and language with respect to community and national belonging. However, the commission did not begin in this way in 1963 as the terms of reference, outlined before the preliminary hearings, specified that the commission was to

> inquire into and report upon the existing state of bilingualism and bicultur-
> alism in Canada and to recommend what steps should be taken to develop
> the Canadian Confederation on the basis of an equal partnership between
> the two founding races, taking into account the contribution made by the
> other ethnic groups to the cultural enrichment of Canada and the measures
> that should be taken to safeguard that contribution.[8]

The first events of the RCBB were the preliminary public hearings, which took place over the course of two days in early November 1963 in Ottawa. Interest in these hearings was extensive, and these sessions laid the groundwork for the regional cross-country meetings to be held the following year. From the start, as co-chair Laurendeau specified, the central idea of the terms of reference concerned the "equal partnership between the two founding races"; moreover, he clarified that "in Canada, there are two main cultures, each related to one of the principal languages."[9]

Although the commission co-chairs were in agreement that the central concern of the RCBB was the relationship between the two founding races, the public forum of the preliminary hearings meant that this framing could be openly challenged. And it was challenged. Over the course of these preliminary hearings, 76 organizations and individuals came out to speak to the commissioners, and many of them challenged the central focus on the English and French as the two founding races as well as the marginal positioning of other ethnic groups as an afterthought of solely cultural concern. Representatives from what were known throughout the inquiry as "the other ethnic groups"[10] spoke of their role in founding the nation by clearing the land, settling communities, and pioneering the work of expansion, and they thereby made demands for concrete forms of recognition, most often in the form of language rights. This is exemplified in a statement made by Dr. Rekem, who came to the preliminary hearings as a representative of the Slovak Parish and the Slovak community of Winnipeg.

> I said in my speech that we are for bilingualism and multiculturalism. I mean, you know, these two groups, English-speaking and French speaking groups they have their historical rights, each other in British, national, safeguarded to them as they should have these rights in all provinces. They should be perfectly bilingual. For example, I am Slovak-bilingual too. We would like to see that our cultures will be organically inter-woven in the Canadian national life and our languages will have at least so much expression of our cultures that they will be taught where our ethnic groups are, that is, in the larger settlements. They will be taught in the secondary schools or at the university level. We would ask at least so much recognition for our ethnic groups and language.[11]

Here Dr. Rekem made a territorial and demographic claim for the substantive recognition of his ethnic group in a demand that linguistic rights be guaranteed through education. Arguing that bilingualism could encompass languages other than English and French, Dr. Rekem also explicitly spoke against the restrictions of biculturalism and for a multiculturalism that could allow for his community's language and culture to be incorporated into Canadian national life. Representatives from many of the other ethnic groups spoke in favour of multiculturalism over biculturalism, arguing often, as Walter Bossey from the Canadian Ethnic Mosaic Confederation did, that in fact "We are Canadians.... This is a mosaic ... and God had one purpose for making this country a multicultural one."[12]

The preliminary report was published on 1 February 1965, and all 5,000 copies sold out within 24 hours. Despite the challenges to the hierarchies outlined in the terms of reference by other ethnic groups at the preliminary hearings, the report reprised the singular notion of a crisis between the two founding races. As the report concluded in its postscript, "The present crisis is reminiscent of the situation described by Lord Durham in 1838: 'I found two nations warring in the bosom of a single state.'"[13] Nevertheless, the challenges mounted against the racialized and ethnicized hierarchy instilled through the bilingual and bicultural framing of the inquiry, embedded in the terms of reference, continued to circulate and would emerge again during the public hearings, couched as demands for multiculturalism and a broader set of language rights.

The public hearings of the RCBB began almost immediately after the publication of the preliminary report as a set of 14 country-wide hearings that lasted from one to four days. These hearings first sought out briefs from communities, groups, and individuals, and it was these submitted briefs that were used to guide the discussions at the hearings. Despite the constraint of having to prepare and submit a brief before appearing at the hearings, the presenters offered the commission a wide range of opinions.

Many of the groups who came to the public hearings to challenge the limited bilingual and bicultural framing of the inquiry began by outlining their community's role in founding the nation. This was exemplified in such briefs as the one from the Canadian Council of National Groups, a Toronto-based umbrella group for a number of European ethnic groups, including the Polish Democratic Association, the United Jewish Peoples Order, and the Association of United Ukrainian Canadians, among others. Beginning with the assertion that Canada was a nation built by immigration – "From the very beginning, immigration has been the major source of Canadian population"[14] – the brief expanded on the idea that all immigrants were settlers and nation-builders.

> Theirs [immigrants] was a life of sweat and tears, and of backbreaking labour. But the forests were felled, the swamps drained, the roads and railways and cities built. In their rough hands the raw materials of Canada took shape, together with the dreams of an emerging nationality.[15]

The claim that the Canadian population had been composed mainly of immigrants and that it had been the labour of all of these immigrants that had settled the nation was a common strategy deployed at the hearings by other ethnic groups to claim a national founding status that was equivalent to that of the English and French. This logic could then be extrapolated to make the claim for a substantive set of rights that were equal to those that the commission sought to accord to the English and French communities.

> Our Council considers it within the democratic rights of the ethnic groups to preserve and exercise their language of origin, as a means of enjoying

their cultural heritage. We further suggest that the desire of Canadians to learn the language of their forefathers, or any languages other than English and French, should be met within the secondary schools and universities where justified and practical.[16]

Thus, language rights were the substantive and equivalent recognition of the claims sought by many of the other ethnic groups. It was also clear that *multiculturalism* began to emerge during these hearings as a term through which the location and inclusion of other ethnic groups could coalesce. This was captured in the brief entitled "Statement of the Mennonite Society for the Promotion of the German Language," which began, "Canada should recognize and accept that it is a multilingual and multicultural country" and then proceeded to outline the concrete provisions the community desired.

Either French, German, Ukrainian, Jewish or Icelandic – depending on the decision of the respective school district – should be introduced in schools as a second language from grade one. The government and peoples of Canada should develop a positive attitude to the teaching of secondary language and to assist peoples of other origins to maintain their cultures…. We would like to draw the attention of the Commission to the fact that in Manitoba alone, over 10,000 students from Mennonite homes study German…. How could any Canadian demand that these our Canadians, just because they belong to a minority group, should not be free to chose [sic] their own language as a second language for their Children.[17]

Beginning with the assertion of the de facto multicultural and multilingual character of the nation, this group – like so many other ethnic groups – supported a broader notion of bilingualism that equated French with ethnic languages and made a claim for demographically based schooling as a right that would maintain community-based language for subsequent generations.

The Canadian Ethnic Press Federation also submitted a brief to the commission.[18] It proclaimed itself the "only nation-wide organization of 'other ethnic' groups in Canada," a claim substantiated by the large volume of ethnic-media clippings and summaries collected by commission researchers during the course of the inquiry. In its brief, the federation pushed for a definition of bilingualism beyond the working definition of the commission: "The word 'bilingual' according to the dictionaries means 'having or using two languages.' In Canada, the word 'bilingual' is given a restricted meaning and is limited to English and French."[19] Following this line of thinking, the federation expanded on the importance of a broader conception of bilingualism not only based on the prevalence of ethnic languages – 14 percent of the population had mother tongues other than English or French, and 26 percent of the population was of non-British or non-French origin[20] – but also because it argued that it was critical for cultural retention and integration.

> The language of origin is the most powerful instrument in the hands of an ethnic group for retaining its cultural heritage ... the selection of English or French (or both) does not mean that the ethnic groups will or should discard their languages – the best media available to them for the preservation of their cultures and integration in to Canadian cultural streams.[21]

Thus, two key elements that emerged from the submissions of the other ethnic groups during the public hearings was the importance of moving beyond biculturalism – as prescribed by the commission's terms of reference – to multiculturalism, as well as the according of multilingual rights – however realized – as the substantive recognition of multiculturalism.

This is not to say that no submissions spoke against multiculturalism or against multilingualism. A good example of this was the submission from the Imperial Order of the Daughters of the Empire (IODE), which stated clearly that "Canada is not a multilingual or multiculturalism society."[22] This rationale was based on a set of durable arguments about immigrant integration.

> It is only natural that, initially, immigrants should wish to speak in their own language and should endeavour to preserve their own culture. However, these contributions are only beneficial and contribute enrichment so long as old prejudices and animosities are not transplanted and perpetuated or nourished in Canada.... This, Canada does not want. It is our experience that immigrants are usually eager and anxious to integrate into English or French speaking communities, because it is to their social and economic advantage to do so. In fact, it is a necessity.[23]

The IODE advanced two key arguments against multiculturalism and multilingualism that still find resonance today. These are concerns about immigrant enclaving and balkanization as well as the argument that immigrant integration requires – even necessitates – speaking only English or French. Also, the IODE foreshadowed the narrow conception of integration that pervades contemporary discourses – that is, as being of economic importance and shifting unidirectionally from the "immigrant" culture into the dominant English and French cultures.

The issue of other ethnic group integration was not just of interest to the IODE; it was in fact a research thread throughout the work of the commission. During its research phase, following the public hearings, the commission examined integration in its reports and research memos. In fact, in a report on a private research meeting with the director of the Citizenship Branch, integration was defined as "language assimilation."[24] However, by the time Book IV of the final report (*The Cultural Contribution of the Other Ethnic Groups*) was published in 1969, integration had been redefined as "acculturation" and specified as "the process of adaptation to the environment in which an individual is compelled to live as he adjusts his behaviour to that of the community.... In adopting fully the Canadian way of life ... those whose origin is neither French nor British do not have to cast off or hide their own culture."[25] In the Canadian context, this meant that "immigrants, whatever their ethnic or national origin or their mother tongue, have the right and are at liberty to integrate with either of the two societies [the English or French]."[26] Thus, integration as acculturation emerged as a social theory to account for a unidirectional shift of ethnic groups into the founding races, even as non-British and non-French other ethnic groups remained differentiated from the founding duality. This differentiation was clearly outlined in the final report.

> We can still state that there are a number of cultural groups in Canada with a clear sense of identity. They want, without in any way undermining national unity, to maintain their own linguistic and cultural heritage. They have their own associations, clubs, parishes, and religious organizations; they maintain their own schools and express their collective views through their own press.[27]

Although integration as acculturation meant that other ethnic groups did not have to cast off or hide their own cultures, it was nevertheless relegated to the private realm; in the final report, therefore, linguistic and cultural preservation for other ethnic groups remained a private concern beyond the commission's mandate.

The articulation of the integration of other ethnic groups in terms of language and culture was a shift that took place during the course of the inquiry. If the RCBB began in 1963 with terms of reference that outlined the different groups through race and ethnicity, by the time *Book I: The Official Languages* was published in 1967, the emphasis had shifted to language and culture. Book I began by clarifying that "in our view, the reference to the two 'founding races' or 'peoples who founded Confederation'[28] was an allusion to the undisputed role played by Canadians of French and British origin in 1867," and, therefore, "The word 'race' is used in an older meaning as referring to a national group, and carries no biological significance."[29] From this, the authors concluded, "Consequently, we feel that language and culture are truly central concepts in the terms of reference. For this reason, we shall give them more emphasis than the notions 'race,' 'people,' or even 'ethnic groups.'"[30]

Now, with language and culture as the central concepts guiding the commission's work, the definition of culture to be used by the commission was presented in Book I of the final report.

> It is a driving force animating a significant group of individuals united by a common tongue, and sharing the same customs, habits, and experiences.

Clearly the two cultures designated in our terms of reference are those associated with the English and the French languages in Canada. But as there are the two dominant languages, there are two principal cultures, and their influence extends, in greatly varying degrees, to the whole country.[31]

Although the centrality of language in culture was affirmed in the report, even as the importance of race and ethnicity were discounted, the hierarchies outlined in the terms of reference were still maintained as the dominance of the languages and cultures of the "founding races" were confirmed. Despite the myriad submissions from other ethnic groups throughout the preliminary and public hearings requesting a substantive recognition of their claims to belonging and equal status, it was clear that for the commissioners, the original hierarchies of the terms of reference were to be maintained, albeit articulated now in terms of language and culture. The inclusion of the other ethnic groups was now also articulated through language and culture.

Canadians who are of neither British nor French origin are covered by our inquiry in two ways: a) to the extent that they are integrated into English- or French-speaking society, all that is said of Anglophones or Francophones applies to them; and b) to the extent that they remain attached to their original language and culture, they belong to other ethnic groups.[32]

Therefore, the integration of other ethnic groups could now be shifted to a linguistic and cultural process, guaranteed through the purported openness of language. However, "ethnic differences" remained, even if specified now as linguistic and cultural differences. Most important, the differentiation between founding and other groups was retained even as the integrative promise of language and culture was asserted.

The original hierarchies of the terms of reference, although now transposed onto language and culture, were concretized through a differential recognition of language rights. Specifically, for the English and French groups, the report specified the collective nature of language and culture.

Languages and cultures are essentially collective phenomena.... The fact is that a given language as means of communication and expression exists to permit the individual to communicate with others.... Hence the great importance of the concept of two distinct societies as developed in our *Preliminary Report*.[33]

However, for the other ethnic groups, the importance of the connection between language and culture was downplayed.

Many seem to believe that the members of a group who have adopted another language have completely lost their original culture. This is yet another illusion which has given rise to many misunderstandings. In Canada we can observe the indisputable survival of some cultural traits among native groups and among a number of groups of other ethnic origins.[34]

The identification on the one hand of the centrality of language to culture for the founding groups and the limited link between language and culture for the other ethnic groups meant not only the consolidation of the groupings – founding and other – laid out in the terms of reference but also the reinscription of the hierarchies between them concretized through a differential recognition of rights to language.

In sum, the final report of the RCBB was able to repeal all traces of substantive recognition raised by other ethnic groups at the hearings and shift the hierarchies of belonging from race and ethnicity to language and culture. This was accomplished by outlining other-ethnic-group integration as unidirectional acculturation into the dominant cultures through language, as well as privatizing the preservation of the other ethnic languages, on the grounds that the link between language and other ethnic cultures was weak – even as the centrality of language for the cultural viability of the founding groups was retained. Thus, it is no surprise to find that the final report recommended an equal partnership between the English and the French, realized both through recommendations for the *Official Languages Act* of 1969 and biculturalism. However, these recommendations were not readily accepted by leaders of all of the other ethnic groups.

Challenges to the bilingual and, particularly, bicultural framing of the RCBB recommendations were exemplified in a statement made by then-senator Yuzyk at the Multiculturalism for Canada conference, held at the end of August 1970 in Edmonton, Alberta. The Citizenship Branch of the Department of the Secretary of State was one of several sponsors of the conference, billed in the summary report as a community-university conference designed to provide a forum to share opinions and analysis of Book IV of the final report. Senator Yuzyk stated,

> The commission does not reject the "melting pot theory," and in adhering to biculturalism advocates the "two melting pots" or the double melting pot theory, advising other ethnic groups to "integrate," but they really mean assimilate them into one of the two pots. Obviously the commission has totally disregarded the numerous briefs that were submitted by the organizations of the ethnic groups. In my opinion, and I am sure that it is the opinion of a large segment of the Canadian population, the premise and basic concept of the Canadian nation that is adhered to by the Bilingual and Bicultural Commission is wrong, as bicultural policies contradict the principles of equality and justice ... multiculturalism is a fact of Canadian life, the very basis of "unity in continuing diversity."[35]

Noting the unidirectional form of integration recommended by the commission, Yuzyk revived the call for multiculturalism that had been voiced during the hearings. This was only one among many other challenges to the RCBB's recommendations for bilingualism and biculturalism that were circulating at conferences and in the media in the period between the tabling of Book IV of the final report in the House of Commons on 15 April 1970 and Pierre Elliott Trudeau's response on 8 October 1971. It is in this response that Trudeau made his famous speech announcing the implementation of a "policy of multiculturalism within a bilingual framework," based on the rationale that "although there are two official languages, there is no official culture." Trudeau elaborated,

> The individual's freedom would be hampered if he were locked for life within a particular cultural compartment by the accident of birth or language. It is vital, therefore, that every Canadian, whatever his ethnic origin, be given a chance to learn at least one of the two languages in which his country conducts its official business and its politics. A policy of multiculturalism within a bilingual framework commends itself to the government as the most suitable means of assuring the cultural freedom of Canadians.[36]

Although the government's implementation of multiculturalism in place of the RCBB's recommendation for biculturalism can be seen as a challenge to the dominant duality put forward by the commission, in substance, Trudeau's formulation still followed the unidirectional logic of integration. The guarantee of the individual right to learn an official language, in contrast with the officialized collective language rights of English and French, only confirmed the original hierarchy of the terms of reference even as it claimed the integrative potential of official languages. This hierarchy was clearly specified and affirmed: "Nor ... should the recognition of the cultural values of many languages weaken the position of Canada's two official languages. Their use by all of the citizens of Canada will continue to be promoted and encouraged."[37]

This hierarchy would be confirmed in the imbalances in government funding for cultural and educational programs between the official-language communities and the other ethnic groups. For example, in the first year of multiculturalism (1971–1972), the Secretary of State spent $78 million on bilingualism but only $2 million on multiculturalism, and under Trudeau, the multiculturalism portfolio would continue to be allocated limited funding under junior ministers, a disparity that would become entrenched and greater in subsequent years.[38]

The RCBB, originally established to address the historical inequities between the English and the French, opened up an opportunity to other ethnic groups in the nation to make a bid for equal and substantive recognition. Despite these efforts, the commission entrenched the original hierarchies of its mandate, and shifted onto the terrain of language and culture, as it asserted a new national narrative of a dually founded white-settler society open to the multicultural "other" through the integrative, yet unidirectional, promise of language. And during this same period, significant changes were taking place in the Canadian immigration system that would have implications for those who would come to inhabit this category of the multicultural other in the nation's racial imaginary. These changes would lay the groundwork for present-day anxieties about multiculturalism and immigrant integration.

CONCURRENT CHANGES TO IMMIGRATION POLICY

The parallel changes that were taking place in immigration policy in this period were also critical in laying the groundwork for how present-day concerns about multiculturalism came to be naturalized as anxieties about the integration of immigrants speaking non-official languages. In 1962, the same year that the RCBB was announced, changes to Canada's immigration policy were also being introduced in the House of Commons, and they would mark a pivotal shift away from Canada's historical immigration policies based on racial and geographical exclusions. In her presentation to the House on 19 January 1962, Minister of Citizenship and Immigration Ellen Fairclough outlined changes in immigration regulations that would emphasize "education, training and skills as the main condition of admissibility regardless of the country of origin of the applicant."[39]

Canadian immigration law, as Taylor states, "from 1885 to 1962, was explicitly racist in wording and intent."[40] Policies such as the "single continuous journey provision," the *Chinese Immigration Act* of 1885, and its various revisions were among the many policies and regulations designed to discourage and/or prohibit non-white and non-European immigration. Even when the "single continuous journey" clause and the *Chinese Immigration Act* were repealed in 1947, Prime Minister Mackenzie King maintained these exclusions through restrictions and quotas on Asian immigration, rationalized on the grounds of maintaining the fundamental character of the population: "There will, I am sure, be general agreement with the view that the people of Canada do not wish, as a result of mass immigration, to make a fundamental alteration in the character of our population. Large-scale immigration from the orient would change the fundamental composition of the population."[41]

In the wake of King's speech, the *Immigration Act* passed in 1952 retained the powers to prohibit admission of persons by reason of "nationality, citizenship, ethnic origin, occupation, class or geographical area of origin" as well as "by reason of probable inability to become readily assimilated or to assume the duties and responsibilities of Canadian citizenship within a reasonable time after admission."[42] However, the decline in

European immigration by the late 1950s meant the need to revise long-term immigration plans, and by 1960, a memo from the Department of Citizenship and Immigration stated that the "need for immigration and its economic advantages should be clearly explained to the Canadian public."[43] This impetus led to the changes in immigration policy outlined by Ellen Fairclough in January 1962, and in 1965, Jean Marchand – until now a commissioner with the RCBB – was appointed the new minister of citizenship and immigration, and the new Department of Manpower and Immigration was created. As Marchand explained, immigration had to be related to the needs of the labour market; therefore, by having both human resources and immigration together in the same portfolio, programs could be designed to achieve optimum economic growth.[44]

On 14 October 1966, the White Paper on Immigration was tabled in the House of Commons, outlining a framework that moved away from overt racial criteria to an emphasis on the economic benefits of immigration: "Without a substantial continuing flow of immigrants, it is doubtful that we could sustain a high rate of economic growth."[45] The white paper went on to specify what this meant.

> Canada has become a highly complex industrialized and urbanized society. And such a society is increasingly demanding of the quality of its workforce. If those entering the workforce, whether native born or immigrants, do not have the ability in training to do the kinds of jobs available, they will be burdens rather than assets. Today, Canada's expanding industrial economy offers most of these employment opportunities to those with education, training, skills.[46]

With the shift from overt racial and geographical criteria to a labour market–oriented emphasis on education, training, and skills, a new points system for immigrant selection was introduced when the new immigration regulations went into effect in October 1967. Points were allocated for a host of desirable characteristics in potential immigrants, including education and degree of fluency in the official languages.

The resulting shift in source countries for immigration was notable: as European-source immigration numbers began their steady decline after a peak in 1967, Asian immigration numbers increased sevenfold between 1963 and 1969[47] and continued to increase thereafter. This change in immigration policy from one based on explicitly racial criteria to one with a focus on the "quality" of the workforce for national economic benefit resulted in a paradigmatic change in immigration source countries and marked an increase of racialized immigrants to Canada. However, the focus on integration had not changed. The concerns before 1962 had been to only accept immigrants who could be "readily assimilated" so that they could "assume the duties and responsibilities" of Canadian citizenship in a timely way without altering the "fundamental character" of the country; however, even after the shift to a points system, the concern lay with ensuring that immigrants would not be burdens but rather could readily assume their place in the labour market as workforce assets. In both eras, a focus on integration remained, and the increase in racialized immigrants arriving after 1967 would continue to trigger concerns about the "fundamental character" of the country, concerns that still find resonance in present-day discourses about immigration.

CONCLUSION

Writing shortly after the effects of changes in immigration policy were becoming apparent, Jean Burnet noted that the visibility of the newer waves of immigrants would present different concerns: "Some of the new visible minorities are of course linguistically and culturally more distinct from older Canadians than earlier immigrants were ... in any event, linguistic and cultural differences tend to be overshadowed by the problem of visibility."[48] Foreshadowing the racialization of issues related to immigration, Burnet predicted the inadequacy of multiculturalism: "The commonplace [idea] that multiculturalism will ease the lot of the visible minorities does not, therefore, seem to be self-evident."[49] Galt Harpham has shown how language can become a proxy for difficult issues that "resist resolution on its own terms" and thereby become a way of "thinking other thoughts and answering other questions."[50] This is reflected by Etienne Balibar, who has argued that the complementarity between language and race roots national character in the people, even as language is tied to the "frontiers of a particular people" by ethnicizing social difference into a division between the "genuinely" and the "falsely" national[51] or, in the Canadian case, the division between official- and non-official-language-speakers.

Thus, a genealogy of the official languages, immigration, and multiculturalism shows how the RCBB ensured that concerns about race, ethnicity, and belonging would come to be articulated as issues of language and culture even as changes to immigration policy ensured that language would continue to function as a proxy for discourses about race and integration. Specifically, the hierarchies of language and culture established through the work of the commission would serve to naturalize, under the rubric of multiculturalism, non-official languages as an index of the unidirectional and instrumental integration of racialized immigrants.

In this way, common discourses in the present, as reflected in the representative quotes at the start of the chapter, can consider non-official languages as a problematic outcome of multiculturalism and their use as a threat to official languages and dual-white-settler harmony as well as a barrier to immigrant integration. In contemporary political discourses, multiculturalism is more commonly spun off from bilingualism, and multiculturalism alone still ostensibly provides a powerful discursive force as an inclusive and equitable model of nation-building. However, as Michelle Anne Lee explains, multicultural nationalism still "purports a discourse that requires 'them' continually to become part of 'us,' as defined by the dominant culture tolerating and choosing to accept, or not, other cultures."[52] This is the dual-white-settler "us" of official bilingualism. Ultimately, the valiant bid made by other ethnic groups for a multilingual future that would signal a more inclusive "us" was not realized, thereafter marking non-official languages as a naturalized site for articulating a host of anxieties about multiculturalism and the integration of racialized "immigrants" in Canada.

NOTES

[1] Statistics Canada, *Linguistic Characteristics of Canadians* (Ottawa: Ministry of Industry, 2012).

[2] Ibid.

[3] All comments have been anonymized by removing identifying online names, tags, and sources.

[4] Site for Language Management in Canada (SLMC), "Canada and Linguistic Policies of Non-Intervention (1867 to 1967)," University of Ottawa, 2013, at http://www.slmc.uottawa.ca/?q=non-intervention_policies, accessed 4 February 2013.

[5] Ibid., n.p.

[6] Frank Scott and Michael Oliver, eds., *Quebec States Her Case* (Toronto: Macmillan of Canada, 1968).

[7] Canada, Parliament, House of Commons, *Debates,* 26th Parliament, 1st Session, May–December 1963, vol. 1 (Ottawa: Queen's Printer, 16 May 1963), 6.

[8] Canada, Royal Commission on Bilingualism and Biculturalism (RCBB), *Report of the Royal Commission on Bilingualism and Biculturalism – Book I: The Official Languages* (Ottawa: Queen's Printer, 1967), 173.

[9] Canada, RCBB, *A Preliminary Report of the Royal Commission on Bilingualism and Biculturalism* (Ottawa: Queen's Printer, 1965), 180.

[10] All non-English and non-French groups were labelled "other ethnic groups" throughout the inquiry.

[11] Canada, RCBB, "Transcripts of Public Hearings" (Ottawa, 1965), microfilm, 58.

[12] Ibid., 461.

[13] Canada, RCBB, *Preliminary Report,* 144. The rest of Durham's statement continues, "I found a struggle, not of principles, but of races"; see Lord Durham's report on the affairs of British North America in *Vol. II: Text of the Report,* ed. Sir Charles Lucas (New York: Sentry Press, 1970), 16.

[14] Canadian Council of National Groups, "Brief to the Royal Commission on Bilingualism and Biculturalism" (Toronto, 1964), 12.

[15] Ibid., 16.

[16] Ibid., 23.

[17] Mennonite Society, "Statement of the Mennonite Society for the Promotion of the German Language," 16 December 1963, Library and Archives Canada, RG 33, Series 80, vol. 115, file 101–125, 2.

[18] Canada Ethnic Press Federation, "Brief Presented to the Royal Commission on Bilingualism and Biculturalism" (Toronto, 1964).

[19] Ibid., 8.

[20] Ibid.

[21] Ibid., 15.

[22] Imperial Order Daughters of the Empire, "Presentation by the Imperial Order Daughters of the Empire (IODE) to the Royal Commission on Bilingualism and Biculturalism" (Toronto, 1964), 10.

[23] Ibid., 9.

[24] A. Stinson, "Confidential: Private Meeting, Department of Citizenship and Immigration, October 11, 1965," Library and Archives Canada, RG 33, Series 80, vol. 122, file 785E, 19 January 1966.

[25] Canada, RCBB, *Report of the Royal Commission on Bilingualism and Biculturalism – Book IV: The Cultural Contribution of the Other Ethnic Groups* (Ottawa: Queen's Printer, 1969), 6.

[26] Ibid., 5.

[27] Ibid., 8.

[28] This is the direct translation from the French terms of reference.

[29] Canada, RCBB, *Book I*, xxii.

[30] Ibid.

[31] Ibid., xxxi.

[32] Ibid., xxv.

[33] Ibid., xliii–xliv.

[34] Ibid., xxxvii.

[35] Multiculturalism for Canada Conference, *Report of the Conference* (Edmonton: University of Alberta, 1970), 14.

[36] Canada, Parliament, House of Commons, *Debates*, 28th Parliament, 3rd Session, 1970–1972, vol. 8 (Ottawa: Queen's Printer, 8 October 1971), 8545.

[37] Ibid.

[38] Kenneth McRoberts, *Misconceiving Canada: The Struggle for National Unity* (Oxford: Oxford University Press, 1997), 128.

[39] Canada, Parliament, House of Commons, *Debates*, 25th Parliament, 1st Session, 1962–1963, vol. 1 (Ottawa: Queen's Printer, 19 January 1962), 9.

[40] K.W. Taylor, "Racism in Canadian Immigration Policy," *Canadian Ethnic Studies* 23, no. 1 (1991):2.

[41] Canada, Parliament, House of Commons, *Debates*, 20th Parliament, 3rd Session, January–July 1947, vol. 3 (Ottawa: Queen's Printer, 1 May 1947), 2646.

[42] Freda Hawkins, *Canada and Immigration: Public Policy and Public Concern*, 2nd ed., Canadian Public Administration Series (Montreal and Kingston: McGill-Queen's University Press, 1988), 102.

[43] Ibid., 105.

[44] Ibid., 158.

[45] Canada, Department of Manpower and Immigration, White Paper on Immigration (Ottawa, 1966), 7.

[46] Ibid., 8.

[47] Hawkins, *Canada and Immigration*, 57.

[48] Jean Burnet, "Multiculturalism, Immigration, and Racism: A Comment on the Canadian Immigration and Population Study," *Canadian Ethnic Studies* 7, no. 1 (1975):38.

[49] Ibid., 39.

[50] Geoffrey Galt Harpham, *Language Alone: The Critical Fetish of Modernity* (New York: Routledge, 2002), 65.

[51] Etienne Balibar, "The Nation Form: History and Ideology," in *Race, Nation, Class: Ambiguous Identities*, ed. Etienne Balibar and Immanuel Maurice Wallerstein (London: Verso, 1991), 100.

[52] Michelle Anne Lee, "Multiculturalism as Nationalism: A Discussion of Nationalism in Pluralistic Nations," *Canadian Review of Studies in Nationalism* 30, no. 1–2 (2003):111.

MULTICULTURALISM: PSYCHOLOGICAL PERSPECTIVES[1]

JOHN W. BERRY[2]

INTRODUCTION

Much of the discussion and debate on multiculturalism has been carried out in the disciplines of political philosophy, political science, and sociology[3] and in general public discourse.[4] However, over the past 40 years, the discipline of psychology (particularly the specialities of cross-cultural and intercultural psychology) has also examined some of the core issues and assumptions surrounding multiculturalism.[5] This chapter examines some of the conceptualizations and empirical research in psychology, both in Canada and in other countries.

CROSS-CULTURAL AND INTERCULTURAL PSYCHOLOGY

The field of cross-cultural psychology seeks to understand the relationships between the development and expression of human behaviour and the cultural contexts in which they take place.[6] Cross-cultural psychology is based on the premise that we cannot understand human behaviour without an understanding of the numerous cultural experiences that influence it. This approach requires the sampling of behavioural expression (through observation, assessment, or experiments), both within particular cultures and across different cultural contexts, and then comparatively examining them for similarities and differences. The goal of this enterprise is to establish some general principles that apply to human behaviour around the world.

The Multiculturalism Question: Debating Identity in 21st-Century Canada, ed. Jack Jedwab. Kingston: School of Policy Studies, Queen's University. © 2014 The School of Policy Studies, Queen's University at Kingston. All rights reserved.

When cultural groups and their individual members come into contact with each other (either across societies or within plural societies), they engage in intercultural relations. The field of intercultural psychology examines the various ways in which groups and individuals can relate to, accommodate to, and adapt to each other. The psychological study of intercultural relations requires the examination of the two core features of cross-cultural psychology that were outlined above: finding links between cultural context and behavioural development and expression, and the use of the comparative method to discern any basic principles that may underpin these links.[7]

Both approaches adopt the perspective of *universalism*, which is rooted in the distinctions among psychological *process, competence*, and *performance*. It asserts that psychological processes are shared, pan-human qualities of all peoples, everywhere. Cultural and intercultural experiences shape the development of behaviour to become competencies. And these competencies are expressed (as performances) in culturally appropriate situations. The existence of universalism is required in order for persons of different cultural backgrounds to interact with, and to adapt to, each other. Even though their competencies and performances may differ greatly across cultures and individuals, these basic psychological features enable individuals and groups to interact with and understand each other and to achieve mutual accommodation within plural societies.

THE MULTICULTURAL VISION

There are two contrasting, usually implicit, models of intercultural relations in plural societies and institutions. In one (the *melting pot* model), the view is that there is (or should be) one dominant (or *mainstream*) society, on the margins of which are various non-dominant (or *minority*) groups. These non-dominant groups typically remain on the fringe unless they are incorporated as indistinguishable components into the mainstream. Many societies have this implicit model, including France (where the image is of the *"unité de l'hexagon"* – that is, of one people with one language and one shared identity, within the borders of the country[8]) – and the United States, where the national motto is *"E pluribus unum."*[9]

In the other (the *multicultural* model), there is a national social framework of institutions (called the *larger society*) that accommodates the interests and needs of the numerous cultural groups that are fully incorporated as *ethnocultural groups* (rather than "minorities") into this national framework. The concept of the *larger society* refers to the civic arrangement in a plural society, within which all ethnocultural groups (dominant and non-dominant, Indigenous and immigrant) attempt to carry out their lives together. It is constantly changing, through negotiation, compromise, and mutual accommodations. It surely does not represent the way of life of the mainstream, which is typically that preferred by the dominant group and which has become established in the public institutions that it has created. All groups in such a conception of a larger society are ethnocultural groups (rather than minorities), who possess cultures and who have equal cultural and other rights, regardless of their size or power. In such complex plural societies, there is no assumption that some groups should assimilate or become absorbed into another group. Hence, intercultural relations and cultural change are not viewed as unidirectional, but as mutual and reciprocal.

These two alternative ways of viewing how groups and individuals can live in plural societies have been examined in the fields of cross-cultural and intercultural psychology.

The multicultural vision was first advanced in Canada in 1971 by Pierre Elliott Trudeau in his announcement to the House of Commons of a multiculturalism policy.

> A policy of multiculturalism within a bilingual framework ... [is] the most suitable means of assuring the cultural freedom of all Canadians. Such a policy should help to break down discriminatory attitudes and cultural jealousies. National unity if it is to mean anything in the deeply personal sense, must be founded on confidence in one's own individual identity; out of this can grow respect for that of others and a willingness to share ideas, attitudes and assumptions.... The government will support and encourage the various cultures and ethnic groups that give structure and vitality to our society. They will be encouraged to share their cultural expression and values with other Canadians and so contribute to a richer life for us all.[10]

An examination of this text reveals three main components to this policy. The first component is the goal "to break down discriminatory attitudes and cultural jealousies" – that is, to *enhance mutual acceptance* among all cultural groups. This goal is to be approached through two main program components. One is the *cultural* component, which is to be achieved by providing support and encouragement for cultural maintenance and development among all cultural groups. The other is the *social,* or *intercultural,* component, which promotes the sharing of cultural expression by providing opportunities for intergroup contact and the removal of barriers to full and equitable participation in the daily life of the larger society. The third component acknowledges the importance of learning one or more common languages in order to permit intercultural participation among all groups.

Over the years, I have been involved in a conceptual and empirical examination of Canadian multiculturalism policy from a psychological perspective. This work was rooted in my earlier research in Australia[11] with respect to how Aboriginal peoples there were seeking to live in the evolving Australian society. I first evaluated the Canadian policy and its implementation after ten years[12] and again after 20 years.[13] In this work, I examined these core elements of the policy (and links among the elements). I proposed that these elements formed a coherent set of psychological concepts and principles and could serve as the basis for developing some testable hypotheses.

Figure 1 portrays some of these core elements and linkages. The clear and fundamental goal of the policy is to enhance mutual acceptance among all ethnocultural groups (on the upper right). This goal is to be approached through three program components. On the upper left is the cultural component of the policy, which is to be achieved by providing support and encouragement for cultural maintenance and development among all ethnocultural groups. The second component is the social (or intercultural) component (on the lower left), which seeks to foster the sharing of cultural expression by providing opportunities for intergroup contact and the removal of barriers to full and equitable participation in the daily life of the larger society. The last feature is the intercultural communication component (in the lower right corner). This represents the bilingual reality of the larger society of Canada and promotes the learning of one or both official languages (English and French) as a means for all ethnocultural groups to interact with each other and to participate in national life.

FIGURE 1
Components and Linkages in Canadian Multiculturalism Policy

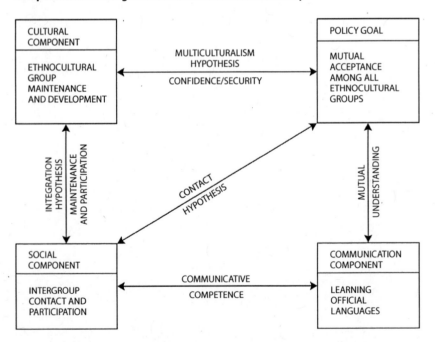

Source: Modified from J.W. Berry, "Multicultural Policy in Canada: A Social Psychological Analysis," *Canadian Journal of Behavioural Science* 16, no. 4 (1984):353–370.

It is essential to note that the Canadian concept of multiculturalism and the multiculturalism policy have two main and equally important emphases: the maintenance of heritage cultures and identities (the cultural component) and the full and equitable participation of all ethnocultural groups in the life of the larger society (the social or intercultural component).

The linkages among these three components are also shown in Figure 1. The first (at the top), termed the *multiculturalism hypothesis*, is expressed in the policy statement as the belief that confidence in one's identity will lead to sharing, respect for others, and the reduction of discriminatory attitudes. Berry, Kalin, and Taylor[14] identified this belief as an assumption with psychological roots and as being amenable to empirical evaluation. A second link (on the left side) is the hypothesis that when individuals and groups are "doubly engaged" (that is, valuing and participating in both their heritage cultures and in the larger society), they will be more successful in their lives. This success will be evidenced by a higher level of well-being, in both psychological and social domains. This is the *integration hypothesis*, in which involvement with, competence in, and confidence in both cultural communities provides the social capital to succeed in intercultural living. A third link (the diagonal) is the *contact hypothesis*, by which contact and sharing is considered to promote mutual acceptance under certain conditions, especially that of status equality and voluntariness of intercultural contact.

Together, and by balancing these components, it should be possible to achieve the core goal of the policy: the improvement of intercultural relations in Canada, where all groups and individuals have a place, both within their own heritage cultural environment and within the larger society. In this sense, multiculturalism is for everyone, not only for nondominant groups. This aspect emphasizes that all groups and individuals are engaged in a process of cultural and psychological change.

Later, in 2005, the European Union (EU) adopted a set of "Common Basic Principles for Immigrant Integration." The first of these principles is:

Integration is a dynamic, two-way process of mutual accommodation by all immigrants and residents of Member States. Integration is a dynamic, long-term, and continuous two-way process of mutual accommodation, not a static outcome. It demands the participation not only of immigrants and their descendants but of every resident. The integration process involves adaptation by immigrants, both men and women, who all have rights and responsibilities in relation to their new country of residence. It also involves the receiving society, which should create the opportunities for the immigrants' full economic, social, cultural, and political participation. Accordingly, Member States are encouraged to consider and involve both immigrants and national citizens in integration policy, and to communicate clearly their mutual rights and responsibilities.[15]

We find in this EU statement the three cornerstones of multiculturalism: the right of all peoples to maintain their cultures; the right to participate fully in the life of the larger society; and the obligation for all groups (both the dominant and the non-dominant) to engage in a process of mutual change. Research on the acceptance of this policy in Europe has only just begun.

However, there is some indication[16] that Europeans make a clear distinction between the right of immigrants to maintain their cultures in *private* (i.e., in their families and communities) and the right to expect changes to the *public* culture of the society of settlement. In much of this research, it was found that it is acceptable to express one's heritage culture in the family and in the community, but that it should not be expressed in the public domains, such as in educational or work institutions. This view is opposed to the basic principles outlined by the EU, where the process is identified as one of mutual accommodation.

There is also a common misunderstanding that multiculturalism means only the presence of many non-dominant cultural communities ("minorities") in a society (i.e., acknowledging the cultural maintenance component), without their equitable participation and incorporation into a larger society (i.e., not accepting the intercultural component). Because of this, many see multiculturalism as leading to social divisiveness and separation. For example, Parekh in the United Kingdom holds to this narrow meaning: "The term 'multicultural' is generally used to refer to societies characterised by diversity, irrespective of whether or not the diversity is exclusively cultural in nature. This is how I use it." [17] It is this erroneous view that has led some in Europe to declare that "multiculturalism has failed." However, in my view, it has not failed because it has not even been tried, having paid little regard to the intercultural component.

INTERCULTURAL STRATEGIES

The question of *how* groups and individuals engage in their intercultural relations has come to be examined with the concept of *intercultural strategies*. Four ways of engaging in intercultural relations have been derived from two basic issues facing all peoples in culturally plural societies. These issues are based on the distinction between orientations toward one's own group and those toward other groups.[18] This distinction is rendered as a relative preference for (i) maintaining one's heritage culture and identity and (ii) having contact with and participating in the larger society along with other ethnocultural groups. These are the same two issues that underlie the multiculturalism policies outlined above (i.e., the cultural and the social/intercultural components). The similarity between the two dimensions in this intercultural strategies framework and the two core elements in the Canadian multiculturalism policy is coincidental and represents some degree of convergence in the *Zeitgeist* in thinking about how to manage intercultural relations in culturally plural societies 40 years ago.

These two issues can be responded to along attitudinal dimensions, ranging from generally positive to negative orientations to these issues; their intersection defines four strategies, portrayed in Figure 2. On the left are the orientations from the point of view of ethnocultural peoples (both groups and individuals); on the right are the views held by the larger society (such as public policies and public attitudes).

Among ethnocultural groups, when they do not wish to maintain their cultural identity and seek daily interaction with other cultures, the *assimilation* strategy is defined. In contrast, when individuals place a value on holding on to their original culture, and at the same time wish to avoid interaction with others, then the *separation* alternative is defined. When there is an interest in maintaining both one's original culture and daily interactions with other groups, *integration* is the option. In this case, an individual maintains some degree of cultural integrity, while at the same time seeking, as a member of an ethnocultural group, to participate as an integral part of the larger social network. Finally,

FIGURE 2
Varieties of Intercultural Strategies in Ethnocultural Groups and in the Larger Society

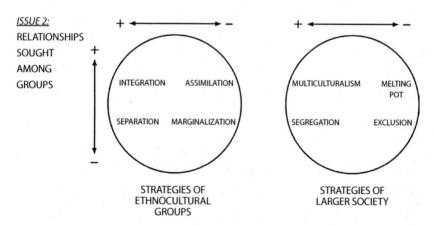

Source: Modified from J.W. Berry, "Marginality, Stress and Ethnic Identification in an Acculturated Aboriginal Community," *Journal of Cross-Cultural Psychology* 1, no. 3 (1970):239–252; and J.W. Berry, "Psychological Aspects of Cultural Pluralism: Unity and Identity Reconsidered," *Topics in Cultural Learning*, vol. 2, ed. Robert W. Brislin (Honolulu: Hawaii University, East-West Center, 1974):17–22.

when there is little possibility or interest in cultural maintenance (often for reasons of forced cultural loss), and little engagement with the larger society (often for reasons of exclusion or discrimination), then *marginalization* is defined.

These two basic issues were initially approached from the point of view of the non-dominant ethnocultural groups. However, the dominant group plays a powerful role in influencing the way in which ethnocultural individuals and groups relate.[19] The views of the larger society are shown on the right side of Figure 2. From the point of view of the larger society, assimilation when sought by the dominant group is termed the *melting pot*. When separation is forced by the dominant group, it is called *segregation*. Marginalization, when imposed by the dominant group, is termed *exclusion*. Finally, when both diversity maintenance and equitable participation are widely accepted features of the society as a whole, integration is called *multiculturalism*.

It is important to emphasize that within this framework, the concept of integration involves engagement with *both* cultures. It is not a euphemism for assimilation, which involves engagement with only the larger society; that is, cultural maintenance is a core part of the concept of integration. Nor does multiculturalism refer only to engagement with members of one's own ethnocultural group (segregation). For there to be integration, members of these communities must also engage with, and become constituents of, the larger society.

These intercultural strategies are related to a number of psychological and social factors. The most important is the discrimination experienced by an individual; less discrimination is usually reported by those opting for integration and assimilation, while more is experienced by those opting for separation or marginalization.[20] In this international study of immigrant youth settled in 13 countries, discrimination was found to contribute to both the experience of marginalization and the lack of psychological and social well-being. This is an example of the reciprocity of intercultural attitudes found in the literature;[21] if persons (such as immigrants or members of ethnocultural groups) feel rejected by others in the larger society, they reciprocate this rejection by choosing a strategy that avoids contact with others outside their own group.

We now examine three hypotheses that lie at the core of intercultural relations research: the *multiculturalism hypothesis*, the *integration hypothesis*, and the *contact hypothesis*. As we shall see, they are very much interrelated, each one influencing the conditions under which the others may be supported by empirical evidence.

MULTICULTURALISM HYPOTHESIS

The multicultural vision enunciated in Canada in 1971 had a key section, one with implications for research on intercultural relations. We[22] developed the *multiculturalism hypothesis* based on the assertion in the policy that freedom from discrimination "must be founded on confidence in one's own individual identity." The basic notion is that only when people are secure in their identities will they be in a position to accept those who differ from them; conversely, when people feel threatened, they will develop prejudice and engage in discrimination.[23] The multiculturalism hypothesis is thus: when people feel secure in their own identity, they will be in a position to accept those who differ from them (i.e., when there is no threat to their culture and identity, they are able to accept "others").

There is now substantial evidence to support this hypothesis. For example, in two national surveys in Canada,[24] measures of cultural security and economic security were created with respect to extant diversity and the continuing flow of immigration. These two security scores were positively correlated with each other and with various intercultural attitudes. Cultural security was negatively correlated with ethnocentrism and positively correlated with both multicultural ideology and perceived consequences of multiculturalism. Economic security had a similar pattern of correlations with these variables. More recently, Annis, Gibson, and Berry[25] have shown that this relationship holds with samples of migrant workers and members of the larger society in rural Manitoba.

In international research, Ward and Masgoret[26] found in a survey conducted in New Zealand that security was positively related to multicultural ideology and attitudes toward immigrants. In Russia, Lebedeva and Tatarko[27] studied migrants from the Caucasus to Moscow and Muscovites. They found that cultural security predicted tolerance, integration, and social equality in both groups, but to a lesser extent among Muscovites.

In Estonia, a representative sample of Russian-speakers was asked about their intercultural strategies, their ethnic self-esteem, their experience of discrimination, and their level of cultural threat, civic engagement, and economic and political satisfaction.[28] The four usual intercultural strategies were found: groups following the separation and marginalization strategies had the highest levels of threat and lowest levels of self-esteem and civic engagement. In contrast, the integration and assimilation groups had the lowest levels of threat and discrimination and the highest civic engagement and satisfaction. Public policy attempts in Estonia (which are largely assimilationist) seek to make the Russian-speaking population "more Estonian," while placing barriers on achieving this. Such a policy appears to have led to the development of a "reactive identity" among Russian-speakers and their turning away from the country of Estonia. Most recently, Cameron, Kocum, and Berry[29] analyzed an international Pew survey for the relationship between cultural and economic security and attitudes toward globalization. They found that when feelings of security are high, then attitudes toward globalization are positive.

From this sampling of empirical studies, it is possible to conclude that security in one's own identity underlies the possibility of accepting "others." This acceptance includes being tolerant, accepting cultural diversity in society, and accepting immigrants to, and ethnocultural groups in, that society. In contrast, threatening an individual's or a group's identity and place in a plural society is likely to lead to mutual hostility.

INTEGRATION HYPOTHESIS

In much of the research on intercultural relations, the integration strategy has been found to lead to better adaptation than other strategies.[30] A possible explanation is that those who are "doubly engaged" with both cultures receive support and resources from both and are competent in dealing with both cultures. The social capital afforded by these multiple social and cultural engagements may well offer the route to success in plural societies. The evidence for integration being associated with better adaptation has been reviewed.[31] For example, considering Indigenous peoples in Canada, studies with James Bay Cree[32] found that those seeking to integrate with the larger Canadian society had better psychological well-being than those using other strategies.

More recently, a study with second-generation immigrant youth in Canada and France were compared.[33] Findings supported the integration hypothesis; in both countries, those who were doubly engaged had higher levels of psychological and social well-being. In both samples, integration was found to be associated with better adaptation, while marginalization was associated with poorer adaptation. However, the magnitude of this relationship was less pronounced in France than in Canada. The national public policy and attitude context was found to influence the young immigrants' intercultural strategies and the relationship with their well-being. In France, there was more discrimination, less orientation to their heritage culture (identity and behaviour), and poorer adaptation (lower self-esteem and higher deviance). This difference was interpreted as a result of it being more psychologically costly to express one's ethnicity in France than in Canada and related to differences in national policy and practices.

Most recently, Nguyen and Benet-Martínez[34] carried out a meta-analysis across 83 studies and over 20,000 participants. They found that integration (*biculturalism* in their terms) had a significant and positive relationship with both psychological adaptation (e.g., life satisfaction, positive affect, self-esteem) and socio-cultural adaptation (e.g., academic achievement, career success, social skills, lack of behavioural problems).

Overall, the integration hypothesis is now well supported in Canadian and international research. It is now clear that when individuals are engaged in both their heritage cultures and the larger society, there are higher levels of both psychological and socio-cultural well-being.

CONTACT HYPOTHESIS

The *contact hypothesis* asserts that "prejudice ... may be reduced by equal status contact between majority and minority groups in the pursuit of common goals."[35] However, Allport proposed that the hypothesis is more likely to be supported when certain conditions are present in the intercultural encounter. The effect of contact is predicted to be stronger when there is contact among groups of roughly equal social and economic status; when the contact is voluntary, sought by both groups, rather than imposed; and when it is supported by society, through norms and laws promoting contact and prohibiting discrimination.

The national surveys in Canada[36] found substantial support for this relationship, especially when status is controlled. For example, overall ratings of mutual *familiarity* (a rating of how much contact and interaction an individual had with members of a specific ethnocultural group) were positively correlated with positive attitudes toward members of that group.

Using data from the two national surveys in Canada, the ethnic attitudes of members of particular ethnocultural groups toward members of other ethnocultural groups were examined. Their attitude data were aggregated by census tracts (essentially neighbourhoods, where status is generally shared), in which the proportion of particular ethnocultural groups was also known from the census. A secondary analysis of data from the first survey by Kalin and Berry[37] found that the higher the proportion of members of a particular group in a neighbourhood, the more positive were the attitudes of non-members toward that group. Analysis of the data from the second survey[38] obtained similar results. In neither study was there evidence of a "tipping point," where a higher presence of a particular group in one's neighbourhood became associated with lesser acceptance of that group. This kind of ecological analysis permits the suggestion that contact actually leads to more positive intercultural attitudes. The alternative possibility is that individuals actually move to particular neighbourhoods where already liked ethnocultural groups reside. More such research is needed, and in other intercultural settings, before firm conclusions can be drawn.

In international research, Pettigrew and Tropp[39] conducted a series of meta-analyses of hundreds of studies of the contact hypothesis, which came from many countries and many diverse settings (schools, work, experiments). Their findings provide general support for the contact hypothesis: intergroup contact does generally relate negatively to prejudice in both dominant and non-dominant samples: "Overall, results from the meta-analysis reveal that greater levels of intergroup contact are typically associated with lower level of prejudice."[40] This effect was stronger when there were structured programs that incorporated the conditions outlined by Allport than when these conditions were not present.

One remaining issue is whether the association between intercultural contact and positive attitudes results from situations where those individuals with positive attitudes seek more intercultural contact or whether more such contact leads to more positive attitudes. Longitudinal studies are very important to the disentangling of the direction of the relationship between intercultural contact and attitudes. One study[41] has shown an interactive effect of contact and intercultural attitudes. The researchers conducted a longitudinal field survey in Germany, Belgium, and England with school-aged samples of members of both ethnic minorities and ethnic majorities. They assessed both intercultural contact and attitudes at two points in time. Contact was assessed by both the quality and the quantity of contact. Attitudes were assessed by social distance and negative feelings. The pattern of intercorrelations, at both times, supported the positive relationship between contact and attitudes. Beyond this correlational analysis, path analyses yielded evidence for the relationship working in both directions: contact reduced prejudice, but prejudice also reduced contact. Thus, in this study, support for the contact hypothesis is partial: contact can lead to more positive attitudes, but initial positive attitudes can lead people into contact with each other.

The evidence is now widespread across cultures that greater intercultural contact is associated with more positive intercultural attitudes and lower levels of prejudice. This generalization has to be qualified by two cautions. First, the appropriate conditions need to be present in order for contact to lead to positive intercultural attitudes. And second, there exist many examples of the opposite effect, where increased contact is associated with greater conflict. The conditions (cultural, political, economic) under which these opposite outcomes arise are in urgent need of examination.

A key element in the contact hypothesis is the set of conditions that may be necessary in order for contact to lead to more positive intercultural relations. The three hypotheses are linked because the first two hypotheses speak to some of these conditions under which contact can have positive outcomes. First, for the multiculturalism hypothesis, we saw that when the cultural identities of individuals and groups are threatened, and their place in the plural society is questioned, more negative attitudes are likely to characterize their relationships. This consequence applies to all ethnocultural groups, both dominant and non-dominant. For example, when members of the larger society feel threatened by immigration, and when members of particular groups are discriminated against, or their rights to maintain their heritage cultures and/or to participate in the larger society are questioned or denied, a mutual hostility is likely to ensue. Under these conditions, increased contact is not likely to lead to more positive intercultural attitudes.

Second, for the integration hypothesis, we saw that double engagement (that is, maintaining contact with and participating in both the heritage culture and the larger society) is associated with better well-being, including greater self-esteem and life satisfaction. When psychological and social well-being are low (e.g., when confidence in one's identity is low), there can be little basis for engaging in intercultural contact. And when contact does occur, as we saw for the multiculturalism hypothesis, it is likely to lead to more hostile mutual attitudes.

GENERAL CONCLUSION

Intercultural relations research in culturally plural societies has been guided by a number of concepts and hypotheses that are linked to Canadian multiculturalism policy. This research has resulted in a number of interrelated findings, both in Canada and around the world. In my view, these findings constitute the kind of general principles that the fields of cross-cultural and intercultural psychology are seeking. This claim is possible because we have been able to understand the cultural underpinnings of individual human behaviour; no person develops or acts in a cultural vacuum. Second, much of the research has been carried out comparatively; research findings from one cultural or social setting alone are never a valid basis for understanding intercultural behaviour in another setting. Comparative research is also required if we are to achieve an understanding of some general principles that underpin intercultural behaviour. Third, policies and programs for improving intercultural relations take many forms. Some have been shown to threaten individuals and groups and provide the conditions that generate mutual hostility (e.g., segregation and exclusion, and possibly assimilation). Conversely, there are policies and programs (integration and multiculturalism) that appear to provide the cultural and psychological bases for enhancing positive mutual intercultural relations.

Plural societies now have the possibility of using concepts, hypotheses, and findings from research to guide the development and implementation of policies and programs that will improve intercultural relations. This way forward stands in sharp contrast to using preconceptions and prejudices that are currently often the basis for intercultural policies. As researchers, we now have the opportunity to provide the information required for such effective policy decisions – and in a form that governments can use.

NOTES

[1] This chapter is dedicated to the memory of my friend and colleague Rudy Kalin, 1938–2011.

[2] Recently appointed research professor at the National Research University Higher School of Economics, Moscow, Russia.

[3] See, for example, Brian Barry, *Culture and Equality: An Egalitarian Critique of Multiculturalism* (Cambridge: Polity Press, 2001); Augie Fleras, *The Politics of*

Multiculturalism: Multicultural Governance in Comparative Perspective (New York: Palgrave, 2009); Will Kymlicka, *Multicultural Odysseys* (Toronto: University of Toronto Press, 2007); Gilles Paquet, "Political Philosophy of Multiculturalism," in *Ethnicity and Culture in Canada: The Research Landscape*, ed. John W. Berry and J.A. Laponce (Toronto: University of Toronto Press, 1994), 60–80; Jeffrey G. Reitz, Raymond Breton, Karen Kisiel Dion, and Kenneth L. Dion, eds., *Multiculturalism and Social Cohesion: Potentials and Challenges of Diversity* (New York: Springer, 2009); and Phil Ryan, *Multicultiphobia* (Toronto: University of Toronto Press, 2010).

    [4] See, for example, Michael Adams, *Unlikely Utopia: The Surprising Triumph of Canadian Pluralism* (Toronto: Viking, 2007); and Jack Jedwab, ed., "Thirty-Five Years of Canadian Multiculturalism (1971–2006): Issues, Ideas and Reflections," *Canadian Diversity* 5, no. 2 (2006).

    [5] See, for example, John W. Berry, Rudolf Kalin, and Donald M. Taylor, *Multiculturalism and Ethnic Attitudes in Canada* (Ottawa: Ministry of Supply and Services, 1976); John W. Berry and Rudolf Kalin, "Multicultural Policy and Social Psychology: The Canadian Experience," in *Political Psychology in Cross-Cultural Perspective*, ed. Stanley A. Renshon and John Duckitt (New York: Macmillan, 2000), 263–284; Richard J. Crisp, ed., *The Psychology of Social and Cultural Diversity* (Chichester, UK: Wiley Blackwell, 2010); and Fathali M. Moghaddam, *Multiculturalism and Intergroup Relations: Psychological Implications for Democracy in Global Context* (Washington, DC: APA Books, 2008).

    [6] For an overview of this field, see John W. Berry, Ype H. Poortinga, Seger M. Breugelmans, Athanasios Chasiotis, and David L. Sam, *Cross-Cultural Psychology: Research and Applications* (Cambridge: Cambridge University Press, 2011).

    [7] For an overview of this field, see David L. Sam and John W. Berry, eds., *Handbook of Acculturation Psychology* (Cambridge: Cambridge University Press, 2006).

    [8] See Colette Sabatier and Virginie Boutry, "Acculturation in Francophone European Societies," in *The Cambridge Handbook of Acculturation Psychology*, ed. David L. Sam and John W. Berry (Cambridge: Cambridge University Press, 2006), 349–367.

    [9] See Huong H. Nguyen, "Acculturation in the United States," in *The Cambridge Handbook of Acculturation Psychology*, ed. David L. Sam and John W. Berry (Cambridge: Cambridge University Press, 2006), 311–330.

    [10] Canada, Parliament, House of Commons, *Debates*, 28th Parliament, 3rd Session, 1970–1972, vol. 8 (Ottawa: Queen's Printer, 8 October 1971), 8545.

    [11] John W. Berry, "Marginality, Stress and Ethnic Identification in an Acculturated Aboriginal Community," *Journal of Cross-Cultural Psychology* 1, no. 3 (1970):239–252.

    [12] John W. Berry, "Multicultural Policy in Canada: A Social Psychological Analysis," *Canadian Journal of Behavioural Science* 16, no. 4 (1984):353–370.

    [13] John W. Berry and J.A. Laponce, eds., *Ethnicity and Culture in Canada: The Research Landscape* (Toronto: University of Toronto Press, 1994).

    [14] Berry, Kalin, and Taylor, *Multiculturalism and Ethnic Attitudes in Canada*.

    [15] Council of the European Union, press release, Brussels, 19 November 2004, at http://www.consilium.europa.eu/uedocs/cms_data/docs/pressdata/en/jha/82745.pdf, accessed 15 January 2014.

    [16] See, for example, Fons J.R. van de Vijver, Seger M. Breugelmans, and Saskia R.G. Schalk-Soekar, "Multiculturalism: Construct Validity and Stability," *International Journal of Intercultural Relations* 32 (2008):93–104.

[17] Bhikhu Parekh, "Multicultural Society and Convergence of Identities," in *The Ties That Bind: Accommodating Diversity in Canada and the European Union*, ed. Erik Fossum, Johanne Poirier, and Paul Magnette (Brussels: Peter Lang, 2009), 33.

[18] John W. Berry, "Marginality, Stress and Ethnic Identification in an Acculturated Aboriginal Community"; John W. Berry, "Psychological Aspects of Cultural Pluralism: Unity and Identity Reconsidered," *Topics in Cultural Learning*, vol. 2, ed. Robert W. Brislin (Honolulu: Hawaii University, East-West Center, 1974), 17–22; John W. Berry, "Acculturation as Varieties of Adaptation," in *Acculturation: Theory, Models and Some New Findings*, ed. A. Padilla (Boulder, CO: Westview, 1980), 9–25.

[19] Berry, "Psychological Aspects of Cultural Pluralism."

[20] See John W. Berry, Jean S. Phinney, David L. Sam, and Paul Vedder, eds., *Immigrant Youth in Cultural Transition: Acculturation, Identity and Adaptation across National Contexts* (Mahwah, NJ: Lawrence Erlbaum Associates, 2006).

[21] John W. Berry, "Mutual Attitudes among Immigrants and Ethnocultural Groups in Canada," *International Journal of Intercultural Relations* 30, no. 6 (2006):719–734.

[22] Berry, Kalin, and Taylor, *Multiculturalism and Ethnic Attitudes in Canada*.

[23] See also Walter G. Stephan, C. Lausanne Renfro, Victoria M. Esses, Cookie White Stephan, and Tim Martin, "The Effects of Feeling Threatened on Attitudes toward Immigrants, *International Journal of Intercultural Relations* 29, no. 1 (2005):1–19.

[24] Berry, Kalin, and Taylor, *Multiculturalism and Ethnic Attitudes in Canada*; Berry and Kalin, "Multicultural Policy and Social Psychology."

[25] Robert C. Annis, Ryan Gibson, and John W. Berry, 2010. "Intercultural Relations in a Prairie Canadian City" (paper presented at the Mi/Más Konferencia ["Us/Them Conference"], Eger, Hungary, 2010).

[26] Colleen Ward and Anne-Marie Masgoret, "Attitudes toward Immigrants, Immigration, and Multiculturalism in New Zealand: A Social Psychological Analysis," *International Migration Review* 42, no. 1 (2009):222–243.

[27] Nadezhda Lebedeva and Alexander Tatarko, "Immigration and Intercultural Interaction Strategies in Post-Soviet Russia," in *Immigration: Policies, Challenges and Impact*, ed. Eugene Tartakovsky (Hauppauge, NY: Nova Science Publishers, 2012).

[28] Jüri Kruusvall, Raivo Vetik, and John W. Berry, "The Strategies of Inter-ethnic Adaptation of Estonian Russians," *Studies of Transition States and Societies* 1, no. 1 (2009):3–24.

[29] Jim Cameron, Lucie Kocum, and John W. Berry, "Security, Ethnocentrism, and Attitude toward Globalization: An International Test of the Multiculturalism Hypothesis" (paper presented at the Annual Scientific Meeting of the International Society of Political Psychology, 2012).

[30] John W. Berry, "Immigration, Acculturation and Adaptation," *Applied Psychology: An International Review* 46, no. 1 (1997):5–34.

[31] John W. Berry and Colette Sabatier, "Acculturation, Discrimination, and Adaptation among Second Generation Immigrant Youth in Montreal and Paris," *International Journal of Intercultural Relations* 34, no. 3 (2010):191–207.

[32] John W. Berry, R.M. Wintrob, P.S. Sindell, and T.A. Mawhinney, "Psychological Adaptation to Culture Change among the James Bay Cree," *Naturaliste Canadien* 109 (1982):965–975.

[33] Berry and Sabatier, "Acculturation, Discrimination, and Adaptation."

[34] Angela-MinhTu D. Nguyen and Verónica Benet-Martinez, "Biculturalism and Adjustment: A Meta-analysis," *Journal of Cross-Cultural Psychology* 44, no. 1 (2013):122–159.

[35] Gordon W. Allport, *The Nature of Prejudice* (Reading, MA: Addison-Wesley, 1954).

[36] Berry, Kalin, and Taylor, *Multiculturalism and Ethnic Attitudes in Canada*; and John W. Berry and Rudolf Kalin, "Multicultural and Ethnic Attitudes in Canada: Overview of the 1991 National Survey," *Canadian Journal of Behavioural Science* 27, no. 3 (1995):301–320.

[37] Rudolf Kalin and John W. Berry, "The Social Ecology of Ethnic Attitudes in Canada," *Canadian Journal of Behavioural Science* 14, no. 2 (1982):97–109.

[38] Rudolf Kalin, "Ethnic Attitudes as a Function of Ethnic Presence," *Canadian Journal of Behavioural Science* 28, no. 3 (1996):171–179.

[39] Thomas F. Pettigrew and Linda R. Tropp, *When Groups Meet: The Dynamics of Intergroup Contact* (London: Psychology Press, 2011).

[40] Pettigrew and Tropp, *When Groups Meet*, 267.

[41] Jens Binder, Hanna Zagefka, Rupert Brown, Friedrich Funke, Thomas Kessler, Amelie Mummendey, Annemie Maquil, Stephanie Demoulin, and Jaques-Philippe Leyens, "Does Contact Reduce Prejudice or Does Prejudice Reduce Contact? A Longitudinal Test of the Contact Hypothesis among Majority and Minority Groups in Three European Countries," *Journal of Personality and Social Psychology* 96, no. 4 (2009):843–856.

"MELTICULTURALISM" IN NORTH AMERICA: CANADIAN AND AMERICAN ATTITUDES TOWARD IMMIGRATION, INTEGRATION, AND RESIDENTIAL CONCENTRATION

JACK JEDWAB AND SUSAN W. HARDWICK

INTRODUCTION

In 1908, immigrant playwright Israel Zangwill coined the term "melting pot,"[1] which proposed a vision of America as an Eden where all races and ethnicities melted happily into a harmonious whole. In his view, this melting pot of immigrants and their descendants were discouraged from maintaining close ties with their countries and cultures of origin and, instead, were encouraged to assimilate into the American way of life. In his 1938 book, *The Canadian Mosaic*,[2] John Murray Gibbon rejected the American melting pot idea and proudly referred to the very different Canadian approach, which encouraged immigrants and their descendants to preserve important aspects of their ancestral cultures if they wished.

Since it was first introduced in 1971, Canada's multiculturalism policy and the discourse accompanying it were invoked to distinguish the country's distinctive national identity from that of the United States.[3] Since then, Canada has been frequently described as a "mosaic" and the United States as a "melting pot." These two contrasting national narratives have long held considerable appeal in Canada (especially with English Canadians outside the province of Quebec). Since 2000,

The Multiculturalism Question: Debating Identity in 21st-Century Canada, ed. Jack Jedwab. Kingston: School of Policy Studies, Queen's University. © 2014 The School of Policy Studies, Queen's University at Kingston. All rights reserved.

the comparison is rarely made as researchers and policy-makers on both sides of the border tend to offer a considerably more nuanced version of their respective approaches to the management of population diversity. In Canada, there is greater recognition of the need for limits to what was previously described as some unfettered expression of minority ethnic cultures, while Americans more readily acknowledge that the process of cultural mixing and/or assimilation do not properly describe the nation's historical or contemporary reality.

In Tamara Jacoby's anthology, *Reinventing the Melting Pot*, nearly all contributors agree that the notion of the melting pot does not fairly characterize the process of immigrant adjustment.[4] Similarly, respected sociologist Herbert Gans has suggested that the ethnic makeup of the United States and the emergent national identity are more like an evolving kaleidoscope.[5] Likewise, William Boelhower and Alfred Hornung state that the image of the melting pot no longer holds but that it has been a long process to get rid of it. The American identity is now sometimes described as a salad bowl, reflecting the diversity of its cultures.[6] According to another American sociologist, Mary Waters, ethnicity has retained its importance across the generations in the United States by allowing Americans to reconcile the contradictory values of choice, individuality, and community.[7]

Moving beyond whether the United States was or is a melting pot, Robert Putnam suggests that there is a need to rethink the effectiveness of this kind of model by addressing immigration and diversity as "best met not by making 'them' like 'us', but rather by creating a new, more capacious sense of 'we', a reconstruction of diversity that does not bleach out ethnic specificities, but creates overarching identities."[8]

An important dimension in the once persistent comparisons between the multicultural model and the melting pot approach is the type of socio-spatial patterns on the neighbourhood scale that are purportedly fostered by each of these two very different paradigms. Historical patterns of newcomer residential concentration in Canada predate the introduction of multicultural discourse and policies. During the first two decades after the introduction of multicultural policies in Canada, the residential concentration of ethnic groups seemed less an object of concern to observers and, instead, tended to be seen as a normal part of the immigrant adjustment process. Since the 1990s, however, the spatial concentration of Canada's ethnic and racial minorities has been described by critics of multiculturalism as one of the many "perverse" effects of the multicultural model. Residential concentration is often described as a threat to neighbourhood and cultural cohesion; consequently, this viewpoint lies at the centre of debates over models of diversity in Canada. In contrast, the relationship between the melting pot model in the United States and the persistent residential concentration of visible minorities has more commonly been regarded as only a "worrisome trend" (as a result of the long history of African American segregation that is a by-product of the nation's racist history).

CANADIAN VERSUS AMERICAN RESIDENTIAL PREFERENCES

To document some of the differences between Canadian and American preferences for residing in ethnically, racially, or culturally homogeneous versus heterogeneous neighbourhoods, we conducted an opinion survey in Canada and the United States in 2009.[9] The results of our survey are discussed below. Overall, we found that Americans were more likely to prefer residing in ethnically and racially homogeneous neighbourhoods than Canadians. This finding may, at first, appear to be counterintuitive since multicultural discourse has long been presumed to encourage precisely this kind of diverse residential space. However, as discussed in more detail later in this chapter, Canadian and American responses to a number of other related questions on our survey indicate that a more nuanced understanding of the differences between Canadian and American residential preferences is needed to more deeply understand the residential impacts of multiculturalism north of the 49th parallel.

What are the differences between Canadians and Americans when it comes to their respective views about immigrant integration, identity, and residential choices? Are there certain attitudes that distinguish Canada from the United States related to the spatial patterns of immigrants in each country? To provide preliminary answers to these questions, we focus here on assessing how and why these two populations view residential space (and not on how the policy frameworks of these two countries compare at the federal and state/provincial levels).

Four questions guide our comparative analysis of the survey data that follow: (i) How do Canadians and Americans compare when it comes to their desire to reside in ethnically and racially homogeneous neighbourhoods or in more diverse neighbourhoods? (ii) How do other related socioeconomic and demographic factors (e.g., age, region, language spoken at home, and income levels) relate to Canadian and American responses to questions about their attitudes and perceptions of immigration and integration on the neighbourhood scale? (iii) Do residential patterns have some impact upon attachment to neighbourhood, ethnic group, or country? (iv) And, if so, do residential patterns correlate in any way with an individual's or group's degree of openness to diversity?

The empirical findings reported below are based principally on the results of the June 2009 binational poll, mentioned above, of 2,500 Canadians and 1,000 respondents in the United States. Questions related to participants' attitudes and perceptions about immigration, integration, diversity, and geographic knowledge were included in this cross-border survey. We also asked specifically whether survey respondents lived (or preferred to live) in a neighbourhood where people shared their same racial and/ or ethnic background. In the United States, survey questions focused on groups that identify as white, African American, and Hispanic, whereas in Canada, we posed questions related to the language identification of the respondents and distinguished between the English, the French, and those whose principal language is neither English nor French (a group known as allophones, which consists largely of people identified as part of an ethnic or racial minority group).

PRIOR STUDIES OF RESIDENTIAL SPACE IN CANADA AND THE UNITED STATES

The abundance of prior research by other scholars on the residential patterns of Canadian and US cities has proven invaluable as a basis for our study.[10] To date, however, almost all of the prior work that has been conducted on residential concentration has failed to document the *residential preferences* of individuals, especially as they relate to perceptions of diversity in their own neighbourhoods. Instead, the socio-spatial research on the patterns and related social, economic, cultural, and environmental processes of immigrants in Canada and the United States has almost all been research on different models of diversity.[11]

The immigration histories of Canada and the United States have a great deal in common. Both countries are long-term immigrant-receiving nations with a high percentage of foreign-born residents. At the present time, Canada has the second-largest per capita population of immigrants of any nation in the world, and the United States is home to the largest total foreign-born population overall. Since the late 1960s, however, a number of significant changes have contributed to the location patterns of immigrants and also the varying policies toward immigrants and immigration.

First, after the passage of more open policies on immigration in both Canada and the United States in the mid-1960s, increasing numbers of immigrants, refugees, and other foreign-born migrants settled in North America. Their arrival resulted in a plethora of new work on both sides of the Canada-US border that focused on the patterns and impacts of these new arrivals, especially in the large metropolitan areas that had served as immigrant gateways for more than a century. As a result, a significantly large body of work has been carried out on the residential patterns of immigrants in these long-term immigrant gateway cities in both Canada and the United States.

Traditional immigrant gateway cities remain powerful magnets for newly arriving groups, much as they did in the past, with most of Canada's smaller cities and towns remaining less ethnically and racially diverse. Ongoing efforts by the Canadian government, social service agencies, and other groups in Canada have continued in recent years to encourage foreign-born groups to relocate to more peripherally located, non-traditional gateways. However, the nation's largest cities of Toronto, Montreal, and Vancouver still attract the largest numbers of new arrivals.

In the United States, in contrast, post-1990s immigration flows have primarily been into what Audrey Singer at the Brookings Institution has called "new immigrant gateway cities."[12] Many of these smaller and increasingly diverse metropolitan areas are located far from traditional immigrant settlement nodes. As a result, cities such as Charlotte, North Carolina; Dallas, Texas; and Portland, Oregon are now home to relatively large populations of foreign-born residents. The emergence of these smaller immigrant gateway cities in the United States has been discussed most recently in two books – *Twenty-First Century Gateways: Immigrant Incorporation in Suburban America* and *Beyond the Gateway: Immigrants in a Changing America.*[13]

Along with the recent preference of immigrants to settle in these kinds of cities in the United States, since the 1990s it has been their preference to reside in what have been called "melting pot suburbs" instead of in more traditional downtown neighbourhoods.[14] In comparison, visible-minority groups in Canada reside in both central-city residential districts and older suburban neighbourhoods.[15]

DEFINING RESIDENTIAL CONCENTRATION

Areas of residential concentration of minority ethnic or racial groups have been referred to interchangeably by scholars over the years as ethnic enclaves, clusters, ghettos, and/or simply as residential segregation. Of particular importance as a foundation for the analysis presented in this chapter is the large body of prior work on processes that have shaped these various types of residential clusters in Canada as compared to the United States. The term *enclave*, in particular, has been used in a wide variety of ways by North American social scientists, policy-makers, and media.[16] Geographers James Allen and Eugene Turner, for example, note that the concept of *enclave* may overlap with the term *residential concentration*, but that *enclave* also has other multiple meanings.[17] Other American scholars such as John Logan, Wenquan Zhang, and Richard Alba use *enclave* to define a residential neighbourhood where one ethnic group – voluntarily or involuntarily – is found in fairly high proportions.[18] In contrast, the work of Peter Marcuse stresses the strictly voluntary nature of contemporary enclaves.[19] Finally, the term *enclave* has also been used by Alejandro Portes and other scholars to refer not only to residentially distinctive spaces, but also to the distinctive ethnic commercial districts that are affiliated with them – places referred to as having an "ethnic enclave economy."[20]

In contrast, the term *ghetto* usually refers to a type of residential concentration that is more often constructed as a result of social or economic restrictions and a lack of other residential choices. In the United States, African American, Hispanic, and Asian groups have often found themselves limited in where they were allowed to live, especially up until a half century ago or so, when government policies and the attitudes of white-majority residents prevented most visible-minority groups from living outside tightly bounded designated neighbourhoods. Compounding the situation was a series of new urban renewal policies and programs in the 1950s and 1960s and the construction of inner-city public-housing projects and new highway programs funded by the US government. These efforts facilitated the persistence of high levels of African American segregation in central city ghettos and encouraged and subsidized white flight to the suburbs. The result (until the mid-1990s, when gentrification processes began to reverse these patterns and attract white residents back to city centres) was stripping many US cities of their downtown middle class. These related economic and social pressures also assured that African Americans would remain trapped in inner-city neighbourhoods.

In the decades that followed, as larger and larger numbers of visible-minority immigrant groups arrived in the United States, at first they, too, faced residential and economic segregation in the central city. However, research on the segregation in US cities of these groups, as compared to African Americans, found that the separation of African Americans and whites remains more severe than the social and geographical distancing of these newest immigrant groups from the majority white population. In the United States in 1980, for example, calculations of average African American isolation indexes remained 2.5 times that of Hispanics and 10 times that of Asians. Shockingly, at the present rate of decline, it would take more than a half-century for African Americans to reach the level of segregation presently experienced by Hispanics and Asians in the United States. The degree of ethnic and racial separation, the inertia of long-term residential restriction, and the relative permanence of economic, social, cultural, and environmental barriers, however, all provide ample evidence that the enclaves that encompass these incoming Hispanic, Asian, and other immigrant groups remain fundamentally different from forced residential clusters known as ghettos.

Traditionally, newly arriving (mostly European) immigrants in North American cities preferred to settle near each other in central-city neighbourhoods because of their limited mastery of the English language, more affordable housing costs, proximity to employment, and a preference for living in close proximity to other newcomers from their homeland. Most were ultimately able to become more spatially dispersed or residentially integrated – but only after they could function economically and socially within mainstream American or Canadian society. During the first half of the 20th century, with increased economic success, proficiency in the English or French language, and the ability to blend into the white mainstream culture because of the invisibility of their skin colour, most of the children and grandchildren of these European immigrants dispersed gradually to the suburbs or other neighbourhoods dominated by white, mainstream residents. This process, first documented by sociologists at the Chicago School in the 1920s and later by Douglas Massey, Richard Alba, and Victor Nee as well as a long list of other scholars, became known as "immigrant spatial assimilation theory."[21] However, the arrival after the mid-1960s of large numbers of visible-minority immigrant groups from Latin America, Asia, Africa, and elsewhere in the world rendered this traditional Chicago School "invasion and succession" model of assimilation obsolete in both Canada and the United States.

Thereafter, new immigration and integration policies that reflected this new diversity were disseminated in Canada under the umbrella term *multiculturalism* and, in the United States, under the rubric of *cultural diversity*. In Canada, ongoing debates about the message to newcomers that arises from multicultural ideology most often centre on whether encouraging individuals and groups to value and preserve their customs and traditions undercuts cross-cultural interaction. Those who may question the principle of multiculturalism often insist that the preservation of minority cultures may reinforce "harmful" spatial patterns characterized by the spatial concentration of distinctive ethnic or racial groups. And, in their view, the spatial concentration of ethnic or racial-minority communities is viewed as one of the "perverse" impacts of multiculturalism and multicultural policies.

However, this view fails to take into account the historical processes and patterns that lie behind such clustered residential patterns in both Canadian and American cities and predate contemporary multicultural discourse. As a result, advocates of multiculturalism have been quick to counter that residential concentration can be a normal part of the early migration and settlement process for certain groups and that over time, as their economic circumstances improve, there is often a shift to more multicultural neighbourhoods that expresses the residential preferences of immigrants and their descendants.

As historian John Zucchi argued, as ethnic groups became more established in the past, they moved from their initial areas of settlement to new areas. Similarly, this observation was confirmed by a number of American sociologists, who observed the same patterns in US cities in the 1920s and 1930s. Just as thousands of post–World War II immigrants sought detached or semi-detached homes in new housing projects being built in Canada and the United States, so immigrants succeeded them in their former neighbourhoods. As a result, according to Zucchi, while some ethnic neighbourhoods have persisted and even flourished since the 1950s, others continue to evolve in terms of their ethnic makeup and ethnic landscapes. This process resulted in 1980s- and 1990s-era suburbs remaining (or becoming) home to concentrations of certain ethnic groups.[22] In sum, contrary to the assumptions made about ethnic concentrations occurring only in inner cities, immigrant groups now also concentrate in these "melting pot suburbs."

According to geographer Daniel Hiebert, an increasingly common pattern of immigrant residency in Canadian cities is the "mixed minority" enclave, where at least 70 percent of a city's population belongs to a visible-minority group.[23]

Generally, such enclaves feature a single group that is at least twice the size of any other. Relatively little diversity might be expected in these types of residential areas; nevertheless, they are characterized by profound ethnocultural diversity, especially in the city of Toronto. Barring a few exceptions, these kinds of enclaves do not have monocultural landscapes.

There are pronounced variations in the ethnic residential patterns of Canada's three largest cities of Montreal, Toronto, and Vancouver. In Montreal, enclaves are most often areas of economic marginalization, something that affects both the white and the visible-minority populations, yet relatively few members of visible-minority groups live in them. Hiebert notes that given the view that equates enclaves with disadvantage, it is ironic that this is only the case in Montreal, the metropolitan area that has the lowest population of visible minorities and the fewest living in enclaves. In comparison, Hiebert's study found that the socio-economic profile of enclaves in Toronto and Vancouver is more complex. Both of these major cities feature large neighbourhoods where visible-minority populations live in extreme poverty. In both places, however, a far larger number of low-income visible minorities live outside enclaves than in them. In fact, the tendency for visible-minority residents of enclaves to be poor in Vancouver is only somewhat higher than for the visible-minority population in the metropolis as a whole.[24]

Underlying any comparison of the residential impacts of multiculturalism and the melting pot paradigm is the importance of the individual migrant's decision-making process. An individual's preference about where to live might, like that of other residents of Canadian and US cities, be reflected in the extent to which a person identifying with an ethnic or racial minority chooses to live alongside members of the community – or to reside in an ethnically or racially mixed neighbourhood.

Residential concentration is often assumed to be a function of the residential preferences of newcomers, and this view is particularly held by observers in Canada. Hence, the phenomenon of ethnic enclaves is often discussed by critics of multiculturalism here. Canadian pollster Allan Gregg claims, "In Canada, we may live in a multicultural society, but the evidence suggests that fewer and fewer of us are living in multicultural neighbourhoods," adding that "we have allowed [our diversity] to slide into self-segregated communities, isolated along ethnic lines."[25]

Adding support to this view, journalist Marina Jimenez found that the total number of ethnic enclaves in Canada has exploded in recent years, despite multiculturalism. In an article in the *Globe and Mail*, she states that "in 1981, there were only six [ethnic enclaves] in Toronto, Montreal and Vancouver. By 2001, there were 254, according to a study by Statistics Canada, which defines ethnic enclaves as communities with 30 per cent of the population from one visible-minority group."[26] Despite the increasingly large number of enclaves documented in Canada in recent years, however, almost all of this prior work on immigrant communities in Canada suggests that newcomers willingly choose to live among members of the same group – an affirmation that has been rarely tested.

Findings from our binational opinion poll provide new insights into the residential preferences of Canadians as compared to Americans. As shown in Table 1 below, the "multiculturally inclined" Canadians are, overall, less likely than Americans to prefer living in ethno-racially homogeneous neighbourhoods. In the United States, we found that it is primarily the white population that is most likely to prefer living in neighbourhoods with persons who share their ethnic and racial background. In Canada, it is the francophone population that is most likely to prefer such neighbourhoods, with the allophone population (which contains a greater share of Canada's minority ethnic groups) least favourable toward doing so.

TABLE 1

Do you strongly agree, somewhat agree, somewhat disagree, or strongly disagree with the following statement?

	I prefer to live in a neighbourhood where most people share my ethnic background					
	United States			*Canada*		
	White	*Black or African American*	*Hispanic/ Spanish/Latino Descent*	*French*	*English*	*Allophone*
	%	%	%	%	%	%
Strongly agree	15.5	7.7	16.7	20.9	8.8	5.7
Somewhat agree	34.0	23.1	24.2	31.9	28.2	17.5
Somewhat disagree	25.1	32.1	25.8	29.5	35.0	49.0
Strongly disagree	12.5	19.2	22.7	13.9	23.6	24.6
Don't know/Prefer not to answer	12.9	17.9	10.6	3.8	4.5	3.2

Source: Authors' compilation.

Most prior analyses of residential concentration have focused on the pattern exhibited by racial and/or ethnic minorities. It is worth noting on this table that when asked about their residential preferences, respondents who identified as white in the United States and French in Canada were most likely to prefer living in a neighbourhood where people share their ethnic background. The least likely to prefer living in a neighbourhood where people share the same background were African Americans in the United States and people in Canada whose first language is neither English nor French.

Table 2 below provides evidence that the white population of the United States, followed by Hispanics, tends to prefer to reside in neighbourhoods where people share their ethnic or racial background. The percentage for each group is somewhat higher than for the group that prefers to live in more "homogeneous" neighbourhoods. When comparing the percentage that live in more homogeneous neighbourhoods versus those who prefer to live with those who share their background, the gap is higher for African Americans than for the other two groups. In the case of Canada, francophones are by far the most likely to live in neighbourhoods where most people share their ethnic background, although they say that they are far less likely to prefer living in such neighbourhoods. Although anglophones are less likely than francophones to live in neighbourhoods where most persons share the same ethnic background, the percentage who live in such circumstances is much higher than those who say that they prefer such neighbourhoods.

TABLE 2

Do you strongly agree, somewhat agree, somewhat disagree, or strongly disagree with each of the following two statements?

	United States			Canada		
	White	Black or African American	Hispanic/ Spanish/Latino Descent	French	English	Allophone
	%	%	%	%	%	%
Most people in my neighbourhood share my racial background	55.4	41.1	47.0	71.0	52.4	22.1
I prefer to live in a neighbourhood where most people share my ethnic background	49.5	30.8	40.9	52.8	37.0	23.2

Source: Authors' compilation.

As to where individuals prefer to live, we found that in the United States, nearly 50 percent of respondents who were native-born expressed a preference for living in neighbourhoods where people share their ethnic or racial background. This compares with nearly 40 percent of the Canadian-born who have this same preference. Related data on Canadians provides the other important distinction: a mere 10 percent of the Canadian-born who identify with an ethnic minority prefer to live in a neighbourhood where most people share their ethnic background; this compares with 33 percent of immigrants. (See Table 3 below.)

TABLE 3
Do you strongly agree, somewhat agree, somewhat disagree, or strongly disagree with each of the following statements?

	I prefer to live in a neighbourhood where most people share my ethnic background			
	United States		Canada	
	Non-immigrant %	Immigrant %	Non-immigrant %	Immigrant %
Strongly agree	15.1	12.3	11.4	8.0
Somewhat agree	33.6	13.1	27.4	24.6
Somewhat disagree	25.3	24.7	35.3	40.9
Strongly disagree	13.0	13.7	21.1	25.9
Don't know/Prefer not to answer	13.0	19.2	4.8	0.7

Source: Authors' compilation.

MAJORITY AND MINORITY RESIDENTIAL CONCENTRATION AND ATTACHMENT TO NATION, NEIGHBOURHOOD, AND ETHNIC GROUP

Several other analysts contend that multicultural models of society encourage the residential concentration of minorities; this, they argue, inhibits attachment to their new country of residence. Until now, however, little or no empirical evidence has been carried out to assess the validity of this claim. As observed below in Table 4, in neither the United States nor Canada does there appear to be any meaningful effect on attachment based on the extent to which people report residing in neighbourhoods where most people share their ethnic or racial background. The one exception is the case of neighbourhoods in the United States where residents' attachment to their host countries is stronger when the majority of people in a neighbourhood share the same background.

TABLE 4
Do you strongly agree, somewhat agree, somewhat disagree, or strongly disagree with the following statement?

	Most people in my neighbourhood share my racial background			
Attached to	Strongly Agree %	Somewhat Agree %	Somewhat Disagree %	Strongly Disagree %
United States	93.8	94.2	91.1	90.5
Neighbourhood	72.6	70.8	58.3	58.9
Ethnic or ancestral group	72.1	69.3	67.2	72.1
Canada	81.0	82.0	92.0	88.0
Neighbourhood	78.0	73.0	73.0	70.0
Ethnic group	65.0	65.0	64.0	65.0

Source: Authors' compilation.

As indicated in the data shown below in Table 5, across the groups examined in our study, those saying that most people in their neighbourhood share their background tend to have a stronger sense of attachment to their neighbourhood. An exception is Canada's francophone population: for this group, most people state that their ethnic background has no bearing on their degree of attachment.

TABLE 5
Do you strongly agree, somewhat agree, somewhat disagree, or strongly disagree with the following statement?

	Most people in my neighbourhood share my racial background			
Attached to Neighbourhood	Strongly Agree %	Somewhat Agree %	Somewhat Disagree %	Strongly Disagree %
White	73	71	57	65
Black	69	63	46	50
Hispanic	80	63	46	50
French	75	70	75	71
English	82	75	69	73
Other	75	66	80	65

Source: Authors' compilation.

Finally, as the summary Table 6 below indicates, when queried about attachment to their own ethnic group, the various groups (with the possible exception of English Canadians) indicate that the composition of their neighbourhood has no meaningful impact on how attached they feel to their ethnic group.

TABLE 6
Do you strongly agree, somewhat agree, somewhat disagree, or strongly disagree with the following statement?

	Most people in my neighbourhood share my racial background			
Attached to Ethnic Group	Strongly Agree %	Somewhat Agree %	Somewhat Disagree %	Strongly Disagree %
White	70	66	67	69
Black	n/s	89	67	86
Hispanic	80	81	75	n/s
French	64	59	59	70
English	65	67	57	55
Other	75	74	79	76

n/s – Count not sufficient to warrant posting a percentage.
Source: Authors' compilation.

CONCLUSIONS

To date, little empirical evidence has been offered to confirm that patterns of residential concentration are related to the societal model of multiculturalism or a melting pot. The assumption that these kinds of spatial concentrations are the preferred condition of the majority of ethnic and racial minority groups remains unfounded (as is the affirmation that, in general, this condition is self-imposed). Such assumptions tend to be based strictly on observable residential patterns – that is, *where* people live as opposed to *why* they live there. Our findings indicate that it is also essential to analyze the attitudes and preferences of individuals in deciding where to live.

Our research provides evidence that the individual preferences of neighbourhood residents from various ethnic and racial groups are far more important than unfounded messages promulgated by supporters or detractors of the multiculturalism or melting pot models. Instead, the results of our binational poll indicate that it is essential for scholars and policy-makers who are interested in the impacts of these two societal models of diversity to examine not only the residential patterns of ethnic and racial minorities but also those of the majority population. Our work also underscores the importance of recognizing that individual and group perceptions and preferences related to residential segregation and diversity are more complex and nuanced than prior studies have indicated.

Of particular interest, based on our findings, is learning more about why most of the American participants in our polls expressed a preference for residing in homogeneous neighbourhoods as compared to the majority of our Canadian respondents. This finding seems paradoxical in light of the notion that multiculturalism presumably fosters ethnic enclaves and, in contrast, the melting pot model encourages ethnic and racial mixing. Thus, we question whether the traditional comparison that suggests Canada is a multicultural mosaic and the United States a melting pot continues to be of value in today's rapidly changing and highly diverse world.

Yet another paradox in the outcome of our study is that Americans tend to more strongly support encouraging immigrants to maintain their distinctive customs and traditions than do Canadians. This, too, seems to run counter to the dominant multicultural policies in Canada that were designed to support, nurture, and maintain the unique customs and traditions of distinctive groups. It is clear that learning more about these unexpected discrepancies in the residential preferences of Americans as compared to Canadians provides a particularly fruitful direction for future research. Do residential patterns arise from particular types of diversity models? Or, conversely, do residential patterns influence the conclusions that have been made about the impact of prevailing models?

Along with expanding on the unexpected outcomes of our study is the need to examine, analyze, and weigh the societal benefits of various models of diversity. We suggest that a new framework or paradigm is needed to rethink future comparative research about Canada and the United States, especially research on the patterns, identities, and integration of new immigrants. As such, we agree with Putnam, Jacoby, and others that there is an urgent need to reinvent the American melting pot paradigm. Likewise, it is essential for scholars to rethink the Canadian multiculturalism model. A broader re-examination of what we might learn from our respective approaches to diversity is long overdue.

NOTES

[1] Israel Zangwill, *The Melting Pot*, 1908.

[2] John Murray Gibbon, *Canadian Mosaic: Making of a Northern Nation* (Toronto: McClelland & Stewart, 1938).

[3] Canadian multiculturalism is defined by Citizenship and Immigration Canada as "fundamental to our belief that all citizens are equal. Multiculturalism ensures

that all citizens can keep their identities, can take pride in their ancestry and have a sense of belonging. Acceptance gives Canadians a feeling of security and self-confidence, making them more open to, and accepting of, diverse cultures. The Canadian experience has shown that multiculturalism encourages racial and ethnic harmony and cross-cultural understanding, and discourages ghettoization, hatred, discrimination and violence. Through multiculturalism, Canada recognizes the potential of all Canadians, encouraging them to integrate into their society and take an active part in its social, cultural, economic and political affairs." (See http://www.cic.gc.ca/english/multiculturalism/multi.asp, accessed 12 January 2014.)

[4] Tamara Jacoby, *Reinventing the Melting Pot: The New Immigration and What It Means to Be American* (New York: Basic Books, 2004).

[5] Herbert J. Gans, *Urban Villagers: Group and Class in the Life of Italian-Americans* (New York: Simon and Schuster, 1982).

[6] William Boelhower and Alfred Hornung, eds., *Multiculturalism and the American Self* (Heidelberg: Winter, 2000), 1–2.

[7] Mary Waters, *Ethnic Options: Choosing Identity in America* (Berkeley: University of California Press, 1990).

[8] Robert D. Putnam, "*E Pluribus Unum*: Diversity and Community in the Twenty-First Century," *Scandinavian Political Studies* 30, no. 2 (2007):163–164.

[9] We appreciate the support of the Association for Canadian Studies and the Association of American Geographers for the development and dissemination of the binational poll reported on in this chapter. Canada's Leger Marketing also helped make this study possible.

[10] See, for example, Richard Florida's book *Who's Your City?* (New York: Basic Books, 2008) for more on the importance of residential choice and an expanded discussion of how the creative economy is influencing the decision about where North Americans are choosing to live in the first decade of the 21st century.

[11] The published literature on processes involved in the construction and maintenance of ethnic enclaves in North America is voluminous. Beginning with the foundational work accomplished by Robert Park and others at the Chicago School of Sociology in the early 20th century, scholars have paid a great deal of attention to the ethnic, racial, cultural, economic, and political factors involved in the formation of enclaves. Since that time, sociologists and other scholars have focused particular attention on the relationship between ethnic enclaves and assimilation and integration, especially in metropolitan settings. The comprehensive historical study of Canadian enclaves by John Zucchi, "A History of Ethnic Enclaves in Canada," ed. Roberto Perm, Canada's Ethnic Groups Series, Booklet No. 31 (Ottawa: Canadian Historical Association, 2007), proved to be especially useful as a precursor for our study, as did other related research on ethnic enclaves in the United States and Canada by scholars such as James P. Allen and Eugene Turner, "Ethnic Residential Concentrations in United States Metropolitan Areas," *Geographical Review* 95, no. 2 (2005):267–285; Daniel Hiebert, *Exploring Minority Enclave Areas in Montréal, Toronto, and Vancouver* (Ottawa: Citizenship and Immigration Canada, 2009), at http://publications.gc.ca/collections/collection_2011/cic/Ci4-30-2010-eng.pdf, accessed 12 January 2014; R. Alan Walks and Larry S. Bourne, "Ghettos in Canada's Cities? Racial Segregation, Ethnic Enclaves, and Poverty Concentration in Canadian Urban Areas," *Canadian Geographer* 50, no. 3 (2006):273–297; Harald Bauder and Bob Sharpe, "Residential Segregation of

Visible Minorities in Canada's Gateway Cities," *Canadian Geographer* 46, no. 3 (2002):204–222; and Mohammad Qadeer and Sandeep Kumar, "Ethnic Enclaves and Social Cohesion," *Canadian Journal of Urban Research* 15, no. 2 (2006):1–17.

[12] Audrey Singer, *The Rise of New Immigrant Gateways* (Washington, DC: Brookings Institution, 2004).

[13] Audrey Singer, Susan W. Hardwick, and Caroline B. Brettell, eds., *Twenty-First Century Gateways: Immigrant Incorporation in Suburban America* (Washington, DC: Brookings Institution, 2008); and Elzbieta M. Gozdziak and Susan F. Martin, eds., *Beyond the Gateway: Immigrants in a Changing America* (Lanham, MD: Lexington Books, 2005).

[14] For more information on melting pot suburbs in US cities, see William H. Frey's analysis of 2000 census data published in his Brookings Institution report, "Melting Pot Suburbs: A Study of Suburban Diversity," in *Redefining Urban and Suburban America: Evidence from Census 2000*, vol. 1, ed. Bruce Katz and Robert E. Lang (Washington, DC: Brookings Institution, 2003).

[15] For a more in-depth comparison of the urban social geography of Canada and the United States, see Carlos Teixeira, Wei Li, and Audrey Kobayashi, eds., *Immigrant Geographies of North American Cities* (Don Mills, ON: Oxford University Press, 2012).

[16] The term *enclave* is often a misnomer. From a research perspective, it simply means an overrepresentation of one ethnic group in a neighbourhood. Sometimes it is used interchangeably with *ghetto*, which is usually associated with lower socio-economic status.

[17] Allen and Turner, "Ethnic Residential Concentrations in United States Metropolitan Areas."

[18] John R. Logan, Wenquan Zhang, and Richard D. Alba, "Immigrant Enclaves and Ethnic Communities in New York and Los Angeles," *American Sociological Review* 67, no. 2 (2002):299–322.

[19] Peter Marcuse, "Federal Urban Programs as Multicultural Planning: The Empowerment Zone Approach," in *Urban Planning in a Multicultural Society*, ed. Michael A. Burayidi (Westport, CN: Praeger, 2000), 225–235.

[20] Alejandro Portes, "The Social Origins of the Cuban Enclave Economy of Miami," *Sociological Perspectives* 30, no. 4 (1987):340–372.

[21] Douglas Massey, "Social Class and Ethnic Segregation: A Reconsideration of Methods and Conclusions," *American Sociological Review* 46, no. 5 (1981):641–650; and Richard Alba and Victor Nee, "Rethinking Assimilation Theory for a New Era of Immigration," *International Migration Review* 31, no. 4 (1997):826–874.

[22] John Zucchi, "A History of Ethnic Enclaves in Canada."

[23] Daniel Hiebert, *Exploring Minority Enclave Areas*.

[24] Ibid.

[25] Allan Gregg, quoted in Marina Jimenez, "Do Ethnic Enclaves Impede Integration?" *Globe and Mail*, 8 February 2007, 1.

[26] Ibid.

Queen's Policy Studies
Recent Publications

The Queen's Policy Studies Series is dedicated to the exploration of major public policy issues that confront governments and society in Canada and other nations.

Manuscript submission. We are pleased to consider new book proposals and manuscripts. Preliminary inquiries are welcome. A subvention is normally required for the publication of an academic book. Please direct questions or proposals to the Publications Unit by email at spspress@queensu.ca, or visit our website at: www.queensu.ca/sps/books, or contact us by phone at (613) 533-2192.

Our books are available from good bookstores everywhere, including the Queen's University bookstore (http://www.campusbookstore.com/). McGill-Queen's University Press is the exclusive world representative and distributor of books in the series. A full catalogue and ordering information may be found on their web site (**http://mqup.mcgill.ca/**).

For more information about new and backlist titles from Queen's Policy Studies, visit http://www.queensu.ca/sps/books.

School of Policy Studies

Rethinking Higher Education: Participation, Research, and Differentiation, George Fallis 2013. ISBN 978-1-55339-333-7

Making Policy in Turbulent Times: Challenges and Prospects for Higher Education, Paul Axelrod, Roopa Desai Trilokekar, Theresa Shanahan, and Richard Wellen (eds.) 2013. ISBN 978-1-55339-332-0

Intellectual Disabilities and *Dual Diagnosis: An Interprofessional Clinical Guide for Healthcare Providers,* Bruce D. McCreary and Jessica Jones (eds.) 2013. ISBN 978-1-55339-331-3

Building More Effective Labour-Management Relationships, Richard P. Chaykowski and Robert S. Hickey (eds.) 2013. ISBN 978-1-55339-306-1

Navigationg on the Titanic: Economic Growth, Energy, and the Failure of Governance, Bryne Purchase 2013. ISBN 978-1-55339-330-6

Measuring the Value of a Postsecondary Education, Ken Norrie and Mary Catharine Lennon (eds.) 2013. ISBN 978-1-55339-325-2

Immigration, Integration, and Inclusion in Ontario Cities, Caroline Andrew, John Biles, Meyer Burstein, Victoria M. Esses, and Erin Tolley (eds.) 2012. ISBN 978-1-55339-292-7

Diverse Nations, Diverse Responses: Approaches to Social Cohesion in Immigrant Societies, Paul Spoonley and Erin Tolley (eds.) 2012. ISBN 978-1-55339-309-2

Making EI Work: Research from the Mowat Centre Employment Insurance Task Force, Keith Banting and Jon Medow (eds.) 2012. ISBN 978-1-55339-323-8

Managing Immigration and Diversity in Canada: A Transatlantic Dialogue in the New Age of Migration, Dan Rodríguez-García (ed.) 2012. ISBN 978-1-55339-289-7

International Perspectives: Integration and Inclusion, James Frideres and John Biles (eds.) 2012. ISBN 978-1-55339-317-7

Dynamic Negotiations: Teacher Labour Relations in Canadian Elementary and Secondary Education, Sara Slinn and Arthur Sweetman (eds.) 2012. ISBN 978-1-55339-304-7

Where to from Here? Keeping Medicare Sustainable, Stephen Duckett 2012. ISBN 978-1-55339-318-4

International Migration in Uncertain Times, John Nieuwenhuysen, Howard Duncan, and Stine Neerup (eds.) 2012. ISBN 978-1-55339-308-5

Life After Forty: Official Languages Policy in Canada/Après quarante ans, les politiques de langue officielle au Canada, Jack Jedwab and Rodrigue Landry (eds.) 2011. ISBN 978-1-55339-279-8

From Innovation to Transformation: Moving up the Curve in Ontario Healthcare, Hon. Elinor Caplan, Dr. Tom Bigda-Peyton, Maia MacNiven, and Sandy Sheahan 2011. ISBN 978-1-55339-315-3

Academic Reform: Policy Options for Improving the Quality and Cost-Effectiveness of Undergraduate Education in Ontario, Ian D. Clark, David Trick, and Richard Van Loon 2011. ISBN 978-1-55339-310-8

Integration and Inclusion of Newcomers and Minorities across Canada, John Biles, Meyer Burstein, James Frideres, Erin Tolley, and Robert Vineberg (eds.) 2011. ISBN 978-1-55339-290-3

A New Synthesis of Public Administration: Serving in the 21st Century, Jocelyne Bourgon, 2011. ISBN 978-1-55339-312-2 (paper) 978-1-55339-313-9 (cloth)

Recreating Canada: Essays in Honour of Paul Weiler, Randall Morck (ed.), 2011. ISBN 978-1-55339-273-6

Data Data Everywhere: Access and Accountability? Colleen M. Flood (ed.), 2011. ISBN 978-1-55339-236-1

Making the Case: Using Case Studies for Teaching and Knowledge Management in Public Administration, Andrew Graham, 2011. ISBN 978-1-55339-302-3

Centre for International and Defence Policy

Afghanistan in the Balance: Counterinsurgency, Comprehensive Approach, and Political Order, Hans-Georg Ehrhart, Sven Bernhard Gareis, and Charles Pentland (eds.), 2012. ISBN 978-1-55339-353-5

Security Operations in the 21st Century: Canadian Perspectives on the Comprehensive Approach, Michael Rostek and Peter Gizewski (eds.), 2011. ISBN 978-1-55339-351-1

Institute of Intergovernmental Relations

Canada and the Crown: Essays on Constitutional Monarchy, D. Michael Jackson and Philippe Lagassé (eds.), 2013. ISBN 978-1-55339-204-0

Paradigm Freeze: Why It Is So Hard to Reform Health-Care Policy in Canada, Harvey Lazar, John N. Lavis, Pierre-Gerlier Forest, and John Church (eds.), 2013. ISBN 978-1-55339-324-5

Canada: The State of the Federation 2010, Matthew Mendelsohn, Joshua Hjartarson, and James Pearce (eds.), 2013. ISBN 978-1-55339-200-2

The Democratic Dilemma: Reforming Canada's Supreme Court, Nadia Verrelli (ed.), 2013. ISBN 978-1-55339-203-3

The Evolving Canadian Crown, Jennifer Smith and D. Michael Jackson (eds.), 2011. ISBN 978-1-55339-202-6

The Federal Idea: Essays in Honour of Ronald L. Watts, Thomas J. Courchene, John R. Allan, Christian Leuprecht, and Nadia Verrelli (eds.), 2011. ISBN 978-1-55339-198-2 (paper) 978-1-55339-199-9 (cloth)

The Democratic Dilemma: Reforming the Canadian Senate, Jennifer Smith (ed.), 2009. ISBN 978-1-55339-190-6